T0345943

Listening

ALSO BY JONATHAN COTT
PUBLISHED BY THE UNIVERSITY OF MINNESOTA PRESS

Pipers at the Gates of Dawn: The Wisdom of Children's Literature

Listening
Interviews, 1970–1989

JONATHAN COTT

University of Minnesota Press
Minneapolis | London

Published by the University of Minnesota Press
111 Third Avenue South, Suite 290
Minneapolis, MN 55401-2520
http://www.upress.umn.edu

Printed in the United States of America on acid-free paper

The University of Minnesota is an equal-opportunity educator and employer.

25 24 23 22 21 20   10 9 8 7 6 5 4 3 2 1

Library of Congress Cataloging-in-Publication Data
Cott, Jonathan, author.
Listening : interviews, 1970–1989 / Jonathan Cott.
Minneapolis : University of Minnesota Press, 2020.
Identifiers: LCCN 2019027091 (print) | ISBN 978-1-5179-0901-7 (hc/j)|
    ISBN 978-1-5179-0761-7 (pb)
Subjects: LCSH: Interviews. | Intellectuals—Interviews.
Classification: LCC CT120 .C675 2020 (print) | DDC 305.5/52—dc23
LC record available at https://lccn.loc.gov/2019027091

To have a dialogue
First: ask a question
Then: listen

—Antonio Machado

Contents

Introduction

It was a long time ago, but in 1952, when I was a fifth grader at P.S. 6 in New York City, I published my first interview in my school's mimeographed newspaper. The subject of my interview was Buffalo Bob Smith, the cowboy-garbed host of the wildly popular children's television program *The Howdy Doody Show*. The program's eponymous star was a red-headed, freckle-faced boy marionette who was a denizen of Doodyville, whose other inhabitants included the grumpy mayor Phineas T. Bluster and his Latin and Anglo brothers, Don Jose Bluster and Hector Hamhock Bluster; Sandra the Witch; the jolly Captain Windy Scuttlebutt; Inspector John J. Fadoozle ("America's number-one private eye"); and the meatball-eating Flub-a-Dub, a hybrid creature with a dachshund's body, a duck's bill, a cat's whiskers, a spaniel's ears, a giraffe's neck, a seal's flippers, a pig's tail, and an elephant's memory.

I was ten years old and hadn't yet outgrown the show, so I asked my father, who worked at NBC television at the time, if he could ask Buffalo Bob if he might let me interview him—and I was overjoyed when the host agreed to see me for half an hour in NBC's Studio 3A at Rockefeller Plaza, where the program was broadcast. I only dimly recall the questions I asked him, but I do remember inquiring about his relationship with my favorite of the show's "human" friends: the mute Clarabell the Clown, who communicated by honking yes-and-no answers on his Harpo Marx–type horn while continually spraying Buffalo Bob with a bottle of seltzer. (Buffalo Bob told me that they were very good friends.)

From the moment that I met Buffalo Bob, I was bitten by the interview bug. While studying at Columbia College I did interviews for the college newspaper and radio station, and for many newspapers and magazines thereafter. I have always loved asking questions, and I was happy to find out that when Nobel Prize–winning physicist Isidor Rabi was a child, his mother didn't ask him, "What did you learn today?" when he came home from school, but rather "Did you ask a good question today?" And that was a very good question. It wasn't just that I loved asking questions, however—I had become fascinated by the very idea of what it means to interview someone, face-to-face, finding one's way toward dialogue. And I became absorbed in what others thought of this act as well.

The journalistic interview was a nineteenth-century invention, and Horace Greeley's interview with Brigham Young, the leader of the Mormon Church, which appeared in the *New York Tribune* in 1859, is widely considered to be the first of its kind published in the United States. (Greeley asked some very good questions.) Ever since the nineteenth century, the interview has become such a ubiquitous and pervasive journalistic form that it is sometimes difficult to see or say exactly what it is. In 1954, the psychologists Eleanor and Nathan Maccoby defined the interview as "a face-to-face verbal interchange in which one person, the interviewer, attempts to elicit information or expressions of opinion or belief from another person or persons." In 1957, social scientists Robert L. Kahn and Charles R. Cannell provided a more delimited definition, proposing that the interview is "a specialized pattern of verbal interaction—initiated for a specific purpose, and focused on some specific content area, with consequent elimination of extraneous material."

Such "interchanges" and "interactions" can be useful not only for gathering quotations for news stories or material for research surveys, or as the basis of, among other things, medical and job interviews; in many instances, they have also enabled the interview to replace the critical essay and the academic paper as a more dramatic and accessible form for investigating and exploring the ideas of men and women in the arts and sciences. Moreover, the interview's Q&A format is, mutatis mutandis, essentially the template for a Buddhist sutra or a Socratic dialogue. As the classics scholar Werner Jaeger points out in his book *Paideia: The Ideals of Greek Culture*, "Socrates taught by question and answer because he held that form of dialogue to be the original pattern of philosophic thought, and the only way for two people to reach an understanding on any subject." He adds: "Socrates never wrote anything down since he held that the only important thing was the relation between the word and the living man to whom it was, at one particular moment, addressed."

The word "interview" is derived from the French *entrevue*, which means "a meeting," which is itself derived from the verb *entrevoir,* meaning "to glimpse, to catch sight of, or to get an inkling of"—like seeing "a house through the trees, a boat in the fog, the faint outline of a person hidden in the dark," as described in one French dictionary. And one may be reminded of the passage in 1 Corinthians: "For now we see through a glass, darkly, but then face-to-face: now I know in part; but then shall I know even as also I am known."

There are meetings that we passively "take" and meetings that we actively "make," and it is in this latter sense that we can best understand the philosopher Martin Buber's profound observation in his book *I and Thou* that "all real living is meeting," and that "if we go on our way and meet a man who has advanced towards us and also gone on *his* way, we know only our part of the way, not his—his we experience only in meeting." When an interview transcends its simply pragmatic function of eliciting information, it can sometimes move into the realm of conversation and dialogue. But, as Buber remarks, "dialogue between mere individuals is only a sketch; only in dialogue between persons is the sketch filled in." In the interviews I most admire, this is exactly what occurs: a person is allowed gradually to fill him- or herself in, and the process by which this takes place is a dramatic face-to-face interchange resulting in a realized embodiment of human personality.

There are some people, of course, who fiercely resist taking part in interviews, considering them to be at best a waste of valuable time and at worst an evisceration of their integral sense of self, not dissimilar to—as the poet Kenneth Rexroth once remarked after attending a particularly noxious cocktail party—"sticking one's tongue on the third rail before dinner." The Italian writer Italo Calvino was one of the waste-of-my-time objectors. In his short text "Thoughts before an Interview," he complained:

> Every morning I tell myself: today has to be productive, and then
> something happens that prevents me from writing. Today . . .
> what is there that I have to do today? Oh yes, they are supposed
> to come interview me. I am afraid my novel will not move one
> single step forward. . . . I have given a lot of interviews and I
> have concluded that the questions always look alike. I could
> always give the same answers. But I believe I have to change my
> answers because with each interview something has changed

either inside myself or in the world. An answer that was right the first time may not be right again the second. . . . But I must go home—the time approaches for the interviewers to arrive. God help me!

More resistant by far, however, was the Nobel Prize laureate J. M. Coetzee, who, in the middle of an interview with David Atwell, announced:

> If I had any foresight, I would have nothing to do with journalists from the start. An interview is nine times out of ten an exchange with a complete stranger, yet a stranger permitted by the conventions of the genre to cross the boundaries of what is proper in conversation between strangers. . . . To me, on the other hand, truth is related to silence, to reflection, to the practice of *writing*. Speech is not a fount of truth but a pale and provisional version of writing. And the rapier of surprise wielded by the magistrate or the interviewer is not an instrument of the truth but, on the contrary, a weapon, a sign of the inherently confrontational nature of the transaction.

Marlon Brando similarly expressed his own disdain for interviews, saying: "I'm not going to lay myself at the feet of the American public and invite them into my soul. My soul is a private place."

I once interviewed one of the greatest singer-songwriters of our time, who famously shared Brando's sense of the interview as a kind of soul violation and who would have unequivocally agreed with the novelist Saul Bellow when he described interviews as being like thumbprints on his windpipe. I was aware that this musician's manager and record company were pressuring him to undergo interview surgery in order to promote his latest album, so I made certain to avoid even the slightest tinge of a personal question, and instead began to ask him about some of the gorgeous images from his songs' luminous poetic world—of fields and gardens wet with rain, country fairs and magic nights, gypsies with hearts on fire, boats in the harbor, cool evening breezes, and rivers flowing. But when I asked him about these images, he told me: "You don't create images, you go *into* them. I don't really know exactly what I'm doing yet, and I don't even know if I have to know."

Some artists appreciate and even encourage examination; others are wary of unweaving the rainbow, of pulling back "enchantment's veil." But rather than use the interview format to project some self-constructed im-

age, or to undermine both the format and the image—as public "personalities" occasionally try to do—this musician made it clear that he was not
at all interested in being caught and confined by other persons' images of
him or by their interpretations of his songs. Someone once remarked that
a rainbow is not an object, it is a vision, and perhaps one should just let it
appear and then vanish. And sometimes perhaps one should let a question
remain unanswered.

One of the most thought-provoking criticisms of the interview form
has been expressed by the psychologist James Hillman. In *Inter Views*,
which is itself a profound, multifaceted book-length interview with Laura
Pozzo as the interlocutor, he declares:

> Interviews belong to an ego genre: one ego asking another ego.
> So one thinks one has to proceed in terms of "I answer a ques-
> tion" and "stick to the topic," "the given subject," and one tries to
> say it . . . you know, nicely, tightly, rationally. "Directed thinking"
> it's called in psychiatry. All ego. Now, the kind of psychology that
> I want to do is not addressed to the ego. It is to evoke imagina-
> tion, it's to be extremely complex, it's to talk with emotion and
> from emotion and to emotion; so how can you, in an interview,
> bring in that complexity? How can you speak to the whole psy-
> che at the same time?

But *Inter Views* ultimately belies Hillman's devaluation of the interview,
and toward the end of the book he unexpectedly talks about the possibility of "re-visioning the genre," declaring to Pozzo:

> Love is one of the forms in which the normal ego has to submit
> to the psyche . . . and the interview itself is a kind of love. . . .
> How can one do an interview without love, without imagination
> working, without this attempt going on all the time as we sit here
> struggling to generate the interview itself into a form, making
> our work as true, as beautiful, as accurate, as well spoken as we
> possibly can . . . and we are both now attached and joined by
> it . . . and it will last longer than we will, sustaining us, loving us
> in return.

Kenneth Rexroth has suggested that the central meaning of the
Hindu scripture the Bhagavad Gita is that "being is a conversation of
lovers," and if an interview can somehow metamorphose into the realm of

conversation, it can perhaps begin to break through the "directed think-ing" and ego rhetoric of a conventional interview. Of course, not just any kind of conversation will do. In another of James Hillman's books, *We've Had a Hundred Years of Psychotherapy and the World's Getting Worse,* cowrit-ten with Michael Ventura, Hillman remarks:

> Not just any talk is conversation, not any talk raises conscious-ness. A subject can be talked to death, a person talked to sleep. Good conversation has an edge: it opens your eyes to something, quickens your ears. And good conversation reverberates: it keeps on talking in your mind later in the day; the next day, you find yourself still conversing with what was said. That reverberation afterwards is the very raising of consciousness; your mind's been moved. You are at another level with your reflections.

And in sharp contrast to J. M. Coetzee, the writer Susan Sontag once told me:

> I like the interview form, and I like it because I like conversa-tion, I like dialogue, and I know that a lot of my thinking is the product of conversation. In a way, the hardest thing about writing is that you're alone and have to set up a conversation with your-self, which is a fundamentally unnatural activity. I like talking to people—it's what makes me not a recluse—and conversation gives me a chance to know what I think. I don't want to know about the audience because it's an abstraction, but I certainly want to know what any *individual* thinks, and that requires a face-to-face meeting.

Plato, who, like Jesus, didn't commit his teachings to the written word—"a fine teacher, but didn't publish," an academic wag once com-mented on Jesus's unfitness for tenure—asserted that only the spoken word and face-to-face communication could elicit truth and guarantee honest teaching; and as the critic George Steiner wittily observed: "The written word does not listen to its reader. It takes no account of his ques-tions and objections." Today one can conduct an interview on the phone or via Skype, but ideally, in order to truly foster reciprocities of rapport and insight in a meeting, one requires a live countenance and a quiet physical space—like the ancient Greek *temenos,* with its sacred enclosure or holy grove or magic circle—in which an interview can live and flourish.

And one also requires time. To say that "time is of the essence" is to enjoin someone to make haste. But in conducting a timeless interview, time *is* essential, and an interviewer always wants to say to an interviewee, as Buddy Holly once sang, "Take your time and take mine too."

Buddy Holly also sang, "Listen to me, hear what I say / Listen to me / Listen closely to me," and an interviewer should never forget to heed these incantatory words. Nor, most indispensably, should an interviewer ever ignore the aphoristic advice given by the Spanish poet Antonio Machado: "To have a dialogue / First: ask a question / Then: listen." But it is easier to "hear" than to "listen." One dictionary in fact defines "listen" as "to make an effort to hear something with thoughtful attention"—and paying attention is a catalyst and a precondition for awareness and awakened consciousness.

However, "listen" can also be used to mean "obey" or "comply," and an admonitory tonal emphasis on that word (*"Listen* to me") is intended to adjure obedience, compliance, and submission. But as the psychologist Kyle Arnold states: "By replacing submissive listening with the art of therapeutic listening, one listens not in order to obey, but to understand. Therapeutic listening is empowering because it is clarifying." He refers to the psychoanalyst Theodor Reik's notion of "listening with the third ear," which, as Arnold explains, proposes that the mind has a natural ability to decipher the deeper emotional meanings conveyed by a speaker, even when those meanings are unstated or unclear; he notes that, from Reik's point of view, "bad listeners are those who do not slow down and pay attention to how they feel when listening, and quickly respond before letting anything sink in."

It seems to me that listening with the third ear is a sine qua non for a successful interview, but as a practicing interviewer, I have to confess that the manner in which I prepare for my interviews often makes me—to use a mixed metaphor—lose sight of that fact. I begin by reading, listening to, and watching as many books, recordings, and films as I can by the person with whom I'll be conversing. In the process of doing so, I often find myself becoming so absorbed and entering so deeply into that person's work that I sometimes perversely imagine that his or her creations are actually my own, and that I therefore have a privileged understanding of them. In a way, of course, each of us does exactly that, since a work of art, once created, contains its own meanings of which even its maker may not be fully aware; discovering and bringing these concealed meanings to light in an interview, while hoping not to murder to dissect, can often surprise even the work's creator. As Carl Jung once observed: "An artist's work takes on a life of its own, and it outgrows him, like a child its mother."

When the moment of reckoning finally arrives, however, and the interview begins, I too often find myself dominating the conversation and talking over the interviewee (as the old Jewish joke goes, "Stop talking to me when I'm interrupting you"). And then the pilfered artistic self that I have come to believe is mine alone inescapably rubs up against the reality of my interviewee's true self, and the ensuing dialogue inevitably reveals the process of that encounter. Occasionally, to my relief, our two selves and perceptions tally, but sometimes my conversational partner will look at me perplexedly, as if to say, "Hey, what are you talking about? That's not me at all, you're way off!!" With a sense of embarrassment, I try to save face, withdraw my projections and preconceptions as quickly as I can, take a deep breath, slow down, pay attention, and just remind myself that all I really need to do is simply ask a question. And then *listen*.

"All conversation," said Ralph Waldo Emerson, "is a magnetic experiment." Over the years, I've been fortunate to have been given "world enough and time," as Andrew Marvell put it, and the opportunity to meet face-to-face with many remarkable people, to ask them questions and listen to the answers. In this volume I present my magnetic experiments with a number of them, including writers, actors, film directors, musicians, interviewers, a choreographer, a Jungian psychologist, a neurologist, an astronomer, and creators of children's books. It seems to me that the common thread running through all of these individuals' lives and work is their unwavering affirmation of the indispensable and transformative powers of the imagination, the "divine faculty," as the French poet Charles Baudelaire called it, "that perceives immediately the inner and secret relation of things." The astronomer Carl Sagan, with whom I converse in one of the interviews here, once remarked: "Imagination will often carry us to worlds that never were. But without it we go nowhere." All of the people who appear in this book have not only gone somewhere but have also taken us along to discover and apprehend those inner and secret relations. Their journeys are not ways *of* life but rather ways *to* life. And it was a joy to have met all of them.

CHINUA ACHEBE
At the Crossroads

London, 1980

"Literature," states I. B. Singer, "is completely connected with one's origin, with one's roots." In his first children's book, *Chike and the River,* the Nigerian writer Chinua Achebe describes the adventures of his young, village-born hero—an eleven-year-old named Chike who, one day, reflects, "So this is me . . . Chike Anene, alias Chiks the Boy, of Umuofia, Mbaino District, Onitsha Province, Eastern Nigeria, Nigeria, West Africa, Africa, World, Universe." And it is this reflection that reveals the roots and the trajectory of all of Achebe's writing for both children and adults.

Born in 1930 in Ogidi, Eastern Nigeria, of devout Christian parents who baptized him Albert Chinualumogu, Achebe "dropped the tribute to Victorian England," as he puts it, when he went to university, and took his first name from his last. "On one arm of the cross," he remembers in his autobiographical essay "Named for Victoria," "we sang hymns and read the Bible night and day. On the other, my father's brother and his family, blinded by heathenism, offered food to idols. . . . If anyone likes to believe that I was torn by spiritual agonies or stretched on the rack of my ambivalence, he certainly may suit himself. I do not remember any undue distress. What I do remember was a fascination for the ritual and the life on the other arm of the crossroads. And I believe two things were in my favor—that curiosity and the little distance imposed between me and it by the accident of my birth. The distance becomes not a separation but a bringing together, like the necessary backward step which a judicious viewer may take in order to see a canvas steadily and fully."

Achebe brilliantly creates and displays this canvas for us in *The African Trilogy,* comprising *Things Fall Apart, Arrow of God,* and *No Longer at Ease.* In

I

addition to his novels, poems, and essays, Achebe has written four works for children. The first of these, *Chike and the River,* is an adventure story about a young boy who goes from the country to the big market town of Onitsha, dreams of crossing the big river (the Niger), finally does so, meets up with a gang of thieves whom he exposes, and in the end becomes a hero.

"The Flute," which Achebe presents in a slightly different version in his novel *Arrow of God,* is his retelling of a folktale about a young boy who, trying to recover something precious to him—a plain, ordinary bamboo flute (a sign of creativity and praise)—goes to the spirit land to reclaim it; and because he is truthful and unselfish he is rewarded, whereas another boy (selfish, proud, greedy, and trying to fool the spirits) winds up destroying himself, his mother, and his brothers and sisters.

Most effective of all are Achebe's two animal stories. *The Drum* is a trickster tale about the wily and ubiquitous Tortoise, who, one day, chasing after some fruits that have fallen into a hole in the earth, comes upon the land of the spirits and winds up the owner of a magic drum that, when played, produces an endless supply of food for the drought-stricken animal kingdom. When the drum is accidentally broken, Tortoise—the now self-proclaimed king—returns to the spirit land, but, as with the second boy in "The Flute," his newly developed greed and pride lead to his obtaining a drum that wreaks havoc and destruction for him and his community.

Achebe's *How the Leopard Got His Claws*—a story that takes its place as one of the most powerful and starkest fables in the tradition that runs from Aesop and Bidpai to Kipling and Orwell—tells of a time "in the beginning" when all the forest animals live as friends; only the dog, with its sharp teeth, acts selfishly and spitefully. Leopard, clawless and gentle, is king. To protect the animals during the rainy season, he suggests that all the animals build a common shelter. But the dog and the duck refuse to help and turn away from the community. Later, one stormy night, when Leopard is out roaming, the dog attacks the animals in their shelter, wounding them severely. Leopard returns, the dog attacks him, too, and when Leopard urges all the animals to stand up to the aggressor as one, they turn into cowards and decide to make the powerful dog their king. Leopard goes into exile, and the new king orders the animals to find Leopard and force him to return to the new totalitarian society. They throw stones at the wounded Leopard, chanting: "No one has a right to leave our village! No one has a right to leave our village!" And "although some of the stones hit the leopard and hurt him, he did not turn round even once. He continued walking until he no longer heard the noise of the animals." Traveling for seven days and seven nights, Leopard meets a blacksmith, who makes deadly bronze claws for him. From Thunder he receives the sound for his voice. And he returns to the village, this time to terrorize, and again becomes king. The dog escapes and servilely offers himself as a slave to the first hunter he meets, promising to help the hunter kill his fellow animals, who have now begun to behave like "animals" to each other. "Perhaps," the story ends, "the animals will make peace among themselves some day and live together again. Then they can keep away the hunter who is their common enemy."

As Achebe explains in the following conversation, both *The Drum* and *How the Leopard Got His Claws*, aside from being striking and enjoyable tales for both children and adults, are connected to the realities of Igbo life and history. And they were written both to delight and to instruct. This dialectical tension between delighting and instructing is at the heart of Achebe's writings, as it is of much of children's literature. "Our ancestors," Achebe affirms, "created their myths and legends and told their stories for a human purpose (including, no doubt, the excitation of wonder and pure delight). . . . Their artists lived and moved and had their being in society and created their works for the good of that society. . . . In a recent anthology, a Hausa folk tale, having recounted the usual fabulous incidents, ends with these words: 'They all came and they lived happily together. He had several sons and daughters who grew up and helped in raising the standard of education of the country.' As I said elsewhere, if you consider this ending a naïve anticlimax, then you cannot know very much about Africa."

* * *

In your fable How the Leopard Got His Claws, *you first describe the animals of the world at peace with one another. "They sat," you write, "on log benches in the village square. As they rested they told stories and drank palm wine." But later, after selfishness and cowardice have upset the animals' communal harmony, the leopard—now forced into the role of violent avenger—says: "From today I shall rule the forest with terror. The life of our village is ended." And this reminds me of the conclusion of your novel* A Man of the People, *in which you write: "The owner was the village, and the village had a mind; it could say no to sacrilege. But in the affairs of the nation there was no owner, the laws of the village became powerless." It seems to me that the idea of the "village"—connected as it is with the notions of the possibilities of community,*

*truthful language, and the attainment of real individuality—is central to all
your work.*

My world—the one that interests me more than any other—is the world
of the village. It is one, not the only, reality, but it's the one that the Igbo,
who are my people, have preferred to all others. It was as if they had a
choice of creating empires or cities or large communities and they looked
at them and said, "No, we think that what is safest and best is a system
in which everybody knows everybody else." In other words, a village. So
you'll find that, politically, the Igbos preferred the small community. They
had nothing to do, until recently, with kings and kingdoms.

Now I'm quite convinced that this was a conscious choice. Some people look at the Igbos and assert that they didn't evolve to the stage of
having kings and kingdoms. But this isn't true—the Igbos have a word
for "king," they have words for all the paraphernalia of kingship—it isn't
as if they don't know about kings. I think it's simply that, looking at the
way the world operates, they seem to have said to themselves: Of all the
possible political systems, we shall insist on the one where there are only
so many people. So that when a man gets up to talk to his fellows they
know who he is, they know exactly whether he is a thief, an honest man, or
whatever. In a city of eight million people, you can't know your neighbor.
And that means you have to set up a system of representation: you choose
a delegate to speak for you. But the Igbos didn't want someone else to
speak for them.

And this is quite central to my fiction and to my analysis of the problems of creating a new nation today. Obviously, we can't go back to a
system in which every man is turning up in the village square—that's in
the past. But we have to find a way of dealing with the problems created
by the fact that somebody says he's speaking on your behalf, but you don't
know who he is. This is one of the problems of the modern world.

In Arrow of God *you write: "The festival brought gods and men together in
one crowd. It was the only assembly in Umuaro in which a man might look to
his right and find his neighbor and look to his left and see a god standing there."
So your idea of the village seems to include the possibility not only of political
participation but of a spiritual one as well.*

Definitely, you're absolutely right. It's a world of men and women and
children and spirits and deities and animals and nature . . . and the dead—

this is very important—a community of the living and the dead and the unborn. So it is both material and spiritual, and whatever you did in the village took this into account. Our life was never compartmentalized in the way that it has become today. We talk about politics, economics, religion. But in the traditional society all these things were linked together— there was no such thing as an irreligious man. In fact, we don't even have a word for religion in Igbo. It's simply *life.*

In Things Fall Apart, *Okonkwo tells his son Nwoye "masculine" stories of violence and bloodshed, but the boy prefers the tales his mother tells him about Tortoise the trickster, about the bird who challenged the whole world to a wrestling contest and was finally thrown by a cat, and about the quarrel between Earth and Sky—stories for "foolish women and children," as Okonkwo thinks of them. But in* No Longer at Ease, *Nwoye—now the father of the protagonist Obi—forbids the telling of folktales to his son because he himself has become a Christian and doesn't want to disseminate what he now thinks of as "heathen" stories. All of this reminds me of the constant attacks against fairy stories in Europe by any number of rigid moralists and educators during the past two centuries.*

I think that stories are the very center, the very heart of our civilization and culture. And to me it's interesting that the man who thinks he's strong wants to forbid stories, whether it's Okonkwo forbidding the stories of gentleness, or whether, later on, it's a Christian who, so self-satisfied in the rightness and superiority of his faith, wishes to forbid the hidden pagan stories. It is there in those despised areas that the strength of the civilization resides, not in the masculine strength of Okonkwo, nor in the self-righteous strength of the Christian faith. The stone the builders reject becomes a cornerstone of the house. So I think a writer instinctively gravitates toward that "weakness," if you like. He will leave the "masculine" military strength and go for love, for gentleness. For unless we cultivate gentleness, we will be destroyed. And this is why you have poets and storytellers.

The psychologist James Hillman has talked of the importance of "re-storying the adult."

This is what I've been trying to say when I talk about weakness and strength. You see, "re-storying the adult" is a very interesting phrase. What, in fact, is the adult as distinct from the child? The adult is someone who has seen it all, nothing is new to him. Such a man is to be pitied. The child, on the other hand, is new in the world, and everything is possible to him. His imagination hasn't been dulled by use and experience. Therefore, when you re-story the adult, what you do is you give him back some of the child's energy and optimism, that ability to be open and to expect anything. The adult has become dull and routine, mechanical, he can't be lifted. It's as if he's weighted down by his experience and his possessions, all the junk he's assembled and accumulated. And the child can still fly, you see. Therefore the story belongs to the child, because the story's about flying.

In your autobiographical essay "Named for Victoria," you've mentioned that, like Nwoye, you were told stories by your mother and older sister. So you were lucky enough to be "storied" at an early age.

I was very fortunate, but I would say that this was traditional. Any child growing up at that time, unless he was particularly unlucky, would be told stories as part of his education. It doesn't happen anymore. The stories are now read in books, and very rarely is there a situation in which the mother will sit down night after night with her family and tell stories, with the young children falling asleep to them. The pace of life has altered. Again, this is what I meant by saying that our generation is unique. And I was lucky to have been part of the very tail end of that older tradition. Perhaps we may not be able to revive it, but at least we can make sure that the kind of stories our children read carry something of the aura of the tales our mothers and sisters told us.

In traditional oral societies, the storyteller would employ intonation, gestures, eye contact, pantomime, acrobatics, and occasionally costumes, masks, and props in his or her dramatic presentation.

Yes, that's right and the loss is enormous. And all I'm saying is that, rather than lose everything we should value the written story, which is certainly better than no story at all. It's impossible in the modern world to have the traditional storytelling. But I think that perhaps in the home we should not give up so quickly. I find, for instance, that when I write a new children's story the best thing I can do is to tell it to my children, and I get remarkable feedback that way. My youngest child, incidentally, writes stories of her own! But the storyteller today has to find a new medium rather than regret the passing of the past. Television is there, we can't do anything about it, so some of us should use this medium, we should do stories for television.

In The Drum, *the tortoise, when retelling to the other animals the story of how he descended into the spirit land to find his magic drum, improvises little dramatic changes in order to make his tale sound more heroic and convincing—which is, of course, what people do quite often in everyday conversation.*

To serve their own ends! *[Laughing]*

It's strange but obvious that it is children—the seemingly least significant members of society—who are given stories about the most important matters: selfishness, pride, greed, the meaning of life and death.

That's right, and this is wonderful for children. I think the adult sometimes loses sight of the nature of stories. But these great fundamental issues have never changed and never will. I mean, children always ask the same questions: Who made the world? How come some people are suffering? Who made death? And to think that we have somehow moved on to more "adult" subject matters is simply self-deception. What we do, of course, is quite often get trapped in trivia masked in highfalutin language. But the basic questions are still the same, and this is what children's stories particularly deal with.

I think that mankind's greatest blessing is language. And this is why the storyteller is a high priest, and why he is so concerned about language and about using it with respect. Language is under great stress in the modern world . . . it's under siege. All kinds of people—advertisers, politicians, priests, technocrats—want to get a hold of it and use it for their own ends: these are the strong people today. The storyteller represents the weakness we were talking about. But of course every poet is aware of this problem. And this is where children come into it, too, because you can't fool around with children—you have to be honest with language in children's stories, mere cleverness won't do.

I wanted to ask you about The Drum, *which begins: "In the beginning when the world was young . . ." Here you conjure a kind of fairy-tale setting in which animals and trees talk to each other. . . . By the way, the number seven seems to come up in your children's books all the time. In* The Drum, *for example, there are seven steps to the underworld, seven times that the drum thanks the tree, and so on.*

Seven is a magical number. And this is almost a formula—crossing the seven rivers and the seven savannas in order to go beyond the world of the human to the world of the spirits. The Igbo week is four days, and seven weeks is one month. Seven weeks is a crucial measure of time. When a child is born, it's not really regarded as fully here until it has lived seven weeks. Then it is human and given a name.

The tortoise, who's the protagonist of the story, follows the fruits he's let fall into the underworld abode of the spirits. And when he returns to his family and friends, he begins to make a grand speech.

Yes, it's like an Igbo meeting. He's trying to become a king, which is anathema to the Igbo.

So here again we discover a parable. And when the tortoise has to repeat his journey to the underworld—since the magic drum has been destroyed and he wants to get another one from the spirits—

He fakes it. So here is a way in which the story of *The Drum* and "The Flute" have the same theme. A true adventure isn't a faked adventure, and there's no mercy shown to the faker. You do something the first time, you do it honestly, that's okay. But then you go back and you plan something which doesn't arise out of necessity—that's fakery. And children understand this because they know about faking. Adults think that they can fool children *[laughing]*, but they don't really succeed.

In "The Flute," the "faked" situation is set up by the greedy first wife, who wants to get something for her son and herself.

Yes. Stories often become far more evil when human characters move in—there's a greater possibility for evil. Somehow there's a limit to how evil the tortoise can be—you know that. He's a rogue, but he's a nice kind of rogue. And in the end he's punished, and that's it.

The Igbo tortoise trickster has been compared to Spider of the African Hausa, Fox of the Toba of Argentina, Maui of the Polynesians, and Rabbit of Afro-American folklore. And their common characteristics, as described by Brian

Sutton-Smith, are as follows: "violation of taboo; impulsiveness; a lack of close, caring relationships; apparent disregard for the feelings of others; an inability to learn from past mistakes; lack of anxiety or remorse; an exhibitionist narcissism; constant use of pretense and trickery; and a demeanor of childlike, innocent charm"—characteristics that Sutton-Smith suggests are reminiscent of the symptoms of the psychopath.

I have to say that the picture painted there doesn't fully account for the role of the tortoise in the Igbo folktales. As I said, he's a nice rogue, because nobody hates him in the end. If you see someone who's always around when something happens, you say, "A story is never complete without a tortoise"—that's one of our proverbs. So Tortoise is a character around whom stories are built. And he tries to get away with more than his fair share. He's smart, sometimes oversmart, and he gets punished. But he's not an evil creature. Certainly not a psychopath! That's too strong.

Children seem to have a special affinity with Tortoise.

Yes, they love him. He's a nice, unreliable kind of rascal, and the village is all the happier for that kind of character—as long as there aren't too many like him in any one community. *[Laughing]* You know the kind of character he is, and when he appears everybody immediately knows that Tortoise is up to his tricks, and they protect themselves. Remember the story in which Tortoise wants to go with the birds to heaven and have a feast? They give him wings, and though he says he's converted, he actually intends to cheat them. As the Chinese say: If you fool me once, shame on you; fool me twice, shame on me. That's a very wise statement. Unfortunately the birds let themselves be fooled three, four, or five times. And so do we.

But getting back to why children, especially, like the trickster: perhaps it's because this figure is very lively, like a child; he's always doing something unexpected. There's a difference between the kind of roguery Tortoise is guilty of and evil. I don't think children like an evil character, they prefer a lively and vivacious one. Even if he's not very honest, they know that anyway, so he can't fool them. And there's room for this kind of person in all stories. Even in adult fiction. Think of a villain like Chief Nanga in *A Man of the People*, who has an attractive character—yes, a trickster, he's really a Tortoise figure. And you're attracted to him in spite of yourself, in spite of what you know. There's always drama around him, something is always happening where he is. As with Tortoise, he isn't going to simply walk down the street and disappear, he's going to start something.

Finally, I think that children like Tortoise because he's a very small fellow—he's weak in relation to the giants of the animal world. The tortoise is the slowest of all slow creatures, and yet he wins the races.

I wanted to ask you about your first children's book, Chike and the River. *The name Chike has* chi *in it, and so does your first name, Chinua. About* chi, *you've written: "There are two clearly distinct meanings of the word* chi *in Igbo. The first is often translated as god, guardian angel, personal spirit, soul, spirit double, etc. The second meaning is day, or daylight, but is most commonly used for those transitional periods between day and night or night and day. . . . In a general way we may visualize a person's* chi *as his other identity in spirit land—his spirit being complementing his terrestrial human being; for nothing can stand alone, there must always be another thing standing beside it."*

When we talk about *chi,* we're talking about the individual spirit, and so you find the word in all kinds of combinations. Chinwe, which is my wife's name, means "*Chi* owns me"; mine is Chinua, which is a shortened form of an expression that means "May a *chi* fight for me." My son is named Chidi, which means "*Chi* is there." So it's almost in everybody's name in one form or the other. Our youngest girl asked me why she didn't have *chi* in her name *[laughing]*, she thought it was some kind of discrimination, so she took the name Chioma, which means "Good *chi.*"

What does Chike mean?

Chike is a shortened form of Chinweike, which means "*Chi* has the strength or the power." And that's what that frail-looking character has—he has the power.

It seems that, in the African tradition, the infant is generally thought of not as a kind of tabula rasa but rather as a messenger whose presence is a gift from the other world.

I think that the idea of the child as messenger is certainly prevalent. Now, my wife has been doing some work on the notion that some children who are born, die, to come back, and to repeat cycles of birth and death—this is a very common and popular belief among the Igbos. In the past, of course, this was meant to explain the high rate of infant mortality. And in doing this research, my wife encountered stories about how children come from the world of "over there" into the world of men. It's very interesting to discover the attributes they're supposed to come with. The fact is that there's a bargain made, there's a discussion concerning what you'd like to be and what you'd like to do that takes place before the child comes over here. So the child is not a tabula rasa, he or she is someone who has already negotiated its entire destiny *over there*. And the child comes to the borderline, and there is somebody there—perhaps a group of people—who tries to talk him out of what he has agreed to be—they want to discourage the child from aspiring too greatly. So what I am saying is that the child comes with a whole realm of experience. Of course, these are really metaphors for explaining reality. But a child isn't a clean slate, it's got all its genes from its ancestors—what he or she is going to be is more or less fixed in the genes, among other things.

In Childhood and Cosmos: The Social Psychology of the Black African Child, *Pierre Erny writes: "The consciousness of receiving into earthly existence a new life which comes from elsewhere, of receiving it much more than molding it, is the very basis of the relationship with the child, who can be made an object of almost fearful respect and gratitude. . . . If an 'angel' . . . is seen in the child, education takes a very specific direction. It becomes humble; it gives way to the revelation of this being who comes to bring eternally young life to the living. . . . The child brings along with it more than can be given to it. It renews those who welcome it, rejuvenates them, regenerates them. Childcare is composed of piety, admiration, freedom, confidence, and gratitude more than authority or a spirit of domination and possessiveness."*

It's true, and had better be, too. What Erny is talking about here concerns the attitude of the *adult* to the child, and I believe that in bringing up children it's the adult who learns. As a parent I know that, and so this leads to the humility Erny mentions—I think this is very real. Now, that's not permissiveness, that's not to say you must never correct a child, because we're not talking about the years of experience the child cannot possibly have. But if you accept that the child comes from somewhere else, you can renew your acquaintanceship with that world through the child. I think this is a very good way of putting it, because these are metaphors for our experience. We really don't know. We're simply trying to use words as images to convey vague but insistent notions that visit us. In the past, when a child was born, our people would go to a diviner, to find out which of the ancestors it was who had come again. So this child was not new. And once they established who the child was, they gave him all that respect.

The Ijo of the Niger Delta have a proverb that goes: "He's of goblin ancestry who knows not whence he came." And this might imply that there is and should be a connection between the adult and his sense of his own childhood, since both connect one to one's past.

Yes, that's right, because if there is a constant coming or going between us and the world of the ancestors, which is what my people believe, then it's in fact the child who can tell you about that world since it's coming from there—it's not the old man who's *going* there but the child who's *coming* from there.

In all your work, the grandfather casts his shadow on the grandchild, the village on the city, and the pagan tradition on the Christian one.

The duality. Things come in twos. "Wherever something stands, something else will stand beside it"—this is another very powerful Igbo statement. It's absolutely true, and it's when someone refuses to see the "other" that you have problems. To my mind, one of the worst and most unimaginative of states is that of single-mindedness. This is the state of a man like Okonkwo in *Things Fall Apart*. In certain limited and restricted spheres this is admirable. But beyond that it becomes a real liability—he cannot see that things come in twos, and in that respect he resembles the British missionaries more than his own people—the way, the truth, and the life. But the old men in the village have no problem with that. They understand that you should have your own God, because it's only natural that if there's one God there must be another. For such people it's easier to accept and appreciate other people. But the single-minded, missionary type, whether he's the Englishman or Okonkwo, doesn't operate on the level of this duality.

Igbo history seems now to be unalterably connected to Nigerian history, and history has brought Nigeria to a critical point—as a country it, too, seems to be at the crossroads. What role do you think stories—and particularly stories for children—can have in these rapidly changing times? And might it not be possible for those of us in the West to learn something from your experience?

Whether or not the West learns anything from the African experience is a matter for the West to decide. I can only say that a major prerequisite to learning is humility, and that on present showing this virtue is extremely difficult for the West, thanks to its immense material success.

But to the main part of your question. Igbo and Nigerian fortunes seem to be indissolubly linked again—for good or ill. Our responsibility as Nigerians of this generation is to strive to realize the potential good and avoid the ill. Clearly, children are central in all this, for it is their legacy and patrimony that we are talking about. If Nigeria is to become a united and humane society in the future, her children must now be brought up on a common vocabulary for the heroic and the cowardly, the just and the unjust. Which means preserving and refurbishing the landscape of the imagination and the domain of stories, and not—as our leaders seem to think—a verbal bombardment of patriotic exhortation and daily recitations of the National Pledge and Anthem.

CHINUA ACHEBE

NOVEMBER 16, 1930 – MARCH 21, 2013

GEORGE BALANCHINE
Dancing with Mr. B

George Balanchine was generally considered the greatest choreographer of modern times. Born in 1904, in St. Petersburg, he studied music and dance in St. Petersburg and made his dancing debut at the age of ten as a cupid in the Maryinsky Theater Ballet Company production of *The Sleeping Beauty.* He later served as ballet master for Serge Diaghilev's famous Ballets Russes de Monte Carlo. At the end of 1933, he traveled to the United States, where, along with the distinguished dance connoisseur and man of letters Lincoln Kirstein, he helped to found both the School of American Ballet and the New York City Ballet, of which he was the artistic director.

For the latter continually inspiring company, Balanchine created scores of masterpieces, including *Serenade, The Four Temperaments, Jewels, A Midsummer Night's Dream,* and *Vienna Waltzes,* whose "dance evolutions and figures"—in the words of the late poet and critic Edwin Denby—were "luminous in their spacing, and of a miraculous musicality in their impetus." Among the greatest of Balanchine's works were his more than thirty ballets to the scores of Igor Stravinsky, with whom he was associated since 1925, when he choreographed a revised version of the composer's *The Song of the Nightingale.* In the collaborations between these two Russian masters, one became ineluctably conscious of "seeing" music and "hearing" movements, as music and dance revealed sound and light to be two manifestations of one vibrational source.

I was fortunate enough to meet with and interview George Balanchine on two occasions. The first was in July 1978, at the opening of the New York City Ballet's annual summer season in Saratoga Springs, New York. Our second meeting occurred exactly four years later, in July 1982, during one of the final performances of the City Ballet's Stravinsky Centennial Celebration, held during that month. It was to be Balanchine's final interview. Several months later he entered New York City's Roosevelt Hospital, suffering from progressive cerebral disintegration.

Mr. B (as Balanchine was known to his colleagues) held at bay almost all kinds of visionary and speculative theorizing about his work, preferring to talk about himself as a craftsman rather than a creator, and comparing himself to a cook and a cabinetmaker (he was apparently extremely adept at both endeavors) and even, as he did once with me, to a horse!

Both of my conversations with George Balanchine were concerned with music. As the composer George Perle states in his liner notes to the marvelous *A Balanchine Album* (Nonesuch Records): "Balanchine was an accomplished musician, but he was much more than this. Just as the words of a Schubert *Lied* have become Schubert's words, whoever the poet may have been, so the music of a Balanchine ballet becomes Balanchine's composition, not because he has appropriated it, but because he seems to have magically re-experienced the creative act, to have relived the decisions, the choices, and eliminations that the composer has lived through in bringing it into being."

Witty, gracious, childlike, and charming, Balanchine conversed with me, in both 1978 and 1982, in his inimitable, idiosyncratically flavored English. During our second conversation, I noticed that Balanchine's mind would occasionally wander, and that he would respond to one question with the answer to another. When asked about Stravinsky's childhood, for example, he proceeded to talk about his own. But as the following two interviews both make clear, Balanchine always refused to dwell on the past or the future. ("I'm not interested in later on. I don't have any later on. We all live in the same time forever.") And the only way to pay tribute to the spirit of this twentieth-century genius is simply to regard his ballets as eternally new creations.

* * *

I

Saratoga Springs, New York, 1978

Of all the art forms, music and dance seem to be the closest—like brother and sister, or like lovers. And whenever I think of your ballets, I hear the dancers and see the music.

Anything that doesn't belong to the world of words, you can't explain.

People say, "What do you feel when you look at this?" We always have to compare with something else. "Is it beautiful?" "Yes." "Well, how beautiful?" "Like a rose, like a taste, like a wine." "And what does wine taste like?" "Like grass." It's always something else. So you describe my ballets in terms of hearing; and you're a writer, so you write. I myself don't have a writing style . . . not at all. Just a few words that I need to remember things.

The French poet Stéphane Mallarmé once talked about a dancer "writing with her body."

Naturally. But not with words. You see, I got a message. Each one of us is here to serve on this earth. And probably I was sent here to see and to hear—that's all I can do. I can't see something that doesn't exist. I don't create or invent anything, I assemble. God already made everything—colors, flowers, language—and somehow there had to be a Mother. Our business is to choose. The more you choose, the more amazing everything is. But I can't explain what I do.

How do you explain a piece by Anton Webern? You can say, mechanically, that it's twelve-tone music, but that doesn't mean anything to anybody. It's like saying something is four-part fugue, but after a while, people listening to it lose hold of it. So the beginning of my ballet *Episodes* to Webern's music *Symphony* [Opus 21] is canonic. I had to try to paint or design time with bodies in order to create a resemblance between the dance and what was going on in sound.

The nineteenth-century theorist Eduard Hanslick said: "Music is form moving in sounds." This would also seem to be your definition of dance.

Absolutely. You have to have sound in order to dance. I need music that's possible to move to. You have to hear the music—the timbre and the use of the sound. Music is like an aquarium with the dancers inside it. It's all around you, like fish moving through water.

Some choreographers take an important piece and then give the ballet an inappropriate title—a Brahms piano concerto, say, and then call it a "Rainbow" ballet by Brahms. He didn't write a rainbow. I, personally, can't do dances to a Brahms symphony or to Beethoven—perhaps little moments from a specific piece. But you can't take one of their symphonies and dance to it.

You've choreographed much Stravinsky, but never Le Sacre du Printemps.

It's impossible, terrible. Nobody can do it. And Stravinsky's *Les Noces* is impossible, too, and it shouldn't be done. The words are tough Russian words, and when at the end of the piece the Bridegroom, very drunk, screams out that he and his Bride will live together forever and that everyone will be jealous of their good life . . . well, he's unhappy when he sings that, because the marriage will be a disaster. He's never seen her and she's never seen him. It's a tragedy, really, when you hear this sung in Russian—those words and that almost funeral music.

Speaking of Stravinsky, someone once described him at a Nadia Boulanger class in Paris, sitting at a piano and "inventing a chord"—playing a chord, then taking one note out and putting another in until he had something very special. Don't you do the same thing?

Absolutely. There's gesture and timing, and I leave things alone or take something out, put something else in instead. I can't take a formula and do just anything with it. Naturally, in a few seconds I can create very banal movements with a formula, but to do something important, to occupy time and space with bodies—several bodies that stop in time and pass—you have to look at them and say: "Not right now, don't do that, get out, do it this way." You have to put things together like a gefilte fish. That's how I do it.

In the second pas de deux of your ballet Stravinsky Violin Concerto, *I get the sense of inert matter being formed—the artist shaping his materials. The dancers' last gestures, especially, suggest this. Did you have this idea in mind?*

To me, it's the music that wants you to do certain things. Dance has to look like the music. If you use music simply as an accompaniment, then you don't hear it. I occupy myself with how not to interfere with the music. And at the end of this pas de deux I made a gesture as if to say, "How do you do, Stravinsky?" That music is very Russian—reminiscent of old, nostalgic Russian folk songs—and I know what Stravinsky meant, I understood and felt it.

It's very difficult to make a gesture such that it looks like a sound. It's also like you're asking and making a question—two people addressing the world. So, at the conclusion, I made a little bow to Stravinsky. And I also did that in the duet to the *Symphony in Three Movements*—there's a little

Balinese-type gesture (Stravinsky loved Balinese culture), like a prayer, and that, too, was for the composer.

Stravinsky's body is gone, but he's still here. What could he leave, his nose? He left me a cigarette case and other things. But the music is really what he left, and when his music plays, he's right here.

There are at least two basic ideas concerning the nature of dance. The first of these is conveyed in a statement by St. Augustine: "All the dancer's gestures are signs of things, and the dance is called rational, because it aptly signifies and displays something over and above the pleasure of the senses." The second is revealed in a statement by the Sufi poet Rumi: "Whosoever knoweth the power of the dance, dwelleth in God."

To me, these are two ways of saying the same thing. Now, the dervishes don't perform specifically for the sake of money or beauty, but personally, I have to do ballets that will attract a public. If people don't come, we don't have a company, dancers and musicians can't get paid. Once they have a salary, they can eat—and then we can tell them: "Don't eat, get thin, do this, put on some makeup, you look like hell!" *Train* them. And then you can do certain dances that aren't meant specifically to entertain the public.

In the great ballroom finale of Vienna Waltzes, *you've created a ballet that entertains but that also suggests a world of waltzing dervishes!*

I agree.

And in the midst of these whirling dancers is the heroine, who just as she seems about to awake—both sexually and spiritually—swoons and faints like the archetypal Victorian maiden.

Or like some of the characters in Turgenev . . . yes, there it is! Hegel once said that people want to see their lives onstage. That means, for example, that one man might think: "I'm married, my wife and children have left me, and I'm unhappy and feel that I'm going to kill myself. And that's what I think Art is—people should play for me my story." Another guy has a bad stomach. So everyone has a different story. Look at *Jesus Christ Superstar*: people say it's very good, they think they get something from it, but they get *nothing* from it, it's miserable. That's no way to find God—going to sleep, having a drink.

I've always wanted to know whether or not you like rock and roll.

It's not my cup of tea, I'm too old. Jazz is my time—and some Gershwin and Rodgers and Hart. But I'm not really American yet. I can't understand rock and roll words: "Auh-uh-er-er-you-er." The boy and girl meet and then never meet again . . . and then . . . what . . . "you went away" . . . er . . . "you and I holding hands . . ." I don't understand it.

Getting back to dance and how you choreograph: When you first hear the opening intervals of a piece of music—Webern's Symphony—*do you immediately visualize these intervals, or feel them in your body?*

No, I feel something can be done, but if I don't try it out, then I can never do it. You can't sit down and think about dancing, you have to get up and dance. You take people and move them and see if their movements correspond to the music. And I have to know the music. In Webern's *Symphony* I made the dancers turn upside down at one point in order to parallel the use of the musical inversion. And near the ending of Stravinsky's *Movements for Piano and Orchestra* I have dancers marking the composer's returning twelve-tone row . . . but now slowed down, spread and stretched out. These certain things I do, naturally, but as little as possible. I don't imitate the notes of a piece.

When you listen to music, you can hear lots of notes in one ear, but you can't see collected movements, as if they were a pill that goes into your eye and dissolves immediately. Léonide Massine used to have people dancing everywhere—he called it contrapuntal ballet. "Contra," which means "against," actually—in reality—means "together." As I've said many times, the movements of arms, head, and feet are contrapuntal to the vertical position of the body.

Writing about Webern's use of retrograde canons, the composer Ernst Krenek once pointed to something extremely fascinating. As Krenek stated it: "The accuracy and elegance with which the reversibility of these models is worked out emanate from a peculiar fascination, seeming to suggest a mysterious possibility for circumventing the one-way direction of time." Does this have any relationship to what you feel about Webern's music or about the way you choreograph a work like Symphony?

Even if it's so, you can't and shouldn't try to effect this. Several years ago I read an article about the reverse-time sense, and I think that the world must have this sense. In the usual time sense, everything decays—what is young gets older and separates—and the world, as we know it, is like that. But there's another world where all this decayed material, in our time sense, goes into . . . whatever it is and reverses. It's as if you're born dead, get younger, and die at birth. Not only that . . . it may be that this time sense is going on at the same time as the other one. Why not? It's everything at once. As you've reminded me before, I still believe what I once said: "I'm not interested in later on. I don't have any later on. We all live in the same time forever." . . . Of course, they talk about the Black Hole. But think: the Black Hole will probably disintegrate, too, because it's part of our world. So the Black Hole feeds himself—it's a *he*, probably, the Black Hole—he eats up the light . . . and then when he's completely fed, he'll explode like mad!

Some of the endings of your Stravinsky ballets, in particular, feel so strongly to me like beginnings that I look forward to the endings.

Like beginnings. Yes. But remember, we have to be thinking of this on the level of particles. And you don't really become aware of it, you only think of it that way. I think that the reverse-time sense is true because I've always thought that it couldn't be that everything goes in just one direction. We know Andromeda goes one way and continues to go that way until it becomes dust. But what else? What about on the level of subatomic particles? I feel something, but as Bottom the Weaver says in *A Midsummer Night's Dream,* "My eye cannot hear and my ear cannot see."

In my ballets, of course, there's an order. A dance must start and go somewhere. I can't start until I know why I have to do something. "Why this?" I say. "Why this way?" If I don't know why, I can't start a ballet. Physically, I do. But before that, I must know, I must be sure why *this* is *that* way. It's inside of me—I have to feel inside of me that this little bundle is right and that it represents something clear, with a beginning, middle, and end.

The painter Paul Klee once wrote about the idea of male sperm impregnating the egg as a way of describing the formal energy of art: "Works as form-determining sperm: the primitive male component."

I don't believe in this at all. It sounds like the painter Pavel Tchelitchew, who once described this idea in reverse. I've often said that the ballet that

I represent makes the woman most important. If the women didn't exist, there wouldn't be a ballet. It would be a man's ballet company, like Maurice Béjart's. That's a good example. There are, of course, women in his company, but it's the men—the way they look—who are most important. His *Le Sacre*, by the way, is the best anyone has done. It has a certain impact, I think, and I was amazed how almost right—physically and musically— his version was. But in my ballet, the man is a consort and the woman is the queen. Terpsichore is our muse, and little Apollo's head is covered with curls. Ballet is a feminine form, it's matriarchal. And we have to serve her.

It's strange, though, when I see your pas de deux—especially those in Agon, Stravinsky Violin Concerto, Duo Concertant, Pithoprakta—*I pay less attention, finally, to the fact that there's a man and a woman dancing, but rather start thinking of things like identity, personality, separation, reflections, duplications.*

That's right. Some people, though, see in these pas de deux only pure man–woman relationships: "The woman didn't have any guts, the man wasn't sexy enough." This isn't my business. And what you're saying is absolutely right. Strange things happen. In the Webern *[Episodes]* pas de deux, for example, it's like a roof . . . raindrops on a crystal roof.

In a pas de deux like that I get a sense of two, or many, parts of myself, and I feel the dance as a kind of energy or electric field, lighting up my emotions.

That's what it is. It exists.

These pas de deux always seem to be distillations and compressions of the whole ballet, incorporating everything that occurs before and after it and raising it to an extraordinary level. "Ripeness is all," Shakespeare said. Moments of ripeness. Which reminds me of the beautiful pas de deux in the second act of A Midsummer Night's Dream.

When Bottom the Weaver is transformed into an ass, he says, "The eye of man hath not heard, the ear of man hath not seen, man's hand is not able to taste, his tongue to conceive, nor his heart to report what my dream was." It sounds silly, but it's full of double and triple meanings. And I think that at moments like this, Shakespeare was a Sufi. It reminds me of St. Paul's First Epistle to the Corinthians [1 Corinthians 2:9]: "Eye hath not seen, nor ear heard, neither have entered into the heart of man, the things which God hath prepared for them that love him." What Bottom says sounds as if the parts of the body were quarreling with each other. But it's really as if he were somewhere in the Real World. He loses his man's head and brain and experiences a revelation.

And then what happens? Bottom wants to recite his dream, which "hath no bottom," to the Duke after his and his friends' play-within-a-play is over, but the Duke chases them away. And the really deep and important message was in that dream.

At one point, when I was choreographing the ballet, I said to myself: "In the last act, I'll make a little entertainment and then a big vision of Mary standing on the sun, wrapped in the moon, with a crown of twelve stars on her head and a red dragon with seven heads and ten horns . . . the Revelation of St. John!"

Why didn't you do it?

Well, because then I thought that nobody would understand it, that people would think I was an idiot.

"The lunatic, the lover and the poet / Are of imagination all compact," Shakespeare says elsewhere in the play.

That's it. I knew it was impossible. I wished I could have done it. But instead in the second act, I made a pretty—not silly or comic—pas de deux to a movement from an early Felix Mendelssohn string symphony [Symphony no. 9 in C]—something people could enjoy.

But that pas de deux is so mysterious and calm . . . perhaps you did, in fact, give us Bottom's dream.

It doesn't matter what it is. What's important is that it's pretty and makes you happy to see it. What it is—a flower or a girl or a dance or music— you can do what you want with it, you can talk about it, take it home with you, think about it, and say it represents this or that . . . that's fine.

So the inexplicability of dance is similar to Bottom's vision.

Absolutely.

You seem to choreograph these pas de deux with a feeling of adoration and of devotion, and the result is a kind of rapturous grace.

23

Naturally, I do it that way . . . but I don't tell anybody. When I was a child, I heard about a kind of enormous water lily—it was called Victoria Regina—that opens only once every hundred years. It's like wax, and everything is in there, everything lives . . . by itself, and it doesn't tell anybody anything. It goes to sleep and then comes back again. It doesn't say "Look at me, now I'm going to wake up, I'm going to jump . . . Look, Ma, I'm dancing!" But if you happen to be around, and are ready, you'll probably see something.

It's like the time capsule with everything in it. Or like the seed that, when you plant it, becomes an enormous tree with leaves and fruit. Everything was in that little seed, and so everything can open. The tree of dance is like that. It just takes a long, long time to blossom.

II

New York City, 1982

Someone once suggested that painting is not a profession but actually an extension of the art of living. Do you think that might be said about dancing?

It's probably true. You see, all I am is a dancer. It started long ago, you know. At first, I didn't want to dance, but I was put in the Imperial Ballet School in Russia. I got accustomed to it and began to like it. Then I was put onstage; everyone was well dressed in blue on a beautiful stage, and I liked participating. And it became a kind of drug. I don't know myself except as a dancer. Even now, though I'm old, I still can move, or at least I can tell exactly how it feels to move, so that I can teach and stage ballets.

You can ask a horse why he's a horse, but he just lives a horse's life. It's like the story of the horse that goes to a bar: The barman serves him, and when he leaves, the people say, "But that was a horse!" And the barman just replies, "I know, and he never takes a chaser!" So it's very difficult to explain why I do what I do. I don't live any other life. It's like a chess player who has a chess player's head.

I can teach and explain to pupils what to do better, but not because there's a reason. I got experience from wonderful teachers in Russia, and then I just started working with my body and discovered that *this* was better than *that*. I improved, I could turn, I could do everything. Now I know *why* it's this way and not that way. But that's all. People like Stravinsky and Vladimir Nabokov studied Roman law or Latin or German.

They knew everything, and I didn't know anything! . . . Actually, though, I do remember that, along with my training as a dancer, I had to recite speeches by Chekhov and Aleksandr Griboyedov, and only today do I remember these. When I talk to myself now, I can recite them and appreciate that beautiful language.

You once said: "Choreography is like cooking or gardening. Not like painting, because painting stays. Dancing disintegrates. Like a garden. Lots of roses come up, and in the evening they're gone. Next day, the sun comes up. It's life. I'm connected to what is part of life."

I don't care about my past. At all. I know people like La Karinska [Barbara Karinska, former head of the NYCB costume shop], who have everything, but only talk about the past: "I remember how I was, I was pretty, I was this and that." I don't give a damn about the past. And the future . . . I wouldn't know what that is. To me, today is everything. Of course, I remember how to cook, I remember the dough that smelled so good. *Today* comes from the past, but in reality, it's all one thing to me.

The New York City Ballet is this year [1982] celebrating the one hundredth anniversary of Igor Stravinsky's birth with a series of old and new ballets set to his music. You and Stravinsky were always collaborators, and it is generally agreed that there was some kind of special affinity you had with his music, and he with your choreography—as if you were soul mates.

It's difficult for me to talk about soul—I just don't know. I know, however, that I liked his music, and I felt how it should be put into movement. But our affinity with each other didn't have so much to do with soul but rather with understanding and eating food! We often had large dinners with "hookers" [Balanchine's term for shots of vodka or whiskey] and caviar, and finally we got so that we could say dirty things, like everybody else. *[Laughing]* But when we met to talk about his music, he'd play something and say, "This should be *this* way"—slow, fast, whatever. That's always what he did, ever since I first worked with him on *The Song of the Nightingale* in 1924 or '25.

What was your first impression of Stravinsky?

First of all, I had great respect for him; he was like my father, since he was more than twenty years older than I. Stravinsky started playing the

25

piece on the piano—*tha ta ta ta, tha tum ta tum* . . . So I choreographed all that, and one day, Diaghilev came to see what I'd been up to and exclaimed: "No, that's the wrong tempo. Much slower!" So I changed the whole thing. Stravinsky came again, we played the piece slowly, and he said, "No, it's not right!" And I said that Mr. Diaghilev had told me to change it. Stravinsky jumped. So I rearranged the choreography again. I didn't know—I was very young, I'd never even heard the piece, I'd just come from Russia! And Matisse, whom I met . . . I didn't know who the heck Matisse was. Raphael, yes, but not Matisse! I didn't speak a word of French, but he seemed like a nice man with a beard.

Anyway, I worked with Stravinsky again on *Apollo,* and then I came to America. . . . Oh, yes, I remember meeting him in Nice, and that was easy because he spoke Russian. I had lunch at his house with his priest and the priest's wife—white clergy were allowed to marry, but not black clergy. My uncle was archbishop of Tbilisi, by the way. And I remember that the first time he learned he was going to be a monk, he went down on the floor and was covered with black crepe. So, at that moment, he was dead to world. Then the people helped him get up, and they took him away.

You were an altar boy at church.

Yes, and I liked it. And at home, I even played priest with two chairs beside me. I liked the ceremony and the way the priests dressed. I was five or six then.

But you became a choreographer instead. Do you think there's a connection?

There is. Our church services were elaborate, like productions. They really were like plays with beautiful singing and choruses. . . . You know, I've just finished choreographing Stravinsky's *Perséphone,* and at the end, I bring the boys onstage—the chorus is there and nobody's doing anything—and I light them from the bottom up, so you can see their faces, as if they're candles in church.

So your childhood love of church influenced your ballets.

Oh, yes.

Stravinsky was religious. Are you?

I don't tell anyone, but I go to church by myself.

Stravinsky used to say that he believed in the Devil.

Not the Devil. The devil exists, but not the Devil. The devil only stands for the negative.

Stravinsky once wrote: "What are the connections that unite and separate music and dance? In my opinion, the one does not serve the other. There must be a harmonious accord, a synthesis of ideas. Let us speak, on the contrary, of the struggle between music and choreography."

Absolutely! Struggle means to be together. It's not so easy to unite and to be together. When you're *immediately* together, it's *[clasps hands]* and you evaporate. Stravinsky's right.

You see, if you look at the dances that most dance makers or ballet masters make, the music is used as background, basically . . . like movie music. Television music. Who are the ballet masters? Unsuccessful dancers. Not all of them, but hundreds and hundreds everywhere. They open a school and teach badly because they didn't dance very well themselves. But to be a choreographer, you must be a great dancer—maybe not great, but better than the dancers who come to you. Because you have to invent and teach these people something that they don't know. Otherwise, you use the steps of somebody else.

I remember that with the G.I. Bill of Rights, the government would send us people they didn't want to take into the army, and they paid us to take them—we *had* to take them. Sixty boys would come to us. And there was one young man who approached me and asked how one became a choreographer. Well, I told him it was very difficult: you had to learn how to dance very well, better than all other dancers. And then, God blesses you, gives you something, helps you to refine what's there. And he replied: "I want to be a choreographer first. I don't want to learn anything. I want to sit and tell everybody what to do." Lots of boys were like that.

So it's no use even to talk about it. It's like everybody wants to write a book. I've even written a book, but I didn't really write it: I sat down and conversed with a nice writer, and he wrote something. So not everybody should be a choreographer. To take music and just use it as a background and have people dance to it . . . it's not right if it doesn't represent anything.

So struggle means respecting dance and music.

Yes, struggle means you have to be right in the way you put them together.

Then each of your works with Stravinsky is a struggle with his music?

Absolutely. After he finished the scores, he gave them to me. I would visit his home in California, and we'd talk. "What do you want to do?" he'd ask, and I'd say, "Supposing we do *Orpheus*." "How do you think *Orpheus* should be done?" "Well," I'd say, "a little bit like opera. Orpheus is alone, Eurydice is dead, he cries, an angel comes and take him to the underworld, and then Orpheus returns to earth. But he looks back, and she disappears forever."

Well, we tried to do that. And Stravinsky said, "I'll write the end first, I sometimes have an appetite to write the end first." And that's what he did, with the two horns—it's a beautiful thing, sad, hair flowing. We couldn't have a river on the stage, but it suggests something like that.

Then he asked "Now, how to begin?" And I said, "Eurydice is in the ground, she's already buried, Orpheus is sad and cries—friends come to visit him, and then he sings and plays." "Well," Stravinsky asked, "how long does he play?" And I started to count *[snaps fingers]*, the curtain goes up. "How long would you like him to stand without dancing, without moving? A sad person stands for a while, you know." "Well," I said, "maybe at least a minute." So he wrote down "minute." "And then," I said, "his friends come in and bring something and leave." "How long?" asked Stravinsky. I calculated it by walking. "That will take about two minutes." He wrote it down.

And it went on like that. He'd say, "I want to know how long it should be." "It could be a little longer," I'd tell him, "but at least it's not forever!" And later he played one section for me, and I said, "It's a little bit too short." "Oh, oh," he'd sigh, "I already orchestrated it, and it's all finished. . . . Well, I'll do something, I know what to do." "Ah, thank you!" I replied. Things like that, you see: "How long?" he'd say. "One minute and twenty seconds," I'd tell him. "Twenty-*one*," he'd say, and smile. And I'd agree, "Fine, twenty-one!"

Stravinsky is more complicated than I am, because the body doesn't have the possibilities that music has in terms of speed. A pianist can play fast, but the body can't go that quickly. The body's different from music. Supposing you start moving fast, like sixty-fourth notes. But you can't, you can't see it. Eyes can't really see peripherally, the movement passes and is gone. So we have to calculate movements. To hear and to see isn't the same thing. You have to have extremely fantastic eyes to see everything.

But perhaps it's better not to talk about. Horses don't talk, they just go!
We want to win the race. And how? With energy, training, and dancing!

GEORGE BALANCHINE

JANUARY 22, 1904 – APRIL 30, 1983

J. G. BALLARD
Halos of Light

Shepperton, 1987

In 1984 a novel titled *Empire of the Sun* was published in England and the United States to great critical acclaim. *The Guardian* called it "the best British novel about the Second World War," the *Sunday Times* called it "an astonishing piece of adventure fiction," and the *Los Angeles Times* praised it as "a profound and moving work of imagination." This partly autobiographical novel describes the life of an eleven-year-old boy named Jim who lives with his British parents, nine servants, and a chauffeur-driven Packard in Shanghai at the outbreak of World War II; his incarceration in a Japanese concentration camp; his witnessing, as if it were a hallucination, of the soundless light of the "second sun" of the atomic bomb at Nagasaki; and his reunion with his missing parents and his plan to return with his mother to England at the end of the war.

Adapted into a 1987 film by Steven Spielberg, with a script by Tom Stoppard and starring Christian Bale as Jim, and shot in Shanghai, England, and Spain, the director explained his admiration for Ballard's novel, telling the *New York Times*'s Myra Forsberg in 1988: "I was attracted to the main character being a child. But I was also attracted to the idea that this was a death of innocence, not an attenuation of childhood, which by my own admission and everybody's impression of me is what my life has been. This was the opposite of 'Peter Pan.' This was a boy who had grown up too quickly, who was becoming a flower long before the bud had ever come out of the topsoil. And, in fact, a flower that was a gifted weed."

J. G. Ballard was a novelist and short story writer who in the 1960s and 1970s was associated with the New Wave of science fiction, a group of writers who evinced a dystopian sensibility that broke from the long-standing traditions of pulp SF. Ballard's own writing was described by Thomas Frick as "situated within the erotic, technical, postholocaust landscape, and so often concerned with the further reaches of postmodern consciousness." As Ballard himself once remarked, "We live inside an enormous novel. For the writer in particular it is less and less necessary to invent the fictional content of his novel. The fiction is already there. The writer's task is to invent the reality."

A student of medicine between 1949 and 1951, Ballard was throughout his life fascinated by advances in science. In the mid-1960s, for example, he arranged with one of his computer-scientist friends to send him the contents of his wastepaper baskets, which included printouts, scientific handouts, giveaway magazines, and laboratory detritus. "These strange crossovers from the communications world," he explained, "were psychopathology, experimental applied psychology, commercialism—you know, the latest stuff the computer firms are trying to sell you. . . . All those, overlaid together, provided a wonderful sort of *compost* which my imagination could feed on."

Ballard once confessed that his two favorite books were the Warren Commission Report ("There's an obsessive concentration on little details") and *Crash Injuries*—a medical textbook that Ballard called his bible ("One should approach the material as, say, an engineer approaches stress deformations of aircraft tail-play—as a fact of life. . . . The human body may crash, so let's look at it anew. Texts like that are a way of seeing the human self *anew*").

Perhaps Ballard's most controversial novel, *Crash,* which was adapted into a 1996 film directed by David Cronenberg, is a work about the psychosexuality of car wrecks. "In his vision of a car-crash with the actress," Ballard writes, "Vaughan was obsessed by many wounds and impacts—by the dying chromium and collapsing bulkheads of their two cars meeting head-on in complex collisions endlessly repeated in slow-motion films . . . by the compound fractures of their thighs impacted against their handbrake mountings, and above all by the wounds to their genitalia, her uterus pierced by the heraldic beak of the manufacturer's medallion, his semen emptying across the luminescent dials that registered for ever the last temperature and fuel levels of the engine."

The novel was praised by William Burroughs and called a masterpiece by the Parisian newspaper *Le Monde,* but the reader for Ballard's London publisher wrote: "The author of this book is beyond psychiatric help." Ballard responded, "The person who wrote that was the wife of a psychiatrist and had some psychiatric training herself. . . . For a *psychiatrist* to say, 'You're beyond psychiatric help'—in a way, that's the greatest compliment you can be paid! You've achieved freedom then—absolute freedom."

J. G. Ballard lived in a two-story house in Shepperton, a nondescript, unfashionable suburb of London in proximity to Heathrow Airport. "In a way," he once observed, "a suburb like this is the real psychic battleground—it's on the wavefront of the future, rather than a city area. . . . I would almost call it an *airport culture* that's springing up in suburbs like this—a very transient kind of world. It's interesting to watch."

The following interview took place on November 19, 1987, in the writer's small study, which was sparsely furnished with a silver-foil palm tree stooping over a reclining aluminum lawn chair, an overstocked bookshelf, and a desk with a manual typewriter. Dominating the room was a five-by-four-foot copy of a painting by the Belgian surrealist painter Paul Delvaux that depicted statuesque nudes in a dreamlike landscape. Ballard commissioned it from a London artist—the original was destroyed during the London blitz— and these nudes in frozen motion seemed to watch over us as we talked.

* * *

The astronomer Carl Sagan tells how, as a child, he eagerly read the novels and stories of Edgar Rice Burroughs, L. Ron Hubbard, Jules Verne, and H. G. Wells. But as he got older, he began to feel frustrated and incredulous when he was asked to believe that the first probe of a neutron star was accomplished by a manned rather than an unmanned spacecraft or when characters were able to build interplanetary cities but had forgotten the inverse-square law. Sagan adds, "I find science more subtle, more intricate, and more awesome than much of science fiction." Do you agree with this?

Yes and no . . . with the emphasis on the *no*. Because science fiction represents a body of popular mythology *inspired* by science, and it isn't necessary for strict scientific accuracy to play a dominant role. For example, the idea, long since exploded, that the Martian canals were constructed by some ancient race *does* have a certain poetic force. It says something to us about our very small place in the great scheme of things. And it inspired at least one great work of literature, Ray Bradbury's *The Martian Chronicles*.

So if you regard SF as the folk literature of the twentieth century, as many people do, its inaccuracies pale into insignificance. Because I think there's something vital about the power of the imagination and its ability to remake the world. You see this, for instance, in the classic surrealist paintings of Max Ernst, Salvador Dalí, Giorgio de Chirico, and Paul Delvaux, where the laws of time and space are constantly being suspended,

33

and where reality is decoded in an attempt to discover the *super*reality that lies behind the façade of everyday life. And that means everything from the world of politics and mass merchandising to something as trivial as the fabrics people have in their homes.

Carl Sagan does say, "The greatest human significance of science fiction may be as experiments on the future, as explorations of alternative destinies, as attempts to minimize future shock."

I think he's right in the sense that science fiction should look at the future and prepare us for it—science fiction puts the emotion into the future, something science tends to leave out. So it can help you to respond emotionally to what it may be like to fly across the Atlantic in five minutes in a rocket plane. But in fact, I think that science fiction is *really* about the here and now—it's a branch of visionary fiction. Remember, I was brought up in the school of British science fiction that goes back to Mary Shelley's *Frankenstein*, Robert Louis Stevenson's *The Strange Case of Dr. Jekyll and Mr. Hyde*, and on through the works of H. G. Wells, Aldous Huxley, and George Orwell. That's the background out of which the British audience reads SF. They don't expect the outer-space, interplanetary-space, far-future approach of SF that seems to be the exclusive monopoly of the science fiction written in the United States. When I first submitted stories to American magazines like *Amazing* or *Astounding Science Fiction*—even in the early 1960s—just setting a story in the present day made editors and readers uneasy.

But here we are in 1987 living, to a large extent, inside an enormous science-fiction novel! SF is a wonderful tool with which to try to make sense of this novel that we all inhabit, and it's a shame that the American view of SF is generally so concentrated on the interplanetary and the far future. Though it's a good sign that the new generation of SF writers, the cyberpunks [William Gibson, Bruce Sterling, Michael Swanwick], have gone back to the original role of science fiction as a direct comment on everyday experience, which today is that communications landscape with its glowing terminals and invisible computer links netting the planet into a McLuhanized village.

But you yourself once wrote, "Modern science fiction became the first casualty of the changing world it anticipated and helped to create. The future envisaged by the science fiction of the 1940s and 1950s is already our past." And you went on to compare the film 2001: A Space Odyssey *to* Gone with the Wind, *commenting that the former seemed to you "a scientific pageant that became a kind of historical romance in reverse, a sealed world into which the hard light of contemporary reality was never allowed to penetrate."*

Sadly, I think that's true. SF as a whole is, of course, time sensitive, and its predictive role means that it can be overtaken by events. It's impossible now, except as a spoof, to write a realistic story or novel about the first landing on the moon, as if it had never taken place. The moment Armstrong put his foot on the turf, that was one piece of possibility deleted from the repertory of SF. And the same will happen as we move into an ever more technological landscape. It's very difficult to grasp how much things have changed just during the past thirty years: TV, computers, heart transplants, extrauterine fetuses, AIDS—which is like a science-fiction disease. It almost seems like a deliberately designed plague by a vengeful deity who has read too much SF. So a lot of SF of the 1940s and 1950s looks like discarded snakeskins. They may glisten a little bit in the deep grass, but the stuff is perishable.

You've commented that SF films of the 1940s and 1950s, like The Day the Earth Stood Still, Them!, *and* The Incredible Shrinking Man, *were masterpieces in which "time suddenly starts accelerating" from their first moments. But you've said that with a film like* Star Wars, *"the moment the film begins, time stops." What did you mean by that?*

Those earlier films sprang out of a period of rapid scientific changes that were taking place, especially in the States. In *The Incredible Shrinking Man*, a man and wife are on a power cruiser, just quietly meandering in the Pacific Ocean. The boat drifts through a cloud of radioactive crop chemicals, and this sets up processes in the man's body that begin to make him shrink. And the movie just *accelerates* away, with the audience thinking, "My God, is *this* what the future is going to be like? Are we all going to be shrunk down to the size of microdots?" In a film like this, one gets the sense of a speeding replica of the twentieth century caught upon a spinning carousel.

Now, in *Star Wars,* there are supertechnologies brilliantly described and realized, but there's no sense of *time.* The action could be in the very far future or the very far past. There's no direct connection with our own world or any other world. The characters inhabit a timeless continuum, such that one senses that any action performed by any one of the characters will have no long-term effect on anything. They're just dealing with events, like speeding dots on a video game.

But you could say that the film's main characters—who are variations on Dorothy, the Tin Man, the Scarecrow, and the Cowardly Lion in The Wizard of Oz*—really make Star Wars a kind of children's literature rather than science fiction.*

Yes, *Star Wars* is a children's movie, and I'm not putting it down as a type of children's literature. But I think there's a great difference between *Star Wars* and, say, *Close Encounters of the Third Kind*, which *does* encourage one's imagination on the deepest possible level, giving a sense of how ordinary lives can be transformed by some unique perception, whatever it may be.

That film seemed to be precisely about the imaginative process itself.

I agree completely. And I'd like to see science fiction moving more in that direction, because it's much more successful and touches much deeper depths. I also, by the way, loved *The Road Warrior*—I thought it was a masterpiece. For ninety or so minutes I really knew what it was like to be an eight-cylinder engine under the hood of whatever car that was. The visceral impact of that film was extraordinary. And seen simply from a science-fiction point of view, it created a unique landscape with tremendous visual authority.

So as you can see, I'm all for variety in science fiction. I'm against the idea of unchanging conventions, which is a form of death. Rules have no business in the realm of the imagination.

It's ironic that you like forties and fifties SF films and at the same time find fault with the books published during that very same period.

Partly because the movies then were low-budget films, and the directors had to make them out in the streets, so to speak—they couldn't afford to build fancy sets the way people like George Lucas can today. And in that way they maintained their contact with reality, as did film noir. It forces a certain relevance on you. Even the recent *Blue Velvet* was shot against a very stylized American suburb—but it's a *real* suburb, and that lends a lot of power to that film. I think the lifeline to reality is all-important, like the umbilical cord between the fetus and the mother.

Empire of the Sun, *your most recent book published in America, is the semi-autobiographical lifeline to the reality of your own childhood. And in reading it in the light of your past work, I recalled a dream I once had in which I saw, at the foot of a crossroads, a sign that read, "Remember the Future!" I recalled that dream because in* Empire of the Sun *there seems to be a kind of remembering of future motifs, images, themes, and obsessions that you would develop in your earlier works: the boy Jim looking at the drained swimming pools by the deserted houses of the International Settlement in Shanghai; the halo of the sun falling from the Mustang fighter plane and the American pilot's body as he's burning to death; and the Japanese soldiers confiscating their prisoners' watches and clocks so that they will lose all sense of time—all of these images correspond to those in your later works. So in a way,* Empire of the Sun *remembers the books you were going to write in the future, though paradoxically, you wrote it after those books . . . if you know what I mean.*

All of my fiction up till *Empire of the Sun* is filled with echoes of my own childhood, and in this book, my dreams of the future and a dream of the past, which is what Shanghai now is to me, came together in a very peculiar way, though it wasn't thought out yet.

But I know what you mean about remembering the future. When one looks back on *authors* from the past—Dickens or Dostoevsky—one doesn't necessarily remember their books in the order in which they were written. In fact, I've often thought that writers don't really produce their works in the order in which they were really written. So that *Empire of the Sun* may really be my *first* novel that just happened to come out rather late. Whereas some of my earlier fiction may be *late* works of mine, drawing on experiences of my first book. In my writing I've made a kind of mythology out of things like drained swimming pools and abandoned hotels and the like, but I was unaware of most of this. What prompts the imagination to put its head above the parapet, God knows! It's a risky business. All I know is that the jigsaw only began to stare back at me in *Empire of the Sun.*

In that book you describe the war newsreels you used to see as a boy in Shanghai, and you even write that it seemed as if "the whole of Shanghai was turning into a newsreel." Today you're living in the suburban town of Shepperton, which is, in fact, famous for its film studios. And it seems as if you've moved from one movie set to another.

It's very strange. And the ultimate strangeness, of course, is that during the filming of *Empire of the Sun* they picked a couple of locations near Shepperton to represent Amherst Avenue—the place in Shanghai where I used to live—and several of the houses that were used in the film were found only a ten-minute drive from here in a place called Sunningdale. And Steven Spielberg very kindly offered me a walk-on part as a guest at a fancy-dress party in Shanghai on the eve of World War II, which, of course, I accepted. I got myself up as John Bull, with Dickensian top hat, Union Jack waistcoat, red cutaway coat, white britches, and boots. And a number of my Shepperton neighbors, whom I've known for about twenty-five years, are *also* in the film. I felt that we had all been recruited to go back to a China of forty years ago, as if in a dream.

I recall a strange moment during the second day of shooting, in which the guests were leaving that fancy-dress party. We, as the guests, were all standing in the large hallway of this house in Sunningdale—the cameras were outside in the drive. At a signal we stepped out of the house, and there, in this large circular drive, were these thirties Buicks and Packards with Chinese chauffeurs—all of them actors—standing beside them. I suddenly felt the wheels were coming full circle. It was like time travel, but the kind of time travel that occurs in the central nervous system. It made me so conscious that there were many layers of time that were being rolled backward to reveal other layers of time beneath, perhaps with their weave running in a different direction.

As you write in Empire of the Sun, *"Jim knew that he was awake and asleep at the same time, dreaming of the war and yet dreamed of by the war."*

And that's the way it felt when I and my neighbors were asked to perform in the movie. People always ask me why I came to live in this nondescript London suburb. But perhaps my life here has been a deep assignment I've been carrying out—like a secret agent—without realizing I was doing it. Perhaps my playing a part in the film has been just a vast therapeutic exercise! But to say that would trivialize it, because it's very difficult, for me and for all of us, to return to one's roots, to go back to one's hometown and see how everything's changed—that your childhood house is now a supermarket or a toothpaste factory and that whole street patterns have been transformed. On the psychological level it's even more difficult to go back to the sources of one's own personality and identity. But thanks to Steven Spielberg's film, I was able to do so. He generously told me he really liked it, and it was clear that his imagination had grasped it in a single swoop. It's so vital to the film to have had a director who was able to enter a child's mind.

In Empire of the Sun, *Jim reads Lewis Carroll's* Through the Looking Glass *and finds it "a comforting world less strange than his own." And you later comment on Jim's ability to double his sense of reality, "as if everything that had happened to him since the war was occurring within a mirror. It was his mirror self who felt faint and hungry."*

I can remember that strongly from my childhood during the war—which was a very strange period. But Shanghai even *before* the war was a strange city, like an elaborate stage set that could be changed overnight—and often was, what with the Chinese, the Japanese, the British fighting for control of it.

You once commented that the only alien planet is Earth.

This planet is genuinely strange. If we were all flown to the moon or to Mars and walked around on them, they wouldn't seem that strange to us because there would be no yardsticks or anything to measure their strangeness by—they're just vast museums of geology. Whereas the earth is a deranged *zoo*, and somebody left the doors of the cages open. We have *real* strangeness because we can measure the degree to which things are or are not what they ought to be.

Against what would we measure this?

Against change, for instance. A mutates so rapidly into B and C. But at least we can remember A. I mean, moral principles survive. If you're bringing up children or looking after the elderly and making something of your own life, whether it's tending a little garden or starting an aircraft company, there are yardsticks that define reality and responsibility. You mustn't lose sight of these. And I hope I've never done so in my work, otherwise I'd consider myself simply a pure fantasist, and I've never wanted to lose the sense of moral compass bearing. I mean, even in a book like *Crash*, which some people consider to be out-and-out pornography, I attempt—

I hope—to make some kind of sense of the marriage of reason and nightmare that has dominated the twentieth century.

At the conclusion of Empire of the Sun, *you tell how Jim, imprisoned in Shanghai's Olympic Stadium, suddenly sees the soundless flash of light of the distant Nagasaki A-bomb—"the light was a premonition of his death, the sight of his small soul joining the larger soul of the dying world"—which seems to him like a "second sun." And one is reminded of the earlier description of the intense "halo of light" emanating from the downed Mustang fighter plane and its burning American pilot.*

I wanted Jim to see light in a special way, because the crash of the Mustang and the burning pilot give him one of those brief glimpses that many of us have had where one is looking through the dimensions of time and space into a reality beyond. And that anticipates the blinding reality of the A-bomb, which Jim sees as the final judgment of the human race.

But the burning light of the Mustang pilot also has a kind of sacrificial quality: as a child I saw the Japanese killing fallen American pilots. Throughout the book, Jim is obsessed with survival on a minute-by-minute basis, but a sense of the larger scheme of things does, I think, come through. Jim imagines seeing his parents and taking them not only away from the war but also away to a world beyond this one. And he catches a glimpse of that world in the burning light of that crashing Mustang. Later, at the Olympic Stadium, he sees the final white light. And from then on he sees ordinary daylight in a different and final sense—there's a sense of an apocalypse that's waiting for him at the end of the book. Even when he's about to take a ship leaving Shanghai for England, he notices in the distance one of the city's outdoor cinemas showing a newsreel. The camera breaks down, there's an enormous white screen and again he sees the white light as a window into another universe.

In your SF novel The Drowned World, *you write of "a second Adam searching for the forgotten paradises of the reborn sun." And in your extraordinary visionary novel* The Unlimited Dream Company, *you describe the townspeople carrying the godlike pagan hero away "toward the sun, eager to lose themselves in that communion of light."*

I'm aware that there's a visionary sense in my work, but I don't have any kind of orthodox or conventional religious feelings, and I can't really call myself "mystical." What I do have is the notion, which I take from modern experimental psychology, that the universe presented to us by our senses is a kind of ramshackle construct that happens to suit the central nervous system of an intelligent bipedal mammal with a rather short conceptual and physical range. We see rooms and people and have perceptions, but it's all a construct. And I see the role of the imaginative writer as an attempt to get through this neuropsychological construct into something closer to the truth.

I've been struck by the extraordinary number of characters in your books who manifest an intense longing to transcend or escape the continuum of time and space.

That's true—it's probably the real matter of my fiction and something I've never been *consciously* aware of. It's a peculiar thing, because as I write, I take it for granted that many of my characters wish to escape the time and space of *these* walls or *this* chair or *this* ballpoint pen, and they try to break out of all of this by some sort of rearrangement of the perceptual apparatus, which they think can be fueled by the imagination.

In my short story "Myths of the Near Future," for example, a character named Sheppard is living alone in a series of deserted hotels near a long-abandoned Cape Kennedy. His wife has died, he has visions of her, he thinks he can bring her back to life by means of a kind of time machine that is powered by the empty swimming pools outside—because the light at Cape Kennedy is extraordinarily intense, partly reflected as it is from these drained concrete swimming pools. But of course it's also an inward light. Sheppard believes his dead wife is trapped in time. So he climbs down into one of these pools with a young woman who has befriended him and tells her, "There's a door out of this pool. I'm trying to find it, a side door for all of us to escape through. This space sickness—it's really about time, not space, like all the Apollo flights. We think of it as a kind of madness, but in fact it may be part of a contingency plan laid down millions of years ago, a real space program, a chance to escape into a world beyond time." Light, time, the attempt to break out of the metaphysical structures that lock us all into our little rooms and mental cubicles and categories—it's a strain that runs through all of my work.

You once commented that "the future is just going to be a vast, conforming suburb of the soul."

I'm afraid that might be so. People have willingly lobotomized themselves with the aid of tools from suburban hardware stores, with TV, with consumerism. In the 1970s, I was invited to make a trip across Germany from Bremerhaven to Stuttgart—this as part of a journalistic junket sponsored by Mercedes-Benz—and we drove along secondary roads. Everything we observed dated from 1945, of course. We trundled through endless immaculate suburbs of executive housing where even a drifting leaf looked as if it had too much freedom. There was a Mercedes or a BMW in every driveway, motorboats on their trailers, identical children identically dressed. We might have been looking at a population of brilliantly designed robots placed there merely to establish a contextual landscape! And this went on and on. I suddenly realized that the future of this planet was not going to be like New York City or Tokyo or London or Moscow but rather like a suburb of Düsseldorf. And you know, most of the Baader-Meinhof gang in fact grew up in these suburbs, and I realized why that kind of terrorism erupted from this kind of landscape. Because in that world, madness is the only freedom.

But think of the nineteen-year-old West German guy who recently flew his Cessna to Red Square.

Yes, it's wonderfully encouraging to see the human imagination still capable of these huge conceptual leaps that leave air-defense systems completely paralyzed! Oddly, I feel that the 1980s are a good time to be alive, because the consumer conformism—"the suburbanization of the soul"—on the one hand, and the gathering ecological and other crises on the other, do force the individual to recognize that he or she is all he or she has *got*. And this sharpens the eye and the imagination. The challenge is for each of us to respond, to remake as much as we can of the world around us, because no one else will do it for us. We have to find a core within us and get to work. Don't worry about worldly rewards. Just get on with it!

J. G. BALLARD

NOVEMBER 15, 1930 – APRIL 19, 2009

RAY DAVIES
Afternoon Tea on Hampstead Heath

London, 1970

"The world keeps going 'round," Ray Davies once sang, and every once in a while you hear the Kinks and wonder where they've been. Ray Davies used to write high-voltage songs about not sleeping at night and getting tired of waiting, but he recently has set forth on a quiet and lonesome path that many people have turned off while the world turned on. With the release of the Kinks' eighth album, *Arthur,* you might feel like catching up.

Many of Ray Davies's songs have set me thinking of the Taoist saint the poet Kenneth Rexroth once wrote about who fished with a pin and a single silk filament. The man caught multitudes of fish because he was perfectly attuned to—contemplating and participating in—the endless flowing. The means of Ray Davies's songs are small—like the persons he sings about—but the effect is that of a small and quiet radiance that would seem to belie the songs' subjects but which in fact light them up from the inside. "Sunny Afternoon," "Waterloo Sunset," or "Sitting by the Riverside" suggest the world of T'ang Chinese poets conversing and drinking wine by moonlight or, closer to home, the streams and meadows of Izaak Walton's angler.

This clarity and directness of feeling imbues even Ray Davies's perceptions of the inhabitants of Dead End Street and suburban England—the anonymous losers of anybody's political program. Thus Arthur, the anti-hero of the new Kinks opera, lies on the opposite side of that musical coin where the Who's Tommy is heads. But together, these two characters not only define English life now but also present a composite awareness of successful and failed attempts at self-realization.

Afternoon tea with Ray Davies took place on November 26, 1970, in the garden restaurant (a converted carriage house) in Kenwood House on

43

Hampstead Heath. The setting might have been a Kinks song: gray-lit cool autumn afternoon, children playing, old persons sitting. Signs on the grass positively read: Please Step on the Paths. And in the toilet, a little boy sang cheerily, "I like you, daddy," as his embarrassed father outside muttered: "Get a move on." As Chekhov once said, almost defining Ray Davies's method, "I imagine people so they can tell me things about themselves."

After tea, we continued the interview on a bench on the heath, and just as Ray Davies was mentioning how he thought people hated the Kinks, my cassette machine broke down. On playback, you heard a sped-up Donald Duck voice augmented by the sounds of a squadron of fighter planes reaching an explosion: then silence, as if the loosing of the apocalyptic beast had terminated the interview, even though Ray Davies and I continued to talk, tapes turning, microphones registering.

* * *

Before your first hit, "You Really Got Me," you recorded "Long Tall Sally" and "You Do Something to Me," the second of which sold something like 127 copies.

Really? Fantastic. How did you know that?

I checked it out.

Then it must be true. . . . I was an art student, like thousands of others. Then I got together with my brother and a friend and we decided to go and play dates. The more we played, the more we wanted to do it. And it got to a stage when we wanted to do it all the time. Our repertoire consisted of rhythm and blues, Sonny Terry things.

For a while when you started, the Kinks were listened to as much as the Beatles and the Stones.

No, we weren't, never. 'Cause I think we were more unpopular than they were. In the States, our old image is still lasting, since the last time we went there that's what they remember us doing—the heavy things, the chunk chunk things, you couldn't really miss it. Those three chords were part of my life—G, F, B♭—yeh, it is, and I can't help noticing it. But there have been other things nearly as close to it which people haven't noticed, other songs we've done.

44

"See My Friends (Playing Cross the River)" moves from those chords to something closer to an Indian drone.

I got the idea from being in India. I always liked the chanting. Someone once said to me, "England is gray and India is like a chant." I don't think England is that gray, but India is like a long drone. When I wrote the song, I had the sea near Bombay in mind. We stayed at a hotel by the sea, and the fishermen came up at five in the morning and they were all chanting. And we went on the beach and we got chased by a mad dog— big as a donkey.

It sounded as if you were singing about an English river.

I think it was the Indian Ocean.

A number of your earlier songs sound not like places, but like other songs: "I'll Remember," for example, like a Beatles' song.

"I'll Remember"? No, no, bullshit. It's a song written on the sixth, Buddy Holly! I wrote it on a harmonica in Seattle, which is in Washington. I'll remember. I liked "Love Me Do." When it came out, I thought it was an American surfing song. Totally unsurfer. But I did think it was an American group. . . . I like surfers. Their imagery, it's great. And that floating feeling . . . I wrote "Holiday in Waikiki" at the Waikiki Hotel in Hawaii, and admittedly it's like Chuck Berry. We used to do a lot of his songs.

One of your songs reminded me of the Ikettes.

Ikettes? Right. Who were the Lennon Sisters? Do you remember? Were they about the same time as the Ink Spots? . . . I think that song writing changed when groups started spending more time in the studio. See, when groups were on the road, they used to go right in the studio and create the same kind of feeling they had on the road, and the stuff they used to cut was influenced by what they did at gigs. But then groups spent more time in the studio and started to change, the atmosphere changed.

When you're making a record, and if you spend more time over it, you have to record it a tone lower or cut the tones lower because you can't reach some of the notes, I find this. But when you go on stage, you have to put the key up and it really changes the whole thing.

A lot of our stuff recently has been routine for the studio, when it should have been routine for the stage, and that's why it sounds so different. I think the writing's the same, maybe, but it's the fact that we spend more time in the studio and less on the road that's changed the sound of it.

You create an easy driving feeling in "Sunny Afternoon." The guy's had to sell his yacht, his money's gone, and he wants to live life pleasantly. How much are you the person you're singing?

Not at all, really. I'm easy driving. But I'm not a person who loves to live pleasantly above everything else. I'm not that way at all. I might think that I'm that, but I'm not really that. I think the person in "Waterloo Sunset" is closer to me.

"Sunny Afternoon" was made very quickly, in the morning, it was one of our most atmospheric sessions. I still like to keep tapes of the few minutes before the final takes, things that happen before the session. Maybe it's superstitious, but I believe that if I had done things differently—if I had walked around the studio or gone out it wouldn't have turned out the same way.

The bass player went off and started playing funny little classical things on the bass, more like a lead guitar; and Nicky Hopkins, who was playing piano on that session, was playing "Liza"—we always used to play that song. Little things like that helped us get into the feeling of the song.

At the time I wrote "Sunny Afternoon" I couldn't listen to anything. I was only playing the *Greatest Hits of Frank Sinatra* and Dylan's "Maggie's Farm"—I just liked its whole presence. I was playing the *Bringing It All Back Home* LP along with my Frank Sinatra and Glenn Miller and Bach—it was a strange time. I thought they all helped one another, they went into the chromatic part that's in the back of the song.

I once made a drawing of my voice on "Sunny Afternoon." It was a leaf with a very thick black outline—a big blob in the background—the leaf just cutting through it.

You sing a lot about sunsets and autumn.

I like autumn things. I did a record called "Autumn Almanac"—I drew pictures of it and everything. After I wrote it, for a whole month I was thinking about it. I wasted a lot of time, really, because I was sweeping up dead leaves and putting them in the sack. I'm susceptible to that sort of thing—to walls and flowers. Walls. You can get probably something more from a wall than from a person sometimes. It's just put somewhere. It's in line, in order, it's in line with the horizon. Ah, ridiculous.

What I try to do probably doesn't come out. What I've worked out, what I do—I might not be right—is to do something very personal, and then suddenly I look at it, up in the air, I look at it. I blow it up and look at it and then I come down again. A better man.

All my records—at one time they've been the most important thing I've ever done. Even the ones that aren't hits. Even the ones that sell a hundred copies. At one time they've been the most important thing to me. So I can't hear our records on the radio, I can't stand it, because they sound to me so *out* of what everyone is doing. You know what I mean? I get embarrassed doing television shows that have lots of people on, compressed, like *Top of the Pops,* one group after another, and we're right in the middle. I feel wrong, not inferior, just wrong. I think we need a bit of time for people to get used to us.

You've also sung about blue skies and suns. "Lazy Old Sun" has what sounds like a hippo groan, almost joking up what you're saying.

Unfortunately, the song just didn't come off, really. When you look at it in writing, it's a lot better. I don't like a lot of the lines. It's nicer when I think about it than when somebody tells me what it's like. I know what I was getting to, but didn't quite get there. It is a joke, it ended up as a joke, a very sad joke . . . too bad. At one stroke it can sound jokey and the next minute I can believe it.

Both at once. As if you're saying something real, don't want to take it seriously, so undermine it with the groan. I could be wrong.

But you're really right.

Are you worried about sentimentality in your songs?

I worry about it because I think other people think I worry. That's the only reason. I like looking at things, remembering things, I like that.

"Dead End Street" sets the theme for a number of your songs. "We are strictly second class." Cracks in the ceiling, sink: leaking. At the end of the song, you sing: "Dead End Street / Head to my feet / I can feel it," so that the personal and the social awareness come together.

47

What you're saying, too, is that it's not only what other people are doing, it's what I'm doing, what I'm feeling. It's a little bit selfish as well. The Beatles are aware that Mr. So-and-so in Northampton is about to buy the record and listen to it while he's having his tea. I think they've always tried to keep that in mind. I'm a little more selfish. I like to do things that involve me a little bit. Sorry, I'm not answering your question directly. We do tend to think about what we're doing . . . too much. And that's what happened to "Dead End Street."

I'll tell you about "Dead End Street." It was about miners, to begin with, because we had a thing in England called Aberfan where a coal tip fell on a school in Wales—they dig for coal and they put all the slack and make a hill. It all fell down on a school and killed 116 little kids. That's where it all started. I wrote the song about that time, and all that time there were news flashes about Aberfan, and also it was the first year of the economic cutback. I felt it was like the days when they had the Depression.

"Big Black Smoke" has that mood, too, about the girl who takes purple hearts and sleeps in bowling alleys.

Yeh, it was written at the same time. But it started off to be something different. The big black smoke was there, and I said, Why can't I just say "Big Black Smoke"? There are some songs that *sound* great. You don't know the words—you don't want to know the words—it's the way they roll off the tongue, they might mean anything. And when you look at the song sheet and the words say "I love you, baby" or something very ordinary, they just sound something good. "Big Black Smoke" had that sound. But I had to put something around it. I had two lines: "Big black smoke" and "She took all her pretty colored clothes," and the song revolves around those lines, really. Because the buildup to the song occurs when she comes into it, or when he comes into it, or when I come into it: "She took all her pretty colored clothes." The beginning builds up to it, and from that line it fades out. There was the first draft, and then I got involved in the story. You've got to have something build up to that line: "She took all her pretty colored clothes."

How did The Village Green Preservation Society *come about?*

Three years ago I wanted it to be *Under Milk Wood*, something like that, but I never got a chance to do it because we had to make albums. Somebody said to me that I preserve things, and I like village green and preservation society. The title track is the national anthem of the album, and I like Donald Duck, Desperate Dan, draft beer.

Johnny Thunder lives on water, he don't eat food, he feeds on lightning. *[Laughing]* Frankenstein. It's not a cowboy song. It would be nice to hear the Who sing it.

Phenomenal Cat went to Singapore and Hong Kong and decided it was just as well to get fat. I didn't, he did, it was completely his own decision. And he came back and sat and ate himself to eternity.

Hope he's there.

He's always there.

In "Animal Farm" you sing: "I want to be back there among the cats and the dogs and the pigs and the goats, where people are people and not just plain."

I like plain Janes. In "Waterloo Sunset" I wanted to use the names Bernard and Dorothy, but it wouldn't work. Terry [Stamp] and Julie [Christie] would have to dog themselves up a bit. They'd have to be less glamorous for a Waterloo Sunset movie. Plain Jane . . . I'd like to hear Burt Lancaster singing "Big Sky."

"Sitting by the Riverside" is similar to "Afternoon Tea" or "Waterloo Sunset." They have that loosened-up, spaces-between feeling.

That's the studio. Maybe people should have a winding down session before listening to our songs. Maybe they should be briefed. Or debriefed. I think they should be debriefed.

Listening to lots of your songs, you get a sense that there's a house on Dead End Street with big black smoke around, a guy upstairs with his Harry Rag, the cat always eating . . .

Do they all live together in a house?

Yes. Plastic Man and Dandy come around to visit. Do you intend to create this kind of world?

I'm not aware of trying to, but it might seem that way. I think on *The Village Green Preservation Society* they were all brothers and sisters. Nobody made love because it was all in the family. I don't think there's a love song on it. Our new record is literally about a family.

You make a perfect family where everyone's friends.

Yeh. The people I'd like to be with are over there—across the river. I'm not left out. I've got a choice, but the easiest one is the one I don't really want. There a line that says: "Wish that I'd gone with her / She is gone / And now there's no one left except my friends." Yeh, she went over there and I stayed here. *[Silence]*

Would you say something about your new opera, Arthur?

The opera is about the rise and fall of the British Empire, which people tend to associate me with. *[Laughing]* You could sum up the British Empire in one song. I haven't written it, but it can be done, a little fifteen-minute thing. *[Laughing]* But about the opera: I decided to make it about one person, someone who didn't really count, that's all, and mixed it with a few people whom I knew, put them into one. I told Julian Mitchell, who wrote the script, a story about somebody I know. We liked it and worked on it and it came from there. He was easy to work with.

Your song "Some Mother's Son" contains the beautiful lines "But still the world keeps turning / Though all the children have gone away" and "One soldier glances up to see the sun / And dreams of games he played when he was young." The ideas of childhood and the sun join each other in that song.

In my song "Lazy Old Sun" I have the lines "When I'm dead and gone / Your light will shine eternally." That idea was right to me, but it didn't work in that song, and there was a vehicle in "Some Mother's Son" for it to work.

I wrote the song in a kitchen. Wrote it at night, it's not a day song. I had a song which I liked, but which nobody else liked very much called "Wonder Boy," and the lines went: "Wonder Boy, some mother's son / Turn your sorrow into wonder." I had to use "some mother's son" again. It was just one line and it was gone and had to be explained, for me, I was interested in that line. And then I wanted to write about how soldiers must have been frightened fighting and killing each other, but they were just some mother's son. Apart from the line "Head blown up by some soldier's gun," the song could be about executives in an advertising agency.

What do you think of the people you sing about in "Shangri-La"?

I played "Shangri-La" to somebody—an old friend of mine—and I knew halfway through it that he was embarrassed by it because it was about him, and he realized it, and I didn't want him to realize it, and I can never sort of talk to him again. I wanted him to hear it, and then I realized: there he is.

I'm not laughing at those people in the song at all. They're brain-washed into that, they brainwash themselves. She says, "That's it, I don't want a new dress," not because she really doesn't want it, but because she can't afford it. Their minds are like that, they're happy, really. It becomes a religion to them. The glory of being boring. It's a glory. He shows you his stamp collection. It's a sense of greatness he's got around him that you can't penetrate because you feel you might upset him, he's got that aura of *stuff.*

The chorus of "Shangri-La" is a bit of a chant—like "See My Friends." It's a religious thing. You accept it as your religion because you can't have anything else, and whatever you've got anyway is what you accept yourself. You let yourself believe it. . . . No, perhaps not. If you lived there *[gestures toward Kenwood House]* and you accepted this, and this was as far as you could go, you'd be a lot happier. Well, no, perhaps not. See, I've tried living in a big house and I can't. I'm going back to a little house. I don't think people really want to live in a posh house, as much as a rich person doesn't want to live in a slum. I don't like to say what I've got and be happy with it. I'd wear hobnail boots by my fire rather than slippers. I can't stand slippers 'cause they symbolize giving up to me. But at the same time, I love the people who are like that. But I hate what's handed down when people get into the state where that's all they want. And that can be anybody—toffs, toffs are the worst offenders. Top hats and walking sticks. Cary Grant's a toff. David Niven.

It's like the song "Princess Marina." My brother David said, "I don't know whether you like these people or you hate them." You don't really hate anybody, do you? You only hate people for an instant. They can't help it. "Princess Marina" starts pretty sad, maybe, then it goes into the bit about what it's all about—"I haven't got any money or anything," they're having a hard time. And then they sing the way they did in the music hall, because that's the way they used to express it: "Don't Have Any More, Mrs. Moore." There was a song about poverty. People think I'm taking it out on ordinary persons. But it's about all people. In fact, it's more about nobs and toffs, executives—"Yes sir, No sir, Three bags full sir."

If people are second-class, and if, when they start making it, they become dedicated followers of fashion, what alternative do they have, given the way things are?

Be like me and be unhappy. . . . We went to Australia and they wanted to take pictures of us surfing, and I thought they only surfed in America. We rolled our trousers up and pulled our overcoats up. It was 100 degrees and we were sweating, but we refused to take our overcoats off. Why should we do it? Surfing in Australia! Rebel at any cost. That's what it seems like, but it isn't really. They'll probably play our song "Australia" at cabaret clubs with maracas and things. That'll be nice. Fabulous!

The line "Australia, no drug addiction" might be too strong for them.

Might have to bleep it out.

The singer in "Driving" sounds like the singer of "Sunny Afternoon."

Can't drive. I probably can. I'm probably a hustler. An American told me I was a hustler: I pretend I can't do things and I can, really. Is that what it means? I probably can drive, but I've never been behind a steering wheel. . . . The song was written for 1938 or '9. "Dead End Street" is written about now, but it could be about the Depression. "Drivin'" is about the thirties, but people still take the attitude: Let's just go driving and get away. I don't 'cause I can't drive.

In "Yes Sir, No Sir," you sing: "You're outside and there ain't no admission to our play." Again, these people aren't part of what's happening.

Superb line the way you said that . . . Nothing's happening. *[Laughing]*

"Now I've got children and I'm going grey / No time for talking I got nothing to say . . ."

Better with an American accent.

Nothin' to say. That's what you tell the cops.

Most certainly. I was in a lift in New York City and wanted to go to the fiftieth floor. A woman came in and wanted to go to the basement. She pressed basement and I said, I was in here first, I want to go to the fiftieth floor, and she said, "Sue me." Great. I accepted it. . . . A lot more casual, the Americans.

Sometimes they shoot you.

In England they just let you live. *[Laughing]* That's the best way to die. The deadest way. Grayness is beauty in boredom. I could have given Arthur a limp, I suppose, made him buy funny books, have a secret life. Then, that isn't the important thing—he'd have had control over his secret life, and he hasn't control over what's happening to him. But he thinks he does. . . . When we play the opera in America, I hope people will accept the opera as a musical thing. There's jamming—we do a lot of that, but people don't think we do, since we don't do it on record. As far as the next thing I'm doing, I'm leaving what I've done. That's why I didn't want pictures taken of me reminiscing. I'm not like that, really. I'm going to try something else next. . . . Someone will get me if I talk about it.

How do you go about writing?

Everything has been thrown at me, and paper boats float past me, but something more direct might hit me and leave its mark. I think the things I write about are the things I can't fight for. There are a lot of things I say that are really commonplace. I can't get rid of them. I go into something minute, then look at it, then go back into it.

Have you been influenced by any poetry?

I like a poet who has the same name as me, someone named Davies. And a crummy eight-line poem that ends up saying "And that lovely woman is my mother." There's a poem I like, too, whose first line goes "Imagine that life was an old man carrying flowers on his head." And it ends up by saying "And death liked flowers." I'm afraid that's as far as my poetic influences go.

How do you feel about the name of your group?

I went to a studio in a gray pullover and horrible tweed trousers, and the next day I went in an orange tie, and a bloke told me, "Now you really look like a Kink." Maybe it was an unfortunate name—the sadistic image or the things in your arm. It's a good name, in a way, because it's something people don't really want. I think people hate us. They think we betrayed them. Perhaps we have.

But when you recorded live at Kelvin Hall people were screaming and adoring you.

Yeah, it was recorded at a cattle show. There was a large metal roof which gave that effect. Someone said that the audience was more in it than the group. The part I enjoyed was when everyone started singing "Sunny Afternoon."

They must love us really.

BOB DYLAN
Behind the Mask

Los Angeles, 1977

We were driving down Sunset Boulevard—Christmastime in L.A.—looking for a place to eat, when Bob Dylan noticed Santa Claus, surrounded by hundreds of stuffed, Day-Glo animals, standing and soliciting on the street. "Santa Claus in the desert," he commented disconcertedly. "It really brings you down."

A few minutes later, we passed a billboard that showed a photo of George Burns pointing to a new album by John Denver and praising it to the skies. "Did you see that movie they appeared in together?" Dylan asked me. "I sort of like George Burns. What was he playing?"

"I saw it on the plane coming out here. He played God," I said.

"That's a helluva role," Dylan replied.

Bob Dylan should know. For years he has been worshipped—and deservedly so. His songs are miracles, his ways mysterious and unfathomable. In words and music, he has reawakened, and thereby altered, our experience of the world. In statement ("He not busy being born is busy dying") and in image ("My dreams are made of iron and steel / With a big bouquet / Of roses hanging down / From the heavens to the ground") he has kept alive the idea of the poet and artist as *vates*—the visionary eye of the body politic—while keeping himself open to a conception of art that embraces and respects equally Charles Baudelaire and Charley Patton, Arthur Rimbaud and Smokey Robinson.

"Mystery is an essential element in any work of art," says the director Luis Buñuel in a recent *New Yorker* profile by Penelope Gilliatt. "It's usually lacking in film, which should be the most mysterious of all. Most filmmakers are careful not to perturb us by opening the windows of the screen onto their world

55

of poetry. Cinema is a marvelous weapon when it is handled by a free spirit. Of all the means of expression, it is the one that is most like the human imagination. What's the good of it if it apes everything conformist and sentimental in us? It's a curious thing that film can create such moments of compressed ritual. The raising of the everyday to the dramatic." And I happened to read these words during my flight to Los Angeles, hardly knowing then that, just a day later, I would be seeing a film that perfectly embodied Buñuel's notion of the possibilities of cinema.

Renaldo and Clara is Bob Dylan's second film. His first, *Eat the Document,* was a kind of antidocumentary, a night journey through the disjointed landscapes of Dylan's and the Band's 1966 world tour, a magic swirling ship of jump cuts, "ready for to fade." It was a fascinating work, but it came and went after only a few showings. And just as it is impossible for Bob Dylan "to sing the same song the same way twice"—as he himself puts it—so his new four-hour film is a departure from *Eat the Document* as it announces the arrival of a visionary cinematic free spirit.

Conceived over a period of ten years and edited down by Howard Alk and Dylan from four hundred hours of footage, *Renaldo and Clara* was shot during the 1975–76 Rolling Thunder Revue, whose participants make up a cast that includes Bob Dylan (Renaldo), Sara Dylan (Clara), Joan Baez (the Woman in White), Ronnie Hawkins (Bob Dylan), Ronee Blakley (Mrs. Dylan), Jack Elliott (Longheno de Castro), Bob Neuwirth (the Masked Tortilla), Allen Ginsberg (the Father), David Blue (David Blue), and Roger McGuinn (Roger McGuinn).

"Who Are You, Bob Dylan?" was the headline in the French newspaper read by Jean-Pierre Léaud in Jean-Luc Godard's *Masculin–Féminin.* And the mystery of *Renaldo and Clara* is: "Who is Bob Dylan?" "Who is Renaldo?" and "What is the relationship between them?"

I decided to ask Bob Dylan himself. "There's Renaldo," he told me, "there's a guy in whiteface singing on the stage, and then there's Ronnie Hawkins playing Bob Dylan. Bob Dylan is listed in the credits as playing Renaldo, yet Ronnie Hawkins is listed as playing Bob Dylan."

"So Bob Dylan," I surmise, "may or may not be in the film."

"Exactly."

"But Bob Dylan made the film."

"Bob Dylan didn't make it. I made it."

"I is another," wrote Arthur Rimbaud. And this statement is certainly demonstrated by *Renaldo and Clara,* in which characters in masks and hats—

often interchangeable—sit in restaurants and talk, disappear, reappear, exchange flowers, argue, visit cemeteries, play music, travel around in trains and vans, and, in one exhilarating scene, dance around at the edge of a beautiful bay, where they join hands and begin singing an American Indian/ Hindu Indian–sounding chant to the accompaniment of a bop-shoo-op-doo-wah-ditty chorus—a spiritual and rock 'n' roll reunion.

To the anagogic eye, however, the film seems to be about just one man—who could pass for the Jack of Hearts, the leading actor of Dylan's song "Lily, Rosemary, and the Jack of Hearts," a card among cards, an image among images—and just one woman. Together they find themselves in the grip of a series of romantic encounters that are reenactments of the Great Mystery, culminating in the confrontation of the Woman in White (Joan Baez), Clara (Sara Dylan), and Renaldo (Bob Dylan)—a meeting at the border of myth and reality.

Using his physical image and name as the raw material of the film, Bob Dylan, like the Renaissance kings of masque and spectacle, moves daringly and ambiguously between fiction, representation, identification, and partici-pation. *Renaldo and Clara,* of course, is a film filled with magnificently shot and recorded concert footage of highly charged Dylan performances of songs like "It Ain't Me, Babe," "A Hard Rain's A-Gonna Fall," and "Knockin' on Heaven's Door"—the last of whose delicate and eerie instrumental breaks makes you feel as if you were entering the gates of paradise. Avoiding all of the cinematic clichés of pounding-and-zooming television rock 'n' roll spe-cials, the cameras either subtly choreograph the songs—revealing structures and feelings—or else look at the white-faced Dylan and the accompanying painted musicians in rapturous and intensely held close-ups.

Around these musical episodes Dylan has woven a series of multilev-eled scenes—unconsciously echoing similar moments in films by Jean Coc-teau, John Cassavetes, and Jacques Rivette—each of which lights up and casts light on all the others. Scenes and characters duplicate and mirror each other, and are disassociated and recombined—all of them, in the words of the director, "filled with reason but not with logic." Thus, when Clara says to Renaldo, "I am free . . . I can change," it brings back to us the words spoken earlier on by the Woman in White to Renaldo: "I haven't changed that much. Have you?" To which Renaldo replies: "Maybe."

And then there are the correspondences and the doubled worlds. The scenes in the bordello, with Joan Baez and Sara Dylan playing prostitutes and Allen Ginsberg playing a kind of Buddhist john, become an image of

Vajra Hell—the Tantric Buddhist idea of the unbreakable diamond netherworld. And a musician blocking someone's way backstage becomes the Guardian at the Gates.

What is most adventurous and mysterious about *Renaldo and Clara* is the way it counterpoints music with action, lyrics with dialogue, songs with other songs. In one scene, for example, Rodeo (Sam Shepard) is trying to win over Clara, and on the soundtrack you hear, almost subliminally, what sounds like the chord progressions of "Oh, Sister," but which you later realize is "One Too Many Mornings"—as if the songs themselves were trying to communicate with each other, as if they were saying goodbye to each other: "You're right from your side, / I'm right from mine. / We're both just one too many mornings / An' a thousand miles behind."

In another scene, members of the Rolling Thunder Revue join in a reception with members of the Tuscarora Indian tribe, while on the soundtrack we hear Dylan's haunting rehearsal tape version of "People Get Ready." Finally, in another scene, Renaldo hurries nervously down a city street—panhandling and making some kind of furtive French connection with the Masked Tortilla (Bob Neuwirth)—to the accompaniment of Dylan's version of "Little Moses," above which we hear powerfully spoken lines from poet Anne Waldman's "Fast Speaking Woman" ("I'm the Druid Woman / I'm the Ibo Woman / I'm the Buddha Woman / I'm the Vibrato Woman").

"Your films make one wonder what's going on in people's minds," says Penelope Gilliatt to Buñuel, to which he responds: "Dreams, and also the most everyday questions: 'What time is it?' 'Do you want to eat?'" And, in spite of the compression and density of most of the scenes in *Renaldo and Clara*, there is also a presentational immediacy and clarity that fixes the scenes in one's mind, like a very special dream one wants to remember.

"I expect this will be a very small film," Buñuel said during the shooting of his recent *That Obscure Object of Desire,* which might, in fact, have served as the title of *Renaldo and Clara.* "One needs just a hole to look out of," Buñuel continued, "like a spider that has spun its web and is remembering what the world outside was like. This hole is the secret of things. An artist can provide an essential margin of alertness."

Renaldo and Clara is a long film, but it is really an intimate and evanescent one. "Art is the perpetual motion of illusion," says Bob Dylan in the interview that follows, which took place a week before Christmas 1977 in Los Angeles. "The highest purpose of art," Dylan commented, "is to inspire. What else can you do? What else can you do for anyone but inspire them?"

* * *

If someone asked me what Renaldo and Clara *was about, I'd say: art and life, identity and God—with lots of encounters at bars, restaurants, luncheonettes, cabarets, and bus stations.*

Do you want to see it again? Would it be helpful for you to see it again?

You think I'm too confused about the film?

No, I don't think so at all. It isn't just about bus stations and cabarets and stage music and identity—those are elements of it. But it is mostly about identity—about everybody's identity. More important, it's about Renaldo's identity, so we superimpose our own vision on Renaldo: it's his vision and it's his dream.

You know what the film is about? It begins with music—you see a guy in a mask [Bob Dylan], you can see through the mask he's wearing, and he's singing "When I Paint My Masterpiece." So right away you know there's an involvement with music. Music is confronting you.

So are lines like "You can almost think that you're seein' double."

Right. Also on a lyrical level. But you still don't really know . . . and then you're getting off that, and there seems to be a tour. You're hearing things and seeing people . . . it's not quite like a tour, but there's some kind of energy like being on a tour. There's a struggle, there's a reporter, who later appears in the restaurant scenes.

All right, then it goes right to David Blue, who's playing pinball and who seems to be the narrator. He's Renaldo's narrator, he's Renaldo's scribe—he belongs to Renaldo.

Yet David Blue talks not about Renaldo but about Bob Dylan and how he, David Blue, first met Dylan in Greenwich Village in the late fifties.

They seem to be the same person after a while. It's something you can only feel but never really know. Any more than you can know whether Willie Sutton pulled all those bank jobs. Any more than you can know who killed Kennedy for sure. And right away, David Blue says: "Well, what happened was that when I first left my parents' house, I bought *The Myth of Sisyphus.*" Now, that wasn't really the book, but it was pretty close. It was actually—so he tells us—*Existentialism and Human Emotions*. So that's it: this film is a post-existentialist movie. We're in the post-existentialist period. What is it? That's what it is.

What could be more existentialist than playing pinball? It's the perfect existentialist game.

It is. I've seen rows and rows of pinball players lined up like ducks. It's a great equalizer.

What about the emotions in Existentialism and Human Emotions?

Human emotions are the great dictator—in this movie as in all movies. I'll tell you what I think of the emotions later. But getting back to David Blue: he's left his home, and right away you're in for something like a triple dimension. Just ten minutes into the movie he says: "I got in the bus, I went down to New York, walked around for four hours, got back on the bus and went home." And that is exactly what a lot of people are going to feel when they walk into the movie theater: they got on the bus, walked around for four hours, and walked home.

There's another guy, later in the film, who walks out into the night and says to a girl: "This has been a great mistake."

Yeah. You can pick any line in a movie to sum up your feeling about it. But don't forget you don't see that guy anymore after that. He's gone. And that means Renaldo isn't being watched anymore because he was watching Renaldo.

Talking about mistakes and seeing double: it's fascinating how easy it is to mistake people in the film for one another. I mistook you, for instance, for the guy driving the carriage (maybe it was you); for Jack Elliott; and I even mistook you for you.

The Masked Tortilla [Bob Neuwirth] is mistaken for Bob Dylan, Bob Dylan is mistaken for Renaldo. And Bob Dylan is the one with the hat on. That's who Bob Dylan is—he's the one with the hat on.

Almost every man in the film has a hat on.

Right.

All those disguises and masks!

The first mask, as I said, is one you can see through. But they're all masks. In the film, the mask is more important than the face.

All the women in the film seem to turn into one person, too, and a lot of them wear hats. It reminds me of "The Ballad of Frankie Lee and Judas Priest":

> He just stood there staring
> At that big house as bright as any sun,
> With four and twenty windows
> And a woman's face in ev'ry one.

This film was made for you. *[Laughing]* Did you see the Woman in White who becomes a different Woman in White? One's mistaken for the other. At first she's only an idea of herself—you see her in the street, later in the carriage. I think the women in the movie are beautiful. They look like they've stepped out of a painting. They're vulnerable, but they're also strong-willed.

"Breaking just like a little girl."

That's the child in everyone. That's the child in everyone that has to be confronted.

"Just Like a Woman" always seemed to me to be somehow about being born: "I can't stay in here . . . I just can't fit." So by confronting the child in you, saying goodbye to childhood, you're born into something bigger. In a way, it's a frightening song.

It always was a frightening song, but that feeling needs to be eliminated.

I was thinking of what looked like a Yiddish cabaret filled with older women listening intently to Allen Ginsberg reading passages from "Kaddish," his great elegy to his mother.

Those women are strong in the sense that they know their own identity. It's only the layer of what we're going to reveal in the next film, because women are exploited like anyone else. They're victims just like coal miners.

The poet Robert Bly has written about the image of the Great Mother as a union of four force fields, consisting of the nurturing mother, like Isis (though your Isis seems more ambiguous); the Death Mother (like the woman in "It's All Over Now, Baby Blue"); the Ecstatic Mother (like the girl in "Spanish Harlem Incident"); and the Stone Mother who drives you mad (like Sweet Melinda who leaves you howling at the moon in "Just Like Tom Thumb's Blues"). Traces of these women seem to be in this film as well.

The Death Mother is represented in the film, but I don't know what I should say or can say or shouldn't say about who is who in the movie. I mean who is the old woman everyone calls Mama—the woman who sings, plays guitar, and reads palms? She reads Allen's palm, saying: "You've been married twice." And me, later on I'm looking at the gravestone marked HUSBAND, and Ginsberg asks: "Is that going to happen to you?" And I say: "I want an unmarked grave." But of course I'm saying this as Renaldo.

In Tarantula you wrote your own epitaph:

> *Here lies Bob Dylan,*
> *killed by a discarded Oedipus*
> *who turned*
> *around*
> *to investigate a ghost*
> *and discovered that*
> *the ghost, too, was more than one person.*

Yeah, way back then I was thinking of this film. I've had this picture in mind for a long time—years and years. Too many years. Renaldo is oppressed. He's oppressed because he's born. We don't really know who Renaldo is. We just know what he isn't. He isn't the Masked Tortilla. Renaldo is the one with the hat, but he's not wearing a hat. I'll tell you what this movie is: it's like life exactly, but not an imitation of it. It transcends life, and it's not like life.

That paradox is toppling me over.

I'll tell you what my film is about: it's about naked alienation of the inner self against the outer self—alienation taken to the extreme. And it's about integrity. My next film is about obsession. The hero is an arsonist . . . but he's not really a hero.

Renaldo and Clara *seems to me to be about obsession, too.*

That's true, but only in the way it applies to integrity.

The idea of integrity comes across in a lot of your songs and in lines like "To live outside the law, you must be honest" and "She doesn't have to say she's faithful / Yet she's true, like ice, like fire."

We talked about emotions before. You can't be a slave to your emotions. If you're a slave to your emotions you're dependent on your emotions, and you're only dealing with your conscious mind. But the film is about the fact that you have to be faithful to your subconscious, unconscious, super-conscious—as well as to your conscious. Integrity is a facet of honesty. It has to do with knowing yourself.

At the end of the film, Renaldo is with two women in a room (the Woman in White played by Joan Baez and Clara played by Sara Dylan), and he says: "Evasiveness is only in the mind—truth is on many levels. Ask me anything and I'll tell you the truth." Clara and the Woman in White both ask him, "Do you love her?" as they point to each other—not "Do you love me?"

Possessiveness. It was a self-focused kind of question. And earlier, one of the women in the whorehouse talks about the ego-protection cords she wears around her neck. Do you remember that? . . . In the scene you mentioned, did you notice that Renaldo was looking at the newspaper that had an article on Bob Dylan and Joan Baez in it? Joan Baez and Bob Dylan at this point are an illusion. It wasn't planned that way. Joan Baez without Bob Dylan isn't too much of an illusion because she's an independent woman and her independence asserts itself. But Joan Baez with Bob Dylan *is.*

So at the moment you open up that newspaper, art and life really come together.

Exactly.

And what about the moment when Joan Baez, looking at Clara, says, "Who is this woman?" and you cut to your singing "Sara"? Talk about art and life!

It's as far as you can take it—meaning personally and generally. Who is this woman? Obviously, this woman is a figment of the material world. Who is this woman who has no name? Who is this woman, she says . . .

who is this woman, as if she's talking about herself. Who this woman is was told to you, earlier on, when you see her coming out of the church carrying a rope. You know she means business, you know she has a purpose.

Another way of putting it is: the singer's character onstage is always becoming Renaldo. By singing "Sara," the singer comes as close to Renaldo as he can get. It brings everything as close as possible without two becoming one.

It was pretty amazing to see you use your personal life and the myth of your life so nakedly in that scene with Renaldo and the two women.

Right, but you're talking to me as a director now.

Still, you do have that scene with Joan Baez and Sara Dylan.

Well, Sara Dylan here is working as Sara Dylan. She has the same last name as Bob Dylan, but we may not be related. If she couldn't have played the role of Clara, she wouldn't have done it.

Is she talking about her real problems or pretending that she's an adventurer?

We can make anybody's problems our problems.

Some people will obviously think that this film either broke up your marriage or is a kind of incantation to make your marriage come back together.

Either one of those statements I can't relate to. It has nothing to do with the breakup of my marriage. My marriage is over. I'm divorced. This film is a film.

Why did you make yourself so vulnerable?

You must be vulnerable to be sensitive to reality. And to me being vulnerable is just another way of saying that one has nothing more to lose. I don't have anything but darkness to lose. I'm way beyond that. The worst thing that could happen is that the film will be accepted and that the next one will be compared unfavorably to this one.

Strangely, the scene where the two women confront Renaldo reminds me of

64

King Lear, *in which each of the daughters has to say how much she loves her father.*

You're right. Renaldo sees himself as Cordelia.

I've always interpreted some of the Basement Tapes *as being concerned with ideas from* King Lear. *"Too much of nothing / Can make a man abuse a king"; "Oh what dear daughter 'neath the sun / Would treat a father so, / To wait upon him hand and foot / And always tell him, 'No'?"*

Exactly. In the later years it changed from "king" to "clown."

King Lear had a fool around him, too, and when the fool leaves, Cordelia comes back. She takes his place, and he takes hers.

The roles are all interchangeable.

As in "Tangled Up in Blue" and as in your movie.

Yes it is.

Were you specifically influenced by King Lear *when you wrote songs like "Tears of Rage"?*

No, songs like that were based on the concept that one is one.

". . . and all alone and ever more shall be so."

Exactly. What comes is gone forever every time.

But one is difficult to deal with, so Christians gave us the Trinity.

The Christians didn't bring in anything—it was the Greeks.

Jesus is a very strong figure in Renaldo and Clara. *There's that song by you called "What Will You Do When Jesus Comes?" There's the woman who says to you in the restaurant: "There's nowhere to go. Just stand and place yourself like the cross and I'll receive you." And then there are the shots of the huge cement crucifix in the Catholic Grotto.*

Right. Jesus is the most identifiable figure in Western culture, and yet he was exploited, used, and exploited. We all have been.

There's also that scene, near the end of the film, where Allen Ginsberg takes you around to see the glassed-in sculptures of the Stations of the Cross, and we see Jesus killed for the second time and then buried under the weight of the cross. On one level, the film is about the Stations of the Cross, isn't it?

Yeah, you're right, like the double vision having to be killed twice. Like why does Jesus really die?

Spiritually or politically?

Realistically. Because he's a healer. Jesus is a healer. So he goes to India, finds out how to be a healer, and becomes one. But see, I believe that he overstepped his duties a little bit. He accepted and took on the bad karma of all the people he healed. And he was filled with so much bad karma that the only way out was to burn him up.

In my film, we're looking at masks a lot of the time. And then when the dream becomes so solidified that it has to be taken to the stage of reality, then you'll see stone, you'll see a statue—which is even a further extension of the mask: the statue of Mary in front of the statue of Jesus on the cross in the Crucifix Grotto.

Throughout the film, I also noticed the continual reappearance of the red rose. Every woman has a rose.

It has a great deal to do with what's happening in the movie. Do you remember the woman in the carriage? She's bringing a rose to Renaldo, who gives it back to her.

But then it appears in your hat when you're singing.

By that time it's all fallen apart and shattered, the dream is gone . . . it could be anywhere after that.

Joan Baez carries one when she's with Mama. And then the violinist Scarlet Rivera gives it to you in your dressing room.

That's right. The rose is a symbol of fertility.

Also of the soul. The Romance of the Rose—the dreamer's vision of the soul.

That's right. . . . The most mysterious figure in the film is the conductor on the train. Do you remember him?

He's the guy who tells the Masked Tortilla—who says he's going to a wedding—that he's only been on the train for four hours (there's that magical four hours again!) and not for the six days that he imagines.

Yeah, he tells him, too, that he's going to possibly the largest city in the East.

I figured it was New York.

No. The largest city in the East!

The Magi!

That's not exactly what he's talking about—it's more like the holy crossroads.

There's another scene like that in which Mick Ronson is blocking Ronnie Hawkins's way to a backstage area. He seemed like some kind of guardian.

He's the Guardian of the Gates. But scenes like these work in terms of feeling. It's like with tarot cards—you don't have to be confused as to what they mean . . . someone else who knows can read them for you.

"Nothing is revealed," you sing at the end of "The Ballad of Frankie Lee and Judas Priest." Is anything revealed at the end of Renaldo and Clara?

Yeah, I'll tell you what the film reveals: this film reveals that there's a whole lot to reveal beneath the surface of the soul, but it's unthinkable.

[Silence]

That's exactly what it reveals. It reveals the depths that there are to reveal. And that's the most you can ask, because things are really very invisible. You can't reveal the invisible. And this film goes as far as we can to reveal that.

Under a statue of Isis in the city of Saïs is the following inscription: "I am everything that was, that is, that shall be. Nor has any mortal ever been able to discover what lies under my veil."

That's a fantastic quotation. That's true, exactly. Once you see what's under the veil, what happens to you? You die, don't you, or go blind?

I wanted to tie in two things we've talked about: the idea of integrity and the idea of Jesus. In your song "I Want You," you have the lines:

> *Now all my fathers, they've gone down,*
> *True love they've been without it.*
> *But all their daughters put me down*
> *'Cause I don't think about it.*

These are some of my favorite lines of yours, and to me they suggest that real desire is stronger than frustration or guilt.

I know. It's incredible you find that there. I know it's true. And in *Renaldo and Clara* there's no guilt. But that's why people will take offense at it, if they are offended by it in any way, because of the lack of guilt in the movie. None at all.

This brings us back to Jesus.

Jesus is . . . well, I'm not using Jesus in the film so much as I'm using the concept of Jesus—the idea of Jesus as a man, not the virgin birth.

But what about the concept of masochism associated with Jesus?

That's what happened to Jesus. People relate to the masochism, to the spikes in his hand, to the blood coming out, to the fact that he was cruci-fied. What would have happened to him if he hadn't been crucified? That's what draws people to him. There are only signals of that in this film—like a fingernail blade at one point.

What about the line in "Wedding Song": "Your love cuts like a knife."

Well, it's bloodletting; it's what heals all disease. Neither aggression nor anger interests me. Violence only does on an interpretive level, only when it's a product of reason.

People are attracted to blood. I'm personally not consumed by the de-sire to drink the blood. But bloodletting is meaningful in that it can cure disease. But we didn't try to make a film of that nature. This film concerns itself with the dream. There's no blood in the dream. The dream is cold. This film concerns itself only with the depth of the dream—the dream as seen in the mirror.

The next film might have some blood. I'm trying to locate Lois Smith to be in it. She would represent the idea of innocence. Do you know who she is? She was the barmaid in *East of Eden*. I'm trying to line up some people for the film, and I can't find her.

For some reason I've just thought of my favorite singer.

Who is that?

Om Kalsoum—the Egyptian woman who died a few years ago. She was my favorite.

What did you like about her?

It was her heart.

Do you like dervish and Sufi singing, by the way?

Yeah, that's where my singing really comes from, except that I sing in America. I've heard too much Leadbelly really to be too much influenced by the whirling dervishes.

Now that we somehow got onto this subject, who else do you like right now? New Wave groups?

No, I'm not interested in them. I think Alice Cooper is an overlooked songwriter. I like Ry Cooder. And I like Dave Mason's version of something, which is on the jukebox right now.

I wonder what you think of the guy who ends your movie singing this fulsome, crooning version of "In the Morning" with those memorable lines: "I'll be yawning into the morning of my life." Why is he there?

The film had to end with him because he represents the fact that Renaldo could be dreaming. And he might be singing for Renaldo—representing him, the darkness representing the light.

He's like what's happened to one sentimental part of rock 'n' roll in the seventies.

He's not rock 'n' roll.

Rock 'n' roll isn't rock 'n' roll anymore.

You're right, there's no more rock 'n' roll. It's an imitation, we can forget about that. Rock 'n' roll has turned itself inside out. I never did do rock 'n' roll, I'm just doing the same old thing I've always done.

You've never sung a rock 'n' roll song?

No, I never have. Only in spirit.

You can't really dance to one of your songs.

I couldn't.

Imagine dancing to "Rainy Day Woman #12 & 35." It's kind of alienating. Everyone thought it was about being stoned, but I always thought it was about being all alone.

So did I. You could write about that for years. . . . Rock 'n' roll ended with Phil Spector. The Beatles weren't rock 'n' roll either. Nor the Rolling Stones. Rock 'n' roll ended with Little Anthony and the Imperials. Pure rock 'n' roll.

With "Goin' Out of My Head"?

The one before that. . . . Rock 'n' roll ended in 1959.

When did it begin for you?

1954.

What is there now?

Programmed music. Quadruple tracking.

What do you think about the seventies?

The seventies I see as a period of reconstruction after the sixties, that's all. That's why people say: "Well, it's boring, nothing's really happening," and that's because wounds are healing. By the eighties, anyone who's going to be doing anything will have his or her cards showing. You won't be able to get back in the game in the eighties.

I came across something you wrote a while back:

> *Desire . . . never fearful*

finally faithful
it will guide me well
across all bridges
inside all tunnels
never failin'.

I even remember where I wrote that. I wrote that in New Hampshire. I think I was all alone.

Here's something else you wrote:

Mine shall be a strong loneliness
dissolvin' deep
t' the depths of my freedom
an' that, then, shall
remain my song.

You seem to have stayed true to that feeling.

I haven't had any reason to stray.

In "The Times They Are A-Changin'" you sing: "He that gets hurt / Will be he who has stalled." What has kept you unstalled?

I don't know. Mainly because I don't believe in this life.

The Buddhist tradition talks about illusion. The Jewish tradition about allusion. Which do you feel closer to?

I believe in both, but I probably lean to allusion. I'm not a Buddhist. I believe in life, but not this life.

What life do you believe in?

Real life.

Do you ever experience real life?

I experience it all the time. It's beyond this life.

I wanted to read to you two Hasidic texts that somehow remind me of your work. The first says that in the service of God, one can learn three things from a child and seven from a thief. "From a child you can learn (1) always to be happy; (2) never to sit idle; and (3) to cry for everything one wants. From a thief you should learn (1) to work at night; (2) if one cannot gain what one wants in one night to try again the next night; (3) to love one's co-workers just as thieves love each other; (4) to be willing to risk one's life even for a little thing; (5) not to attach too much value to things even though one has risked one's life for them—just as a thief will resell a stolen article for a fraction of its real value; (6) to withstand all kinds of beatings and tortures but to remain what you are; and (7) to believe that your work is worthwhile and not be willing to change it."

Who wrote that?

A Hasidic rabbi.

Which one?

Dov Baer, the Maggid of Mezeritch.

That's the most mind-blazing chronicle of human behavior I think I've ever heard. . . . How can I get a copy of that? I'll put it on my wall. There's a man I would follow. That's a real hero. A real hero.

Another Hasidic rabbi once said that you can learn something from everything. Even from a train, a telephone, and a telegram. From a train, he said, you can learn that in one second one can miss everything. From a telephone you can learn that what you say over here can be heard over there. And from a telegram that all words are counted and charged.

It's a cosmic statement. Where do you get all of these rabbis' sayings? Those guys are really wise. I tell you, I've heard gurus and yogis and philosophers and politicians and doctors and lawyers, teachers of all kinds . . . and these rabbis really had something going.

They're like Sufis, but they speak and teach with more emotion.

As I said before, I don't believe in emotion. They use their hearts, their hearts don't use them.

In one second missing everything on a train . . . do you think that means that you can miss the train or miss seeing something from the train window?

That's a statement of revelation. I think it means that in one moment you can miss everything because you're not there. You just watch it, and you know you're missing it.

What about the telephone—what you say here is heard over there?

That means you're never that far away from the ultimate God.

And words being counted and charged.

That's very truthful, too. That's everything you say and think is all being added up.

How are you coming out?

You know, I'll tell you: lately I've been catching myself. I've been in some scenes, and I say: "Holy shit, I'm not here alone." I've never had that experience before the past few months. I've felt this strange, eerie feeling that I wasn't all alone, and I'd better know it.

Do you watch what you say?

I always try to watch what I say because I try not to say anything I don't mean.

Maybe Renaldo has that problem at the end of your movie?

No, Renaldo's on top of it, he's on top of circumstance. He's not going to say too much 'cause he knows he doesn't know much. Now me, obviously I'm talking and saying things, and I *will* talk and say things, but that's because I think I'm going to mean them . . . or I feel I mean them now. I'm not just talking to hear myself. But Renaldo is *not* saying anything just because he knows that *what* he says is being heard and that therefore he doesn't know what to say. No, he says some very incredible and important things when he's confronted with his *allusion*. You know, he does say: "Do I love you like I love her? No." "Do I love her like I love you? No." He can't say any more than that . . . you don't have to know any more about him than that. That's all you have to know about him, that's all you have to know about Bob Dylan.

*At that moment in the film, you cut into a performance of your song "Catfish"—
"Nobody can throw the ball like Catfish can." It's almost jokey after that intense
preceding scene.*

It's treated more in the way of music, getting back to the idea that music
is truthful. And music is truthful. Everything's okay, you put on a record,
someone's playing an instrument—that changes the vibe. Music attracts
the angels in the universe. A group of angels sitting at a table are going to
be attracted by that.

So we always get back to the music in the film. We made a point of
doing it, as if we had to do it. You're not going to see music in the movies
as you do in this film. We don't have any filler. You don't see any doors
close or any reverse shots, which are just there to take up time until you
get to the next one. We didn't want to take time away from other shots.

A lot of hold shots, not enough of them. When the woman is walking
down the street with that rope, that's a hold shot. David Blue is on a hold
shot for six minutes the first time you see him. I know this film is too long.
It may be four hours too long—I don't care. To me, it's not long enough.
I'm not concerned how long something is. I want to see a set shot. I feel
a set shot. I don't feel all this motion and boom-boom. We can fast cut
when we want, but the power comes in the ability to have faith that it is
a meaningful shot.

You know who understood this? Andy Warhol. Warhol did a lot for
American cinema. He was before his time. But Warhol and Hitchcock
and Peckinpah and Tod Browning . . . they were important to me. I figured Godard had the accessibility to make what he made, he broke new
ground. I never saw any film like *Breathless*, but once you saw it, you said:
"Yeah, man, why didn't I do that, I could have done that." Okay, he did it,
but he couldn't have done it in America.

But what about a film like Samuel Fuller's Forty Guns *or Joseph Lewis's* Gun
Crazy?

Yeah, I just heard Fuller's name the other day. I think American filmmakers are the best. But I also like Kurosawa, and my favorite director
is Buñuel—it doesn't surprise me that he'd say those amazing things you
quoted to me before from the *New Yorker*.

I don't know what to tell you. In one way I don't consider myself a filmmaker at all. In another way I do. To me, *Renaldo and Clara* is my first real film. I don't know who will like it. I made it for a specific bunch of people and myself, and that's all. That's how I wrote "Blowin' in the Wind" and "The Times They Are A-Changin'"—they were written for a certain crowd of people and for certain artists, too. Who knew they were going to be big songs?

Your film, in a way, is a culmination of a lot of your ideas and obsessions.

That may be true, but I hope it also has meaning for other people who aren't that familiar with my songs, and that other people can see themselves in it, because I don't feel so isolated from what's going on. There are a lot of people who'll look at the film without knowing who anybody is in it. And they'll see it more purely.

Sergei Eisenstein talked of montage in terms of attraction—shots attracting other shots—then in terms of shock, and finally in terms of fusion and synthesis, and of overtones. You seem to be really aware of the overtones in your film, do you know what I mean?

I sure do.

Eisenstein once wrote: "The Moscow Art Theater is my deadly enemy. It is the exact antithesis of all I am trying to do. They string their emotions together to give a continuous illusion of reality. I take photographs of reality and then cut them up so as to produce emotions."

What we did was to cut up reality and make it more real. . . . Everyone from the cameramen to the water boy, from the wardrobe people to the sound people, was just as important as anyone else in the making of the film. There weren't any roles that well defined. The money was coming in the front door and going out the back door. The Rolling Thunder tour sponsored the movie. And I had faith and trust in the people who helped me do the film, and they had faith and trust in me.

In the movie, there's a man behind a luncheonette counter who talks a lot about truth—he's almost like the Greek chorus of the film.

Yeah, we often sat around and talked about that guy. He *is* the chorus.

That guy at one point talks about the Movement going astray and about how everyone got bought off. How come you didn't sell out and just make a commercial film?

I don't have any cinematic vision to sell out. It's all for me so I can't sell out. I'm not working for anybody. What was there to sell out?

You could have sold out to the vision of the times.

Right. I have my point of view and my vision, and nothing tampers with it because it's all that I've got. I don't have anything to sell out.

Renaldo and Clara *has certain similarities to the recent films of Jacques Rivette. Do you know his work?*

I don't. But I wish they'd do it in this country. I'd feel a lot safer. I mean I wouldn't get so much resistance and hostility. I can't believe that people think that four hours is too long for a film. As if people had so much to do. You can see an hour movie that seems like ten hours. I think the vision is strong enough to cut through all of that. But we may be kicked right out of Hollywood after this film is released and have to go to Bolivia. In India, they show twelve-hour movies. Americans are spoiled. They expect art to be like wallpaper with no effort, just to be there.

I should have asked you this before, but how much of the film is improvised and how much determined beforehand?

About a third is improvised, about a third is determined, and about a third is blind luck.

What about, for instance, the scene in which Ronnie Hawkins tries to get a farm girl to go on tour with him, trying to convince her by saying something like: "God's not just in the country, God's in the city, too. . . . God's everywhere, so let's seize the day."

In that scene, Ronnie was given five subjects to hit on. He could say anything he wanted as long as he covered five points. Obviously, God was a subject relevant to the movie. Then he talked about the Father. Now get this: in the film there's the character of the Father played by Allen Ginsberg. But in Ronnie's scene, the farmer's daughter talks about *her* father. That's the same father.

Another half-improvised scene is the one in which Ramone—the dead lover of Mrs. Dylan [played by Ronee Blakley]—appears as a ghost in the bathroom, and they argue in front of the mirror.

How does the audience know that that's "Mrs. Dylan"?

She's so identified later on in the film. It's just like Hitchcock. Hitchcock would lay something down, and an hour later you'd figure it out—but if you want to know, you wait and find out. It's not given to you on a platter.

Hitchcock puts himself into each of his films—once. You put yourself in hundreds of places and times!

Right. *[Laughing]* I've tried to learn a lack of fear from Hitchcock.

Did the John Cassavetes movies influence you at all in scenes such as the one in the bathroom?

No, not at all. But I think it all comes from the same place. I'm probably interested in the same things Cassavetes is interested in.

What are those?

Timing, for example, and the struggle to break down complexity into simplicity.

Timing of relationships?

The relationships of human reason. It's all a matter of timing. The movie creates and holds the time. That's what it should do—it should hold that time, breathe in that time, and stop time in doing that. It's like if you look at a painting by Cézanne, you get lost in that painting for that period of time. And you breathe—yet time is going by and you wouldn't know it, you're spellbound.

In Cézanne, things that you might take as being decoration actually turn out to be substantial.

That's exactly what happens in *Renaldo and Clara*. Things which appear merely decorative usually, later on, become substantial. It just takes a certain amount of experience with the film to catch on to that. For example, Allen Ginsberg. You first hear his name, just his name.

77

And then you get a glimpse of him at that weird, monomaniacal poetry reading.

It's not as weird as it should be. Weirdness is exactness.

One quick question about Hurricane Carter, whom you show in the film. Do you think that he was guilty?

I don't personally think he is. I put that sequence in the film because he's a man who's not unlike anyone else in the film. He's a righteous man, a very philosophic man—he's not your typical bank robber or mercy slayer. He deserves better than what he got.

You told me that you plan to make twelve more films, but I gather you're not giving up on songwriting and touring.

I have to get back to playing music because unless I do, I don't really feel alive. I don't feel I can be a filmmaker all the time. I have to play in front of the people in order just to keep going.

In "Wedding Song" you sing: "I love you more than ever / Now that the past is gone." But in "Tangled Up in Blue" you sing: "But all the while I was alone / The past was close behind." Between these two couplets lies an important boundary.

We allow our past to exist. Our credibility is based on our past. But deep in our soul we have no past. I don't think we have a past, any more than we have a name. You can say we have a past if we have a future. Do we have a future? No. So how can our past exist if the future doesn't exist?

So what are the songs on Blood on the Tracks *about?*

The present.

Why did you say, "I love you more than ever / Now that the past is gone"?

That's delusion. That's gone.

And what about, "And all the while I was alone / The past was close behind"?

That's more delusion. Delusion is close behind.

When your "Greek chorus" restaurant owner talks about the Movement selling itself out, you next cut to your singing "Tangled Up in Blue," which is, in part, about what has happened in and to the past.

But we're only dealing with the past in terms of being able to be healed by it. We can communicate only because we both agree that this is a glass and this is a bowl and that's a candle and there's a window here and there are lights out in the city. Now I might not agree with that. Turn this glass around and it's something else. Now I'm hiding it in a napkin. Watch it now. Now you don't even know it's there. It's the past. I don't even deal with it. I don't think seriously about the past, the present, or the future. I've spent enough time thinking about these things and have gotten nowhere.

But didn't you when you wrote "Blood on the Tracks"? Why is it so intense?

Because there's physical blood in the soul, and flesh and blood are portraying it to you. Willpower. Willpower is what makes it an intense album, but certainly not anything to do with the past or the future. Willpower is telling you that we are agreeing on what is what.

What about "Idiot Wind"?

Willpower.

Why have you been able to keep so in touch with your anger throughout the years, as revealed in songs like "Can You Please Crawl out Your Window?" and "Positively 4th Street"?

Willpower. With strength of will you can do anything. With willpower you can determine your destiny.

Can you really know where your destiny is leading you?

Yeah, when you're on top of your game. Anger and sentimentality go right next to each other, and they're both superficial. Chagall made a lot of sentimental paintings. And Voltaire wrote a lot of angry books.

What is "Idiot Wind"?

It's a little bit of both because it uses all the textures of strict philosophy, but basically it's a shattered philosophy that doesn't have a title, and it's driven across with willpower. Willpower is what you're responding to.

79

In your film you show a bearded poet in Hasidic garb who speaks in an Irish brogue and carries a gun. He tells us that he doesn't care about being fast but about being accurate. Is that how you feel now?

Yeah. Everyone admires the poet, no matter if he's a lumberjack or a football player or a car thief. If he's a poet he'll be admired and respected.

You used to say you were a trapeze artist.

Well, I see the poet in every man and woman.

Rimbaud's grave doesn't even mention the fact that he was a poet, but rather that he was an adventurer.

Exactly. But I don't try to adopt or imitate Rimbaud in my work. I'm not interested in imitation.

I've always associated you with Rimbaud. Illuminations and Fireworks. Do you believe in reincarnation?

I believe in this: If you want to take reincarnation as a subject, let's say a child is conceived inside of a woman's belly, and was planted there by a man. Nine months before that seed is planted, there's nothing. Ten, twelve, thirteen months . . . two years before that seed is planted, maybe there's the germination of that seed. That comes from food intake into the bloodstream. Food can be a side of beef or a carrot on a shelf. But that's what makes it happen.

In another lifetime, you're in a supermarket and there's a package of carrots right there . . . *that* possibly could be you. *That* kind of reincarnation. . . . And how did that carrot get there? It got there through the ground. It got there through the ground with the help of a piece of animal shit. It has to do with the creation and destruction of *time*. Which means it's immense. Five million years is nothing, it's a drop in a bucket. I don't think there's enough time for reincarnation. It would take thousands or millions of years and light miles for any real kind of reincarnation. I think one can be conscious of different vibrations in the universe, and these can be picked up. But reincarnation from the twelfth to the twentieth century—I say it's impossible.

So you take reincarnation on a cellular level, and when I say "Rimbaud and you," you take it as an affinity.

Maybe my spirit passed through the same places as his did. We're all wind and dust anyway, and we could have passed through many barriers at different times.

What about your line: "Sweet Goddess / Born of a blinding light and a changing wind" in the song "Tough Mama"?

That's the mother and father, the yin and yang. That's the coming together of destiny and the fulfillment of destiny.

George Harrison once said that your lines

> *Look out kid*
> *It's somethin' you did*
> *God knows when*
> *But you're doin' it again*

from "Subterranean Homesick Blues" seemed to be a wonderful description of karma.

Karma's not reincarnation. There's no proof of reincarnation and there's no proof of karma, but there's a *feeling* of karma. We don't even have any proof that the universe exists. We don't have any proof that we are even sitting here. We can't prove that we're really alive. How can we prove we're alive by other people saying we're alive?

All I have to do is kick a rock.

Yeah, you're saying *you're* alive, but the rock isn't going to tell you. The rock don't feel it.

If you take reality to be unreal, than you make unreality real. What's real to you? Art?

Art is the perpetual motion of illusion. The highest purpose of art is to inspire. What else can you do? What else can you do for anyone but inspire them?

What are your new songs like?

My new songs are new for me, and they accomplish what I wanted to accomplish when I started thinking about them. Very seldom do you finish something and then abandon it, and very seldom do you abandon something with the attitude that you've gotten what you started out to get. Usually you think, "Well, it's too big," you get wasted along the way someplace, and it just trails off . . . and what you've got is what you've got and you just do the best with it. But very seldom do you ever come out with what you put in. And I think I've done that now for the first time since I was writing two songs a day way back when. My experience with film helped me in writing the songs. I probably wouldn't have written any more songs if I hadn't made this film. I would have been bummed out. I wouldn't have been able to do what I knew could be done.

I know I'm being nostalgic, but I loved hearing you sing "Little Moses" in Renaldo and Clara.

I used to play that song when I performed at Gerde's Folk City. It's an old Carter Family song, and it goes something like:

> Away by the waters so wide
> The ladies were winding their way,
> When Pharaoh's little daughter
> Stepped down in the water
> To bathe in the cool of the day.
> And before it got dark,
> She opened the ark,
> And saw the sweet infant so gay.

Then little Moses grows up, slays the Egyptian, leads the Jews—it's a great song. And I thought it fit pretty well into the movie. Everybody's in this film: the Carter Family, Hank Williams, Woody Guthrie, Beethoven. Who is going to understand this film? Where are the people to understand this film—a film which needs no understanding?

Who understands "Sad-Eyed Lady of the Lowlands"?

I do. . . . It's strange. I finally feel in the position of someone who people want to interview enough that they'll fly you into town, put you up in a hotel, pay all your expenses, and give you a tour of the city. I'm finally in that position.

I once went to see the King of the Gypsies in southern France. This guy had twelve wives and a hundred children. He was in the antique business and had a junkyard, but he'd had a heart attack before I'd come to see him. All his wives and children had left. And the Gypsy clan had left him with only one wife and a couple of kids and a dog. What happens is that after he dies they'll all come back. They smell death and they leave. That's what happens in life. And I was very affected by seeing that.

Did you feel something like that in the past five years?

You're talking about 1973? I don't even remember 1975. I'm talking about the spring of 1975. There was a lack of targets at that time. But I don't remember what happened last week.

But you probably remember your childhood clearly.

My childhood is so far away . . . it's like I don't even remember being a child. I think it was someone else who was a child. Did you ever think like that? I'm not sure that what happened to me yesterday was true.

But you seem sure of yourself.

I'm sure of my dream self. I live in my dreams. I don't really live in the actual world.

* * *

> "I'll let you be in my dreams
> If I can be in yours.
> I said that."
> —Bob Dylan, 1963

ORIANA FALLACI
The Art of Unclothing an Emperor

Little man whip a big man every time if the
little man's in the right and keeps a' comin'.

—motto of the Texas Rangers

New York City, 1976

When Oriana Fallaci went to interview Ethiopia's Haile Selassie, the emperor's two pet Chihuahuas, named Lulu and Papillon—sensitive antennae of the monarch's autonomic nervous system, Geiger counters registering the presence of friend or foe—stopped dead in their tracks. And after this interview (in which the emperor sounded "sick or drunk") was published in Italy, the Ethiopian ambassador in Rome was recalled to his homeland, and no word of or from him was ever heard again.

It is not uncommon for political repercussions to result from a Fallaci interview. The original tapes of her conversation with Golda Meir, Fallaci claims, were stolen by agents of Libya's Colonel Qaddafi. Her interview with Pakistan's Ali Bhutto delayed a peace agreement between Pakistan and India. And Henry Kissinger paid Oriana Fallaci one of her greatest compliments, saying that his having consented to an interview with her was the "stupidest" thing he had ever done.

Like the child in "The Emperor's New Clothes," and like the "Plain Dealer" of Restoration comedy, whose unremitting rudeness signified to the audience that this stock character was being true to himself, Oriana Fallaci has, simply with a tape recorder, exposed the inanities and pretensions of those contumelious rascals and fat-hearted popinjays who pose and act as the powerful leaders and manipulators of the world's destiny.

After years of interviewing "vacuous" movie stars, this slight (in stature), passionate, and mettlesome woman—who speaks in a candent, husky tone—has become the greatest political interviewer of modern times. The Oriana Fallaci Tape Collection is now housed in humidified shelves at Boston University. And this year [1976] Liveright is publishing *Interview with History*—a book consisting of fourteen of Fallaci's interviews with persons such as Kissinger, President Thieu, General Giap, Golda Meir, the shah of Iran, Archbishop Makarios, and Indira Gandhi. As an international correspondent for the Italian magazine *L'Europeo,* she has become a star throughout Europe (where her articles, interviews, and books appear regularly in translation) and she has attracted a devoted following in this country through the publication of her interviews in magazines and newspapers such as the *New Republic,* the *Washington Post,* the *New York Review of Books,* and the *New York Times Magazine.*

Oriana Fallaci claims that she prepares herself for her interviews "as a boxer prepares for the ring," but it is as a "midwife"—as she defines her role in the following interview—that she has drawn from her subjects many astonishing revelations. Through her gentle ministration, Kissinger finally explained the reason for his abiding popularity: "Well, yes, I'll tell you. What do I care? The main point arises from the fact that I've always acted alone. Americans like that immensely. Americans like the cowboy who leads the wagon train by riding ahead alone on his horse, the cowboy who rides all alone into the town, the village, with his horse and nothing else. Maybe even without a pistol, since he doesn't shoot. He acts, that's all, by being in the right place at the right time. In short, a western."

From the shah of Iran, Fallaci received the following remarks concerning the role of women in his life: "Women, you know . . . Look, let's put it this way. I don't underrate them; they've profited more than anyone else from my White Revolution. . . . And let's not forget I'm the son of the man who took away women's veils in Iran. But I wouldn't be sincere if I stated I'd been influenced by a single one of them. Nobody can influence me, nobody. Still less a woman. Women are important in a man's life only if they're beautiful and charming and keep their femininity and . . . This business of feminism, for instance. What do these feminists want? What do you want? You say equality. Oh! I don't want to seem rude, but . . . You're equal in the eyes of the law, but not, excuse my saying so, in intelligence."

From the tortured leader of the Greek Resistance, Alexandros Panagou-lis, Fallaci elicited his haunting description of how it felt to rediscover space after years sequestered in the darkness of prison: "I made a terrible effort to go forward in all that sun, all that space. Then all of a sudden, in all that sun, in all that space, I saw a spot. And the spot was a group of people. And from that group of people a black figure detached itself. And it came toward me, and little by little it became my mother. And behind my mother, another figure detached itself. And this one too came toward me. And little by little it became Mrs. Mandilaras, the widow of Nikoforos Mandilaras, murdered by the colonels. And I embraced my mother, I embraced Mrs. Mandilaras."

And at the conclusion of her conversation with the ill-fated President Thieu, Oriana Fallaci presented the following dialogue that extends the interview form into the realm of the greatest comic farce:

THIEU: *Voyez bien, mademoiselle,* anything I do I like to do well. Whether it's being converted, or playing tennis, or riding a horse, or holding the office of president. I like responsibility more than power. That's why I say that power should never be shared with others. That's why I'm always the one to decide! Always! I may listen to others suggest some decision, and then make the opposite decision. *Oui, c'est moi qui décide.* If one doesn't accept responsibility, one isn't worthy to be the chief and . . . mademoiselle, ask me this question, "Who's the chief here?"

FALLACI: Who's the chief here?

THIEU: I am! I'm the chief! *Moi! C'est moi le chef!*

FALLACI: Thank you, Mr. President. Now I think I can go.

THIEU: Are you leaving? Have we finished? Are you satisfied, mademoiselle? Because if you're not satisfied, you must tell me. Mademoiselle, I hope you're satisfied because I've hidden nothing from you and I've spoken to you with complete frankness. I swear. I didn't want to in the beginning. But then . . . what can I do? That's the way I am. Come on, tell me. Did you ever expect to find such a fellow?

FALLACI: No, Mr. President.

THIEU: *Merci, mademoiselle.* And, if you can, pray for peace in Vietnam. Peace in Vietnam means peace in the world. And sometimes I feel as though there's nothing left to do except pray to God.

At their best, Oriana Fallaci's brilliantly theatrical interviews remind us of the aims of historians and playwrights such as Thucydides and Ben Jonson, in whose works history and human relations are seen as nothing less than moral drama.

Interviewing Oriana Fallaci is an instructive and reassuring experience. She approved of the kind of cassette recorder I use (she has the same model) and, as well, my 90-minute tapes (120-minute tapes jam up, as interviewers learn not soon enough). Throughout the interview, she positioned the machine and checked the battery indicator, turned over the tapes while remembering and repeating the last words of her unfinished sentences on the new side, then numbered the tapes for me. She suggested that I learn how to ask one question at a time instead of rambling and ranging over a series of suggestive ideas, and she turned the recorder off when she wanted to say something off the record. "Only Nixon," she once stated, "knows more about tape recorders than I do."

* * *

It wasn't so long ago that advice-to-the-lovelorn columnists used to suggest that all a woman had to do to get a man interested in her was to cajole him gently into talking about himself all evening, thereby flattering him and bolstering his sense of self-importance. In your interviews you seem, almost unconsciously, to have taken this piece of folk wisdom and pushed it very far down the line, using it in order to expose your grandiloquent subjects for what they really are.

I've never thought of that. Neither in my private nor my public life have I ever thought in terms of "seducing" somebody, using what are called the "feminine arts"—it makes me vomit just to think of it. Ever since I was a child—and way before the recent feminist resurgence—I've never conceived of . . . I'm very surprised by what you say. There might be some truth here, but you've really caught me by surprise.

What you're talking about implies a kind of psychological violence which I never commit when I interview someone. I never force a person to talk to me. If he doesn't want to talk, or if he talks without pleasure, I just walk out. I've done that many times. There's no courting or seducing involved. The main secret of my interviews lies in the fact that there's no trick whatsoever. None.

You know, there are many students who write about my interviews—in Italy, France, and America, too. And they always ask me how I go about it and if I could teach them to do it. But it's impossible, for these interviews are what they are, good or bad, because they're made by me, with this face, with this voice. They have to do with my personality, and I bring too much of myself into them to teach them.

When I was reading Interview with History, *I began thinking of the great Enlightenment author Diderot, who, it's been said, had an "instinctual" urge to expose what was concealed. And it seems to me that one of the underlying impulses of your work—along with your unmediated hatred for fascism and authoritarianism—is exactly this instinctual urge to expose. Do you feel that this is true?*

All right. You must give me a little time to answer, as I do with the people I interview. It's a difficult question, very difficult. As I told you before, I bring myself into these interviews completely, as a human being, as a personality, I bring what I know, what I don't know, what I am. Oriana is in there, as an actor. And I bring into these encounters all my choices, all my ideas, and my temperament as well. So, being at the same time very antifascist and very passionate, it's very difficult for me to interview the fascist, in the broad sense of the word. And I say it with shame, since I'm perfectly aware of how ridiculous this is. If I am, as I claim to be, an historian as much as a journalist—I claim that a journalist is an historian of his time—how can I reject at least half of humanity? Because at least half of humanity is fascist.

And when I happen to be interviewing a fascist, and if he really "counts" in history and the interview is going well, I get fascinated. I want so much to know *why* he's a fascist. And this "fascination" on my part then leads to what Socrates called *maieutica*—the work of the *midwife,* whose role becomes especially interesting when I have in front of me someone like Thieu. You see, I think that *power* itself is in some sense fascist by definition (I'm not speaking here of the Mussolini type of fascism but am rather referring to it in the philosophical sense of the word). And I almost always end by being captivated by it.

I say "almost," because I did once walk out during an interview with Giorgio Almirante. Almirante's that nice gentleman whom the Americans invited to Washington, the man who's reconstructed the Fascist party in Italy. And I really did violence to myself when I asked to interview him. He received me immediately, he was happy to see me, of course—an interview with me is always publicity, even if it's negative. The more negative, the better for Almirante! So I went to see him, and he was immensely polite, most intelligent, and I started with my *maieutica.* And my *maieutica* was working so well that at a certain moment he said: "Oh yes, sure I was a Fascist, sure I was, I'm very proud of it." And I said: "Well, listen . . . Mussolini, what about Mussolini?" Believe me, I was very nervous, I was suffering like hell, I was hiding my head and suffering. And he said: "I *love* Mussolini, I loved him, I still love him." And I got up and said: "That's enough! I refuse to stay one second more. This bullshit—you don't think I'm going to *publish* this!" It was such a wild thing. Almirante first became pale, then red, then green, and all he could say was: "I'm sorry, you're not going, you're not really . . ." Argh argh, argh! And after that, for five years, Almirante has tried to see me again, to be interviewed by me. He wrote me a letter: I didn't answer. He sent me messages through two people: "You know, he would like so much to be interviewed by you. You can do the nastiest of interviews to him, he doesn't mind. He's so sorry that you walked out like that." And I believe he would like that, sure he would like it. But I'm not going to do it, I'm not going to give him an interview.

He's obviously suffering from an unrequited interview.

Unrequited interview! *[Laughing]* That it was. And it happened again with Mujib Rahman, the man who was martyred in Bangladesh. I started the tape recorder, and all at once he started behaving so badly. He was so arrogant and so stupid—one of the most stupid men I've ever met in my life, maybe the most stupid. So I said: "Listen, Mujib, I'm not going to go on like this, you know. If you're not polite, I'm not going to do this interview." Argh, argh, argh . . . he started yelling. We both yelled, there was a big fight, and he said: "Get out of my country, don't come back again, leave my people, leave us alone, leave us alone!" And I yelled back: "Be sure I'll leave you alone!" It went on and on and on like that. The Mukti Bahini— the guerrillas—almost lynched me because of that, and I was only saved by two Indian officers. So these "unrequited" interviews, as you call them, are always very dramatic and always end tragically because I'm passionate and I'm not able to control myself sometimes.

In your book you often talk about your desire to "remove the veils" masking the politicians you're interviewing. And when you've done that, what often appears before you and us are characters straight out of Alice in Wonderland *or* Ubu Roi. *(I'm thinking here of your interviews with Kissinger, Thieu, and the shah of Iran.) But with persons such as Helder Camara—the leftist archbishop of Brazil—and Alexandros Panagoulis—the jailed and tortured head of the Greek Resistance—you are clearly presenting portraits of two unalterably heroic human beings.*

You see, I think that each of us is Dr. Jekyll and Mr. Hyde. But with Dom Helder and . . . Panagoulis . . . well, maybe I didn't want to look for that in them. I am the judge, I am the one who decides. Listen: if I am a painter and do your portrait, have I or haven't I the right to paint you as I want? It's my interpretation. I've seen the last portrait that Pietro Annigoni painted of Queen Elizabeth, and it's really cruel. I said: "Annigoni, how could you do that, she's not like that!" And he said: "Yes, maybe she's not." "Then why did you do it like that?" "Because that's the way I saw her." So if this is permitted to a painter, why shouldn't it be permitted to us? I saw Dom Helder as a saint, and I portrayed him as one, Panagoulis as a hero, and I portrayed him as a hero. By the way, they *are* two very decent people. *[Laughing]* It's not my fault. But I'm sure that they have their Dr. Jekyll and Mr. Hyde sides, too, which I didn't look for. Maybe Dom Helder goes around in the nighttime stealing the virginity of the girls of his village. I doubt it very much. But I saw him as a saint.

Improbable as it might seem, might there have been a saintly side to someone like President Thieu?

Thieu is very far from being a saint. I interviewed him when Kissinger had just taken him by the nose. And Thieu was damn right when he realized that Kissinger only looked at the world in terms of global strategy. "I give you Russia, you take China, I go to America, add a little salt and then some onion, a little of Guatemala and then some parsley, and maybe some Brazil." That's the way Kissinger cooks the destiny of people. And Thieu said: "I'm not that. If Kissinger cooks like that, I'll fall immediately. I'm Vietnamese, I'm small, if they give me a slap—boom—I fall. I'm left here with 300,000 North Vietnamese and their tanks inside South Vietnam. What kind of an armistice is that?" And he was right! He was a victim of Mr. Kissinger, of American power, of American arrogance—as much as the people of Hanoi were victims of American bombings. And naturally I pointed that out.

But in the introductory essay to your Thieu interview, you finally judged him harshly, saying: "Almost every time that I have tried to give compassion and respect to a government leader, almost every time that I have tried to absolve even partially some famous son of a bitch, I have later been bitterly sorry." And I wanted to ask you about your unmitigated sense of justice and your inevitable judgmental assessments. It's obvious that you view people in strict moral terms—almost as if they represented physiological humors like choler, phlegm, or black bile.

Yes, you're right, and that's terrible. It's very Protestant. I guess it's the destiny of atheists to become moralists. And the more they age, the more moralistic they become. I think that it helps to dramatize things but I don't do it because of that, unfortunately. I'm *really* a moralist. It's a defect I have, and it limits freedom, it limits *my* freedom. Imagine, I don't feel free to go and interview a son of a bitch, I suffer when I do it. But I am a moralist.

Do you know Lenin's dictum: "Ethics will be the aesthetics of the future"?

No I didn't. That's interesting, but my moralism is not of the Leninist kind. I'm too much of a liberal to see things . . .

You really are full of contradictions—an anarchist in spirit, a socialist in theory, a liberal . . .

Listen, Jonathan, in my last book, *Letter to a Child Never Born*, I have brought to such a paroxysm exactly what you're saying—a book that's the apotheosis of doubt. Every time the female character says something, she soon thereafter says the contrary of that, and then the contrary of *that* without denying the original statement. And it goes on in this way. Antithesis and synthesis occur here at the same time, all at once. The woman keeps contradicting herself, keeps being controversial with herself, and in the end she is terribly human.

Speaking of the "terribly human," I was struck by a moving moment during your interview with Mrs. Gandhi when you talked about "the solitude that oppresses women intent on defending their own destinies." You mention that Mrs. Gandhi, like Golda Meir, had to sacrifice her marriage for her career. And I got the feeling that here you were somehow also talking about your sense of yourself.

The first difference between me and them is that I never give up. Marriage is an expression that to me suggests "giving up," an expression of sacrifice and regret. I never wanted to get married, so I didn't make that sacrifice—it was a victory for me. The solitude I was referring to wasn't a physical solitude. Nor was it, for instance, for Indira Gandhi, because everybody knows that at the time I interviewed her she wasn't alone at all. She likes men, thank God, and she makes use of that. It was an internal solitude that comes about from the fact of being a woman—and a woman with responsibilities in a world of men.

That kind of solitude is a victory for me, and I've been searching for it. Today, you are interviewing me in 1976. If you had interviewed me in '74 or '73 or '65, I would probably have answered a little differently—but not too much. Like a photograph, an interview has to crystallize the moment in which it takes place. Today. I need that kind of solitude so much—since it is what moves me, intellectually speaking—that sometimes I feel the need to be physically alone. When I'm with my companion, there are moments when we are two too many. I never get bored when I'm alone, and I get easily bored when I'm with others. And women who, like Indira and like Golda, have had the guts to accept that solitude are the women who have achieved something.

You must also consider that, in terms of the kind of solitude we've been talking about, women like Golda and Indira are more representative because they are old. A person of my generation and, even more so, a woman younger than myself really *wants* that solitude. Golda and Indira were victimized by it, since they belonged to a generation in which people didn't think as we do today. They were probably hurt, and I don't know how much they pitied themselves. Golda cried at a certain moment during the interview. When she spoke of her husband, she was regretting something.

As for myself, in the past I felt less happy about this subject. It was still something to fight about inside myself, trying to understand it better. But today I'm completely free of it, the problem doesn't exist anymore. And I don't even gloat over the fact that what could have been considered a sacrifice yesterday is today an achievement. We must thank the feminists for this, because they've helped not only me but everybody, all women. And young people, both men and women, understand this very much.

Golda spoke of having lost the family as a *great* sacrifice—she was crying then. But to me, the worst curse that could happen to a person is to *have* a family.

That's not a very Italian attitude, is it?

You'd be surprised. We know about Marriage Italian Style. But people in Italy today are getting married less and less. We have an unbelievable tax law that makes two persons who are married and who both work pay more taxes than they would if they were single. So they get separated or divorced. And there's nothing "romantic" or "Italian" about this. No, the family, at least morally and psychologically, is disappearing in Italy, as well as all over Europe.

What should exist in its place?

Free individuals.

But no community.

You ask me too much. If I could answer you I would have resolved the problem. If you said to me: "All right, socialism as it's been applied until now hasn't worked. Capitalism doesn't work. What should we do?" I'd have to respond: "My dear, if I could answer these questions, I'd be the philosopher of my time."

In the introduction to your interview with Golda Meir, you comment on the resemblances you noticed between Meir and your own mother, writing: "My mother too has the same gray curly hair, that tired and wrinkled face, that heavy body supported on swollen, unsteady, leaden legs. My mother too has that sweet and energetic look about her, the look of a housewife obsessed with cleanliness. They are a breed of women, you see, that has gone out of style and whose wealth consists in a disarming simplicity, an irritating modesty, a wisdom that comes from having toiled all their lives in the pain, discomfort and trouble that leave no time for the superfluous."

And in the introduction to your interview with Henry Kissinger, you tell how you were immediately reminded of an old teacher of yours "who enjoyed frightening me by staring at me ironically from behind his spectacles. Kissinger even had the same baritone, or rather guttural, voice as this teacher, and the same way of leaning back in the armchair with his right arm outstretched, the gesture of crossing his legs, while his jacket was so tight over his stomach that it looked as though the buttons might pop." It's at special moments like these in your book that I get the sense of a little girl looking at the world so clearly because she remembers so much—a sense one usually finds in the best literature and films, but almost never in interviews.

Do you understand now why I can't teach someone how to make these interviews? Do you understand now why they are what they are because I do them? Kissinger was sitting on this raised armchair, having asked me to sit down on the sofa. So he was up there and I was down here, and it was like seeing . . . Manchinelli was his name, that professor of physics and mathematics. He was a real bastard who used to sit up high and mighty at his podium like God, judging us instead of teaching us, and from there cursing and reproaching us, making us suffer. He made me suffer particularly because I was the only one who answered him back. Oh, I was terrible in school. Poor people, poor professors, I made them suffer so much. Because I was very clever, I was always the first of my class, but I was terrible. Because if they said something wrong, I didn't keep my mouth shut. Anyway, when I saw Kissinger sitting like that—poor man, he wasn't aware of it, of course, and he didn't do it on purpose, he is what he is and was showing what he is—I said: "Oh God. Here we go with Manchinelli again."

I associated the two things, and I always do. I always go back to childhood. But do you know why I make these comparisons? Not only because they come spontaneously to me but because I like to be simple when I write, I want to be understood, as I used to say, by my mother when I write about politics. How can my mother understand me? And my audience is made up mostly of people who have not been to university. So in order to simplify things, I use everyday facts, "human" facts—that word is overused, but I'll use it here again. So you associate Kissinger with a nasty old professor, or Golda with your mother, the same wrinkles, the same irritating modesty. And then people understand. My use of associations is a result both of spontaneity and tactics.

I didn't start writing about politics until fairly recently—until Vietnam, in fact. But I've always been a very politicized person because of the family I was born into—I'll come back to this in a minute—and because of my experiences. I was a little girl during the Resistance—and a member of the Liberal Socialist party—and I spoke in public the first time when I was fifteen at a political rally. I'll always remember—I had pigtails and was trembling: "PEOPLE OF FLORENCE . . . A YOUNG COMRADE SPEAKS TO YOU . . ."

And I kept saying to my editors: "I want to write about politics, I want to interview politicians in the same way that I interview actors. Because it's boring when we read politics, it must be done in another way." But they didn't let me do it because I was a woman. (There we go again.) And only when I demonstrated that I could be a good war correspondent in Vietnam did they allow me to do interviews with politicians in the same way that I'd done them with astronauts, soldiers, and actors.

Do you think that your forceful way of doing interviews was in any way determined by the humiliation and contemptuousness you might have felt being a girl growing up in a world of political men?

Absolutely not. I can't complain too much about men because, number one, I had the luck to be born into a feminist family—they didn't know it, but indeed they were. To begin with: my father. He always believed in women. He had three daughters, and when he adopted the fourth child, he chose a girl—my youngest sister—because . . . he trusts women. And my parents educated me with the attitude of: you *must* do it because you are a woman. It was, for sure, a challenge, which implies the recognition of a certain reality. But they never thought that I couldn't do it.

In the beginning I wanted to become either a surgeon or a journalist. And the only reason why I didn't choose medicine was because we were too poor to afford six years of medical school. So then it seemed obvious for me to get a job as a reporter when I was sixteen. I gave up medicine because I was poor, not because I was a woman. What I never forget is that I was *poor*. And this is probably at the roots of my moralistic attitude that we were speaking about before. Not the fact that I was a woman.

I noticed that you dedicated your book to your mother. Was she a strong influence on you?

She pushed me. She pushed all of us. But my father did, too. I dedicated it to her more than to him because she's dying from cancer, but I should have dedicated it to both of them, because the person who gave me my political ideas was my father. I've changed my mind about many things, but not about my belief in freedom, social justice, and socialism—*that* came from him. And when we get to this point, it doesn't matter whether one is a man or a woman.

We were speaking before of Golda and Indira. The feminists are wrong to say: "Ha, ha! Indira behaves the way she does because she lives in a society of men." No, sir. She does it simply because she's a person of power who wanted more power. She wasn't ready to give it up and she acted as a man would have acted. At that point, it was the moment of truth—*el momento de la verdad,* as the Spanish call it. She could have said goodbye, sir, thank you very much. *That* means democracy to me. But instead she became a dictator, she demonstrated that being a woman makes no difference, she was no better because she was a woman. . . .

I want to return to something I spoke to you about earlier—about my obsession with the fascist problem and how it relates to my family experiences. I've just said that I come from an antifascist family, and this was important for me because, to me, being fascistic means making *anti*politics, not *politics.* The fascist—as I once told an interviewer—is someone who resigns, who obeys, who doesn't talk, or who imposes himself with violence and avoids the problematic. The antifascist, on the contrary, is a naturally political person. Because being antifascist means to fight through a problem by means of a discussion that involves everybody in civil disobedience. And this atmosphere of disobedience . . . I've breathed it since I was a little girl. My mother's father was an anarchist—one of those who wore a black ribbon and the big hat. He was a deserter in World War I, and I remember my mother proudly saying: "My father was a deserter in the Great War"—as if he had won some kind of medal. In fact, he was condemned to death because he was a deserter, but they couldn't catch him. And my father's father was a Republican follower of Mazzini, when being that meant one was an extreme leftist. And my father was a leader in the Resistance. It's really in the family.

As you stated it so movingly in the introduction to your book: "I have always looked on disobedience toward the overbearing as the only way to use the miracle of having been born."

That's socialism, Jonathan. Being a socialist, or wanting socialism, doesn't mean just the distribution of wealth. It *should* work, but it doesn't in the so-called socialist countries. And for sure not in the capitalistic regimes. Socialism means much more to me. One of the great victories has been what we call the *spirit of socialism* with its sense of equality. When I was a little girl, the reality of hierarchy was so strong—the teacher above the pupil, the rich above the less rich, the bourgeoisie above the proletariat. In Europe we had it, we still have it, but we have it much less. And this was brought about by socialists and is why, for me, socialism is synonymous with freedom.

Socialism is freedom. When I say this, I imagine that if I were a peasant of Chianti and you were a landowner, I'd look at you like this *[fearless and skeptical look]* because of my belief in socialism, in freedom. And this spirit has such deep roots in me that when I go to interview a person of power, the more power this person has—would you believe me?—the more I intimidate him. And inevitably, this personal attitude of mine is transferred mentally and technically in the interview. So I undress them. I say: "Come on, come on, maybe you're better than you look, or maybe you're worse."

This is interesting: I've noticed that when a person goes to interview someone, he often sees himself in a position of inferiority. It's a nuance, it's very subtle, it's difficult to explain. And this feeling increases when this someone being interviewed is a person of power. If you're observant, you can see the eyes tremble and something in the face and the voice changing. That's never happened to me. *Never.* I'm tense. I'm worried because it's a boxing match. Oh ho! I'm climbing, I'm going into the ring, I'm nervous. My God, who's going to win? But no inferiority complex, no fear of the person. When someone starts acting superior, then I become dangerous, then I become nasty.

In a recent interview with Jean-Paul Sartre on his seventieth birthday, he stated: "I believe that everyone should be able to speak of his innermost being to an interviewer. I think that what spoils relations among people is that each keeps something hidden from the other, something secret, not necessarily from everyone, but from whomever he is speaking to at the moment. I think transparency should always be substituted for what is secret."

I don't believe it. He's not sincere, he's acting. Noble, intelligent, yes . . . he's playing the philosopher. But I can't conceive for a second that he means what he's saying because his daily life is the contrary of that. He's a superb man, often proud, and he can be very cruel and cold to people. He never forgets to be Sartre.

You want to know what I think of his idea? You cannot deny a human being his right to his privacy, to his secrets, to himself. When I speak of socialism, I don't mean that. I am mine, and to hell with the others: at a certain point I have the right to say that. What he's saying is pure intellectualism. If he had said that to me, I would have replied: "Come on, that's enough of that bullshit, you don't believe that. Come on now." I really believe so little in what he says. You know, there's always a moment during an interview, during my research into the soul of the person, when I stop. I voluntarily stop. I don't want to go on, I haven't the guts to invade further the soul of that person.

Listen, I'll give you an example. I've had two moments of great embarrassment. Not superficial embarrassment, because I'm a tough person, but here, inside. One was with Golda, when I asked her about her husband and she cried. And I felt—I'll make a confession now—a sort of shame. It was far from the vulgar way that journalists put questions, you know: "Tell me about Mr. So-and-so." I'd done it very sweetly, very elegantly, but all the same I felt ashamed of myself when she was crying. And the other moment was with Thieu, when he started crying while talking about being just a little man. And God knows, I was against everything he represented, but I saw a man, a person, and again I felt a sort of shame.

There are moments when I listen with an internal embarrassment that you'd never notice, but I have it very deep. For instance, with Kissinger—when we got to the problem of women he was like that, he didn't want to talk about it. But I didn't want to either. Even with Hussein, when he spoke of the fear of his being killed, I felt uncomfortable, uncomfortable.

I think it's important to make a distinction between "mystification" and "mystery," and I feel that you respect the latter.

Ah, you see how coherent I am for once in my life? The way I reacted to Sartre . . . well, the explanation is here. Because I wouldn't like them to do it with me. I wouldn't.

The duty of a journalist is to reveal everything that's possible. Not to leave any interrogation point. To wipe out all curiosity. But I'm not a journalist 100 percent. I'm a writer, and I bring that into the journalism. I much prefer to have something well written, well built from a literary and a dramatic point of view, so that it can be read as a piece of literature—and this necessarily includes the *mystery.* I'm more interested in doing that than in telling everything as a good journalist should.

And when I'm asked, "What do you prefer to be, a journalist or a writer, and what is the difference between them?" I reply that there is no difference for me. And I mean that. My approach is to see the president of Angola, for example, as if he were a character in a novel rather than just an important name mentioned in the *New York Times.*

It might sound a bit far-fetched, but while reading Interview with History,

I was reminded of Plutarch's Lives—*though I know that you are hardly a propagandist for the ancient Roman senatorial caste or Spartan despots.*

Don't forget that they've broken my balls with Plutarch for years in school. It's part of our culture. And they tortured us with Herodotus, too. But listen, these idiots who want to get rid of these things from the school curricula—it's nonsense. It was good to study Plutarch, Herodotus, and even Cicero.

A lot of the things from my book that you've liked and quoted to me today come out spontaneously, but they come out that way because we have a "classical" culture. Thank God you studied literature! You should listen to Panagoulis when he talks. One day he was in Bologna for a speech, and he hadn't prepared it. And I said: "Oh God, what are you going to do now?" And he replied: "Something will happen." So he went up to the platform and he began: "I did not want to kill a man. I cannot kill a man. I wanted to kill a tyrant, and I can kill a tyrant." And I complimented him: "My God, it was great when you said that." "Ah, come on!" he retorted. "We say it in school when we're children." Another time, at a rally in Florence, he said: "Freedom has no country. The country of freedom is each of us." "You prepared that, didn't you?" I asked him. "No, I didn't," he replied. "I hadn't the slightest idea what I was going to say." "But how did it come off so well?" "Because . . . because I felt it, no? Because I say things like that on other occasions." You see, he has classical culture. This is a richness that you don't have much of in the United States. I agree that it's good in high school to learn how to drive a car. I'm still not able to drive a car because I'm too lazy to learn, and I would like to have been in a school where they taught me how to drive. However, a little Plutarch when you're thirteen, fourteen, fifteen years old, it's not bad. And I defend our Italian school system, which is going to be destroyed because they want to follow the American style. I think they're committing a crime. Maybe we'll have better drivers and more technicians, but we'll have fewer poets and writers—and also, which counts more, fewer people with the sense of history. I know that I have this sense. When I see things, when I judge a situation—personal and overall political situations—I always see it as if I were at a window very far away in the space and time. I have the sense of perspective.

So I see things in perspective, and when I perform my work as a journalist, I do it in that way. And this is another secret of these interviews: being able to see people from afar. I always say when I ask for an interview: "I need time, I'm not looking for scoops, I'm not looking for sensationalism." If I ever went to Brezhnev, who'll never see me, of course, I wouldn't go with the idea of asking him: "What will you discuss tomorrow with Dr. Kissinger?" I don't give a damn what he's discussing with Dr. Kissinger. I want to do an interview which will be interesting in ten, possibly twenty years.

Are you going to continue doing interviews?

It's becoming more and more difficult for me and I'll tell you why. First, I've launched a fashion and now everybody does it, or tries to do it. There are more people requiring those interviews and so you see more of them around. And second, it's become more difficult because people are stupidly scared of me. They're worried. And if they decide to do an interview with me, it's because they think the moment is good for them, I'm a good vehicle for publicity. And then they act too nice. I have one to do soon, and when I telephoned yesterday, the people said: "Oh, Oriana Fallaci, we're *so* honored," and I thought: "Oh, no, *Madonna mia.*" Others like Qaddafi, for example, don't want to see me. (I accused him of having stolen my Golda Meir tapes—which is true.) Some persons really don't have the guts to see me.

In the preface to your book, you regret that no one had tape recorders during the time of Jesus, in order to "capture his voice, his ideas, his words." Were you being hyperbolic or serious? And if serious, what would you have asked Jesus if you had had the chance to interview him?

I meant it seriously. For sure! Today we think and speak of Jesus as he's been told to us. So now, after two thousand years, I'd like to know how important he was at the time or find out how much he was built up. Of course, I reject the concept of Jesus as God, Christ/God. I don't even pay attention to that for one second. But as a leader, was he that important? You know, he might very well have been a little Che Guevara.

And a deeply enlightened person.

He might have been, but not the only one. Because many of those people were crucified just as he was. We make all this fuss about him, but it would be like saying: "Jesus Christ has been executed by Franco!" What about the others? For Christ's sake, how many people have been executed in Spain? *La garotta!* What about Paredez Manot, called Txiki—one of the five Basques who was executed in the fall of 1975 in the cemetery of Barcelona, in front of his brother Miguel. He's the one who died singing, "Free, free the country of the Basques," smiling all the time and singing, then waving goodbye to Miguel. And that was Txiki. But there were four others who were executed, and hundreds of others all these years. So I don't know if Christ was that important later on.

One of the first things I would have asked him was: "Where have you been all those years, where have you been? Did you go to India?" Ooh-la-la! That would have been the first question. Then I would have asked if he really behaved chastely or if he had women, if he slept with women, if he went to bed with Mary Magdalene, if he loved her as a sister or as a woman. I would have asked that. And I would have loved to have found the grave of Jesus Christ—that would have been good *reportage*. And those who had stolen the corpse and reported he had flown to heaven: "*Who* told you to do that? For *whom* did you do that?"

That might have ended Christianity then and there.

It might have been a good thing.

I imagine that you'd have one question to ask the Virgin Mary.

[Laughing] Certainly one.

This is getting a bit sacrilegious.

Well, why be scared of that?

Don't you think it's possible that Jesus was an avatar?

Listen, I don't know how much about Jesus is just the image created by Mark, Luke, Matthew, and John. They were so damn intelligent, those four. And I'm afraid . . . listen, Jonathan, do you know how many times I make people more interesting than they are? So what if Mark or Matthew did the same thing with Christ, huh? What about if this Jesus Christ was much less than Luke or John? I have no evidence, I have no tapes . . .

I guess you don't believe in miracles.

Oh no, come on, come on. You must be very religious, no?

I believe that some people have certain special powers. And I've always loved the simple and radiant view of the miraculous as depicted in films like Rosselli-ni's The Miracle and The Flowers of St. Francis.

Well, remember Kazantzakis's book on Christ and that scene where Christ dreams of making love with Martha and Mary, the sisters of Lazarus!

Who else in history would you have liked to interview?

Julius Caesar, very much. And the Emperor Augustus, because he was such a damn fascist Nazi. He was a real Nazi, that man. Unbearable. And Cleopatra—Ahhhh! *Simpatica! Che simpatica,* Cleopatra! Intelligent. I'm sure she was extremely intelligent, with enormous culture.

You don't think that she was like Mme Chiang or . . .

Those are puppets, little puppets. Just think of what Cleopatra did with the library at Alexandria! She put together . . . I mean, it would take the National Library in Florence and your library . . . My God, she did mar-velous things. Think of the scientists she called upon. And although she was obsessed with her own beauty, she had people who studied cosmetics. *Nothing* was banal in that fantastic woman.

Then, of course, there's Joan of Arc. With Joan of Arc, however, I would have gotten myself in trouble. Because I would have forgotten my duty as a journalist—that is, as an historian—and I would have tried to free her. The moment she was condemned to death. I would've done ev-erything to free her. This is the way I feel. I am not able—and *this* explains my interviews, all of this explains my interviews, of course—I am not able to see things in a cold way. Looking at things from afar doesn't mean looking at them coldly.

For instance, when I was in Bolivia—Juan José Torres was the presi-dent at that time until your CIA got him out—there were three brothers named Peredo. Two had already been killed. The third and youngest one was leading a group of guerrillas in the center of Bolivia, and the group was surrounded and caught. So the students of the opposition whom I was interviewing and working with came to me and said: "Fallaci, Fallaci, they've caught Chato Peredo." And I started working like hell. I went looking for a certain Major Sanchez, who was Torres's man, and with him I went around to the presidential palace to get the news to Torres, who stopped the execution. I wasn't thinking a second of the newspapers I was writing for. Afterward, I wrote up the story, of course, but at that moment I got very much involved. . . . And I would have tried to save Joan of Arc.

But just to go back in time for a minute: I would have loved to interview Dante, for sure. Not as an artist, but as a politician. You know, Florence of that time seduces me. I'm Florentine, and that was the very first experiment in democracy—in the commune at Florence, not in Periclean Greece.

How about Dante's Beatrice?

Who cares about Beatrice? . . . But you don't have to go so far back, because I've missed some recent ones. I missed Chou En-lai because the Chinese never gave me a visa, they didn't want me. I almost cried when he died. He was the person of our times whom I wanted to interview more than anybody else. And he died without seeing me. Oh God, he shouldn't have done it to me! They were too intelligent to invite me because they knew I'm too unpredictable. If I arrived there and I saw all those red this and red that, I would have really started carrying on, giving them problems. . . . And so I lost Chou En-lai. And of course I can't see the pope, but I would have loved to interview John XXIII. Ahhh, another one.

You'd be the person I'd choose to interview the first being we met from outer space.

And I would do it like a *child*. That's the secret. . . . I'll tell you something. During the first moon shot, there was a press conference just before the launch. There was a group of Very Important American Journalists there, and, thank God, there was also my dear friend Cronkite among them. And Cronkite sent me a note—we were in the same room because the press was interviewing the astronauts via TV—asking me if I wanted to ask them a question. "Put a question to them? Thank you." And I wrote down my little question—three words—and sent it to Cronkite. The other questions went on and on . . . about the fuel and not the fuel, about the gas and the starter and the trajectory. . . . I didn't understand anything being said. You know, I wrote a book about the conquest of the moon and I still don't know how and why a rocket goes up. I'm very proud of that. And I didn't understand the questions of the journalists, who were extremely pompous. Everybody was pompous. And then Cronkite said: "I have a question here from Oriana Fallaci." Pause. And he didn't ask the question.

(He was marvelous, he was a real actor.) Then, dramatically: "The question is: ARE YOU SCARED?"

Well, after discussing it with Aldrin and Collins, Neil Armstrong was elected to take the walk: "Well," he hesitated, "you know, the adrenalin goes up." "Ah, bullshit. Say you're scared!" I yelled out loud to everybody in the press room. "Who cares about the adrenalin! Tell me, tell me, fear, *fear*! Walter, ask them about *fear*!"

And that was the question of the child. If you asked my youngest sister to put a question to the astronauts, she'd say: "Are you afraid going to the moon?" Of course. That's what she'd want to know.

ORIANA FALLACI

JUNE 29, 1929 – SEPTEMBER 15, 2006

FEDERICO FELLINI
The Language of Dreams

Rome, 1984

One sunny morning, when he was nine years old, filmmaker Federico Fellini ran away from his religious boarding school in Fano, Italy. Next to the market in the town square was a small circus. As Fellini remembers it, he went into an empty tent, breathed in the odor of sawdust, noticed the hanging trapezes, and caught sight of "a fat girl with beautiful plump bare legs who was sewing spangles on a tutu." Hearing a moan, the young Federico followed the sound to another tent. "And I saw before me a scene from the Nativity," Fellini writes in a memoir. "A zebra was stretched out on the ground. And around the zebra was, first, an old man, wearing the great collar of the clown, whose face bore the marks of deepest despair; then there was an old lady who was whimpering, and three or four children . . . all in a state of suspense and tender solicitude toward the animal. While I was standing there, fascinated by the sight, I felt myself violently shoved aside, and I saw a man enter carrying a valise, who was revealed to be the veterinarian."

The veterinarian discovered that the zebra had eaten a chocolate bar that had made it sick, and he asked that someone bring a pail of water to the ailing animal. Federico quickly did so, and the zebra eventually revived. "Finally, two hours later," Fellini recalls, "I found myself sitting in their caravan; they fed me, gave me a slice of sausage, and nobody asked me who I was. Then, at twilight, they began to play music; they put on their costumes. I saw the girl with the beautiful thick legs; she had put on a skintight costume that had a lot of feathers. . . . I felt I had come home at last. But then, just as the performance was about to begin, the old clown, who was called Pierino, said to me: 'But what are you doing here? Who are you?' So I said to him, 'Me, I'm the one who went to get water for the zebra,' and he answered, 'Ah, yes, that's right, that's right,' and he kept me beside him, like a father. Then I saw him go into the ring to perform his number; he made me laugh and cry a lot . . . I was truly exalted. Nobody asked me anything."

Ever since making such extraordinary films as *I Vitelloni, La Strada, Nights of Cabiria, La Dolce Vita, 8½,* and *Amarcord,* Federico Fellini has been habitually asked questions about the meanings of the characters and images in his work, the seeds of which are easily discovered in the director's early memory of his deeply dreamlike encounter with the circus in Fano.

It has been suggested that dream interpretation arises when we have lost touch with our inner nighttime images, when we no longer experience them as fully real. In the same sense, Fellini has always insisted that we observe the images in his films not with cultural preconceptions and theoretical biases but with the innocent eyes of children. And, as he once said, "It is necessary to understand childhood as the possibility of maintaining an equilibrium between the unconscious and the conscious, between 'real' life and the life of memory." It is in this light that one recalls the images of the deserted piazza at night in *I Vitelloni,* the sea at dawn at the end of *La Dolce Vita,* the holy Fool in *La Strada* grieving over his broken watch, the heroine of *Nights of Cabiria* wandering alone through the forest, and the peacock in *Amarcord* opening out its wings in falling snow . . . and one is reminded of the psychologist James Hillman's remark that "dreams call from the imagination to the imagination and can be answered only by the imagination."

In his most beautiful and imaginative film since *Amarcord,* Fellini's *And the Ship Sails On* takes place in 1914 on the eve of World War I, as opera singers, impresarios, aristocratic guests, a group of Serbian refugees, and a lovesick rhinoceros (perhaps an unconscious remembrance of the sick circus zebra of Fellini's childhood) find themselves together on a luxury liner that sets out to fulfill the last wish of a world-renowned diva to have her ashes scattered over the Adriatic. Opening with haunting black-and-white silent movie images that are slowly transformed into sepia and dreamlike colors, *And the Ship Sails On* was filmed entirely at Cinecittà—the famous Roman film studios that are a veritable dream factory—in which Fellini has created a magical "unreal" world (the sea is made of cellophane and the moon of paper) that seems more real than reality itself.

The following interview took place in 1984 in the director's office in Rome. Hanging on the walls were a Möbius strip, Indian paintings, a photograph of Carl Jung, and three tarot cards (Strength, the Stars, the Fool). And in one corner of the room, resting on a small table, were a small Buddha and a marionette—a microcosm of the Fellinian world.

* * *

In thinking about your first encounter with the circus, I was moved and struck by the sense you had of "coming home at last."

When you're a child, there's a possibility of foreseeing what your future life will actually be, of recognizing an atmosphere and a dimension that, mysteriously, somehow seem very familiar to you. So when a child who will later become a priest first steps into a church, he will be overwhelmed by the attraction he feels there. I only remember the coldness and gloominess I experienced being in church, but when I discovered that circus, I had the impression of something that seemed more familiar to me than school, even than my own family. So now, when I think back on that moment, I see that it must have been some kind of announcement. It's very strange that a nine-year-old boy stepping into a circus should feel so protected and invaded by such a warmth. Circus people are never very surprised by things that happen to them. I was a child and they—in particular, the clown Pierino, who was the boss of that circus—simply accepted me. I really felt that I was in the center of a town that was my town. And it was the same feeling I had many years later when I went to Cinecittà.

Clowns and children seem to understand each other—fools to some, Fools to others.

A fool is someone who has lost his rationality, lost a part of himself. To be consciously a Fool, however—that is the great challenge, the great realization. But I feel a little bit stupid saying things like that so I would prefer that we talked about movies. About my job.

"Roll away the reel world, the reel world, the reel world!"
Who wrote that?

James Joyce.

It's a very appropriate pun. Somebody once said that no one is more realistic than the person who has visions because he intensifies the most profound reality, which is his reality. The expression of the visionary—the painter or director—is a translation of his vision. And the result of this operation is absolute reality.

Certain people have criticized you for having given up the neorealistic vision of La Strada *and* Nights of Cabiria *in favor of the vision of artifice that one finds in your new film,* And the Ship Sails On, *in which the sea is made out of cellophane and the moon out of paper.*

This is a very silly accusation. First of all, I don't see the difference between neorealism and artifice. But even if one accepted these kinds of statements, it would be like accusing a person of having gone from the age of twenty to the age of forty. It's just a path that you have to follow. What people call artifice is the only way I can express my interior reality. It's like accusing an artist who paints a picture of a field of working with colors instead of using the real grass.

Thoreau once said, "Our truest life is when we are in dreams awake."

Yes, in a certain sense, though ultimately I think I disagree with this. Because very often in a dream you're not really aware of what is happening. It would be more appropriate to be able to live as if you were watching yourself live—becoming more aware of what is going on. In the dream, however, this kind of awareness is lacking, even if it may be the intention of the dream to tell you through symbols what is happening to you, in order to get you to be a bit more detached from your emotions, while representing them to you as if you were watching a movie. Because it's true that talking about dreams is like talking about movies, since the cinema uses the language of dreams: years can pass in a second, and you can hop from one place to another. It's a language made of images. And in the real cinema, every object and every light means something, as in a dream.

And that's why television has killed movies—it has wounded the cinema in its most precious part. Because it uses the language of film, but in a different context, and it reduces its proportions. So you don't have the same impression of sleep that you get when you step into a movie theater—that solemn, almost religious ritual of stepping into the realm of visions, as when you go to sleep and start to dream . . . like stepping into the cinema and suddenly the lights go off and you start watching this enormous screen. Television, on the other hand, constantly projects images through that little box, and while watching TV, people chat, eat, et cetera, et cetera. It's as if you were dreaming by being awake, but in such a way you actually can pay no attention to your dream because you're awake. And in that way, TV has killed the heart of the movies.

You once commented: "Going to the cinema is like returning to the womb. You sit there still and meditative in the darkness, waiting for life to appear on the screen. One should go to the cinema with the innocence of a fetus."

Maybe my mother, when I was a fetus, brought me to the cinema. I don't remember. *[Laughing]* But what I meant is that I think an audience should see a picture without any kind of bombardment of advice or interpretation. When I speak of the innocence of the spectator, I'm thinking of someone who goes into the theater because he's attracted by the poster. He doesn't know who did the movie, he just looks—and here we are again—like a dreamer. If a dreamer were warned beforehand that what he was about to dream meant this or that—the blue horse means this, the blood that—he wouldn't go to bed because he wouldn't want to dream anymore. It often happens that the spectator is scared off by knowing that he has to see a movie by Bergman or Buñuel. And when he sits there, trying to figure out what they're trying to say, he doesn't see the film.

What was the first film that you remember seeing? The first that gave you the feeling you wanted to be a director?

The first film that I saw—I was seven years old, and I didn't imagine it could concern me in any way—was called *Masciste Inferno.* Masciste was someone like Hercules—a character taken from a poem by Gabriele D'Annunzio—a very strong, almost-naked man who was in hell. And I remember that the movie theater was very crowded and outside it was raining, so most of the people were standing up in wet coats. I remember smelling all that wet cloth. It was a silent movie, a little man was under the screen playing the piano, and I was on the arm of my father. It was the first time I saw these big shadows moving. The room was full of cigarette smoke that passed through the beam of light and I was much more interested in watching the smoke and the movement and all the curls that it made in the light than in the film itself. But I was affected and touched by a big woman—it was Proserpina, the Queen of the Underworld, with big fat eyes, big breasts, and very made up like a singer. She made a sudden gesture, and suddenly there was a circle of flames all around Masciste. And probably this image of that strong, beautiful woman—like a big, regal, royal whore—must have struck me, because I put her into all my films after that.

Watching movies, I never thought that I was going to be a director. I knew that I wasn't going to be a lawyer, an engineer, or a doctor, as my mother would have liked. But I never imagined that I would become a director. I knew in a sort of vague and confused way that I would like to be an actor or a puppet master or a painter or a sculptor—an artist of some sort. Because when I was in Rimini as a child, I saw that the artists, who were painters and sculptors on the whole, were looked upon with both diffidence—a sort of moralistic judgment—and envy at the same time. Anyway, they were considered different from everyone else, so I was particularly attracted to these characters. They dressed in a different way, they had big ties, they didn't go to school, they had models coming around, they ate at hours no one else did—they had this freedom of life, and they were always spending time together. My father, and especially my mother, used to speak very badly of them, and that, of course, made them very likable. These people with long hair and beards were more familiar to me than my own family, and when I was with them, I felt the same way as I had felt at the circus. And from the age of ten or eleven, I began going into the artists' ateliers and played with colors and made little sculptures.

So when I finished school, I thought I'd be a journalist or a writer or an actor. And eventually, I managed to find my work, which united all these things. In my job, you can be a bit of a journalist, a bit of a painter, a bit of a puppet master, an actor—you're a bit of everything. In fact I started as a screenplay writer, and sometimes I was called into the studio to correct or add some dialogue. But I always entered the studio with an uneasy feeling, because the crowd, the screaming, all that confusion made me very unhappy. So I never thought I could be a movie director.

But it happened, and in a very spontaneous way, without my thinking that that was to be my real life. I just started to help a friend of mine, for whom I wrote a screenplay called *Closed Shutters*. It was the first time that he had the job of director, and he had a breakdown—Monday, Tuesday, Wednesday, Thursday—he couldn't work. He was overcome by anxiety and the anguish of being responsible for a hundred persons. The producer insisted that I try to give him some confidence. So I went to Turin, where he was supposed to be shooting, and saw that this poor man was totally impotent. I tried to help him and spent hours talking to him. Then we went together for the first day on the set and it was very difficult because my friend had to film a scene—that I had written!—in which someone had drowned in the river. There were all these people on the beach, and the police were arriving with their boats. And I saw that my friend was desperate on the set, so I took the loudspeaker and ordered the camera to move here and there. I was doing the job for someone else, so I was extremely relaxed and natural about it. And probably, at that moment, the spirit of the director emerged from inside me. I became a director by doing exactly all those things that used to bother me: I was arrogant, yelling, insulting, commanding, treating actors badly, having houses moved, telling the sun to move a little bit further down! And I directed until evening. The producer obviously wanted me to go on, but since I didn't want to hurt my friend, another director came and took his place. At that moment, however, I understood that I was able to direct. And maybe in a few years' time when I become completely incompetent, the producer will call *another* director to help me and then *he* will start directing, and the chain will go on. Maybe.

Aside from the circus and the artists of Rimini, what else influenced you creatively as a child?

Fairy tales. My grandmother used to tell them to me. She was a farmer, a peasant, and her stories—since she lived in the country and was surrounded by animals—always concerned horses, cats, owls, bats. So we grew up to respect and be very curious about them. And still today, when I eat a chicken, I'm afraid that suddenly it will become a prince once it's inside me! *[Laughing]* I've always had—and still have—this feeling.

Also, when I was eight or nine, *Pinocchio* was an enormous influence. It isn't just a wonderful book, for me it's one of the great books—equal to the *Odyssey* and Franz Kafka's *The Trial*. And for my generation, it was our first happy encounter with a book. When you're small, a book is something very strange that belongs to the world of adults—something that has to do with school, something that takes away your freedom—unless there are beautiful pictures inside. And mostly it was something you could throw at your brother when you were fighting. *[Laughing]* But ultimately, it was something that didn't belong to you. The encounter with *Pinocchio* was like coming upon a magical object—it was a big bridge between life and culture—so it had a special meaning, almost exorcistic.

Now the author, Carlo Collodi, lived in the nineteenth century, so he had to conclude the book in a certain moralistic way. It ends with the transformation of the puppet into a boy. That, however, is the least interesting, and even the saddest, part of the book. But, of course, it's true that we all lose the magical, childhood, Pinocchio part of our being—being in touch with animals, with the night, with mystery . . . contacting with life the way it should be. And with this loss, we become good idiots, good students, good husbands, good citizens.

Pinocchio is a marvelous book because you can read it forever—when you're a child, when you're young, when you're old. It has the simplicity of the Bible and lacks all presumptuous consciousness. And, indeed, it really is a work of magic. You can open it like a book of oracles, read just one line, and it will help you. All your doubts and problems find an answer on those pages.

You once mentioned three other books that had a strong influence on you: Franz Kafka's Metamorphosis, *Ludovico Ariosto's sixteenth-century epic poem* Orlando Furioso, *and the French occult author Éliphas Lévi's* Dogma and Ritual of High Magic. *I'm curious about your interest in magic.*

A creative person—to use the awful word—can be seen to make what we call magical operations because he takes something that lives only in his imagination, totally hidden and unimaginable to others, and with his talent and experience and artisanal sense of working—with materials or colors or whatever—materializes that dream, that fantasy, and makes what doesn't exist, or just confusedly exists in a very vague way, concrete. When an artist makes a painting or a melody or a book or a film that didn't exist before, then, in a sense, that's a magical operation. The artist lives somewhere between the unconscious and the normative cultural standards and tries to combine those two things. That's the ground where a magician lives, works, and operates.

The novelist Italo Calvino has written, "You reach a moment in life when among the people you have known, the dead outnumber the living. And the mind refuses to accept more faces, more expressions: on every new face you encounter, it prints the old forms, for each one it finds the most suitable masks." Is this true for you when you look for the "faces" for your new films?

When a character is born in your imagination, it has a certain function in the story that you want to tell, and the face has to express this character. So you tend to look for one that can immediately suggest to the spectator who this person is. I don't tell psychological stories—stories in which characters develop throughout the film—so the character has to declare himself right from the start. For that reason, I try to find faces that are immediately believable and fascinating. And that is the reason why, when making a picture, I spend most of my time in testing, in order to discover the right facial materialization and incarnation of the role—an expressive mask. And of all the phases of the preparation, choosing the faces is perhaps the most anxious and even dramatic one, because what you're looking for is in your mind.

I'll try, for example, to represent on a piece of paper with pen and ink and colors the kind of faces I imagine. I'll think of, say, the captain of the boat in *And the Ship Sails On*. I'll make a sketch at my desk, then people will start coming into my office. And the fact that someone is there, alive, with a real voice, with a particular slight accent . . . the fact that he's smoking, that I see his hands, his flesh, suggests to me that, even if he isn't right for the part, even if he's exactly the opposite of what I'm looking for, the fact that he's alive creates a very strong temptation for me. I say to myself, "What I have in mind is just a sketch, a phantom, but here is a real creature." But then another person appears, completely different. "So why not?" I say. "Maybe this is the one." And then comes another, and another.

So to try to be faithful to what you had in mind and not to refuse any new suggestions that life gives you is sometimes very difficult. For that reason, I have a folder into which I put many different photographic solutions for each character: one actor is little, another tall, another fat, another thin, another has a nice face, another is ugly. Sometimes an actor seems right by himself, but not when put together with someone else. The captain's face might be good for one century, but the face of the second officer might be the face of two centuries before—so they can't stay together. This kind of dialectical joke sometimes makes me feel lost, and my ship may have fifteen or twenty captains. But, finally, I have to decide. And at that moment, I have confidence that my labyrinthine research will have paid off.

For instance, I started *And the Ship Sails On* without having chosen all the characters. Even during the third week of shooting, I hadn't cast the blind Austro-Hungarian princess, and the production was going crazy because the day of the first scene with the princess was coming up, and I still didn't know who it was going to be. It's like landing an airplane when you can't see any sign of an airport. But I always have confidence, even when everybody around me gets crazy. But two nights before the shooting of the first scene with the blind princess, I was still feeling very unsure and lost, because I didn't know where to find a blind princess of an empire that no longer existed. But then that night, a friend of mine took me to see the dance company of Pina Bausch, a German choreographer, who had come to perform for the first time in Rome. Usually, I don't go to the dance or ballet—I feel a little bit foreign to that. But I went to see this show, it was excellent, and afterward we went backstage to say hello to her. And as I walked into the dressing room, there was the blind princess who was waiting for me with a pale face and a detached, cruel smile—someone who was a cross between a saint and a madwoman. So, this is just to say that if you really put yourself honestly and sincerely, with childish enthusiasm, into the trip or voyage, things will always come to you.

There's an old text from India that gives three rules for the theater: (1) that it must be encouraging and amusing to the drunk; (2) that it must respond to someone who asks, "How to live?"; and (3) that it must answer the one who asks, "How does the universe work?" What do you think?

I'm not Indian . . . I was born in Rimini. *[Laughing]* So I have a completely different . . . well, not completely different, but a slightly different attitude to this. First, I don't think a drunk needs to go to the theater or the movies, because once he's drunk, he sees everything he wants to anyway. So when I'm working, I don't have the thought of making a picture for a drunk. . . . I don't know, I'll think about it.

You know, I've sometimes been accused of not thinking enough about the audience. But I find that a really goofy and strange accusation. For if one pretends to be a person who can speak and tell stories to someone else . . . if one believes in and has chosen the profession of a storyteller, then it's clear that inside of oneself there must be this sort of push, this drive to be clear to others. But apart from that, it's impossible for me to try consciously, practically, technically to make a film for an audience. You don't know who that is, and it's a silly pretension. If you have a restaurant, you naturally can think of the various tastes of the people who come. But if you intend to make culture or express your fantasies, then you can't expect to think of an audience. The only things you have to be faithful and loyal to are the characters of the story. You have to obey them. The characters are the real audience to which one must pay attention. And if you can satisfy their demands, then you have created the proper ground for the audience to receive and understand them. But if you have to think of a particular audience—and an audience of drunks—never!

Now, as far as thinking of satisfying someone who wants to know how the universe works, I can't imagine why a person would go to a movie expecting that kind of explanation.

In And the Ship Sails On, *I thought I found out a little bit about how the universe works—what with the cosmic music played by several passengers on the ship's kitchen glasses and the mantric* om *intoned by the basso profundo who hypnotizes a chicken.*

You did?

Maybe I was drunk.

Maybe. *[Laughing]* But I didn't have that in mind when I made the movie. And as far as answering the question "How to live?"—if a work of art is honest and sincere and loyally expresses the problems, emotions, and experiences of the author's life, then it will always have something in it that concerns and affects the person in the audience who is looking to find some point in common.

When once asked, "What is requisite for an entertainer?" you replied: "A mixture of magician and prestidigitator, of prophet and clown, of tie salesman and priest who preaches."

I think that someone who pretends to be a storyteller has to be a prophet, clown, trickster, and magician. A creative person—let's say that awful word: an artist—makes what we call magical operations. Because if something lives only in his imagination, totally hidden to others, then people won't be able to imagine it. So, with his talent, experience, artisanal sense, materials, and colors, an artist makes things visible for everybody, like the magician in a fairy tale who makes something that wasn't there suddenly appear. Because the artist always lives somewhere in between the unconscious and the prevailing cultural standards, and he attempts to combine the two. Or one could refer to the twilight zone between the sun and the moon, which is the same borderline between what is unconscious and what is real. And so the artist is particularly moved by the light that is between—between two attitudes, two sets of behavior, two dimensions. He is moved by the twilight because then one finds the union of contrasts. And the ground on which the artist stands and works is also like that of the magician who operates on what doesn't exist—or just confusedly exists—and turns it into something concrete and ordered.

Do you think there's a connection between the magician and the tribal shaman or medicine man who, through the overcoming of his own psychic wounds, is able to heal others?

You could say that the process of creativity is, in a certain sense, a kind of sickness or illness. You're invaded by a germ, something that has to grow inside you and that makes you completely sick, and the therapy is to materialize the germ of the fantasy so that you become cured. And it's possible that what you've done can turn out to be therapeutic for other people.

In And the Ship Sails On, *when you show everyone—the Serbian refugees and the upper classes—dancing together on the lower deck, I felt a kind of curative power at work.*

You know, when I make a picture I want to tell a story. And I'm glad and sometimes even a little bit surprised by different interpretations and points of view. But I feel a little bit ridiculous encouraging this kind of approach to my films. What you said now about the dance may be true. But for me, the important thing about a creation is whether it's alive or not. I don't care about aesthetical, philosophical, or ideological points of view. But if I had to say something about the dance you referred to, I'd say it's simply a moment of drunkenness, of pure and innocent energy that breaks down the barriers and defenses between the bourgeoisie and the slaves. All that detachment and distance is transcended by means of music. It's a moment of life that suggests that things could be better if we broke through our defenses and egotism.

But basically, I don't like to say stupid things about what is done. Do, don't talk. And do it while being awake—even if sleepily awake—and, as the ancient Chinese used to say, "intentionally without intention."

FEDERICO FELLINI

JANUARY 20, 1920 – OCTOBER 31, 1993

THEODOR GEISEL
The Good Dr. Seuss

La Jolla, California, 1980

"You're going to see the good Doctor?" asked the cab driver cheerily as we drove up the La Jolla hills to Theodor Geisel's home. "He's full of character and brings joy—unlike most doctors!" the driver adds. "My children love his books, and so do I."

It was July 1980, a typically beautiful Southern California morning—sunshine, warm breezes, and a perfect blue sky—the kind of weather that makes you feel as if you've finally arrived in Dr. Seuss's mythical city of Solla Sollew, "where they *never* have troubles! At least, very few" *(I Had Trouble in Getting to Solla Sollew).*

The good Doctor met me at the gate, with a twinkle in his eye and sporting a white beard that reminded me of the high-spirited, white-bearded figure pictured in the trailer in *And to Think That I Saw It on Mulberry Street,* who oversees the wondrous, multispangled parade scene with exorbitant delight. I told Geisel about the cab driver's exuberant characterization of him, which he appeared pleased by, saying modestly and with a smile, "I'm probably just a good tipper."

He led me through the front door of his spacious, pink-stucco house built around a converted watchtower overlooking La Jolla and the Pacific—a house he shares with his second wife, Audrey, and Sam (short for Samantha), a twelve-inch Yorkshire terrier almost as tiny as a Who. Geisel took me into the living room, and we sat down and began to chat.

He pointed through the window to the dozens of sailboats out on the Pacific below, saying, "Those are some of my retired friends down there, but retirement's not for me! [Geisel was seventy-six when I saw him in 1980.] For me, success means doing work that you love, regardless of how much you make. I go into my office almost every day and give it eight hours—though every day isn't productive, of course. And just now," he added, putting on a pair of glasses, "I've slowed down because of my second cataract operation. It was impossible for me to mix a palette—I didn't know which colors were which. With my cataract I had two color schemes—red became orange, blue became slightly greenish: my left eye was like Whistler and the right one was like Picasso—seeing things straight and clear in primitive colors."

"I was just thinking of your book *I Can Read with My Eyes Shut!*" I said, "with those lines: 'If you keep / your eyes open enough, / oh, the stuff you will learn! . . . Keep them open . . . / at least on one side.'"

"That book was dedicated to my surgeon, by the way," Geisel replied, smiling. "Now I have to learn to focus my pen—it'll take about a month."

"You once said that your career began at the zoo. What did you mean by that?" I asked.

"When I was young," Geisel explained, "I used to go to the zoo a lot, and when I returned home I would try to draw the animals. . . . You see, my father, among other things, ran a zoo in Springfield, Massachusetts. He was a guy who became president of a Springfield brewery the day Prohibition was declared (this was wartime prohibition). So he became very cynical and sat for days in the living room saying 'S.O.B., S.O.B.' over and over—he didn't know what to do with himself. But he had been honorary head of the Parks Department, and there had been a mix-up with the books and he had to straighten them out. At that time the superintendent left the park system, so my father took the job permanently. And at a salary of five thousand dollars a year he became a philanthropist. He built tennis courts, trout streams, three golf courses, bowling greens—he changed people's lives more than he would have done if he'd been a millionaire; he used WPA funds and government money to put people to work. So he ended up as a very worthwhile guy."

"Imagine what you might have conceived in that position!" I said.

"I would have been fired if I'd had that job!"

"Would your father have been critical or approving of Marco's imaginative powers in *Mulberry Street*?" I wondered.

"My mother would have loved it," he said. "My father would have been critical. But he was a remarkable man. Let me tell you a story: My father's hero was a person named Cyril Gaffey Aschenbach, who had been captain of the first Dartmouth football team that beat Harvard. When I lived in New York City, I mentioned to my father that Cyril lived near me. So one night we all had dinner together. My father would ask all night long: Tell me how you scored that winning touchdown. And Cyril would say: 'Look at these sconces, they're two hundred and fifty years old'—all he talked about was antiques. So when my father was heading back to Springfield, he said, 'I'm going to send you an antique that will shut Cyril Gaffey Aschenbach up forever!' He found a dinosaur footprint—a two-hundred-and-fifty-pound slab showing three toes—which is hanging outside next to the swimming pool—you can see it through the window. It was found around Holyoke, Massachusetts, near a shale pit. My father sent it to me in New York in a truck, but on the way down he stopped off at Yale and had it appraised—and he found out that it was a hundred and fifty million years old.

"My father, as you see, had an unusual sense of humor. And every time I've moved I've taken that footprint with me: it keeps me from getting conceited. Whenever I think I'm pretty good, I just go out and look at it. Half the people I show it to think I've made it myself."

"The Glunk might have made a similar footprint," I suggested.

"I think they're related," Geisel was happy to agree. He pointed to a shelf across the room on which were resting various baked-clay imaginary animals. "They were made a couple of hundred miles from Kabul, Afghanistan," he told me, "at a place the American diplomats call Dr. Seussville—they've had this craft going on for a thousand years. Someone at the embassy sent me these weird animals—a lot of two-headed beasts."

"Where *do* you suppose he gets things like that from? / His animals all have such very odd faces. / I'll bet he must hunt them in rather odd places!" I said, quoting from *If I Ran the Zoo*. "What is it with you and the animals?" I asked him.

"Let's just say I find them more compatible than most people," he said, smiling.

In reading a number of articles about Geisel, I'd discovered that he had been drawing "his" animals since his childhood days at the zoo; had done animal cartoons for Dartmouth's humor magazine *Jack-o-lantern*, which he edited for a while, as well as for magazines such as *Judge*, *Vanity Fair*, and *Saturday Evening Post*; had doodled winged horses in his class notebooks at Oxford; had painted pictures of donkeys for a month in Corsica after leaving academia; had used animals for his political cartoons for *P.M.* magazine—depicting a Nazi as a dachshund, Pierre Laval as a louse on Hitler's finger—as well as for his famous advertising cartoons that accompanied his "Quick, Henry! The Flit!" insect-spray caption; and had created many bizarre animals for Standard Oil billboards, including the Moto-Munchus, the Oilio-Gobelus, and the Zerodoccus. As a child once wrote to him: "Dr. Seuss, you have an imagination with a long tail!"

"My style of drawing animals," Geisel now explained, "derives from the fact that I don't know how to draw. I began drawing pictures as a child—as I mentioned before—trying, let's say, to get as close to a lion as possible. People would laugh, so I decided to go for the laugh. I can't draw normally. I *think* I could draw normally if I wanted to, but I see no reason to re-create something that's already created. If I'd gone to art school I'd never have been successful. In fact, I did attend one art class in high school. And at one point during the class I turned the painting I was working on upside down—I didn't exactly know what I was doing, but actually I was checking the balance: if something is wrong with the composition upside down, then something's wrong with it the other way. And the teacher said, 'Theodor, real artists don't turn their paintings upside down.' It's the only reason I went on—to prove that teacher wrong.

"I'm fascinated by all kinds of animals. When I was at Oxford, I read *The Travels of Sir John Mandeville*, which describes weird animals and a race of people who lived in a desert. They had enormous feet, which they put up in the air over their heads to give them shade. I was bogged down in Old High German, and Mandeville sort of opened up a door for me. That's one reason I left Oxford—in order to go in that direction.

"I met a professor there who suggested that I leave Oxford and come study with him in Paris. He was a Jonathan Swift scholar, and I thought he had a bright, original mind. So I packed up and went to the Sorbonne. I had fifteen minutes with him in his study, and I almost went crazy. Instead of the wild, exciting things I expected to be studying, he asked me to investigate whether Swift wrote anything between the ages of sixteen and a half and seventeen—something like that—and I was to research all the obscure libraries in England, Scotland, and Ireland to find out. And, I said, supposing I found out that he didn't write anything? Well, the professor said, you will have had a lovely time in Paris and in traveling. That was when I booked myself on a cattle boat to Corsica—it was my final revolt against academicism."

"I wanted to bring up a slightly 'academic' point of my own"—

I hesitated—"about the possibility of *Mulberry Street* and Goethe's 'The Erl-King' being somewhat similar, for both of them are about a father and a son and about the exigencies and power of the imagination. In 'The Erl-King,' the son's imagination transforms a dog into the Erl-King's crown and train, and the Erl-King's daughters into gray, shimmering willow trees. And in *Mulberry Street* the young Marco transforms a dumpy horse and wagon into a howdah-caparisoned blue elephant marching astride two crocked-looking yellow giraffes pulling a seven-piece brass band."

"It's interesting you say that," Geisel replied, as he broke into German: "'*Wer reitet so spät durch Nacht und Wind?/ Es ist der Vater mit seinem Kind.*' . . . I was brought up in a German-speaking home, I minored in German in college, and I learned 'The Erl-King'—I still remember those first two lines—when I was still in high school. It could tie up, though I never thought of it before. It's very odd that you discovered that. I've learned something. Back to the psychiatrist's couch!"

"I was wondering what books you read as a child," I said. "I've brought along a few pages from two books about freedom-loving creatures that I thought might have influenced you a bit—Palmer Cox's *Brownies: Their Book* and Gelett Burgess's *Goops and How to Be Them.*"

"Both books were very popular when I was a kid," Geisel replied. "My parents bought them and I read and loved them, though I haven't seen them for years. They bring back a lot. The Goops were a little too moralistic for me, but I loved the Brownies—they were wonderful little creatures; in fact, they probably awakened my desire to draw.

"I also remember liking Wilhelm Busch's *Max and Moritz,* and when I was six or seven years old I read Peter Newell's *The Hole Book,* which I remember very well. It had a die cut through the whole thing, from the cover to the end, and it began: 'Tom Potts was fooling with a gun / (Such follies should not be), / When—bang! The pesky thing went off / Most unexpectedly!' And it followed the course of that bullet, which went through a hot water boiler—and the house got flooded—then through ropes people were swinging on . . . it just raised hell. And it ended with what was then considered to be one of the funniest things in the world: the bullet hit a cake made by a bride, and the cake was so hard that the bullet flattened out . . . which was very fortunate, because otherwise it would have gone completely around the world and come back and killed Tom Potts on the spot!"

"Aside from Newell and Cox—and, best of all, Carroll, Lear, and

Busch," I added, "you've consistently written some of the greatest comic verse for children. Peter Slade, in his book *Child Drama,* states that 'after the age of six of so, this gift of rhythm appears naturally in child work, but the adult has to toil hard "for it" and often does not attain it. Those who are most successful in doing so are, for the most part, those who have actually retained it from childhood. We call them great artists.' And I wanted to know how you've managed to keep your rhythmic and rhyming impulses intact."

"It's so ingrained in me," Geisel replied, "that I now have trouble writing prose. I find that if I'm writing a short letter, it comes out in verse. It's become a normal method of expression.

"I hate making speeches, incidentally, but several years ago I solved my problem: in 1977, for a commencement address at Lake Forest College, I read an epic poem of fourteen lines entitled 'My Uncle Terwilliger on the Art of Eating Popovers.' The kids in the graduating class are probably still cheering because they thought I'd speak for hours. The *New York Times* picked it up and said that there should be a law that no commencement speech should be longer than that. And the *Reader's Digest* even 'digested' it by cutting out the three short introductory paragraphs."

"Is it easy or hard for you," I asked, "to write the kind of verse in your books—like the following stanza, say, from *On Beyond Zebra*—a stanza, by the way, that sounds like a perfect description of the apartment situation in New York City":

> The NUH is the letter I used to spell Nutches
> Who live in small caves, known as Nitches, for hutches.
> These Nutches have troubles, the biggest of which is
> The fact there are many more Nutches than Nitches.
> Each Nutch in a Nitch knows that some other Nutch
> Would like to move into his Nitch very much,
> So each Nutch in a Nitch has to watch that small Nitch
> Or Nutches who haven't got Nitches will snitch.

"It's hard," Geisel said, laughing. "I'm a bleeder and I sweat at it. As I've said before: the 'creative process' consists for me of two things—time and sweat. And I've also said that too many writers have only contempt and condescension for children, which is why they give them degrading corn about bunnies. The difficult thing about writing in verse for kids is that you can write yourself into a box: if you can't get a proper rhyme for a quatrain, you not only have to throw that quatrain out but you also have to unravel the sock way back, probably ten pages or so . . . you find that you're not driving the car, your *characters* are driving it. And you also have to remember that in a children's book a paragraph is like a chapter in an adult book, and a sentence is like a paragraph."

"In 1925," I mentioned, "the Russian children's poet Kornei Chukovsky wrote an important book that in English is called *From Two to Five,* and in it he formulated a set of rules for the composing of verse for children. I wanted to find out what you thought of these rules."

"I'd love to hear what they are!"

"Chukovsky's first rule is that poems for children must be *graphic,* and by that he meant that every stanza must suggest an illustration, since children think in terms of images."

"I agree," Geisel said, "and one should add the importance of eliminating the nonessentials."

"Two," I continued, "there must be a rapid change of images— movement and change."

"He's talking about progression," Geisel responded, "and I agree entirely."

"Three, that this verbal painting must be lyrical—so that a child can sing and clap to the verse."

"I'll go along with that," said Geisel.

"Four, that there be a moving and changing of rhythm."

"Definitely a change of pace," Geisel allowed. "I'll get going at a certain pace and meter, and I'll turn the page and then have one line in prose to break up what I've been doing and then start building up again from there."

"Five, that there be a heightened musicality of poetic expressiveness."

"What does that mean?"

"He's referring to what he calls the flow and fluidity of sound—the avoidance of cluttered-up clusters of consonants, for example."

"Okay," Geisel assented.

"Six, that there be frequent rhyming."

"Yes."

"Seven, that the rhyming words carry the meaning."

"That's *very* true," Geisel insisted. "I find that a lot of authors will use convenience rhymes and not positive thought rhymes. And the child's interest disappears entirely."

"Eight," I continued, "that every line must have a life of its own, with no internal pauses."

"Yes."

"Nine, that the author not crowd the poem with adjectives—*more verbs and fewer adjectives.*"

"He's definitely right about the adjectives," Geisel explained. "If I'm supplementing the words with pictures and if I can substitute the adjectives with a picture, I'll leave them out of the text."

"Ten, that the predominant rhythm be that of the trochee."

"That could be true in Russian," Geisel suggested, "it could come out of the way the Russian language sounds. In most of my work I use anapests. But in any case, I think the subject matter is more important than what meter you use."

"Eleven, that the verse be suitable for play and games."

"All of my books," said Geisel, "are informally dramatized in schools. And recently, the Children's Theater Company in Minneapolis did a wonderful adaptation of *The 500 Hats of Bartholomew Cubbins*—an amazing production."

"Twelve, that verses for children have the skill, the virtuosity, the technical soundness of poetry for adults."

"I think so," Geisel agreed.

"And thirteen," I concluded, "that through your verse you try to bring children within reach of adult perception and thoughts."

"I don't know how far you can bring them to it," said Geisel, "but you can try to initiate them. . . . I like this guy, and I think that what he says holds up."

About the first years of his life, Tolstoy wrote: "Was it not then that I acquired all that now sustains me? And I gained so much and so quickly that during the rest of my life I did not acquire a hundredth part of it. From myself as a five-year-old to myself as I now am there is only one step. The distance between myself as an infant and myself at five years is tremendous." And following Tolstoy's notion, Chukovsky states: "It seems to me that, beginning with the age of two, every child becomes for a short period of time a linguistic genius." Throughout his book, the author makes many fascinating observations, among them:

Two-and three-year-old children have such a strong sensitivity to their language—to its many inflections and suffixes—that the words they construct inventively do not seem at all distorted and freakish but, on the contrary, extremely apt, beautiful, and natural.

In the beginning of our childhood we are all "versifiers"—it is only later that we begin to learn to speak in prose. The very nature of an infant's jabbering predisposes him to versifying.

Another quality of children's rhymes and nonsense verse is that they are saturated with joy. They do not show a trace of tears or a whisper or a sigh. They express the child's feeling of happiness with himself and his world which every healthy child experiences so much of the time. This is the reason that their rhymes and nonsense verse have such a zestful spontaneity.

It is high time to promote these "nonsense" verses into the category of educationally valuable and perceptive works of poetry. . . . With the help of fantasies, tall tales, fairy tales, and topsy-turvies of every type, children confirm their realistic orientation to actuality.

All of these observations make it clear that Chukovsky would undoubtedly have greatly approved of the works of Dr. Seuss, who has never severed his connection with the child's ways of being in and conceiving the world. As Goethe wrote: "Every child is to a certain extent a genius and every genius to a certain extent a child. The relationship between the two shows itself primarily as the naïveté and sublime ingenuousness that are a fundamental characteristic of true genius."

Geisel's illustrative style, for example, has its roots in the naïve and sublimely ingenuous manner with which young children create their own drawings. Unlike the child, however—about whom André Malraux once wrote: "His gift controls him, not he his gift"—Geisel is always in command of his idiosyncratic style. As he once told Michael J. Bandler: "Schools send me hundreds of drawings each year, and I find most kids draw as I do—awkwardly. I think I've refined my childish drawing so that it looks professional. But kids exaggerate the same way I do. They overlook things they can't draw, their pencils slip, and they get some funny effects. I've learned to incorporate my pencil slips into my style." As he later told me: "Technically, I'm capable of doing more complicated things. But every time I try to do something sophisticated in a children's book, it fails—it doesn't attract kids. This is due to the fact that I work the way they work. A child's idea of art is a pen-and-ink drawing filled in with flat color, with no modulation and no subtlety. *McElligot's Pool,* which has modulation of tones, isn't as successful as the books with hard black outlines and flat color. That's just the way kids see things."

And concerning the little stories very young children themselves make up, Brian Sutton-Smith, in his essay "The Child's Mind as Poem," has noted certain recurring features in these stories—their verse-like quality (rhythm, alliteration, and rhyme); their simplified syntax and use of nonsense; their expressive as opposed to referential features (melody preceding meaning); their use of exaggeration and of emphatic and pantomimic effects; and their reliance on theme-and-variation, repetitive, and cyclical forms of organization. And Sutton-Smith concludes his discussion by affirming that "the child's mind is like a poem."

One might even suggest that the child's mind is indeed like many a Dr. Seuss book, for his poetic style—although more controlled—has its roots in these characteristic modes of children's storytelling: simply and unselfconsciously, Dr. Seuss has retained a fresh perceiving system, naturally communicating and understanding of children's energies, needs, and desires.

Nowhere is this more obvious than in *The Cat in the Hat* (1957). "It's the book I'm proudest of," Geisel told me, "because it had something to do with the death of the *Dick and Jane* primers. In 1954 John Hersey wrote an article in *Life* that suggested something to the effect that we should get rid of the boredom of Dick and Jane and Spot and hand the educational system over to Dr. Seuss! William Spaulding, who was then the textbook chief at Houghton Mifflin, read the article and asked me if I'd like to try to do a primer, and he sent me a list of about three hundred words and told me to make a book out of them.

"At first I thought it was impossible and ridiculous, and I was about to get out of the whole thing. Then I decided to look at the list one more time and to use the first two words that rhymed as the title of the book— *cat* and *hat* were the ones my eyes lighted on. I worked on the book for nine months—throwing it across the room and letting it hang for a while— but I finally got it done. Houghton Mifflin, however, had trouble selling it to the schools—there were a lot of Dick and Jane devotees, and my book was considered too fresh and irreverent. But Bennett Cerf at Random

House had asked for trade rights, and it just took off in the bookstores."

And just as Theodor Geisel, during his one and only art class, turned his painting upside down, so Dr. Seuss, in *The Cat in the Hat,* created one of the great bouleversements in the history of children's reading.

"The sun did not shine. / It was too wet to play. / So we sat in the house / All that cold, cold, wet day" is the way the book begins, as two children—brother and sister—and a surprised goldfish in a bowl suddenly hear the *bump* that announces the dramatic arrival of the Cat in the Hat, who, in the absence of the children's mother, tells them: "I know it is wet / And the sun is not sunny. / But we can have / Lots of good fun that is funny!"

And then the fun begins!

John Hersey has called *The Cat in the Hat* a "gift to the art of reading" and a "harum-scarum masterpiece." And Alison Lurie, in her essay "On the Subversive Side," has seen *The Cat in the Hat* as being part of the subversive tradition of children's literature represented by books such as *Huckleberry Finn* and *Alice's Adventures in Wonderland.* As she writes: "It is the particular gift of some writers to remain in one sense children all their lives: to continue to see the world as boys and girls see it, and take their side instinctively. One author who carries on this tradition today in America is Dr. Seuss, who like Twain and Carroll has adopted a separate literary personality."

"It's interesting," I mentioned to Geisel, "that after Samuel Clemens and Charles Dodgson, you are the most famous and most popular pseudonymous writer for children."

"I never thought of that," he replied. "Twain and Carroll are both a couple of phonies, masquerading under false colors. It's not bad company at all. I'm very flattered to be included. When I received an honorary Doctor of Humane Letters from Dartmouth in 1955, the president of the college, in his conferral speech, said that this would make an honest man of me, and no longer would I have to masquerade under a phony doctorate."

"You seem quite recusant yourself, and I think a lot of your books *are* subversive," I added. "Don't you?"

"I'm subversive as hell!" Geisel replied. "I've always had a mistrust of adults. And one reason I dropped out of Oxford and the Sorbonne was that I thought they were taking life too damn seriously, concentrating too much on nonessentials. Hilaire Belloc, whose writings I liked a lot, was a radical. *Gulliver's Travels* was subversive, and both Swift and Voltaire influenced me. *The Cat in the Hat* is a revolt against authority, but it's ameliorated by the fact that the Cat cleans everything up at the end. It's revolutionary in that it goes as far as Kerensky and then stops. It doesn't go quite as far as Lenin."

"Like many of your books," I suggested, "*The Cat in the Hat* is quite anarchistic."

"It's impractical the way anarchy is, but it works within the confines of a book," Geisel agreed.

"Without pushing you further down the revolutionary path," I said, laughing, "I've always wondered about the concluding lines of *Yertle the Turtle*: 'And today the great Yertle, that Marvelous he, / Is King of the Mud. That is all he can see. / And turtles, of course . . . all the turtles are free / As turtles and, maybe, all creatures should be.' Why 'maybe' and not 'surely'?"

"I qualified that," Geisel explained, "in order to avoid sounding too didactic or like a preacher on a platform. And I wanted *other* persons, like yourself, to say 'surely' in their minds instead of my having to say it."

"Within the confines of your books," I added, "you've written some very moral and political tales. The two books about Horton the elephant praise the virtues of loyalty and faithfulness. And you once said that the idea for *The 500 Hats of Bartholomew Cubbins* came about when you were 'taking a railroad train through Connecticut, sitting in a smoky, stuffy car, and ahead of me sat a smoky, stuffy Wall Street broker, wearing a derby and reading the *Wall Street Journal*. I was fascinated with his hat, and wondered what his reaction would be if I took his hat off his head. And then, half an hour later, I wondered how he'd react if there was still another hat on his hat.'"

"Yes," Geisel responded, "children's literature as I write it and as I see it is satire to a great extent—satirizing the mores and the habits of the world. There's *Yertle the Turtle* [about the turtle dictator who becomes the 'ruler of all that I can see' by sitting on the backs of hundreds of subject turtles, his throne brought down by the simple burp of the lowliest and lowest turtle], which was modeled on the rise of Hitler; and then there's *The Sneetches* [about Star-Belly Sneetches who ostracize Plain-Belly Sneetches who pay to become Star-Belly Sneetches who then have to become Plain-Belly Sneetches, etc.], which was inspired by my opposition to anti-Semitism. These books come from a different part of my background and from the part of my soul that started out to be a teacher. Every once in a while I get mad. *The Lorax* [about a rapacious Once-ler who despoils the land of its Truffula Trees, leading to the total pollution and destruction of the environment] came out of my being angry. The ecology books I'd read were dull. But I couldn't get started on that book—I had notes but was stuck on it for nine months. Then I happened to be in Kenya at a swimming pool, and I was watching a herd of elephants cross a hill. Why that released me I don't know, but all of a sudden all my notes assembled mentally. I grabbed a laundry list that was lying around and wrote the whole book in an hour and a half. In *The Lorax* I was out to attack what I think are evil things and let the chips fall where they might, and the book's been used by ministers as the basis of sermons, as well as by conservation groups."

"Aside from works like *Yertle the Turtle* and *The Sneetches,* which have the power of the great fables," I said, "there's a certain folktale quality to a few of your stories—I'm thinking particularly of 'The Big Brag' in *Yertle the Turtle*—about the pomposity and egomania of a bear and a rabbit and of how they are cut down to size by a little worm—and 'The Zax' in *The Sneetches*—about two Zaxes who bump into each other in the prairie and who each stubbornly refuse to let the other one pass until, eventually, highways are built over and around them. This last tale is similar to an African tale I recently read about two goats who bump into each other on a bridge and refuse to budge, each of them finally throwing the other into the water below."

"It just proves that there's nothing new," Geisel replied. "People are always reacting to the same stimuli. You could probably find duplications of all of my stuff. But I used to read a lot of Uncle Remus and a lot of Belloc, as I mentioned before, so maybe there's some influence there.

"Anyway, to get back to what we were talking about earlier," Geisel said: "*The Cat in the Hat* was an immediate best seller. And at that point Bennett and Phyllis Cerf of Random House conceived the idea of starting a publishing house just for the lower graders which we called Beginner Books."

"It's interesting," I interrupted, "that a Zen Buddhist monk once said: 'If your mind is empty, it is always ready for anything; it is open to everything. In the beginner's mind there are many possibilities; in the expert's mind, there are few. . . . That is always the real secret of the arts: always be a beginner'" (Shunryu Suzuki).

"But to create a book," Geisel said, "you have to have an ability and a technique, which you don't have in an empty mind. So maybe we should change 'empty' to 'receptive.' . . . Anyway, when we started Beginner Books we had no idea what we were doing—it was *really* an 'empty' mind. And when we began Beginner Books, we found out that *The Cat in the Hat* was at that time hard for first graders to read. It all depended, of course, on what experts you talked to—how many words a kid could read. But I realized that there was a level below Beginner Books, so we began making things simpler and simpler; and then we set up Bright and Early Books for younger and younger readers. At the moment I'm working on something I call Prenatal Books *[laughing]*, but there are a few little difficulties we haven't yet solved.

"When I first started doing children's books I knew nothing about the market. But, obviously, parents read my earlier books to their kids. Did the parents like them? In his autobiography, Prince Rainier of Monaco says something like: 'My children insist that I read those silly Dr. Seuss books to them—I don't care for them, but my kids do.' In those earlier and regular-sized books I'm writing for people. In the smaller-sized Beginner Books I'm still writing for people, but I go over them and simplify so that a kid has a chance to handle the vocabulary. But, basically, I've long since stopped worrying about what exact ages the books are for—I just put them out. Sometimes the more complex books can be the simplest ones to read because the clues given in the pictures are stronger. You can't base it entirely on words."

Along with "imagination," "play" is the cornerstone of Dr. Seuss's world. And its importance is specifically revealed in one of Seuss's early fairy-tale-type prose works, *The King's Stilts* (1939), which seems to illustrate Nietzsche's comment that "in any true man hides a child who wants to play."

The Kingdom of Binn, we are told, is surrounded by mighty Dike Trees that hold back the sea from engulfing the land. But since the roots of these trees are extremely tasty to the rapacious Nizzard birds, King Birtram has gathered an army of a thousand Patrol Cats, who guard the kingdom both day and night. The Changing of the Cat Guard takes place at seven each morning, and once King Birtram reviews the Guard, he rushes off to a special castle closet where he keeps his beloved red stilts, grabs them, and begins leaping around the palace grounds on them: "This was the moment

King Birtram lived for. When he worked, he really worked . . . but when he played, he really PLAYED!" ("The essence of kingship is childlikeness," wrote Georg Groddeck, adding: "The greatest monarch is the infant.")

The townsfolk do not really understand, but they approve of their king's playful ways, until one day the malicious, curmudgeonly Lord Droon ("Laughing spoils the shape of the face" is his motto) steals the stilts and has them secretly buried. King Birtram grows sadder and sadder and finds it impossible to take care of his Patrol Cats, who in turn become lazy and apathetic. The Nizzards, of course, start ravaging and destroying the roots of the trees, and the kingdom is in danger. But with the help of his courageous page boy Eric ("Quick, Eric! The Stilts!" shouts the king— parodying Geisel's "Quick, Henry! The Flit!" insect-spray commercial), he regains his stilts and leads the Patrol Cats to victorious battle. And the book ends with Lord Droon imprisoned and Eric rewarded with his own pair of stilts, on which he races around the kingdom with King Birtram every afternoon: "And when they played they really PLAYED. And when they worked they really WORKED. And the cats kept the Nizzards away from the Dike Trees. And the Dike Trees kept the water back out of the land."

Play allows us to innovate, test, accept, and reject; to explore and integrate different forms of behavior; and to envisage and to conceive of new ideas, new theories, new creations, new discoveries, and new societies. Imagination and play are at the basis of all our hope. In the words of the psychologist D. W. Winnicott: "One has to allow for the possibility that there cannot be a complete destruction of a human individual's capacity for creative living and that, even in the most extreme cases of compliance and the establishment of a false personality, hidden away somewhere there exists a secret life that is satisfactory because of its being creative or original to that human being."

In the words of the good Doctor Seuss: "There is no one alive who is you-er than you!"

THEODOR GEISEL

MARCH 2, 1904 – SEPTEMBER 24, 1991

RICHARD GERE
Face-to-Face

New York City, 1985

People who think of the Bible's King David simply as the shepherd boy who killed the giant Goliath with a slingshot or as a bearded man in flowing robes strumming a harp are in for a shock. In the film *King David,* directed by Bruce Beresford *(Breaker Morant, Tender Mercies),* viewers are confronted with an intense, disturbingly real portrait—based on the biblical text—of one of the most complex and fascinating characters of ancient history. As portrayed by Richard Gere, David is at once shepherd, poet, warrior, lover, traitor, out-law, king, and spiritual seeker. Beautifully shot in the southern Italian town of Matera—one of the oldest villages in Europe—*King David* presents with startling clarity this 3,000-year-old story that has so often been glossed over and sentimentalized by generations of Sunday-school-book accounts and retellings.

Gere's performance marks the twelfth film appearance of the thirty-five-year-old actor, whose roles up to now have ranged from big-city, streetwise, macho-yet-vulnerable protagonists *(Bloodbrothers, American Gigolo, Cotton Club)* to American innocents insistently trying to live out their dreams and romantic commitments *(Days of Heaven, Yanks, An Officer and a Gentleman).* But in *King David,* he has taken on what is perhaps the most challenging and risk-taking role of his career.

* * *

What do you say to people who think it takes a lot of chutzpah to play the role of King David?

135

Well, who has a right to play anyone on that level? Who has the chutz-pah to play any other life and think you can fulfill it? But as with other professions, you take on the largest challenge in order to expand yourself. It would be foolish for anyone to think he could be King David or Jesus Christ or Freud or whomever. What you can do, though, is to explore some of the territory and hope that, momentarily, through craft and hard work, you can coax out some of the essence of the material. And that's it. There's really no pretense about it. I approached the role of David like any other character. You can't do it any other way. If you start playing the king, then you don't play the person. You never play the king. It's the people around you who play you as if you were the king. So, as with any character, you find the essential human being there—the situation, the mind-set, the spiritual point of view. By keying into those aspects of the character, you can then deal with it dramatically.

What first got you interested in the character of David?

He was the golden boy, he was someone who could do everything. He was the poet, the lover, the chosen one, the madman, the womanizer, the warrior, the rebel, the political thinker, the philosopher, the priest, the prophet. He had touches of all these things within him, and they were all explored and expressed. We have the whole legacy of his military and po-litical thinking. And in the Psalms, we see a guy who's psychologically very similar to us, who's dealing with self-knowledge and guilt, who's aware of his shortcomings and is trying to overcome them, but is very honest about them, who's saying, basically, "I'm fucked, I've sinned, forgive me." It's his sense of self-awareness, I think, that's interesting about his character.

I've always wanted to know, what was the first role you ever played?

You mean besides Santa Claus?

Santa Claus?

Yeah, Santa Claus. I was in the first or third grade, and my mother made the costume. I had a pillow over my belly and a big black belt, and my mother pasted cotton on my red jacket.

How did you do?

I think it was a huge success. *[Laughing]*

Then what happened?

My second role was the funniest one, actually. I was in junior high—and wasn't exactly student council material—but I was playing the president of the United States in *The Mouse That Roared*. So you can imagine this fourteen-year-old kid coming out onstage and playing the president, with everybody knowing that he was a fuckup. So I went from Santa Claus to King David in thirty years!

A very religious career.

It's the beard *[laughing]*—that must really be the key. Maybe it's the same essential character I'm perfecting now.

What were your first serious roles?

The first time I was ever paid for this line of work was at the Province-town Playhouse one summer when I was nineteen. It was a two-week rep—that is, you rehearsed for two weeks and played for two weeks, and while you were doing one role, you rehearsed the next one. So it was really a twenty-four-hour nightmare. No sleep. You never learned the lines. You were always on the edge of a nervous breakdown.

   I was ill equipped, I'm sure, to play any of the roles, but for some reason they allowed me to do them. And I covered an incredible range of things. The first play I was in was Eugene O'Neill's *The Great God Brown*. We wore plastic masks through which we spoke our lines in normal, prosaic ways, and then we'd take the masks off and speak our innermost feelings.

As Santa Claus, you had a beard, and in The Great God Brown, *you wore a mask. When did you show your true face?*

I don't know if one ever does that. Maybe when you die—that's about it.

Sometimes a mask allows you to be truly yourself.

I think the gig is either to have no mask at all or else to have an infinite number of them and keep shuffling them. It's probably more fun to have an infinite number of masks.

What were some of the other masks you were trying on at that time?

I remember being in Tom Stoppard's *Rosencrantz and Guildenstern Are*

Dead, Peter Shaffer's *The White Liars,* Edward Albee's *Everything in the Garden,* and Tennessee Williams's *Camino Real.* In that last one, I played the roles of Lord Byron and Lobo, the beach boy!

Where did your acting career go from there?

After Provincetown, I spent a season in Seattle, then later moved to New York City, where I lived in a fifth-floor walk-up—no heat, no water—on Sixth Street between Avenue C and Avenue D. When I took the place, I told the landlord, "Look, the only thing I can't take is roaches." He said, "No problem with roaches." But as soon as I wrote him a check and he left, four million roaches jumped out of every nook and cranny in the place. Meanwhile, outside on the street, I learned drums and Spanish.

This was in the early seventies, and it was a time when rock operas like *Hair* were popular. I played instruments and sang and had long hair, so I fit right in and started working immediately. The first thing I did was something called *Soon, a Rock Opera*—that's how they billed it. It was on Broadway, and I was making money, and a lot of good people were in it—Peter Allen, Barry Bostwick, Marta Heflin, Nell Carter. Nell Carter played my girlfriend.

It was a very *deep* piece about country musicians who come to the big city to make it. All of a sudden, their acoustic instruments are taken away from them, and they're playing electric instruments. The songs were supposed to come out sounding like disco, but unfortunately, when we prerecorded the music, instead of it sounding awful, it actually sounded great *[laughing]*—like Leon Russell, which at the time was the hippest stuff going. I was playing slide guitars and basses and everything. Hardly anyone who was in those kinds of musicals felt they were great art, but they kept the wolf away and gave you money for your rent and acting classes.

Soon led to *Grease,* which took me to England, where I met Frank Dunlop, who was then running the Young Vic. He asked me to work in a production of Shakespeare's *The Taming of the Shrew,* in which I played Christopher Sly. The concept of the role was that I was a member of the audience, a drunk in the lobby causing trouble before the play began. Then when everyone was seated, Jim Dale—the actor playing Petruchio—made an announcement, saying, "We're terribly sorry, but we've had this terrible disaster—our sets and our costumes have been destroyed in a fire, but we're going to go ahead and do what we can." And then I shouted out from the audience: *[drunken voice]* "Whahthafuckareyatalkinabout . . ." So the actors kind of pacified me, brought me up onstage, and at that point I became part of the drama—which, in fact, honors the essence of the play, since it was supposed to be performed for this drunk named Christopher Sly, though that suggestion is normally cut out in most productions.

So here I was stuck up on the stage in various stages of stupor. And at a certain point, the other actors decide to let me play the role of an old man who's pretending to be the father of some other character. It was quite fun, actually. And I got arrested the first night we did it, because the guards didn't know that I was supposed to be part of the production.

You're playing a role, and they arrest you. It could be your life story!

Arrested because they didn't know. *[Laughing]* And the audience would think it was kind of funny that I was falling off the chair, being an asshole. But when I'd speak up, they'd get embarrassed, especially those sitting next to me. Some nights I fooled people, some nights I didn't. I remember one performance when there was a little girl up in the balcony who called out, "He's not drunk!" *[Laughing]*

Your first critic . . . she's still around.

She's still here. *[Laughing]* She grew up to be Pauline Kael!

Some critics and gossip writers seem to forget that you've performed a broad spectrum of fascinating film roles, and they tend to stereotype you as a one-dimensional kind of magnetic, provocative character whom girls get crushes on, boys feel resentful toward, mothers get nervous about, and fathers get scared of.

I think that somewhere along the line, the people who have to market and sell things—people who sell Tupperware and plastic—decided this was a way to sell whatever it is I represent. And it's got nothing to do with me. It's very bizarre. They seem to have bent things in order to make me fit a certain kind of argument they have about me.

You should talk to the people I work with, because my essential self comes out in that process. I like working with people, I enjoy group enterprises. And that's the joy of making films. You're dealing with so many elements—most of which I'm a novice at—but, I mean, film fulfills so many drives with regard to music, photography, writing, philosophy, world movements, metaphysics *[laughing]*—they're all involved. As for my roles,

I've tried not to repeat myself. My static media image bothered me for a little while, because I felt I was being incredibly misconceived. But then I realized that it really had nothing to do with me, that I was happy with what I was doing, proud of the work that I was doing and the choices I was making.

It's interesting that you choose to play characters who, no matter how different each one may seem from the other, are all, in a sense, lunatics, lovers, and poets, to quote Shakespeare.

I've always thought of these roles as being that way, too. But some people don't notice those aspects because they don't get past the obvious attributes of the characters to see what's really motivating them. All of them are leaning in a certain direction. They're people who are trying to grow in some way, trying to figure out what they're involved with, trying to figure out what is this universe. They all reflect different intellectual, spiritual, and economic points of view, but they're all basically unencumbered human beings—lunatics, lovers, and poets.

Do you think of yourself as a lover, lunatic, and poet?

Me. I'm nothing. I'm an empty creature. *[Laughing]*

So how does an empty creature go about preparing for the part of King David?

The way I work is to pull back and find neutral, to clean myself out of me, Richard. Then, on neutral ground, I start building the pieces of the character, and also try to coax in whatever can come through me from other levels. And you can only do that if you're empty. If you're filled, there's no room for something else to come through. That goes without saying.

Did you know much about the David story before you started work on the film?

The Goliath story was just about it. Marty Elfand, who produced *An Officer and a Gentleman,* sent me the script, which was written by the English author Andrew Birkin. The first version—there were, finally, ten drafts—was huge and filled with everything one could say on the subject. But it was done with such invention and texture that I was immediately drawn to it, just as I had been drawn to the movies of Bruce Beresford, who was going to direct. We tried to avoid overpoeticized spiritual digressions and the kind of style typified by the biblical engravings of Gustave Doré—you know, Moses with the beard, holding a stone. We also tried to steer clear of any kind of mock-Shakespearean attitudes. But we had to find some kind of heightened way of dealing with the language so that it would convey the weight of the material—the Bible—and at the same time still be within the realm of believability, so that characters would be talking to one another like friends to friends.

Not being Jewish, how did you feel playing a Jewish king?

At the time of David, people didn't understand the sense of Jewishness the way they do now, which is informed by the whole European experience of exile. So I related to the role completely divorced from the oy veys of Yiddish New York and saw the story simply as being about people trying to survive in a desert society, like the Bedouins I visited in Morocco. Before shooting the film, I went to the edge of the Sahara and spent some time in the Atlas Mountains with the Berbers and Bedouins. We had a Berber guide who took us into Bedouin tents. One isn't normally invited into Bedouin tents. In fact, it's highly dangerous to go near them. But our guide spoke the language and got us in. In one tent, we met a girl who was in a lot of trouble. She had been in labor for days, and everyone feared for her life. So we got her to our vehicle and took her to the nearest town, which opened up the possibilities of dealing with the Bedouins on a day-to-day basis. Which is really ground-level stuff. I mean, it's a totally transient, nomadic life. Tents and animals. A little taste of that, and you begin to sit differently, your concept of time becomes different, and you start to live that way. I think it's important to explore that way of living. How do you protect yourself at night? How cold is it? How do you deal with women? How do you deal with men? Do men touch? You have to confront all those kinds of physical realities. So that was essential. And on top of that, doing all the reading and research I could, and then going to Israel and visiting the places that are described in the Bible and in the script. I walked the riverbed, for example, where, the archaeologists tell us, David and Goliath supposedly had their encounter.

All of these events were supposed to have taken place around 1000 B.C.

To simplify the story: Saul was the first king of the Jewish tribes, and was chosen by God through the prophet Samuel. The Jews hadn't had a king before. God was their ruler, and he was an all-encompassing concept for them. But the people were having lots of problems with the neighboring Philistines, so they felt they needed one leader to command the standing army—a temporal king, one they could see. Samuel chose Saul—who he thought was just a big dumb soldier from the small Benjamite tribe. In fact, however, he turned out to be not only a good soldier but also a powerful man who began to question the authority of Samuel and of the revealed God through him. So Samuel began to have problems with his protégé—the issue being the division of church and state—and had him excommunicated. In the film, we show Samuel using two divinatory gems, by means of which he chooses the young shepherd boy David to be the future king.

It's been pointed out that the Bible, which is the basic source for the story of David, reveals him to be guilty of extortion and robbery, high treason, consorting with the enemy, and conspiracy with intent to murder.

It's there in the Bible. This guy who's grown up very innocent, a poetic soul, is brought into court, becomes the king's armor carrier and then a captain in Saul's standing army, one who rides a chariot into town as the girls line up, cheering, "Saul has killed his thousands, David his tens of thousands." Saul tells David to go out to kill one hundred Philistines as the bride price for his daughter Michal, thinking he will surely die in the process, but he comes back with a box of two hundred foreskins. So this is a brutal time, Jack. And this young poet has taken quite a voyage into the realm of death and killing.

The film itself begins in an extremely brutal way.

Saul has won the war against the Amalekites. He's happy. He's got Agag—the king of the Amalekites—before him. And, spying Samuel, he asks him to come in to observe the negotiations, because his basic idea is to buy the Amalekite land for a low price in order to obtain a deed of ownership so that it could never be argued that the land was obtained illegally. But Samuel, as the Word of Yahweh, says: "This is blasphemy. The word of God is clear: Kill every man, woman, child and beast; take no prisoners; do not negotiate; the enemy is unworthy and unclean." And he then personally cuts off Agag's head.

It's pretty shocking.

It's pretty shocking for a god to be interpreted by a prophet in that way, and to be believed . . . by both sides. Each side was fighting for its god, and the same edict was down: Kill every man, woman, child, and beast . . . the other side is unclean. This story, to me, represents a transitional phase between the biblical accounts of Moses and of Jesus, who, the Bible tells us, is said to be descended from the House of David, because the history of David represents the change that occurred between the conception of the strict and punishing God of Moses and the loving and compassionate God of Jesus, the God who basically says, "Look, I know you're fucked, but I love you anyway." And David is the key character who explores that new territory which no one had been in before. His own hands are bloodied, but he's also torn by the compassionate and giving side, for of course he's a poet and musician as well.

The hard side of the story—as it's written in the Bible and as we portray it in the film—is that of Samuel and the prophet Nathan, who are upholding the word of the God of Moses. And Saul and David are continually questioning that word and saying, "Look, if God wants us to do something, let him speak to us face-to-face." They've been commanded to kill, and they want to know that the command is a direct communication from God.

To me, the key to the whole story is hidden in that phrase "face-to-face." "Let me see you face-to-face," David is saying to his God. "Let there be no separation between my life and yourself. If you're going to use me, use me fully, take the whole thing, you and me, face-to-face." And on his deathbed, David says, "Hide your face no more."

These are characters whose unbridled emotions are openly on display. Saul loves David, even when Saul tries to kill him. And David loves Saul's son, Jonathan.

It's clear to me that the characters in the Bible knew that something was going on between David and Jonathan. Saul tells Jonathan that he has chosen David "to your own shame and the downfall of us all." Don't forget, too, that David is married to Saul's daughter, Michal. He's the best soldier, he's loved by the people, and he has a special relationship with God, which torments Saul. The one smile that David and Saul share together at their first meeting says it all. They understand each other immediately. Saul loves him, he's jealous of him, he's attached to him.

Now the movie doesn't get into this heavily. If you want to see the relationship in the way it's suggested in the Bible, you won't find it in the film such that people could walk out of the theater saying: *[Borscht Belt voice]* "Do you think David and Jonathan were *shtupping* each other?" Rather, there's a gentleness of spirit, an ease of touch, poetry whispered in the ears, tearful runnings-away—it's that kind of thing. And yes, it's men doing this. But we found that it was better to show it in this fashion, with a purity of expression devoid of any coy sexuality. All of the relationships among the male characters are extraordinarily strong and bizarre, and none of these characters could exist without the others. Look at Nathan and David—they're like Hermann Hesse's Narcissus and Goldmund.

King David *accurately re-creates the passions and violence and political realities and spiritual yearnings of the biblical story. Which side is the film ultimately on?*

Basically, I was free from dogma and had no religious or political ax to grind and was as confused as anybody else about the issues involved. Everyone working on the film entered into it in order to explore the territory. Of course, there's ammunition for anyone's ideas or ideologies in this movie. But clearly there's a message that we all wanted to communicate, and that has to do with the face-to-face notion I mentioned earlier. If you're going to be doing something in God's stead, make sure you have direct communication with him, not via some self-proclaimed prophet, who may be a false prophet anyway. As David whispers on his deathbed to his son Solomon, "No matter what the prophets may tell you, be guided by the instincts of your own heart, for it's through the heart and the heart alone that God speaks to man."

So after immersing yourself in the role of King David and his story, what did you learn?

You want to know what I learned? "Who knows the meaning of anything? God has so ordered the world that man cannot find the answer. However hard a man may try, he will not find God. The wise man may think he knows, but he knows no more than the fool, who knows nothing. Emptiness, emptiness, all is emptiness and a striving after wind. What has happened will happen again, and what has been done will be done again. And there is no new thing under the sun." Ecclesiastes. . . . Just kidding, folks!

STÉPHANE GRAPPELLI
The Prince of Violins

Paris, 1977

My grandmother used to tell me that, when I was three years old and on an outing with her to a toy store, I grabbed and tried to make off with a pretty, stuffed, violin-playing monkey—much like the storybook chimpanzee that throws itself on ladies' hats decorated with artificial fruit. In fact, it wasn't the monkey I wanted, but rather that irresistible violin which I tried, unsuccessfully, to wrench from the prehensile grasp and chin of that obdurate and well-made creature.

Three years old is the beginning of the end. At home I pined away, comforting myself with a little 78 rpm phonograph on which I incessantly played a recording of Mischa Mischakoff performing treacly standards like Dvořák's "Humoresque" and Fritz Kreisler medleys. Six months later, however, my weltschmerz vanished upon my receiving from my grandmother an eleven-inch-long Mexican wooden toy violin (a relic that my mother, obviously sensing a legendary career in its formative stages, still keeps in one of her closets).

At seven, two things happened to change my life: first, I discovered Jascha Heifetz, whose electrifying recordings suggested to me, then and even now, the possibility of perfection. And second, my mother bought me a quarter-size violin, and I began taking lessons and practicing, scratchily and irritably, those miserable Ševčík exercises that are the bane of parents and next-door neighbors. I progressed from first to fifth positions, but prodigy I was not.

I was eventually to enjoy the communal experience of performing Haydn and Schubert string quartets with my thirteen-year-old colleagues (though the arguments over who would play first violin were hardly harmonious). But aside from the Bach unaccompanied sonatas and partitas (which I attempted to struggle through later) and the Brahms, Schoenberg, Berg, and Stravinsky violin concertos (which were always beyond my technical command), I began to lose interest in what I considered to be the mostly sentimental Romantic violin repertoire. And when, at fourteen, I flubbed my way through a Vivaldi concerto in front of an audience of parents and peers, I turned to "Heartbreak Hotel" and "Roll Over Beethoven" for solace. I started having fantasies about and casting furtive glances at sensual-sounding oboes and English horns, and realized that my love affair with the violin was over.

Or so I thought until January 1976, when, almost by accident, I went to Carnegie Hall to hear the great jazz violinist Stéphane Grappelli performing with the Diz Disley Trio. I had, of course, earlier admired Django Reinhardt and Grappelli's Quintet of the Hot Club of France's recordings of "Mystery Pacific," "Nuages," "Ain't Misbehavin'," and "Hot Lips," among others. But I hadn't quite expected the faultless intonation, crisp upper-register sonorities, wine-dark lower-string timbres, rhapsodic phrasing, and vespertine lyricism of that shining, graceful, Pierrot-like figure—reminding me lightly of my grandmother in former times—playing the most mellifluent version of "Body and Soul" I had ever heard.

That night at Carnegie Hall brought on one of those Proustian moments of involuntary memory, taking me body and soul back to my three-year-old's obsession, as I repressed the thought of dashing onstage and running off with that beautiful violin.

In December of last year I was on the phone to Paris. "Hello, is this Stéphane Grappelli?"

"You're calling from New York? You want to see me in Paris? *Incroyable! Bien sûr,* you're invited, my dear, and bring Rockefeller Cen*taire* when you come!"

* * *

"Jazz violinists have always had to be unusually resilient to survive," Nat Hentoff has put the matter bluntly, "because until recent years their instrument has not been regarded as a legitimate jazz axe." Considering the dominant position held by the piano and reed instruments, it is important to remember the efflorescence in the twenties and thirties of such inventive pioneer jazz violinists as Joe Venuti, Eddie South, and Stuff Smith (once described as the "palpitating Paganini"), who in turn inspired Svend

Asmussen and Ray Nance and, more recently, Michael White, Leroy Jenkins, and Jean-Luc Ponty.

Stéphane Grappelli not only partakes of this hardly superannuated tradition—a tradition he himself has shaped and developed—but today [1977], at sixty-nine, the violinist is at the height of his imaginative and technical powers. He lives in a compact, modest Upper West Side–looking apartment on the Rue de Dunquerque—an apartment filled with books, records, and souvenirs from his travels. It is just one of Stéphane's home bases (he has a room in Amsterdam and apartments in London and Cannes, where his daughter lives) and, in fact, he is continually traveling at a clip that would exhaust a person half his age. During the last three months of 1976, for example, Stéphane played in eight American and seven Canadian cities, then flew off for performances in Edinburgh, London, Amsterdam, Lyon, Stuttgart, and Hamburg.

"We are all gypsies, my dear," Stéphane says to me as we sit down in his study. "As a matter of fact, I don't like living in any one place. I don't like doing the same thing every day. The only thing in this life is to find people to have a little talk to . . . *that's* agreeable. I really don't envy [pronounced en-*vee*, lovely is lov-*lee*, chopped liver is shopped lee-*vair*] people staying in the same place. I'm not blasé at all. I prefer to be an *ignorant* and be amazed when I see something that's new to me. Sometimes it helps to be an imbecile: you don't need a name or a tax collector coming after you.

"I like New York in June (though I once got the most celebrated flu of my life there), San Francisco in the summer. But best of all I love New Orleans in the fall. I was there a few weeks ago and it's the best thing I ever saw in my life. We played at Rosy's Jazz Hall. Rosy is the woman who owns the club, she likes music very much and she even sang 'Summertime' with us. 'Summertime' in a cool night."

"The great French writer, jazz critic, and singer Boris Vian, who died in 1959, loved New Orleans, too," I mention to Stéphane.

"Oh, I knew him and loved his books," Grappelli says enthusiastically. "Do you know about the Clavicocktail Machine that he describes in his novel *L'Écume des Jours [The Froth of Days]*? It reminds me of your playing."

"I read that book so long ago. It's a machine?"

"A machine that makes drinks to music," I say. "For each note there's a corresponding drink—either a wine, spirit, liqueur, or fruit juice. The loud pedal puts in egg flip and the soft pedal adds ice. For soda you play a cadenza in F-sharp. And if you feel like a dash of fresh cream, you just play a chord in G major. The quantities depend on how long a note is held, but the alcoholic content remains unchanged. So you can make a 'Weather Bird' drink or a 'Loveless Love' potion. Imagine what cocktails you could concoct with your music!"

"A marvelous contraption," says Stéphane. "You know, Boris Vian used to play the trumpet, and I was pinching myself not to laugh. But what a brain! He was a very spiritual man, and he used to compose some very light but amusing songs. In fact, I have a rare edition of *I Spit on Your Grave,* the detective novel he wrote which was banned in France. He used to come to Club St. Germain about twenty years ago almost every night when I was playing there. I'll never forget him. Near the end, he was completely white. I think he was suffering with his art [heart] a long time before. It was not very *solide.*

"Me, I'm A-okay. I was just checked up. I used to smoke a lot, but no more. I started when I was ten. It was during World War I so, *alors,* when I see an American I ask him, but they didn't often give a cigarette to me because I was too small. So I smoked the leaf of the chestnut tree . . . *maronnier.* But I stopped cigarettes in 1970. It was easy, and now my cerebral is clearer.

"Do I smoke anything else? Well, I've tried like everybody, but I'm not a *dope.* One thing that helps me through when I'm playing something that I've done over and over for fifty-four years is a couple of whiskies before I go on the stage. When I'm at Carnegie Hall, for example, I get a little nervous, it's normal. But when you must *attack*—bang!—you need a little support behind. I always arrive one hour before I'm supposed to perform, put my fingers into good order—maybe it sounds pretentious—I take a little drink, some quick conversation like that, and then I'm onstage. Maurice Chevalier once told me: 'You must start very well, finish very well, and in the middle it's nobody's business.' But me, I try to do the business in the middle, too."

"Whiskies or no," I say to Stéphane, "I'm amazed that you can play those same pieces and make them sound new after all these years."

"The big groups of today," he replies, "like the Rolling Stones, always do the same thing: 'I love you, I love you, I love you.' . . . You see what I mean? Any time you go to see those people they're always saying: 'I love you, baby.' I try to catch them changing, but it's *impossible.* I can't bear those screams for nothing at all without *nécessité*. If I did that on my violin, it would be in pieces! I recently heard Morgana King singing 'You Are the Sunshine of My Life.' Now, I could listen to *her* say 'I love you' for one month! But she's intelligent, she doesn't say 'I love you' for one month. She says: 'You are the sunshine of my life,' which at least is a change. But I don't want to criticize too much because these people do their best to please a certain clientele.

"*Alors,* me . . . I, too, am saying 'I love you' or 'I don't love you' with my violin. It's basically the same program every night, but sometimes we start with the entrée and end up with the appetizer. And we've got the dessert as well. No dessert in the middle, though—that would be a bad menu. And when the public is nice, we add a little salt, pepper, and a better bottle of wine. *Voilà!*

"I prefer performing for young people than for the people who ask for mustard when I'm playing 'Nuages.' That's why I like performing at the Bottom Line in New York or at the Great American Music Hall in San Francisco. A lot of atmosphere and no soup.

"I like my programs to have something *soft,* something *energetic,* something *slow,* something *blue,* something *red,* something *burning.* And it's quite difficult to do that with just two guitars, string bass, and violin. We are a bit victimized by the new aspects of electric music. We're playing like classical people except that we're doing jazz music. Segovia or Ike Isaacs—one of the guitarists I play with—is to me the same sound. I don't dare to say I'm playing like Heifetz. I play my own style—I bought it myself from my body—but I'm trying to get that sound. Those classical guys go very fast, but I go fast, too, in my music. Why not? It keeps you alive."

Stéphane has some errands to do and asks if I'd mind joining him on a little walk around the neighborhood. When we get outside—a chilly December day—he mentions that we're just a couple of minutes away from the first apartment he ever lived in as a child.

"My childhood was like a Dickens novel," Stéphane says as we start walking. "I lose my mother, who was French, in 1911 when I was three. And my father had no choice but to put me in a very poor *Catholique* orphanage. My father, who was Italian, was a very strange and interesting person. He was the first *heepie* I ever met, a Latinist and a teacher of philosophy. He did translations from Virgil and Italian into French, and he spent most of his time in the Bibliothèque Nationale. Occasionally he worked as an instructor in a place like Berlitz, but he was incapable of making a penny. We were very good friends. But I'm the opposite of him. I'm very practical, he was *theoretique,* always reading and writing. He thought he could get well by reading a book instead of going to a doctor, but he died in 1939. You know, my father got remarried, but I didn't get on with my stepmother. It's probably the reason I never got married.

"My first impression of live music was when I was six. My father wanted to take me out of that orphanage, and since he knew Isadora Duncan, who had a school then, he asked her if she wanted another student. 'Bring me the child,' she said. Of course, in those days, I was not looking like what I look like today. So she said: 'Oh, yes, I like him!' But I wasn't very successful as a dancer. I played an angel, but when you're not an angel it's *difficile.* I did, however, hear some grand music there. Musicians used to play in her garden, and I remember hearing Debussy's *Afternoon of a Faun* and the music made me *feel* the faun.

"After Isadora Duncan I had to go to another orphanage because the war was breaking out. We slept on the floor and I suffered from under-nutrition. That's why I like desserts now. I never ate much of anything there, and I wasn't very sunny. So I escaped that damned place and wandered in the streets. Finally I move back with my father. And because of him I become a musician. Every Sunday he used to take me to hear orchestras, and that's when I first become acquainted with a lot of Debussy and Ravel. I wanted to play something. And my father wanted to distract me and keep me a bit quiet. So he took me into a store on Rue Rochechouart and bought me a three-quarter violin. All the way home I hugged it so hard I almost broke it. In fact, I still have that violin in my desk at home— there are no cracks in it and it is one of the only things of mine that wasn't destroyed during World War II. I'll show it to you. It's my only fetish.

"There was no money for lessons, so my father takes out a book from the *bibliothèque,* and we learn solfeggio together. I never had a teacher, so I learn good position and posture from sheer luck. The technique came along slowly. When I needed some more notes I had to wait. I can't play the notes with the correct classical fingering. On the other hand, a classical musician can't play jazz easily either. It's a different way. Maybe if I practiced I could succeed in playing the Beethoven concerto from beginning to end, but I'd never play like Isaac Stern or Yehudi Menuhin because my hand is deformed, my brain is deformed. I love bluegrass fiddling, but maybe I could catch it if I lived down South for six months. Because learning to play music is like a language—you've got to learn it on the spot. But you can't catch anything on the street except a cold.

"At fourteen I got a job in a pit band in a cinema. That's where I really learned to play and to read music—three hours during the day, three in the evening. I played in tune, and that's why they kept me."

We reach Stéphane's dentist's office, and he goes upstairs to give the dentist—"a nice guy"—two of his albums *(Stéphane Grappelli Plays Cole Porter* and *Stéphane Grappelli Plays George Gershwin)*. When he comes smiling back down the stairs, I suddenly realize how much his bearing and music remind me of Charlie Chaplin and Buster Keaton.

"Did you ever play music for Chaplin films?" I ask.

"Oh yes, my dear, I was dying of love for his films. I used to love so deeply that sometimes I was sick. But I can't love like that today. Rarely do I have what we call *fou rire*. But, you know, the only kind of movie I don't like is those family-affair films in which they dispute and go back with everybody kissing at the end. I can't bear that.

"It's interesting that just about this time I heard my first jazz. I don't want to sound stupid or pretentious, but I think I'm more near the black beat than the white. I was first attracted to black musical interpretation and atmosphere by chance. I remember hearing a tune called 'Stumbling' on a record performed by a group called Mitchell's Jazz Kings. It drive me insane. Soon after that I listen through the door of a nightclub to a pianist, saxophone, and drums playing 'Hot Lips,' and that drive me mad, too. Practically just two notes and the chords change all the time. So when Char*lee* Chaplin comes on the screen in that cinema, I start playing 'Stumbling' with the other musicians.

"Then one day I went out and saw musicians playing in a courtyard and decided I wanted to earn some pocket money for some pastry, so why don't I try it? I remember concierges chasing me out with their brooms, but one or two accepted me, and I got a little money. I did this two years—though I never tell my father—and I earn more than I make from playing in silent-movie cinemas.

"In the courtyards I play little classical tunes—*Berceuses* by Fauré, melodies from *Thaïs* and the *Serenade* by Toselli, which was a great success. It was the 'You Are the Sunshine of My Life' at the time, and if you wanted to make money you had to play that. So I begin to make some money, and my father and I move into a bigger apartment. About this time I hear Louis Armstrong and Bix Beiderbecke and teach myself the piano. I like its *harmonique* aspect and discover that I can make money playing it at private parties."

Stéphane and I have now arrived at the local optometrist, who chats with Stéphane as he loosens the violinist's glasses ("I'm very farsighted"), and out we go again.

"When did you meet Django Reinhardt?" I ask.

"Oooh, more questions about Zhango! Information about him is *everywhere*. In the subways even! One day I may sit down and write things no one knows about him. He was a very secret person. But I meet him casually when I am playing piano in southern France in 1930 or '31. I had been playing piano at the Ambassadeurs in Paris—where I hear Paul Whiteman, Bing Crosby, Oscar Levant, and George Gershwin perform—and then with Gregor and his Gregorians in Nice. Gregor got me playing the violin again, and one day I meet Zhango, who was looking for a violinist to 'play hot.' But I lose touch with him. Then at Hotel Claridge in Paris in 1933 we both met up again in the same hotel orchestra. One day when the tango orchestra was on we find each other backstage. I had broken a string and was tuning up, and all of a sudden we start fooling around playing 'Dinah' together—pretending we are Eddie Lang and Joe Venuti."

Stéphane is tired of telling Django stories, so I fill in the rest. Django, his brother, his cousin, and bassist Louis Vola formed the legendary Quintet of the Hot Club of France, which, as Ralph J. Gleason once wrote, was the first and only European group of that time "accorded major-league status in jazz by musicians and fans alike."

Reinhardt was a Gypsy whose third and fourth fingers on his fretting hand were left withered and paralyzed by a fire in his caravan, forcing the guitarist to develop a unique "cross-fingering" technique with which he created a dazzling musical style. A man who told time by the sun, Django, more often than not, was off playing billiards, fishing, or painting when he was supposed to be onstage.

In fascinating interviews with Whitney Balliett in the *New Yorker* and with Dan Forte in *Guitar Player*, Stéphane remembers Django as "a great artist but a difficult man. His chords were always there, but he was not there himself." Stéphane was constantly trying to get Django to gigs on time. "But when he was annoyed with me," Stéphane recalls, "he would give me some funny chords."

They were in London together just about the time the Germans invaded France. "I used to get up very late," Stéphane told Dan Forte, "six o'clock in the afternoon. Django, as a Gypsy, would always get up early. Any time, he'd get up. Three in the morning, he'd go be listening to a bird somewhere. He'd hear a bird and say, 'Oh, it's the spring.' The spring was my worst enemy, because when the new leaves came on the trees, no Django. During the war we were in London, but the first siren Django heard, he said, 'We must go, we must go!' He was in the street when he called me, and I said, 'Fuck off, I'm not going to get up. We'll see you later on.' But when I got up, it was too late. And that was good for me, because at least I was not with the Germans."

During the war, Stéphane played in London with pianist George Shearing. "I played with George for the troops. And the bombs dropped quite often. I remember one time we finished up playing in a club in Golders Green. The sirens started, so we flew out of there to get to the deepest underground station nearby, which was Hampstead Heath. We started walking fast down the street, and George said: 'There's no need to run, we're underground.' He didn't know where we were because he was blind.

"One Friday night when we were performing, there was a terrible bombing. I didn't want to disturb George, who was playing his solo, so I ask the manager of the club if we should stop. 'Keep blowing forever!' he shouted. And I didn't dare go because he had our check! Another time I remember a singer we were accompanying who was singing 'As Time Goes By' as the bombs came down. You should have heard the tremor— 'Ti-iy-i-me go-oo-es bi-yi.' It was awful! We laugh now, but those damn V-2s could drop anywhere. Always that bloody blitz started when *we* started. It was a signal."

After the war Stéphane rejoined Reinhardt in Paris, but they played less frequently together. In 1953, Reinhardt died of a cerebral hemorrhage while playing billiards. Stéphane kept a low profile for a while, performing at nightclubs, then for five years at the Paris Hilton and later at Ronnie Scott's Jazz Club in London. During the past ten years he has performed all over the world and has recorded prolifically, releasing at least five albums a year with musicians as diverse as Duke Ellington, Jean-Luc Ponty, Gary Burton, Bill Coleman, Paul Simon, Stuff Smith, Baden Powell, Barney Kessel, George Shearing, and Yehudi Menuhin. Two of the most wonderful of Grappelli's post-Reinhardt albums are *Duke Ellington's Jazz Violin Session* (Atlantic Records SD 1688), with Svend Asmussen, Ray

Nance, Billy Strayhorn, and Grappelli himself; and *Stéphane Grappelli— I Got Rhythm* (Black Lion Records BL-047), recorded live in London in 1973 with the Hot Club of London. With Menuhin he has collaborated on two scintillating albums of music of the thirties (*Jalousie* and *Fascinating Rhythm,* both on Angel Records), eliciting the following comments from his classical friend: "Stéphane Grappelli is a colleague whom I admire and would love to emulate. Although his repertoire is entirely different from mine and he plays the violin in a different style, he brings to it an imagination, a perfection of technique and a spontaneous expression of feeling which would be the envy of every violinist."

"Where will you be playing next?" I ask Stéphane as we continue our walk.

"A trip to Tunisia and then in March I'll be performing at the Hong Kong festival, and back to the States again in May. I do get about. By being hectic I keep young. But here we are at Anvers Square—it's the highlight of our little stroll. I wanted to show you this square because I used to play here as a child. It's changed a lot since then: there's an underground parking lot now, and the statues have been torn down. I used to hang around here and do little things to earn some money, like opening doors of taxis, helping people with luggage, working in a laundry nearby, and delivering hats. One day I delivered a hat to a prostitute at her home. Her boyfriend and a friend of his were there playing banjos, and that woman had a violin around, so the three of us had a wonderful concert that afternoon."

Back in Stéphane's study, I notice a framed photograph of a beautiful woman hanging on the wall. "She was a close friend of mine," Stéphane says, "a hostess in one of the clubs I played at in London during the war. One night a bomb dropped and killed her. I lost another friend—an ice-skating champion—at that time, but in a different way. I was the Prince of Violins, but one day she met the King of Sardines, and I couldn't compete. He was an American colonel and he took her to America after the war, but a year later I received an announcement from her saying that she was marrying *another* guy. By that time I forget.

"In 1975 I was confined in New Zealand and Australia, the most faraway places in the world. And for some reason I had a desire to read something—anything, it could have been the telephone directory. I was feeling homesick and worried about my daughter and grandsons. And by chance I found a copy of *Madame Bovary,* which I read as a child. But in New Zealand I came across two lines in the book which told me exactly what I was feeling: 'How to describe that elusive sickness whose aspects change like clouds in the sky and which whirl around like the wind.' When you feel something like that, it's an impalpable disease. It's dreadful. But it wasn't too bad and I soon forget. One gets fed up with the same thing.

"Unlike Zhango, I like a classical life. I like everything classical. I don't like that abstract business. I like Louis Quatorze, the music of Couperin and Rameau. But I always come back to jazz music. Not so much to the great jazz violinists, but rather to pianist Art Tatum. For me, my god is Art Tatum [pronounced Ta-*toom*]. Tatum's melodic line is influenced by Ravel and Debussy, you know, and by orchestral work. Art Tatum *is* an orchestra. I've played with Count Basie, Joe Turner, John Lewis, Duke Ellington, Oscar Peterson, Erroll Garner, Fats Waller . . . but, alas, never Art Tatum. My greatest ambition is to be the Art Tatum of the violin. That's why I want to keep good health and try to go on."

It was time for me to leave. Stéphane, too, had an appointment, so we walked to the Metro together, and he treated me to a ticket for the first-class section.

"It's our type of chic," he said smiling.

I noticed the red French Legion of Honor stripe in his lapel. "I wear it, my dear, so that I don't have to carry identification papers."

For some reason I also noticed what large ears Stéphane has. "Did you know, Stéphane, that Stravinsky once said that musicians have bigger ears than most other people?"

"A donkey as well," he replied, giving me a warm bear hug as he got up to say goodbye, beaming the way my grandmother used to, the way Stéphane always does when he plays his beautiful violin.

"When I'm playing I'm blissful, I'm happy,
I improvise."

STÉPHANE GRAPPELLI

JANUARY 26, 1908 – DECEMBER 1, 1997

WERNER HERZOG
Signs of Life

New York City, 1975–76

Rabbi Nachman of Bratslav, the eighteenth-century Hasidic master, once told the following story. One day a king summoned his counselor. "I have read in the stars," he said, "that all who eat of the next harvest will be driven mad. What shall we do?" To which the counselor advised that he and the king should eat the previous year's dwindling reserves and let the populace eat the tainted food. "I don't wish to remain lucid in the midst of a people gone mad," replied the king, "so we shall all enter madness together. When the world is in a state of delirium it is senseless to watch from the outside: the mad will think that we, too, are mad." Yet the king also desired to keep alive the memory of his decision and of his former state. Putting his arm around his friend's shoulder, he said: "You and I shall therefore mark each other's forehead with a seal, and every time we look at one another, we shall know that we are mad."

"Make my tales into prayers" was one of Rabbi Nachman's last wishes. And perhaps no contemporary filmmaker has so devotedly and rapturously made these kinds of tales into movies than the thirty-four-year-old German director Werner Herzog, whose cinematic depictions of the autistic, the deaf, the dumb, the blind, ski jumpers, dwarfs and midgets, and inspired and deranged prophets remind us of the deeply longed-for and remembered state of cosmic sanity and unity betokened and embodied by those who, living on the brink of experience, reveal to us the seals of our own madness.

Throughout Europe, Herzog's films are considered visionary masterpieces (*Aguirre, the Wrath of God* played in Paris for eighteen months). But in the United States his movies—in spite of the support of a director like Francis Ford Coppola, an actor like Jack Nicholson, film critics like Amos Vogel,

Manny Farber, and Jack Kroll, and admirers like the New York Film Festival's Richard Roud and Tom Luddy of the Pacific Film Archive in Berkeley—either show up infrequently or else open and close almost as quickly as it takes moviegoers to wait in line for the latest Hollywood action film. (San Francisco is the one city in this country where it appears that *Kaspar Hauser* has developed a considerable theatrical following.)

Herzog, of course, is not the only young German filmmaker whose works remain relatively unknown in this country. And it is interesting to point out that after a creative void in German cinema for thirty years, the most vital and innovative areas of contemporary moviemaking are currently being explored and developed by a remarkable group of directors including Wim Wenders, Volker Schlöndorff, Werner Schroeter, Jean-Marie Straub, and Rainer Werner Fassbinder, who, along with Herzog, is one of the most fascinating filmmakers in the world today. But just as the techniques, styles, and concerns of older German masters such as Pabst, Murnau, and Lang differed from each other, so too those of the practitioners of the new German cinema.

Unlike the other important members of this multifaceted group, Werner Herzog shares less of an affinity with the political aesthetics of Bertolt Brecht and the German New Left than with the mystical tradition of Master Eckhart and Jacob Boehme, as well as of the *Märchen,* or supernatural fairy tale tradition of the German Romantic poet Novalis. Like Herzog, Novalis was especially interested in the idea of the artist as magical synthesizer whose "eye stirs with the desire to become a true eye, a creative instrument," and whose ultimate aim—like the Gnostic-influenced Boehme—is that of perceiving and reaching out for our true home. As Herzog's Kaspar Hauser says: "It seems to me that my coming into this world was a terrible fall."

Signs of Life, Herzog's first feature, made when he was twenty-four, is about a wounded German officer stationed on Crete during World War II who goes mad in a valley of windmills; *Fata Morgana,* the director's most abstract film, was shot almost entirely in the Sahara Desert and is divided into three sections ("The Creation," "Paradise," "The Golden Age"), presenting a few isolated human beings surrounded by sand and sky and the mirages created by their union; *Even Dwarfs Started Small* features a cast of both midgets and dwarfs (Herzog uses the word "dwarf" to include both midgets and dwarfs) in an isolated Borstal-type prison at Lanzarote, one of the volcanic Canary Islands, who riot and run amok as if out of a Wilhelm Busch cartoon book, starting cockfights, burning a palm tree, pouring gasoline in flowerpots and setting them aflame ("When we're well behaved, nobody cares; but when we're trouble, nobody forgets"); *Land of Silence and Darkness* is a magnificent documentary about the deaf, dumb, and blind, smelling and feeling flowers and trees, "hearing" poems through the hand signals of others, feeling the vibrations of radios through their chests, describing the imagined "real" world as if it were paradise; *Aguirre, the Wrath of God*, filmed mostly in the Peruvian Amazon, opens with indescribably beautiful shots of insurrectionary conquistadors and Indian slaves coming down a mist-enshrouded mountain, follows the adventures of the deranged Aguirre's small band of followers floating down the river in search of the lost city of Eldorado, and ends with what seems to be hundreds of chattering monkeys dancing wildly over dead bodies and the remains of the drunken raft; *The Great Ecstasy of the Sculptor Steiner* is a documentary about Walter Steiner, whom Herzog considers the world's greatest ski jumper ("ski flyer" is what the director calls him), whose glorious trajectories, seen in a succession of slow-motion zooms, reveal the impassioned relationship between camera and flyer; *Kaspar Hauser* (the original title is *Every Man for Himself and God against All*), Herzog's best-known film in America, is the director's romantic and meditative adaptation and interpretation of the famous story of the young man who, brought up chained in a dungeon without ever seeing a human being, was discovered in 1828 standing in the Nuremberg town square holding an anonymous note. Knowing only one sentence ("I want to be a gallant rider like my father before me"), Kaspar Hauser is taught to speak, is exhibited as an example of "natural" man, and is then mysteriously murdered.

"Mother, I am far away from everything," are Kaspar's first, halting words when a woman places her baby in his awkward arms. Like almost all of Herzog's characters, Kaspar Hauser is only the most recent of the director's extraterritorial creatures. Far away from their origins, their seeming inarticulateness is in fact the mark that reveals their childlike nature and their sense of homelessness. All of Herzog's characters are spiritual infants. Significantly, the derivation of the word "infancy" comes from the idea of the "inability to speak," and the obsession with language itself is at the heart of Herzog's work, for it is here that one discovers the line where communication, being, imagination, and perception touch, define, and color each other.

In June of this year [1975], Herzog flew to the United States in order to film a forty-five-minute television documentary about the world championship of livestock auctioneers in New Holland, Pennsylvania. "Theirs is like a new language, it's like the last poetry, the last incantations," the director told me a few days after the auction. "To me it's somehow the ultimate of human communication, showing us how far our capitalist system has taken us. It's very frightening and very beautiful at the same time. One of the auctioneers told me that as a child he would drive in a car and at each telephone pole he'd sell livestock to the poles as they passed by very quickly. Another one trained by reciting tongue twisters: 'If it takes a hen and a half a day and a half to lay an egg and a half, how long does it take a broken wooden legged cockroach to kick a hole in a dill pickle?'"

In *Signs of Life*, a young Greek boy, a little bird in his hand, suddenly says to the hero: "Now that I can talk, what shall I say?" And in *Kaspar Hauser*, the delineation of the boy's education simply acknowledges the ineradicable power of preoperational infant thinking and speaking. As an apple rolls down a path, Kaspar says: "The apples are tired, they would like to sleep." When he has a dream, he tells us: "It dreamed to me." When he listens to the piano, he says: "The music feels strong in the heart." And, finally: "Nothing lives in me except my life."

"Kaspar was between fourteen and seventeen when he was discovered," Herzog explains. "Bruno S., who plays him in my film, is forty-three. I don't care at all." Herzog chose Bruno for the part after seeing a documentary made about his life. His prostitute mother had deposited him in an institution for the retarded when he was three years old. Although not retarded, Bruno lived in the hospital until the age of nine, by which time he was psychically maimed for life. Herzog found him living like a bum in a shack, occasionally playing an accordion in backyards. His performance as Kaspar Hauser comes close in intensity to Falconetti's portrayal of St. Joan in Carl Dreyer's *The Passion of Joan of Arc*. To perform the scene in which he learns to walk, Bruno knelt for three hours with a stick behind his knees until his legs were too numb to stand. Exhausted after filming each shot, he fell immediately asleep.

Herzog's concern with the extremities of experience is meant to bring to light what Master Eckhart called the *scintilla animae*—the spark of the soul. The director wants to reveal this light in and by means of his denounced and renounced characters, and at the same time to bring us to an understanding of the birth of the word in the soul that is the light itself. By means of an uncanny admixture of montage, mise-en-scène, music, silence, and language (with its hesitations, gaps, and distortions), Werner Herzog has fashioned a spiritual and aesthetic program similar to the great magus Giordano Bruno: that of opening the "black diamond doors" within the psyche and of returning the intellect to unity through the organization of significant images.

Herzog made his first short films when he was nineteen years old. "I never had any choice about becoming a director," he says. "It was always clear, ever since I was fourteen years old. I converted to Catholicism at fourteen—my father was a militant atheist, and it was an enormous battle against my father. It was at that time that, too, I wanted to go to Albania, which was completely closed off to the rest of the world. So I walked along the Albanian–Yugoslavian border. I can't tell you why I wanted to do this, but Albania was *the* mysterious country in Europe. . . . I wrote scripts at school and submitted them, but there was a long chain of humiliations and failures, so I decided to work at a steel factory at night to make money to produce my first short films."

His sense of resolution and determination has become legendary. At the end of 1974, Herzog walked six hundred miles from Munich to Paris—it took him three weeks—as a tribute to the great German film historian Lotte Eisner, to whom he dedicated *Kaspar Hauser*. "She was in a hospital in Paris, and I was afraid she was going to die," Herzog explains. "And somehow, out of protest, I started to walk, thinking that when I arrived in Paris she would be out of the hospital. And she was. It was just some crazy thought in the back of my mind.

"I'm a friend of hers. But she's important not only to me personally but to the whole of German filmmaking. You know, she was chased out of Germany in 1934 during the years of barbarism, and she remained the historical and cultural link to the great and legitimate German cinema of the twenties and thirties. Filmmakers like myself started from zero—we didn't have the cultural continuity of France or the United States. And Lotte Eisner witnesses for us that we are legitimate again. She is the only person alive who knows film history in person from the Lumières and Méliès to Eisenstein and Pudovkin and the early Chaplin. She's like the last surviving mammoth. And when she dies, something unique will be gone forever. It will be the tragic hour of my life."

Herzog's films share certain visual and thematic concerns with the work of Luis Buñuel, Tod Browning, Georges Franju, and Ruy Guerra, but, most especially, with the films of F. W. Murnau. "*Nosferatu* in particular," the director agrees. "It's the most incredible film ever made in Germany. Once I make a film on that level, I'll be able to step back and be satisfied with my work. But I don't feel any continuity of culture with Murnau—he could have been from Japan or anywhere else, it's his way of seeing things, his narration, that I feel close to. I just see something at the horizon and try to articulate it."

Of all the major directors, Werner Herzog is perhaps the first to use music in such a way that the visual integument of his films at moments seems almost to become transparent as the exorcistic, floating, and numinous sounds of chorales, chants, and motets lead us inward to the mysterious foundations of being. The night before I went to interview Herzog, I made a little cassette tape of pieces by Francesco Landini (the blind fourteenth-century organist and composer) and Don Carlo Gesualdo (the mad sixteenth-century composer-prince), both of them musically and emotionally akin to Herzog's own work and obsessions. The interview began with my playing this tape for him (this was, in a sense, the real interview), and it turned out that both composers were among Herzog's favorites. ("Some people have written that I'm a figure out of the nineteenth century," the director says in the following interview, "but the appropriate time for me would be the late Middle Ages.")

As the tape neared the end, on came a minute-and-a-half lullaby sung by a little Balinese girl (I'd forgotten I'd recorded it), whose tiny, disembodied voice ravished us completely. Suddenly, Herzog said: "I hear a rooster in the background!" And there it was, crowing somewhere in the Balinese countryside.

"It's strange," I said to him, "I've noticed that there are lots of chickens and roosters in your films, and in fact I was planning on telling you a Rabbi Nachman story about a prince who became a rooster."

"Please, I must hear it," Herzog insisted.

"In a distant land, a prince lost his mind and imagined himself a rooster. He took refuge under the dining room table, stripped naked and refused to eat anything but grain. The king called in magicians and doctors to cure his son, but to no avail. One day an unknown sage arrived, took off his clothes and joined the prince under the table, saying that he, too, was a rooster. Eventually, the sage convinced the prince to get dressed and finally to sit down to eat with the others. 'Don't ever think,' the sage told the prince, 'that by eating like man, with man, at his table, a rooster ceases to be what he is. You mustn't ever believe that it is enough for a rooster to behave like a man to become human; you can do anything with man, in his world and even for him, and yet remain the rooster that you are.'"

Werner Herzog made me promise to include this story here, along with our conversation that began in September 1975 and concluded in June 1976.

* * *

In your films you always show chickens and roosters as malevolent, scavenger-like creatures. You seem to be obsessed with them.

I've been searching all over the United States for the most gigantic rooster I could find, and recently I heard about a guy in Petaluma, California, who had raised a rooster named Weirdo. Weirdo weighed thirty pounds, Weirdo had died, but his offspring were alive and as big as he. So I went out to see Ralph, a thirty-one-pound rooster, and then found a horse that stood only twenty-two inches high. I wanted to film them—the rooster chasing the horse with a midget rider on it (the horse and midget rider together were shorter than Ralph)—but the guy who owned the horse refused to allow it to be taken to a sequoia tree forest, about 150 miles away.

I *am* obsessed with chickens. Take a close and very long look into the eye of a chicken and you'll see the most frightful kind of stupidity. Stupidity is always frightful. It's the devil: stupidity is the devil. Look in the eye of a chicken and then you'll know. It's the most horrifying, cannibalistic, and nightmarish creature in this world.

Once I had a dream. I dreamt that one of my girlfriends got married—I had wanted to marry her myself—and I was standing in the rear aisle of the church, while she was being interrogated by the priest, who held a big book and asked stereotyped questions like: "Do you reject all the powers of the demons?" and she replied: "Yes, I reject all of the powers of the demons," after which he intoned: "Do you reject all the tricky devices of the devil?" and so on. And all of a sudden I walked up the aisle, closed the book, and said: "There is no devil, there's only stupidity." They chased me out of the church, I fled with the bride, and at the corner of a street I took a left turn and went up the hill, and she took the right turn, and after twenty steps I realized that she was gone. So I ran back down this hill and just at the corner a mule came galloping by and hit me so hard that I woke up. . . . That's the dream.

In your films, I always get a sense of secret correspondences between animals and states of mind. The kneeling camel, for example, is another ubiquitous creature in your movie—in Kaspar Hauser *and, most powerfully, as the presiding presence over the final scenes of madness in* Even Dwarfs Started Small.

We tried out about sixty camels until we found one that was obedient enough to freeze in a position half between sitting and standing up. When a camel sits down it falls to its front knees and then sits down completely. And we had one camel whose owner would say, "Sit down," and before it sat down he'd then say, "Get up," "Sit down," "Get up"— and finally the camel was so confused that it froze halfway in this awkward position. The smallest dwarf begins his horrible laughing fit and the director of the institution goes berserk and points with his finger at a branch, demanding the branch to lower its arm while he himself raises his arm and says: "I will hold my arm out longer than you and I will stand longer than you." It seems as if this will go on for weeks and weeks, and that when you return three weeks later they will still be there, the camel kneeling. It's so pathetic, it really moves me. And I only know the camel has to be there. Without the camel the film is nothing.

Animals are so important in my films. But I have no abstract concept that a particular kind of animal signifies this or that, just a clear knowledge that they have an enormous weight in the movies.

Giordano Bruno wrote: "The forms of deformed animals are beautiful in heaven." A number of persons have wondered why you seem fascinated with "deformed" people in your movies.

That's a great statement, but there are no deformed people in my films. The dwarfs, for example, are well proportioned. What *is* deformed are the very normal, average things: consumer goods, magazines, a chair, a doorknob—and the religious behavior, table manners, educational system. *These* are the monstrosities, not the dwarfs.

But there's another aspect to the way you present animals in your films. Sometimes—as with the turtle in Fata Morgana, *the swan in* Kaspar Hauser—*they appear as creatures whose presence conveys a sense of liberation suggested in one of the most famous passages from Walt Whitman's* Song of Myself:

> *I think I could turn and live with animals, they are so placid*
> *   and self-contain'd,*
> *I stand and look at them long and long.*
> *They do not sweat and whine about their condition,*
> *They do not lie awake in the dark and weep for their sins,*
> *They do not make me sick discussing their duty to God,*
> *Not one is dissatisfied, not one is demented with the mania of*
> *   owning things . . .*

Yes, Whitman can say it in words, I can't. I can show it only. But it comes very close to what my animals are about . . . But not the chickens: they're vicious, neurotic, the Real Danger.

Chickens are birds, but birds that can't fly. Perhaps that's one reason you dislike them so much.

Yes, maybe it has some significance, because I myself can't fly. I used to love ski jumping, but I had to give it up. I was so deeply shocked by an accident that happened to my best friend who almost died.

I have to tell you the story that's in my film *The Great Ecstasy of the Sculptor Steiner*. Steiner—who's a woodcarver and, in my opinion, the world's greatest ski jumper—had a photo album that I happened to leaf through, and there were pictures in it of when he was a kid, and one strange shot of a raven. So I asked him about the raven, I kept bothering him about it, and finally he told me the story.

When he was twelve, his only friend was a raven, which he raised and fed. And both the raven and Steiner were embarrassed by their friendship, so the raven would wait for him far away from the schoolhouse, and when all the other kids were gone it flew onto his shoulder and, together, they'd walk through the forest. Finally the raven lost its feathers and the other ravens started to pick on him and hack him. The raven wanted to flee, it fell down from the tree because it couldn't fly anymore, and Walter Steiner shot his own raven because he couldn't stand the cruelty any longer.

At this point in the film there's a cut, and you see Steiner flying in slow motion for more than a minute. On skis he flies. An incredible man, he flies in complete ecstasy, as if into a ravine, as if he were going into the darkest abyss that is imaginable. He flies into it, and he flies and flies and then lands, he is all alone on that slope, and you see him in a blurred, very strange way. Then a text appears, a written text based on words by Robert Walser, over the image. And it says: "I should be all alone in this world, I, Steiner, and no other living being. No sun, no culture, I naked on a high rock, no storm, no snow, no streets, no banks, no money, no time, and no breath. Then I wouldn't be afraid anymore."

In Goethe's novel Elective Affinities, *one of the characters says: "We may imagine ourselves in any situation we like, but we always think of ourselves as seeing. I believe that the reason man dreams is because he should not stop seeing. Some day perhaps the inner light will shine forth from us, and then we shall need no other light." I quote this because it seems to me that the mystery of your films lies in the way you reveal this special inner light emanating from the autistic, the deaf, the dumb, and the blind.*

Yes, I always try to go to the innermost light that is burning inside of us. In *Kaspar Hauser,* Kaspar is writing his name with weeds in the grass, and his face reveals this light. Or when Kaspar says, "I dreamt of the Caucasus"—you see it then, too.

I hardly ever dream in my life, I have a dream maybe once in a year. But when I walk, for example, I live whole novels. Or when I drive for a long time in the car I see whole films, and I get afraid. And one time I almost had an accident in my car because there were hundreds of butterflies in the car and they wouldn't get out. I knew they weren't real so I stopped the car and let them out. I opened the door, but still they wouldn't go. I was on the Autobahn in the country, but it was as if I were on a big street in Vienna, with old-fashioned houses and hundreds of people leaning out, staring at me, and I was frightened, and I was driving and there were these butterflies around my head . . . and whole stories developed out of it.

There's also an extraordinary dreamlike quality to your directing and editing. In the beginning of Even Dwarfs Started Small, *for example, you show Hombre, the smallest midget, sitting between the windows as he's being interrogated, and when he says, "My ears are ringing. Someone is thinking of me," the camera . . .*

Yes, that's the only time the camera moves, the camera starts to move toward the window and looks out of the window because Hombre looks at the window and says, "Someone is thinking of me," and then you see that barren place as the camera moves away in a half circle.

At that moment you hear on the soundtrack that otherworldly malagueña melody sung by a young Spanish girl, and then you see the landscape again, but this time from a distance and almost in a mist, as if the landscape were now being seen by a different and higher consciousness.

Yes, I direct animals and I also claim that you can even direct a landscape.

In Fata Morgana, *the narrator says: "In paradise you cross the sand without seeing your shadow. There is landscape even without deeper meaning."*

It's even stated twice. . . . There is something visionary about these landscapes, the way they're shown. Most of my films have their origins in locations and landscapes, and then they start to build up around those locations.

I'm looking for new images in film. I'm sick of the images in magazines, I'm sick of postcards, I'm sick of walking into a travel agency and seeing a Pan Am poster of the Grand Canyon: it's a waste of worn-out images. And somehow I have the positive knowledge of new images, like a far-distant strip of land on the horizon—I see new images and try to articulate them. I've tried to do this in *Fata Morgana* and in the dream sequences in *Kaspar Hauser*. I'm trying to discover our innermost conditioning, it's a very deep-down brooding knowledge.

We were listening before to some music of the thirteenth and fourteenth centuries: *that's* my time. Every person can be identified with a certain type of landscape or season. A man like de Gaulle—his landscape is Lorraine, and to me he's a November person. And perhaps a certain epoch of time would apply as well.

Some people have written that I'm a figure out of the nineteenth century, but they're wrong. The appropriate time for me would be the late Middle Ages. I feel close to the music and painting of that time. It would also fit the concept of my work. I don't feel like an artist, I feel like a craftsman. All the sculptors and painters of that period didn't regard themselves as artists, but rather as craftsmen, and they did professional work as craftsman. That is exactly how I feel about my work as a filmmaker—as if I were anonymous, I couldn't even care.

I knew, for instance, that *Fata Morgana* was very frail, that the film itself was like a cobweb and very sensitive. I said to my friends: I've made a film now, but it has to be untouched. There shouldn't be any brutality. It shall be untouched, anonymous, I will keep it and show it only to my very best friend before I die. And this friend has to keep and before he dies must show it and hand it over to his best friend, and it should go on like that for a few generations . . . and only then might it be released. I kept the film for almost two years without showing it, and then I was somehow pushed into it, tricked into it. It makes sense that it's being shown, but I did have that idea of never releasing it. And in fact I have a short film that I've not shown to anyone for twelve years—it's called *Game in the Sand*. A rooster is the leading character in the film, by the way. It's about four children and a rooster.

There's one scene in Kaspar Hauser *showing a carnival in which we see Kaspar hired out as a freak-show oddity;* Hombre, *who appeared in* Even Dwarfs Started Small; *and the young Mozart in a trance, peering into the deep holes of the earth, "his mind engrossed in his own twilight." It's interesting that this little scene by itself seems to contain in microcosm most of the thematic cells and motifs of all your films.*

It was in fact the idea for an entire movie that I was thinking of making. Kaspar Hauser literally comes out of darkness, dwarfs come out when night is at its darkest, and many of my figures come from the very deep night. It is the dark night that's in my films.

I couldn't help feeling that Kaspar Hauser's impassioned and craggily imperfect piano performance of the Mozart sonata suggested that the spirit of Mozart was somehow entrapped in the sonata-allegro form itself.

Exactly, I feel so much compassion when I hear how Bruno played the piece. That's exactly right. People used to laugh at his performances because they'd say, "Oh, this is ridiculous and dilettantish," and I'd say, "No, this is the great cultural event of the year, it's not Bernstein or von Karajan: this agitation, this sheer agitation of the mind is culture. This is the true culture, that's what culture is, and therefore he's a great man, he is really great." People don't understand it, but they will.

There are two other wonderful scenes in Kaspar Hauser: *the desert dream sequence, for one, in which Kaspar is told that the mountains are just his imagination . . .*

The blindness of that old leader of the caravan . . . that's his virtue because he cannot be misled. He tastes the sand as if it were food and leads the people out of the desert because he's blind. This is his virtue . . .

And then the scene on the lake with the swan gliding . . .

And the boat. The boat drifts into it, but they don't row, they stopped rowing just outside the frame, and it just drifts into the frame. . . . For five consecutive nights the crew went to the lake at 3:00 a.m., and we waited until 4:00, and each time there was something wrong—we wanted it a little foggy and there was no fog. That swan rests calmly at one point, and all of a sudden it starts to move, and the music . . . by Albinoni . . . we organized the music to the movement of the swan. Just look at how the animal starts to swim away and how the music pulls with it.

The most beautiful and privileged moments in your films either occur in silence ("Can't you hear that terrible screaming all around us that men call silence?" are the words that appear at the beginning of Kaspar Hauser*) or are accompanied by a music that seems to represent a kind of audible silence.*

Silence is very important in *Aguirre,* for example. We spent weeks recording birds' voices, and I composed the soundtrack out of eight tapes, and there isn't one single voice of a bird that isn't properly placed as if in a big choir. All of a sudden there is silence. And when there's silence, someone is going to die on the raft because it means that Indians must be hiding in the trees, and all the birds stop singing. Everybody's so afraid that they start to scream and shout and to fire their rifles in order not to hear the silence.

I also remember the eerie, noisy silence when the soldier goes mad in Signs of Life, *walking in that field filled with what looks like thousands of whirring windmills—I think that's one of the most haunting moments I've ever experienced in films.*

Yes, it starts with silence and then there's a very strange sound. I took a recording of the applause of about fifteen hundred people after a concert and distorted this applause electronically in such a way that it sounds like the clacking of wood. Have you ever placed your ear against a telephone pole when there was a lot of wind? As children we used to call it the "angels singing." And that kind of sound goes over it. There were ten thousand windmills. People ask me what kind of trick I used, but it was nothing but a normal camera that looked across this field with ten thousand windmills. This is exactly what I was referring to before with regard to the new images I'm after: something that is even beyond what one can dream, something beyond our dreams.

I also remember one powerful scene in Even Dwarfs Started Small *in which you see scavenger chickens, then a willowlike tree with leaves in mist, then goggle-helmeted dwarfs with their sticks, sitting like little boys pretending to be kings in the stone garden . . .*

I really like that scene. You can't describe it and there are no words to explain the strength of those images. I'm glad you've seen these things.

And then there's that first image in Land of Silence and Darkness—*a ski jumper flying through the air and the innocent, wavering voice of a deaf and blind woman saying: "When I'm touched I jump."*

I asked the woman to say this line—she'd never seen a ski jumper—and I said: "This is going to be important for the film, maybe you don't understand but please say this text for me as if you'd seen the ski jumper." I'm not a cinéma vérité person, I hate cinéma vérité, by the way. There is such a thing as the plain truth, but there are also different dimensions in truth—and in film there are more dimensions beyond the cinéma vérité truth. That's where it starts to become exciting.

In your films, these new forms of truth often occur when language disintegrates. There's that scene in Signs of Life *when the soldiers meet this young autistic girl . . .*

The two soldiers are on this reconnaissance, and they meet a shepherd who gives them water to drink. And there's that little girl, and he says: "This girl, my daughter, can hardly speak at all because it's so lonely up here. I'm out at night with the sheep and my wife is away during the day and we don't talk, so, even though she is seven years old, she can hardly talk at all. Sometimes she picks up a few words down in the town when she sees her aunt." And then all of a sudden, the father wants to demonstrate that his daughter is really all right, and he asks her: "Please, won't you say the words of a song for those gentlemen." And the girl starts to recite the text of a song, but all of a sudden she gets stuck, she loses her speech, and she starts to twist her skirt in despair, she's so upset. It's a poem I wrote myself about sheep, ninety-eight sheep in Lasithi Mountain (it's a mountain range in Crete), and one of them got lost. The text goes: "Hurry ye shepherds, hurry. For over the range, there are circling the vultures." And she doesn't remember the word "vultures," so she hesitates on that word.

It's important that she loses her speech only minutes before the soldier goes insane. The same thing almost occurred to me when I climbed up that mountain and looked down into that valley with the ten thousand windmills. I sat down and it was at that very moment when I was sure I was insane. And I had a very hard time getting out of that place. . . . I claim that I'm not insane. I think the others are, or most of the others are. I think I make sense to some extent. But that was a moment when I felt I must be insane: it can't be true, it can't be real.

In all of my films, in moments of utmost despair, there's silence and an exchange of signals—people exchange some kind of signals. You don't see the soldier anymore as a private person, as a psychological figure. You see him from a distance of four hundred yards away, like an ant, as little as that. And he gives signals or signs—the same kind of signs of violence and despair that he himself had received all the time. He wants to destroy the whole town with toy rockets. It's humiliating for him. It's such a humiliation that he only scorches a chair and he only manages to kill a donkey. And that's all, and then he's captured by his own people.

He lacks the divine madness of Kaspar Hauser, doesn't he?

But they are close to each other, too, because both try to articulate themselves and their loneliness.

The overwhelming intensity of your films makes some people feel that you lack a sense of irony.

I don't understand irony. I recently received a national film award, which gave me a lot of money for my next film. So two days after I had received a letter from the minister of the interior, the phone rang and I picked it up and a voice said: "This is the minister of the interior." And I said, "Well, sir . . ." And that guy started to stutter: "I'm so sorry. We've made such a mistake that I personally had to call you up. We sent you a letter saying that you've received a big award, but it's a mistake. And I had to tell you." So I said: "Sir, how could this have happened? I mean, there are three signatures on this letter. It must have passed through three departments. It's all right, I accept this, but how can this have happened? How can this occur?" Then, after ten minutes of talking, this guy started to scream with laughter. And then I found out it was a friend of mine who was just pulling a trick on me. It's a habit to kid each other in the United States. But I'm just like a fool, I'm sitting around like a fool because I take it all literally. There are things in language that are common to many people, or to almost all, but they are lost on me. I have some defects of communication in the form of language.

I was very silent as a child, and violent. I was very choleric and really dangerous to other kids because I didn't speak for days, and they kept singing around me and just pulling on me, and all of a sudden there was an outburst of rage and violence and despair.

I read that after you finished making Even Dwarfs Started Small, *you jumped into a giant, seven-foot cactus.*

There were always catastrophes. During the shooting of that film, I was so shocked by the fact that one of the dwarfs caught fire—you know, they take gasoline to water the flowers and they set a flowerpot aflame, and all of a sudden one of those guys was just burning like a tree. And all of the rest of the crew looked at him as if this guy were a Christmas tree, with open eyes and giving them a beautiful stare. So I was the first one to react. I jumped over that little guy, buried him under me, and extinguished the flames—his face was only a little scorched. And then two days later the same guy was hit by the car that was circling around him. The guy fell and the empty car went right over him. That man just stood up and walked away, but when that occurred I couldn't continue and had to stop shooting.

There was a big field of cactuses, each with long spines as long as my finger. And I said to them: "If all of you survive this shooting, if all of you get out of it unhurt, I will do the big cactus leap, and you can have the camera." And so, the last day of shooting, when it was all over, they took the super-8-millimeter camera. I put on big goggles to protect my eyes, and I really took a big jump. Today there are still some spines in my knee sinews from the jump. The bad thing wasn't the leap itself but the getting out of it . . . that's painful. I suffered for half a year. I didn't imagine beforehand how painful it would be.

There were many catastrophes during the shooting of *Fata Morgana*, too. In the Cameroons, we wanted to cross the country to get to an eastern Congolese province for some locations there. Unfortunately there was an aborted coup d'état a few weeks before we arrived. Some mercenaries had been involved in the whole thing, one of them was condemned to death in absentia, and unfortunately, the cameraman had almost an identical name as one of the mercenaries. So we were captured at night and dragged into prison, I had malaria and a very bad parasitic disease. We were hardly able to hold the camera still because we were shaking with fever and we were locked into a room that was maybe fifteen by eighteen feet, but there were more than seventy people cramped together in that room. There was no light, no water, and people were tortured to death, two of them died. And we were very badly mistreated there. It went on like that, too. There was a warrant out for us all over the country. And either on purpose or out of slovenliness the officials forgot to destroy that warrant. So every time we passed through a town, we were arrested.

Just before the shooting of *Signs of Life*, the military coup d'état occurred in Greece, and everything was forbidden to us. I was forbidden to have fireworks in my film. I told the army major: "It's so essential, it's the main motif in the film. This film is more important than your private life and my private life. And you're just scared because you might do something wrong when you allow this. I will do it, even though it's forbidden." And he said: "Then we'll arrest you." And I said to him: "Go on and arrest me. But I won't be without a firearm tomorrow. Keep in mind that the very first man who touches me, who lays a hand on me to arrest me, will drop down dead with me." And I was not unarmed next morning. There were fifty policemen and soldiers who watched us, and three thousand people of the town who wanted to see the fireworks—they all watched us and nobody dared to touch me.

It seems to me that Aguirre *is about a man who takes his imagination to be reality and that* Kaspar Hauser *is about a person who takes reality to be his imagination.*

That's a good formula. And my new film is in between *Aguirre* and *Kaspar Hauser*—both stylistically, in terms of the images and action, and thematically, in terms of the idea of the striving for something . . . not for Eldorado this time but for a special ruby glass.

The film is called *Heart of Glass*, and it's about a legendary prophet in Bavarian folklore—a shepherd with prophetic gifts and visions. The story is mine and tells of a disaster at a glass factory. The prophet is called in because the secret required for the mixture of this very valuable glass has been lost. Everyone becomes halfway insane and the prophet foresees that the factory is going to burn down. At the end, the factory owner performs a ritual murder of a fifteen-year-old servant girl, thinking that virgin blood in the mixture will create rubies. He burns his own place down, as foreseen, but the prophet is blamed for it and is imprisoned. Here he has a vision of a place so remote from the inhabited world that the few people living there haven't learned that the world is round. And the prophet has a vision of a man standing on the cliff and staring for years over the ocean. And years later a second person joins him, then another, until four men stand over the ocean, which, for them, ends in an abyss. And after many years of hypnotic staring, they decide to take a rowboat and find the end of the world. . . . Most of the film was shot in a glass factory and in a forest in northern Bavaria. And the prophet's vision was shot fifteen miles off the west Irish coast on a little island where monks built a settlement fourteen hundred years ago.

I've heard that you hypnotized the members of your cast for this film.

I have to say that I was interested in hypnosis mainly for the way it could be used as a means of stylization. We tested out about 450 people and we needed persons who could be hypnotized under very difficult circumstances—standing around with reflectors shining on them and with a lot of activity going on. And they had to be hypnotized so deeply that they could open their eyes without waking up. However, we rehearsed the basic movements and lines of the dialogue without hypnosis.

During the tryouts, I wanted to find out about the poetic quality of the cast, so I hypnotized them and said: "You are in a beautiful and exotic land which no person from our country has ever set foot on. Look in front of you—there is an enormous cliff, but on looking at it more closely you'll find that it's actually one solid piece of emerald." And I continued: "In this country, a couple of hundred years ago, a holy monk lived here and he was a poet and he spent his entire life engraving just one inscription into this emerald cliff." And I said: "Open your eyes, you can read this inscription."

And one of the men there who tends to the horses in the police stable—he took a look, opened his eyes, and read: "Why can't we drink the moon? Why is there no vessel to hold it?" And the guy next to him was a law student. He took a look and started to read: *"Dear Mother, I am doing fine, I just don't know where we're going, but I think everything is all right. Hugs and kisses, Your Son."*

MICK JAGGER
Some Girls

A certain prudent man, when he felt himself to be
in love, hung a little bell round his neck to caution
women that he was dangerous. Unfortunately for
themselves they took too much notice of it, and he
suffered accordingly.

— A. R. Orage

Paris, 1978

I've been missing the Rolling Stones for years—ever since they released *Exile
on Main Street,* as a matter of fact. Of course, I've seen them on their occasional concert tours, which have become more and more circus-like, and enjoyed
a number of their mid-seventies songs ("Star Star," "If You Really Want to Be
My Friend," "Time Waits for No One," "Fool to Cry," and "Memory Motel"). But
during their post-*Exile* period, the Stones seem to have been around more in
body than in spirit.

But now we have *Some Girls*—an album that draws on, in a remarkably
unhackneyed way, the Stones' love for blues, the Motown sound, country
music, and Chuck Berry, and that combines and transforms these elements
into the group's most energized, focused, outrageous, and original record
since the days of *Between the Buttons, Beggar's Banquet, Let It Bleed,* and *Exile
on Main Street.* And it is an album that crystallizes the Stones' perennial obsession with "some girls"—both real and imaginary. After years of standing

in the shadows, the soul survivors are back on their own, with no direction home, sounding just like . . . the Rolling Stones.

* * *

You've been a Rolling Stone for about fifteen years. How does it feel?

What a funny question! It's a long time, maybe too long. Maybe it's time to restart a cycle—yeah, restart a five-year cycle.

Maybe we can start talking about "Miss You," which you've released in three versions: a 45 disc, an LP track, and a twelve-minute version on which there's a fantastic harmonica solo by a guy named Sugar Blue, who plays like a snake charmer.

Yeah, my friend Sandy Whitelaw discovered him playing in the Paris Metro. He's a blues harpist from America, and he plays not only in the subway but in a club called La Vielle Grille. He's a very strange and talented musician.

The lines in the song about being called up at midnight by friends wanting to drag you out to a party remind me of "Get Off of My Cloud."

I've a limited number of ideas. *[Laughing]*

You once sang: "I only get my rocks off while I'm dreaming."

I don't dream more than anybody else. But dreams are a great inspiration for the lowliest rock 'n' roll writer to the greatest playwrights. Chaucer was a great one for dreams. He was a great one for explaining them and making fun of the astrological explanations. He used to take the piss out of most of them, but some of them he took seriously. Shakespeare, too, knew a lot about early English witchcraft and religion, and Chaucer had some sort of similar knowledge. Today we have psychiatrists to interpret dreams.

Have you ever been to one?

Never, not once. I've read a lot of Jung, and I would have gone to see him because he was interesting. . . . Anyway, dreams are very important, and I get good ideas from them. I don't jot them down, I just remember them— the experiences of them—they're so different from everyday experiences.

In "Moonlight Mile" there's the beautiful line, "I'm hiding sister and I'm dreaming."

Yeah, that's a dream song. Those kinds of songs with kinds of dreamy sounds are fun to do, but not all the time—it's nice to come back to reality.

What about the girl with the faraway eyes on your new album ("Faraway Eyes")? The lines "And if you're downright disgusted and life ain't worth a dime / Get a girl with faraway eyes" make it sound as if this dreamy truck-stop girl from Bakersfield, California, is really real.

Yeah, she's a real girl.

Is she a girl you know?

Yeah, she's right across the room . . . a little bleary-eyed.

Well, there's no one else here except for that poster of a Japanese girl. Is that whom you mean?

Naw, she's not in a truck stop.

Right she's standing under a parasol, in fact . . . Let me have another glass of wine and maybe I'll see her, too!

You know, when you drive through Bakersfield on a Sunday morning or Sunday evening—I did that about six months ago—all the country-music radio stations start broadcasting black gospel services live from L.A. And that's what the song refers to. But the song's really about driving alone, listening to the radio.

I sense a bit of a Gram Parsons feeling on "Faraway Eyes"—country music as transformed through his style, via Buck Owens.

I knew Gram quite well, and he was one of the few people who really helped me to sing country music—before that, Keith and I used to just copy it off records. I used to play piano with Gram, and on "Faraway Eyes" I'm playing piano, though Keith is actually playing the top part—we added it on after. But I wouldn't say this song was influenced specifically by Gram. That idea of country music played slightly tongue-in-cheek—Gram had that in "Drugstore Truck Drivin' Man," and we have that sardonic quality, too.

The title of your new album is the title of one of your most powerful and out-rageous songs—"Some Girls"—and I wanted to ask you about some of the girls in your songs. Here are a few lines taken at random from several of your older albums: "Who's that woman on your arm / All dressed up to do you harm?" ("Let It Loose"); "Women think I'm tasty / But they're always trying to waste me" ("Tumbling Dice"); "But there is one thing I will never understand / Some of the sick things a girl does to a man" ("Sittin' on a Fence").

I didn't write all those lines, you know. *[Laughing]*

All right, we'll reduce the charge. But obviously, in your songs of the mid-sixties, you were at pains to accuse girls of being deceptive, cheating, greedy, vain, af-fected, and stupid. It was a list of sins. Whether you were singing about rejecting the girl ("Out of Time," "Please Go Home") or about the girl rejecting you ("All Sold Out," "Congratulations") or about both ("High and Dry," "Under My Thumb"), almost all the songs from that period . . .

Most of those songs are really silly, they're pretty immature. But as far as the heart of what you're saying, I'd say . . . any bright girl would under-stand that if I were gay I'd say the same things about guys. Or if I were a girl I might say the same things about guys or other girls. I don't think any of the traits you mentioned are peculiar to girls. It's just about people. Deception, vanity . . . On the other hand sometimes I do say nice things about girls. *[Laughing]*

Some of those other girls—Ruby Tuesday, Child of the Moon, or the girls in songs like "She's a Rainbow" and "Memory Motel"—are all very elusive and mystical.

Well, the girl in "Memory Motel" is actually a real, independent Ameri-can girl. But they are mostly imaginary, you're right. . . . Actually, the girl in "Memory Motel" is a combination. So was the girl in "Faraway Eyes." Nearly all the girls in my songs are combinations.

What about in "Till the Next Goodbye"?

No she was real *[laughing]*, she was real. . . . If you really want to know about the girls on the new album: "Some Girls" is all combinations. "Beast of Burden" is a combination. "Miss You" is an emotion, it's not really about *a* girl. To me, the feeling of longing is what the song is—I don't like to interpret my own fucking songs—but that's what it is.

You mentioned Jung before, and it seems to me that your "dream" girls are what Jung called anima figures. Do you ever think in those terms?

My anima is very strong . . . I think it's very kind. What you're saying, though, is that there are two different types of girls in my songs: there's the beautiful dreamy type and the vicious bitch type. There are also one or two others, but, yeah, you're right—there are two kinds of girls . . . only I never thought about it before.

You don't have too many girls in your songs that share both qualities.

Ah, I see, I'm not integrating them properly. Maybe not. Maybe "Beast of Burden" is integrated slightly: I don't want a beast of burden, I don't want the kind of woman who's going to drudge for me. The song says: I don't need a beast of burden, and I'm not going to be your beast of burden, either. Any woman can see that that's like my saying that I don't want a woman to be on her knees for me. I mean, I get accused of being very antigirl, right?

Right.

But people really don't listen, they get it all wrong; they hear "Beast of Burden" and say, "*Argggh!*"

They sure heard "Under My Thumb" ("Under my thumb's a squirming dog who's just had her day").

That's going back to my teenage years!

Well, it's both a perverse and brilliant song about power and sex.

At the time there was no feminist criticism because there was no such thing, and one just wrote what one felt. Not that I let it hinder me too much now. . . . Did you hear about the dinner honoring Ahmet Ertegun [president of Atlantic Records]? Some feminists were giving out leaflets saying what terrible things he'd done, saying that the Average White Band's new cover depicts a naked woman standing in a steaming bath of water, which could cause "enormous pain and possible death" *[laughing]*—things like that.

How about your woman-in-bondage poster for your Black and Blue *album?*

Many people may have a deep masochistic streak, but that poster and some of your songs certainly seem hung up on that.

Yeah, we had a lot of trouble with that particular poster. As far as the songs go, one talks about one's own experience a lot of the time. And you know, a lot of bright girls just take all of this with a pinch of salt. But there are a lot of women who *are* disgraceful, and if you just have the misfortune to have an affair with one of those . . . it's a personal thing.

And the "squirming dog" image?

Well, that was a joke. I've never felt in that position vis-à-vis a person—I'd never want to really hurt someone.

That bondage poster, though, was pretty blatant.

Well, there are a lot of girls into that, they dig it, they want to be chained up—and it's a thing that's true for both sexes.

But why use it to advertise a record?

I don't see why not. It's a valid piece of commercial art, just a picture.

Would you show yourself getting whipped and beaten?

Sure, if I thought it was more commercial than a beautiful girl!

People are obviously going to take a few of these songs on the new LP as being about your domestic situation.

Well, I actually mention "my wife" in "Respectable."

"Get out of my life, go take my wife—don't come back." And there's also "You're a rag trade girl, you're the queen of porn / You're the easiest lay on the White House lawn."

Well, I just thought it was funny. "Respectable" really started off as a song in my head about how "respectable" we as a band were supposed to have become. "We're" so respectable. As I went along with the singing, I just made things up and fit things in. "Now we're respected in society . . ." I really meant *us*. My wife's a very honest person, and the song's not "about" her.

But people will probably take this song, as well as the album, to be about you, in the same way they took Blood on the Tracks *to be about Dylan or John Lennon's "I don't believe in Beatles" song to be about him.*

But it's very rock 'n' roll. It's not like "Sara." "Respectable" is very light-hearted when you *hear* it. That's why I don't like divorcing the lyrics from the music. 'Cause when you actually hear it sung, it's not what is, it's the way we do it. "Get out of my life, go take my wife—don't come back" . . . it's not supposed to be taken seriously. If it were a ballad, if I sang it like: "*Pleeease,* taaake my wiiiiife"—you know what I mean?—well, it's not that, it's just a shit-kicking rock 'n' roll number.

Keith Richards once said something to the effect that rock 'n' roll really is subversive because the rhythms alter your being and perceptions. With your words and your rhythms, your stuff could do and has done that, don't you think?

Rhythms are very important. But subvert what?

Well, Keith Richards's implication was that words could be used to lie, but that what the Stones did was just to let you see clearly the way things were. And that that vision—or so I inferred—was what was subversive.

Maybe Keith did mean that. Music is one of the things that changes society. That old idea of not letting white children listen to black music is true, 'cause if you want white children to remain what they are, they mustn't.

Look at what happened to you. [Laughing]

Exactly! You get different attitudes to things . . . even the way you walk . . .

And the way you talk.

Right, and the way you talk. Remember the twenties when jazz in Europe changed a lot of things. People got more crazy, girls lifted up their dresses and cut their hair. People started to dance to that music, and it made profound changes in that society. . . . That sounds awfully serious.

To keep on the semi-serious keel for a second, the song "Some Girls" seems to be about what happens when hundreds of idealized twenties girls—like the ones drawn by Guy Peellaert on your It's Only Rock 'n' Roll *album—decide to come to life, and, like maenads, try to eat you, destroy you—taking your money and clothes and giving you babies you don't want.*

Well, it could be a bad dream in a way. I had a dream like that last night, incidentally, but there were dogs as well as girls in it.

Maybe you can call your next album Some Dogs.

[Laughing] I'd get in trouble with the anti-dog defamation league.

I wonder what the girls and women, of all races, are going to think of lines like: "Chinese girls, they're so gentle—they're really such a tease."

I think they're all well covered—everyone's represented. *[Laughing]* Most of the girls I've played the song to *like* "Some Girls." They think it's funny. Black girlfriends of mine just laughed. And I think it's very complimentary about Chinese girls, I think they come off better than English girls. I really like girls an awful lot, and I don't think I'd say anything really nasty about any of them.

Are you running for president?

[Laughing] The song's supposed to be funny. I remember that when I wrote it, it was very funny. 'Cause we were laughing, and the phone was ringing, and I was just sitting in the kitchen and it was just coming out . . . and I thought I could go on forever!

The first time I heard it, I started making up my own lyrics: "Green girls get me anxious / Blue girls get me sad / Violet girls get me silly / And red girls make me mad." It's like a kid's song.

[Laughing] That's why I said it wasn't serious, it's just anything that came to my head.

Do you remember the Beach Boys' "California Girls"?

Yeah, I love that song.

Well, it seems to me that instead of all the girls in your song being California girls, they've all turned into a different type of girl, and certainly from another state.

I know what you mean. I never thought of it like that. I never thought that a rock critic of your knowledge and background could ever come out with an observation like that. *[Laughing]*

You mean it's pretentious?

Not at all. It's a great analogy. But like all analogies, it's false. *[Laughing]*

On your It's Only Rock n' Roll *album you did a great version of the Temptations' "Ain't Too Proud to Beg," and now you're doing a version of "Just My Imagination."*

It's like a continuation, and I've always wanted to do that song—originally as a duet with Linda Ronstadt, believe it or not. But instead we just did our version of it—like an English rock 'n' roll band tuning up on "Imagination," which has only two or three chords . . . it's real simple stuff.

I like the lines: "Soon you and me will be married and raise a family / Two boys for you, what about two girls for me?" There are those girls in there again.

Yeah, I made that up. In reality the girl in the song doesn't even know me—it's a dream . . . and we're back where we started this conversation.

"Of all the girls in New York she loves me true" is one of the lines from "Imagination." And in fact the entire album is full of New York City settings and energy.

Yeah, I added the New York reference in the song. And the album itself is like that because I was staying in New York part of last year, and when I got to Paris and was writing the words, I was thinking about New York. I wrote the songs in Paris.

It's a real New York record.

Hope they like it in South Jersey. *[Laughing]*

There's the gay garbage collector on Fifty-third Street in "When the Whip Comes Down," Central Park in "Miss You," the sex and dreams and parties and the schmattas on Seventh Avenue in "Shattered"—and there's a distinct Lou Reed-cum-British vaudeville tone to some of your singing on "Shattered."

Every time I play guitar my engineer, Chris Kimsey, says: "Oh, here comes Lou Reed again." But I think a lot of English singers do that—there's a kind of tradition, it's natural. In "Shattered," Keith and Woody [Ron Wood] put a riff down, and all we had was the word "shattered." So I just made the rest up and thought it would sound better if it were half talked. I'd written some of my verses before I got into the studio, but I don't like to keep singing the same thing over and over, so it changed. And I was noticing that there were a lot of references to New York, so I kept it like that. *Some Girls* isn't a "concept" album, God forbid, but it's nice that some of the songs have connections with each other—they make the album hold together a bit. . . . But then there's the girl with faraway eyes!

JOHN LENNON
December 5, 1980

New York City, 1980

"Welcome to the inner sanctum!" said John Lennon, as he greeted me with high-spirited, mock ceremoniousness at the entrance to Yoko Ono's office in their ground-floor apartment in the Dakota—the quasi-Gothic, castle-like edifice, with its gables, gargoyles, and wrought-iron gates on New York City's Upper West Side. It was Friday evening, December 5, 1980.

I removed my shoes and entered an iridescent, white-carpeted room and saw Yoko sitting on an enormous pearl-white plush couch. I sat down next to her, and when I looked up I noticed that the entire ceiling was in fact a trompe l'oeil sky filled with what uncannily appeared to be floating and drifting gossamer clouds. Yoko began explaining to me how the collaborative new album, *Double Fantasy*, had come about. Last spring, John and their son, Sean, were vacationing for three weeks in Bermuda while Yoko stayed home "sorting out business," as she put it. While in Bermuda, John phoned her to say that he had taken Sean to the Botanical Gardens, where, under a cedar tree, he had come across some delicate white-and-yellow flowers called a Double Fantasy. "It's a type of freesia," John would later say, "but what it means to us is that if two people picture the same image at the same time, that is the secret."

John now entered the inner sanctum, and Yoko said that she'd be leaving us for a while so that we could chat. John sat down on the couch and explained: "I was at a dance club one night in Hamilton when I was in Bermuda. Upstairs, they were playing disco, and downstairs I suddenly heard 'Rock Lobster' by the B-52s for the first time. Do you know it? It sounds just like Yoko's music, so I said to meself, 'It's time to get out the old axe and wake the wife up!'" She and John spoke on the phone every day and sang the songs that would ultimately be included on *Double Fantasy* and which they had composed in between their phone calls.

"Someone mentioned to me," I said to John, "that you've had a guitar hanging on the wall behind your bed for the past five or six years, and that you only recently took it down to play on *Double Fantasy.* Is that true?"

"I bought this beautiful electric guitar, round about the period I got back with Yoko and had the baby," John explained. "It's not a normal guitar; it doesn't have a body; it's just an arm and this tube-like, toboggan-looking thing, and you can lengthen the top for the balance of it if you're sitting or standing up. I played it a little, then just hung it up behind the bed, but I'd look at it every now and then, because it had never done a professional thing, it had never really been played. I didn't want to hide it the way one would hide an instrument because it was too painful to look at—like Artie Shaw went through a big thing and never played his clarinet again. But I used to look at it and think, 'Will I ever pull it down?'

"On the top of the guitar I'd placed a wooden number nine that some kid had sent me and a dagger Yoko had given me—a dagger made out of a bread knife from the American Civil War to cut away the bad vibes, to cut away the past symbolically. It was just like a picture that hangs there but you never really see, and then recently I realized, 'Oh, goody! I can finally find out what this guitar is all about,' and I took it down and used it in making *Double Fantasy.*"

"So that guitar wasn't gently weeping behind you for five years?" I asked.

"Mine *never* weeped," he replied. "Mine screams or it's not on at all!"

"I've been playing *Double Fantasy* over and over," I started to say to John overexcitedly, "and it's fantastic, but I've only heard it for the past three or four days and I wish I had it before—"

"How are you?" John interrupted, and looked at me with a time- and interview-stopping smile. "You don't have to rush, we've got hours and hours and hours. It's been like a reunion for us these last few weeks. We've seen Ethan Russell, who's doing a videotape of a couple of the new songs, and Annie Leibovitz was here. She took my first *Rolling Stone* cover photo. It's been fun seeing everyone we used to know and doing it all again—we've all survived. When did *we* first meet?"

"I met you and Yoko on September 17, 1968," I said, remembering the first of many future encounters. I was just a lucky guy, at the right place at the right time. John had decided to become more "public" and to demystify his Beatles persona. He and Yoko, whom he'd met in November 1966, were preparing for the Amsterdam and Montreal bed-ins for peace, and were soon to release *Two Virgins,* the first of their experimental record collaborations, with its Shakespearean "noises, sounds, and sweet airs." The album cover—the infamous frontal nude portrait of them—was to grace the pages of *Rolling Stone*'s first-anniversary issue. John had just discovered the then-impoverished, San Francisco–based magazine, and he'd agreed to give *Rolling Stone* the first of his "coming-out" interviews. As "European editor," I was asked to visit John and Yoko and to take along a photographer (Ethan Russell, who later took the photos for the *Let It Be* book that accompanied the album). So, nervous and excited, we met John and Yoko at their temporary basement flat in London.

First impressions are usually the most accurate, and John was graceful, gracious, charming, exuberant, direct, witty, and playful; I remember noticing how he wrote little reminders to himself in the wonderfully absorbed way that a child paints the sun. He was due at a recording session in a half hour to work on the White Album, so we agreed to meet the next day to do the interview, but John and Yoko unexpectedly now invited Ethan and me to attend that day's session for "Glass Onion" and "Helter Skelter" at Abbey Road Studios. (I remember making myself scarce behind one of the giant studio speakers in order not to raise the hackles of the other at first visibly disconcerted three Beatles.) Only my attending a rehearsal for a Shakespeare play at the Globe Theater might have made me feel as imparadised as I did at that moment.

Every new encounter with John brought a new perspective. Once, in 1971, I ran into John and Yoko in New York City. My friend Ann Druyan and I had gone to see the film *Carnal Knowledge,* and afterward we bumped into the Lennons in the lobby. Accompanied by the yippie activist Jerry Rubin and one of his fellow travelers, they invited us to drive down with them to Ratner's restaurant on the Lower East Side for blintzes, where a beatific, long-haired young man approached our table and wordlessly handed John a card inscribed with a pithy saying of the inscrutable Meher Baba (the self-proclaimed Indian Avatar of the Age who supposedly kept a forty-four-year vow of silence until his death) and walked back to his table. Rubin took one disparaging look at the card, drew a swastika on the back of it, then got up and gave it back to the man. When the gloating Rubin returned, John admonished him gently, saying that wasn't the way to change someone's consciousness. As far as I was concerned, an audible avatar was sitting just beside me; and acerbic and skeptical as he could often be, John Lennon never lost his sense of compassion.

Almost ten years later, I was again talking to John, and he was as gracious and witty as the first time I met him. "I guess I should describe to the readers what you're wearing, John," I said. "Let me help you out," he offered, then intoned wryly: "You can see the glasses he's wearing. They're normal plastic blue-frame glasses. Nothing like the famous wire-rimmed Lennon glasses that he stopped using in 1973. He's wearing needle-cord pants, the same black cowboy boots he'd had made in Nudie's in 1973—"

"What's Nudie's?" I asked him.

"It's the famous cowboy shop in Hollywood where Elvis got his gold lamé suit. It's the place with the bull horns on the front, and everybody knows it."

"Except me."

"Now you do. . . . And he's wearing a Calvin Klein sweater and a torn Mick Jagger T-shirt that he got when the Stones toured in 1970 or so. And around his neck is a small, three-part diamond heart necklace that he bought as a makeup present after an argument with Yoko many years ago and that she later gave back to him in a kind of ritual. Will that do?

"But I know you've got a Monday deadline, so let's get boogieing!"

* * *

Double Fantasy is the first recording you've made in five years, and, to quote from your song "The Ballad of John and Yoko," "It's good to have the both of you back."

But the illusion that I was cut off from society is a joke. I was just the same as any of the rest of you, I was working from nine to five—baking bread and changing some nappies and dealing with the baby. People keep asking, "Why did you go underground, why were you hiding?" But I wasn't hiding. I went to Singapore, South Africa, Hong Kong, Bermuda. I've been everywhere in the bloody universe. And I did fairly average things, too . . . I went out to the movies.

But you weren't writing a lot of songs during those years.

I didn't write a damn thing. . . . You know, it was a big event for us to have a baby—people might forget how hard we tried to have one and how many miscarriages we had and near-death scenes for Yoko . . . and we actually had a stillborn child and a lot of problems with drugs, a lot of personal and public problems brought on by ourselves and with help from our friends. But whatever. We put ourselves in situations that were stress-ful, but we managed to have the child that we tried to have for ten years, and my God, we weren't going to blow it. We didn't *move* for a year, and I took up yoga with the gray-haired lady on TV. *[Laughing]*

*You can't really win. People criticized you for not writing and recording, but it's sometimes forgotten that your three previous albums—*Some Time in New York City, Walls and Bridges, *and* Rock 'n' Roll—*weren't universally praised . . . especially the agitprop* Some Time in New York City, *which in-cluded songs like "Attica State," "Sunday Bloody Sunday," and "Woman Is the Nigger of the World."*

Yeh, that was the one that really upset everyone. Yoko calls it "Bertolt Brecht," but, as usual, I didn't know who he was until she took me to see Richard Foreman's production of *The Threepenny Opera* four years ago, and then I saw the album in that light. I was always irritated by the *rushness* of sound on it, but I was consciously doing it like a newspaper where you get the misprints, the times and the facts aren't quite right, and there's that you've-got-to-get-it-out-by-Friday attitude.

But I've been attacked many, many times . . . and right from the be-ginning: "From Me to You" was "Below Par Beatles," don't forget that. That was the review in the *NME [New Musical Express]*. Jesus Christ, I'm *sorry.* Maybe it wasn't as good as "Please Please Me," I don't know, but "below par"? I'll never forget that one. And you know how bad the reviews were of our Plastic Ono albums? They shredded us! "Self-indulgent sim-plistic whining"—that was the main gist. It's the same assholes that booed Dylan for playing electric. Because those albums were about ourselves, you see, and not about Ziggy Stardust or Tommy. . . . And *Mind Games,* they *hated* it.

But it's not just *me.* Take Mick, for instance. Mick's put out consis-tently good work for twenty years, and will they give him a break? Will they ever say, "Look at him, he's Number One, he's thirty-six and he's put out a beautiful song, 'Emotional Rescue.'" I enjoyed it, a lot of people enjoyed it. And God help Bruce Springsteen when they decide he's no longer God. I haven't seen him—I'm not a great "in"-person watcher—but I've heard such good things about him from people I respect, and I might actually get out of bed to watch him. Right now his fans are happy. He's told them about being drunk and chasing girls and cars and everything, and that's about the level they enjoy. But when he gets down to facing his own success and growing older and having to produce it again and again, they'll turn on him, and I hope he survives it. All he has to do is look at me or at Mick. So it goes up and down, up and down—of course it does, but what are we, machines? What do they want from the guy, do they want him to kill himself onstage? Do they want me and Yoko to kill ourselves onstage? But when they criticized "From Me to You" as below par Beatles, that's when I first realized you've got to keep it up, there's some sort of system where you get on the wheel and you've got to keep going around.

Watching the wheels. What are those wheels?

The whole universe is a wheel, right? Wheels going round and round. They're my own wheels, mainly, but, you know, watching meself is like watching everybody else. And I watch meself through my child, too.

The thing about the child is . . . it's *still* hard. I'm not the greatest dad on earth, I'm doing me best. But I'm a very irritable guy, and I get depressed. I'm up and down, up and down, and he's had to deal with that, too—withdrawing from him and then giving, and withdrawing and giving. I don't know how much it will affect him in later life, but I've been *physically* there. We're all selfish, but I think so-called artists are *completely* selfish: to put Yoko or Sean or the cat or anybody in mind other than meself—me and my ups and downs and my tiddly problems—is a strain. Of course, there's a reward and a joy, but still . . .

So you fight against your natural selfish instincts.

Yeh, the same as taking drugs or eating bad food or not doing exercise. It's as hard as that to give to a child, it's not natural at all. Maybe it's the way we were all brought up, but it's very hard to think about somebody else, even your own child, to *really* think about him.

But you're thinking about him in a song like "Beautiful Boy."

Yeh, but that's easy . . . it's *painting.* Gauguin was stuck in fucking Tahiti, painting a big picture for his daughter—if the movie version I saw was true, right? So he's in fucking Tahiti painting a picture for her, she dies in Denmark, she didn't see him for twenty years, he has VD and is going out of his mind in Tahiti—he dies and the painting gets burnt anyway, so nobody ever sees the masterpiece of his fucking life. And I'm always thinking things like that. So I write a song about the child, but it would have done better for me to spend the time I wrote the fucking song actually playing ball with him. The hardest thing for me to do is *play* . . . I can do everything else.

You can't play?

Play, I can't. I try and invent things, I can draw, I can watch TV with him. I'm great at that, I can watch any garbage, as long as I don't have to move around, and I can talk and read to him and go out and take him with me for a coffee and things like that.

That's weird, because your drawings and so many of the songs you've written are really playful.

That probably came from Paul more than from me.

What about "Good Morning Good Morning"? That's one of yours. It's a great song, a kind of playful day-in-the-life of this older guy who's roaming aimlessly around town after work because there's nothing happening and everything's closed and everyone's half asleep and he doesn't want to go home, so he takes a walk by his old school and starts checking out the girls and then goes to a show and has nothing to say but it's okay.

Oh, that was just an exercise. I only had about a week to write songs for *Pepper.* "Good Morning Good Morning" was a Kellogg's Corn Flakes ad at the time—that's how desperate I was for a song. What I realized when I read *Lennon Remembers* [John's legendary 1971 interview with Jann Wenner] or the new *Playboy* interview [conducted by David Sheff between September 8 and 28, 1980] was that I'm always complaining about how *hard* it is to write or how much I *suffer* when I'm writing—that almost every song I've ever written has been absolute torture.

Most of them were torture?

Absolutely. I always think there's nothing there, it's shit, it's no good, it's not coming out, this is garbage . . . and even if it does come out, I think, "What the hell is it anyway?"

That sounds a bit constipated, in a way.

It's just *stupid.* I just think, "That was tough, Jesus, I was in a bad way then." *[Laughing]* And then I realize that I've been saying that all these years about every session and every song, you know, except for the ten or so songs the gods give you and that come out of nowhere.

Did the songs you wrote for Double Fantasy *come easier?*

Not really, it actually took me five years for them to come out. Constipated for five years, and then diarrhea for three weeks! *[Laughing]* The physical writing was within a three-week period. There's a Zen story that Yoko once told me—and I think I might have told it in *Lennon Remembers* or *Playboy Forgets*: A king sent his messenger to an artist to request a painting, he paid the artist the money, and the artist said, "Okay, come back." So a year goes by, and the messenger comes back and tells him, "The king's waiting for his painting," and the artist says, "Oh, hold on," and whips it off right in front of him and says, "Here." And the messenger says, "What's this? The king paid you twenty thousand bucks for this shit, and you knock it off in five minutes?" And the painter replies, "Yeah, but I spent ten years thinking about it." And there's no way I could have written the *Double Fantasy* songs without those five years.

At this point, Yoko comes into the room to announce that someone who says he's George Harrison just telephoned and wanted to come over. "Of course it's not George," John mutters. "He was probably on acid," says Yoko. "I said to him, 'Can I ask you some questions?' 'No,' the guy said, 'I can't be bothered with all that, Yoko.' So I hung up and made a call to George's number and found out that George was in fact sleeping." I start to laugh, and John says, "We laugh at it, too, you know. Jesus Christ. If it wasn't a laugh, we'd go crazy, wouldn't we?"

Yoko takes this opportunity to hand John a recent copy of Japanese *Playboy* that features an article about them. "It's nice of them to show just the back of the baby," John remarks about one of the photos. "I don't want pictures of Sean going around. Most stars, as soon as they have a baby, put it on the front page: *We've just had a baby!* I'm not interested in that. It's dangerous. You know, we make no pretense of being average Tom, Dicks, or Harry—we make no pretense of living in a small cottage or of trying to make our child into an average child. I tried that game with my son Julian, sending him to a comprehensive working-class school, mixing with the people, but the people spat and shit on him because he was famous, as people are wont to do. So his mother had to finally turn around and tell me to piss off: 'I'm sending him to a private school, the kid is suffering here.'"

John now thumbs through *Playboy*. "Take a look at these tits in the front half of the magazine," he says, as he generously shares the issue with me. "They're beautiful. They're not allowed to show pussy, only breasts. Before the Christians got there, the Japanese were absolutely free sexually, like the Tahitians—not in an immoral way, it was natural to them." "And it's the Christians that changed that?" I asked. "Yeh," John replied, "the Christians don't let you have cock and balls. It's the *Judeo*-Christians, just to get *you* in it, too." "You're right," I confess, "it's all my fault!" "Never mind, never mind," John says, patting me on the shoulder. "But we'd better get on with this since you've only got until Monday. Ask away!"

It's interesting that no rock 'n' roll star I can think of has made an album with his wife or whomever and given her 50 percent of the disc.

It's the first time we've done it this way. I know we've made albums together before, like *Live Peace in Toronto 1969*, where I had one side and Yoko had the other. But *Double Fantasy* is a dialogue, and we have resurrected ourselves, in a way, as John and Yoko—not as John ex-Beatle and Yoko and the Plastic Ono Band. It's just the two of us, and our position was that, if the record didn't sell, it meant people didn't want to know about John and Yoko—either they didn't want John anymore or they didn't want John with Yoko or maybe they just wanted Yoko, or whatever. But if they didn't want the two of us, we weren't interested. Throughout my career, I've selected to work with—for more than a one-night stand, say, with David Bowie or Elton John—only two people: Paul McCartney and Yoko Ono. I brought Paul into the original group, the Quarrymen; he brought George in and George brought Ringo in. And the second person who interested me as an artist and somebody I could work with was Yoko Ono. That ain't bad picking.

Right now, the public is our only criterion: you can aim for a small public, a medium public, but for meself, I like a large public. And I made my decision in art school, if I'm going to be an artist of whatever description, I want the maximum exposure, not just paint your little pictures in the attic and don't show them to anybody.

When I arrived in art school, there were lots of artsy-fartsy guys and girls, mainly guys, going round with paint on their jeans and looking just like artists. And they all had lots to talk about and knew all about every damn paintbrush, and they talked about aesthetics, but they all ended up being art teachers or Sunday painters. I got nothing from art school except for a lot of women, a lot of drink, and the freedom to be at college and have fun. I enjoyed it like hell, but for art, I never learned a damn thing.

You've always had a unique, playful drawing style—just think of your book In His Own Write *or the album cover and inner sleeve of* Walls and Bridges *or your immediately identifiable "Lennonesque" cartoons.*

I did the *Walls and Bridges* drawings when I was eleven. But I found at art school that they tried to knock it out of me, they tried to stop me from drawing how I draw naturally, which I wouldn't let them do. But I never developed it further than cartoons. Somebody once said that cartoonists are people with a good creative gift who are scared of failure as painters, so they make it comedic. My cartoons, to me, are like Japanese brush paintings—if you can't get it in one line, rip it up. Yoko got me into that notion a little when we met, and when she saw that I drew, she'd say, "That's how they do it in Japan, you don't have to make changes . . . *this is it!*"

Yoko and I come from different kinds of backgrounds, but basically, we both need this communication. I'm not interested in small, elite groups following or kowtowing to me. I'm interested in communicating whatever it is I want to say or produce in the maximum possible way, and rock 'n' roll is it, as far as I'm concerned. It's like that image of watching a giraffe going by the window. People are always just seeing little bits of it, but I try and see the whole, not just in my own life, but the whole universe, the whole game. That's what it's all about, isn't it? So whether I'm working with Paul or Yoko or Bowie or Elton, it's all toward the same end, whatever that is—self-expression, communication, or just being like a tree, flowering and withering and flowering and withering.

On Double Fantasy, *I noticed a mysterious and magical little sound-collage that segues between your song "Watching the Wheels" and Yoko's charming, thirties-like "Yes, I'm Your Angel." One hears what seem to be a hawker's voice, the sounds of a horse-driven carriage, then a door slamming and a few musical phrases played by a piano and violin in a restaurant.*

I'll tell you what it is. One of the voices is me going, "God bless you, man, thank you, man, cross my palm with silver, you've got a lucky face," which is what the English guys who beg or want a tip say, and that's what you hear me mumbling. And then we re-created the sounds of what Yoko and I call the Strawberries and Violin Room—the Palm Court at the Plaza Hotel. We like to sit there occasionally and listen to the old violin and have a cup of tea and some strawberries. It's romantic. And so the picture is: There's this kind of street prophet, Hyde Park corner–type guy who just watches the wheels going around. And people are throwing money in the hat—we faked that in the studio, we had friends of ours walking up and down dropping coins in a hat—and he's saying, "Thank you, thank you," and then you get in the horse carriage and you go around New York and go into the hotel and the violins are playing and then this woman comes on and sings about being an angel.

In "Yes, I'm Your Angel," Yoko sings that she's in your pocket and that you're in her locket, and the song then segues into "Woman," which sounds a bit like a troubadour poem written to a medieval lady.

"Woman" came about because, one sunny afternoon in Bermuda, it suddenly hit me what women do for us. Not just what my Yoko does for me, although I was thinking in those personal terms . . . but any truth is universal. What dawned on me was everything I was taking for granted. Women really *are* the other half of the sky, as I whisper at the beginning of the song. It's a "we" or it ain't anything. The song came as it was, I didn't try to make it artsy-fartsy or clever, and it reminds me of a Beatles track, though I wasn't trying to make it sound like a Beatles track. I did it as I did "Girl" many years ago—it just sort of hit me like a flood, and it came out like that. "Woman" is the grown-up version of "Girl."

I know that Yoko is deeply interested in ancient Egyptian art and antiques, and that you have a small collection of it in your home. Regarding "the other half of the sky," it's interesting that in ancient Egyptian mythology, the Sky was personified as the goddess Nut—she wasn't Mother Earth—and the Earth was personified as the god Neb. And in fact in your song "Yer Blues," you say "My mother was of the sky / My father was of the earth."

But I *do* call Yoko "Mother," like our president-elect [Ronald Reagan] calls his wife "Mommy." And for those childless people who find that peculiar, it's because, in general, when you have a child around the house, you tend to refer to each other that way. Yoko calls me "Daddy"—it could be

Freudian but it could also mean that Sean refers to me as "Daddy." Occasionally I call her "Mother," because I used to call her Mother Superior—if you check your Beatles Fab Four fucking records, "Happiness Is a Warm Gun." She is Mother Superior, she's Mother Earth, she's the mother of my child, she's my mother, she's my daughter . . . the relationship goes through many levels, like most relationships. But it doesn't have any deep-seated strangeness about it.

People are always judging or criticizing you, or focusing on what you're trying to say on one little album, on one little song, but to me it's a lifetime's work. From the boyhood paintings and poetry to when I die—it's all part of one big production. And I don't have to announce that this album is part of a larger work: if it isn't obvious, then forget it. But I did put a little clue on the beginning of *Double Fantasy*—the bells on "(Just Like) Starting Over." The head of the album is a wishing bell of Yoko's. And it's like the beginning of "Mother" on the Plastic Ono album, which had a very slow death bell. So it's taken a long time to get from that slow church death bell to this sweet little wishing bell. And that's the connection. To me, my work is one piece.

In "Woman," you also sing about how Yoko allowed you to express your inner feelings and then thank her "for showing me the meaning of success."

I'm not saying success as a famous artist and star is no good, and I'm not saying it's great. The thing about the "Working Class Hero" song that nobody ever got right was that it was supposed to be sardonic—it had nothing to do with socialism, it had to do with, "If you want to go through that trip, you'll get up to where I am, and this is what you'll be—some guy whining on a record, all right? If you want to do it, do it." Because I've been successful as an artist and have been happy and unhappy, and I've been unknown in Liverpool or Hamburg and been happy and unhappy. But what Yoko's taught me is what the *real* success is—the success of my personality, the success of my relationship with her and the child, my relationship with the world . . . and to be happy when I wake up. It has nothing to do with rock machinery or *not* rock machinery.

What am I supposed to be, some kind of martyr that's not supposed to be rich? Did they criticize me when I was a Beatle for making money? In retrospect, a lot of money came our way, and I spent a lot of it, I sure as hell had a lot of fun with it. But through ignorance, I lost a lot of it and gave a lot of it away through maybe a misplaced charitable heart, I don't know. So why are they attacking me for making money now? Because we were associated with radical causes, feminism, and the antiwar movement. To be antiwar you have to be poor? There's many a socialist in the House of Lords, what are they talking about? I mean, if they want a poor man, they can follow Jesus. And he's not only poor, he's dead!

Some asshole recently wrote a cover story about me in *Esquire*. [Journalist Laurence Shames's virulent article "John Lennon, Where Are You?" appeared in the November 1980 issue of the magazine. In it, Shames wrote: "I was looking for the Lennon who had always shot his mouth off, who had offended everyone without having to try. My Lennon was a bitter clown, a man of extravagant error and vast resilience, a big baby, an often pathetic truth-seeker whose pained, goofy, earnest, and paranoid visage was the emblem and conscience of his age. . . . The Lennon I would have found is a forty-year-old businessman who watches a lot of television, who's got $150 million, a son he dotes on, and a wife who intercepts his phone calls. . . . Is it true, John? Have you really given up?"] This guy spent twenty months chasing cows and gardeners and deeds. I'm busy making a record, and that asshole's looking at cows. For fuck's sake, man, what are they talking about? What should I have bought—slaves? Hookers? *[Laughing]* They've got minds like fucking sewers to sell magazines, to sell products that people can't afford to buy, that they don't need and have to replace every three months . . . and they're accusing me of what? That guy is the kind of person who used to be in love with you and now hates you—a rejected lover. I don't even know the asshole, but he was chasing an illusion, fell out of love with it, and now hates another illusion. Neither one of the people he's describing ever existed, it's only in his head. It had nothing to do with me—it could be Greta Garbo he's talking about, right?

These critics with the illusions they've created about artists—it's like idol worship. Like those little kids in Liverpool who only liked us when we were in Liverpool—a lot of them dropped us because we got big in Manchester, right? They thought we'd sold out. Then the English got upset because we got big in . . . What the hell is it? They only like people when they're on the way up, and when they're up there, they've got nothing else to do but shit on them. They like to imagine they create and break people, but they don't. I cannot be on the way up again, and I cannot be twenty-five again. I cannot be what I was five minutes ago, so I can't waste the time on considering what they're going to say or what they're going to do. Most of them are now half my age and know shit from Shinola about anything other than from 1970 on. What they want is dead heroes, like Sid Vicious and James Dean. I'm not interested in being a dead fucking hero. . . . So forget 'em, forget 'em.

You know what Eugene O'Neill said about critics? "I love every bone in their heads." You see, the only way to deal with critics is to go *over* their heads *direct* to the public. That's what we did with the bed-ins and with our *Two Virgins* and Plastic Ono albums, and that's what we're doing now. And we hear from all kinds of people. One kid living up in Yorkshire wrote this heartfelt letter about being both Oriental and English and identifying with John and Yoko. The odd kid in the class. There are a lot of those kids who identify with us—as a couple, a biracial couple, who stand for love, peace, feminism, and the positive things of the world. They're the ones we're talking to.

But the press are always looking at the neck of the giraffe as it goes past the window—that's how the game goes. So there's absolutely no way they can ever keep up. And does anybody ever look at the writing of these critics? You'd think nothing had happened in writing—no William Burroughs, no Ginsberg, no Dylan, no *nothing* if you look at the way these people write. They're criticizing us for what we're doing and how we're doing it, and they do so in schoolboy-essay style with three-syllable words.

Most of the petty resentment is mainly from the sixties rock critics who are reaching that age where the beer belly is getting larger. The younger ones are into the New Wave, and some of the older ones are trying to get into it, but they don't really appreciate it, they'd just as soon be listening to *Sgt. Pepper* and *Exile on Main Street* and *Highway 61 Revisited* or whatever it was. And the sixties rock critics are locked into the sixties more than they'd like to admit, and they're becoming our parents . . . and the artist's job is not to get locked into *any* period, whether it's the sixties, the seventies, or the eighties. Most of those critics haven't got the guts of someone like Jon Landau [music critic, record producer, and Bruce Springsteen's manager] to get out there and *do* it. I admire Lester Bangs, who's a musician as well as a critic, and I'm sure there's many times he shit all over me, and I'm sure Landau must have, in his time, both praised and hated me. I've had it both ways from all the major critics. But at least some of them *do it*. And as I said in *Lennon Remembers*, and as I said in art school, I'm a doer, not a voyeur. . . . And I've got nothing to hide. Remember the song?

"Everybody's Got Something to Hide Except Me and My Monkey," where you sing about your inside being out and your outside being in, and your outside being in and your inside being out.

Right, but what did the critics say? "A bit simplistic, no imagery in it." Perhaps I should have said: *"Your inside is like a whale juice dripping from the fermented foam of the teenyboppers' VD in Times Square as I injected my white clown face with heroin and performed in red-leather knickers."* Maybe then they'd like it, right?

That's great, that sounds like Allen Ginsberg.

Right, we can all do Ginsberg—and I like Ginsberg. But try shaving it all off and getting down to the nitty-gritty—that's what I always tried to write . . . except for the occasional "Walrus" bit. I'm not interested in describing a fucking tree. I'm interested in climbing it or being under it.

"No one I think is in my tree."

Yeh, well, that was imagery. Because I was more self-conscious then and paranoid. It was that bit about not knowing "Am I crazy or what?" The eternal questions.

All the way through your work, there's this incredibly strong notion about inspiring people to be themselves and to come together to try to change things. I'm thinking here, obviously, of songs like "Give Peace a Chance," "Power to the People," and "Happy Xmas (War Is Over)."

It's still there. If you look on the vinyl around the new record's logo [on the twelve-inch single "(Just Like) Starting Over"]—which all the kids have done already all over the world from Brazil to Australia to Poland—inside is written: ONE WORLD, ONE PEOPLE. So we continue. "Give Peace a Chance," not "Shoot People for Peace." "All You Need Is Love": it's damn hard, but I absolutely believe it.

We all want war to go away, but you can't just sit around waiting for it to happen. It's like what they said after the Holocaust. "First they came for the Jews and I did not speak out because I was not a Jew. Then they came for me, and there was no one left to speak out for me." It's that same thing today, only not such a pressured, horrific scene. But you first have to be *conscious* and imagine there's no countries, not "This is the answer to the universe, let's get rid of the passports tomorrow."

First of all, *conceive* of the idea of no nation, no passport. If you're not defending a nation there's nothing to fight about. We've said it a million times—first of all we conceived of flying, then we flew. It took a long time to get up in the air, and it was a lot of sticking feathers together and melting under the sun and all that, but conceiving the idea is the first move.

We're not the first to say "Imagine No Countries" or "Give Peace a Chance," but we're carrying that torch, like the Olympic torch, passing it hand to hand, to each other, to each country, to each generation . . . and that's our job. Not to live according to somebody else's idea of how we should live—rich, poor, happy, not happy, smiling, not smiling, wearing the right jeans, not wearing the right jeans.

I'm not claiming divinity, I've never claimed purity of soul, I've never claimed to have the answers to life. I only put out songs and answer questions as honestly as I can, but *only* as honestly as I can—no more, no less. I cannot live up to other people's expectations of me because they're illusionary. I cannot be a punk in Hamburg and Liverpool, because I'm older now, I see the world through different eyes now. But I still believe in peace, love, and understanding, as Elvis Costello said. What's so fucking funny about peace, love, and understanding? It's fashionable to be a go-getter and slash thy neighbor with a cross, but we're not one to follow the fashion.

It's like your song "The Word" . . .

Yes, the word was "love."

"Why in the world are we here, / Surely not to live in pain and fear"—that's from "Instant Karma." And that's an idea in all of your and Yoko's work . . . as when she tell us in her new song "Beautiful Boys" that we should never be afraid to cry or be afraid to be afraid. I found that beautiful.

That is beautiful. I'm often afraid, but I'm not afraid to be afraid, though it's always scary.

When Yoko sings "Hard times are over," she adds, "for a while." She doesn't say they're over forever.

No, no. She knows better. *[Laughing]* But at least when it's all right, let's enjoy it! What's more painful is to try *not* to be yourself. People spend a lot of time trying to be somebody else, and I think it leads to terrible diseases.

Maybe you get cancer or something. A lot of tough guys die of cancer, have you noticed? John Wayne, Steve McQueen. I think it has something to do—I don't know, I'm not an expert—with constantly living or getting trapped in an image or an illusion of themselves, suppressing some part of themselves, whether it's the feminine side or the fearful side.

I'm well aware of that because I come from the macho school of pretense. I was never really a street kid or a tough guy. I used to dress like a Teddy boy and identify with Marlon Brando and Elvis Presley, but I was never really in any street fights or real down-home gangs. I was just a suburban kid, imitating the rockers. But it was a big part of one's life to look tough. I spent the whole of my childhood with shoulders up around the top of me head and me glasses off because glasses were sissy, and walking in complete fear, but with the toughest-looking little face you've ever seen. I'd get into trouble just because of the way I looked. I wanted to be this tough James Dean all the time. It took a lot of wrestling to stop doing that, even though I still fall into it when I get insecure and nervous. I still drop into that I'm-a-street-kid stance, but I have to keep remembering that I never really was one.

That's what Yoko has taught me. I couldn't have done it alone—it had to be a female to teach me. That's it. Yoko has been telling me all the time, "It's all right, it's all right." I look at early pictures of meself, and I was torn between being Marlon Brando and being the sensitive poet—the Oscar Wilde part of me with the velvet, feminine side. I was always torn between the two, mainly opting for the macho side, because if you showed the other side, you were dead.

I once heard some Blue-Meanie-type person say, "You know, that John Lennon really has a super-enlarged sense of himself."

Explain.

I think that he was referring to a comment you once made to the effect that sometimes you thought you were a loser and other times that you were God almighty

Well, we all think that, don't we? Everybody goes through that. When something is put down in print, it looks like it's being writ by Moses on the tablets. One has to deal with the reality that when it comes out of your mouth and it goes into print—and after years and years of answering the same questions, basically, over and over again—one tends to get it down into the simplest form, and the simplest form is that we all feel almighty some days and we all feel no-mighty other days, and that's all that's saying. Sometimes you look in the mirror and "Oh, isn't it wonderful?" And other times "What is *that*, I hate it!" I don't know anybody who isn't like that. Sometimes you love yourself, sometimes you hate yourself, and as I believe that we all contain God and we are all God, so the fact that I think I'm God almighty some days is fine, because I think we're *all* God almighty. I'll compare myself with any creature, living or dead, the potential's in me just as it's in any one of us to be God or the devil, Picasso or Norman Rockwell or the *Peanuts* artist Charles Schulz.

I notice that in nearly every interview you've done, you're continually asked, "What do you think of Paul, George, and Ringo?"

Right. Journalists used to ask me to tell the story of how I wrote "Strawberry Fields," and I used to say, "Okay, I was making the film *How I Won the War* in Almería in Spain, the Beatles had just stopped touring, I was going through this trauma, and then when we got in the studio I didn't like Paul's attitude." But that was *then*, I'm not telling that *now*. I just saw Ringo two days ago, and I can tell you hundreds of things I might have been mad at him about when something happened in the past, but I'm not carrying any cross. It's the press that wants to know about the fucking Beatles. You ask me about the Beatles, I'll tell you what I feel about them. But if you look in the new *Playboy* interview I did a couple of months ago, *carefully*, you'll see that I said, "I love those guys, I love the Beatles, I'm proud of the music. I admire a lot of what Paul's done since we split up, I think a lot of it is shit." What do they want from me? So maybe it was sibling rivalry then. Maybe it's still in my subconscious—who gives a shit? Paul doesn't really give a shit. George doesn't really give a shit, and Ringo doesn't really give a shit. It's *you* assholes always talking about it—I don't mean *you* personally. Do you understand? Do you understand what the game is? The press come up, ask us about each other just to get some quote to go back and sell newspapers with, and then tell us we're a lot of rich farts bitching about each other.

Okay, let's get back to reality for a moment. And speaking of reality, there's another aspect of your work, which has to do with the way you continually question what's real and what's illusory, such as in "Look at Me," your new

"Watching the Wheels," and, of course, "Strawberry Fields Forever," in which you sing: "Nothing is real."

In a way, *no thing* is real, if you break the word down. As the Hindus or Buddhists say, it's an illusion. It's *Rashomon*. We all see it, but the agreed-upon illusion is what we live in. And the hardest thing is facing yourself. It's easier to shout "Revolution" and "Power to the People" than it is to look at yourself and try and find out what's real inside you and what isn't, when you pull the wool over your own eyes, your own hypocrisy. That's the hardest.

I used to think that the world was doing it to me and the world owed me something, and that either the conservatives or the socialists or the fascists or the communists or the Christians or the Jews were doing something to me. And when you're a teenybopper, that's what you think. But I'm forty now, and I don't think that anymore, 'cause I found out it doesn't fucking work! The thing goes on anyway, and all you're doing is jacking off, screaming what your mommy or daddy did . . . but one has to go through that. For the people who even bother to go through that—most assholes just accept what is and get on with it, right?—but for the few of us who did question what was going on . . . well, I've found out for me personally—*not* for the whole world—that I am responsible for me, as *well* as for them. I am part of them. There's no separation: we're all one, so in that respect I look at it all and think, "Ah, I have to deal with me again in that way. What is real? What is the illusion I'm living or not living?" And I have to deal with it every day. The layers of the onion.

"Looking through a glass onion."

That's what it's about, isn't it?

Yoko now comes into the room to say that she and John have to leave for the Record Plant—the legendary, now defunct recording studio on West Forty-fourth Street where albums like *Electric Ladyland, Born to Run, Rumours,* and *Hotel California* were recorded, and where, for the past couple of weeks, John and Yoko have been remixing some of Yoko's old songs and putting finishing touches on her new single, "Walking on Thin Ice." They'll be working there throughout the night . . . and why didn't I join them? It's around 10:00 p.m. when we leave the Dakota and get into the waiting car. Arriving at the Record Plant a half hour later, we enter the main studio and are immediately greeted by a sonic blast whose force almost sends me reeling backwards, as, out of the speakers, comes the shattering cascade of the accelerated high-energy vocal particles of Yoko's inimitable, primordial voice—intersected by John's forward and backward guitar tracks—screaming out for us to open our boxes, our trousers, our thighs, our legs, our ears, our noses. And over the next six hours, and as two sound engineers and producer Jack Douglas (who co-produced *Double Fantasy* with John and Yoko) remix a number of Yoko's songs ("Open Your Box," "Kiss Kiss Kiss," "Every Man Has a Woman Who Loves Him"), John and I continue our conversation till 4:00 in the morning, by which time Yoko is napping on a studio couch.

Is Yoko thinking of putting out a disco album?

I can't really verify what we're doing yet, because with Yoko, you never know until it's done. But we did come in here to make this string of songs that might go to the rock and disco clubs.

And what about your new songs?

No, because I don't make that stuff. *[Laughing]* I mean, what way could I have come back into this game? I came back from where I know best, as unpretentious as possible . . . and with no experimentation, because I was happy to be doing it as I did it before. My song "(Just Like) Starting Over"—I call it "Elvis–Orbison" [sings: "Only the lonely / know why I cry / only the lonely"].

There's a bit of slap-back echo on your recording.

Well, the tape echo is from the fifties. A lot of the records I made had the same echo on them . . . all the way back to "Rock and Roll Music." I love it. And my voice has always sounded pretty much the same. I'm going right back to the roots of my past. It's like Dylan doing *Nashville Skyline*. But I don't have any Nashville, being from Liverpool, so I go back to the records I knew, which is Elvis and Roy Orbison and Gene Vincent and Jerry Lee Lewis. If I felt like making one, I could make a disco record, I could make a waltz, I could make a country record, but my interests happen to lie in fifties rock 'n' roll and blues. "I'm Losing You" is a kind of blues. It's just the style of the song, it's like a watercolor as opposed to oil.

I like to dabble. And I occasionally get tripped off into a "Revolution 9," but my far-out side has been completely encompassed by Yoko.

You know, the first show we did together was at Cambridge University in 1969, when she had been booked to do a concert with some jazz musicians. That was the first time I had appeared un-Beatled. I just hung around and played feedback, and people got very upset because they recognized me: "What's *he* doing here?" It's always: "Stay in your bag." So, when she tried to rock, they said, "What's *she* doing here?" And when I went with her and tried to be the instrument and not project—to just be her band, like a sort of Ike Turner to her Tina, only her Tina was a different, avant-garde Tina—well, even some of the jazz guys got upset.

Everybody has pictures they want you to live up to. But that's the same as living up to your parents' expectations, or to society's expectations, or to so-called critics who are just guys with a typewriter in a little room, smoking and drinking beer and having their dreams and nightmares, too, and getting paid once a week or once a month, watching TV, but somehow pretending that they're living in a different, separate world. That's all right. But there are people who break out of their bags.

I remember years ago when you and Yoko appeared in bags at a Vienna press conference.

Right. We sang a Japanese folk song in the bags. "Das ist really you, John? John Lennon in zee bag?" Yeh, it's me. "But how do we know ist you?" Because I'm telling you. "Vy don't you come out from this bag?" Because I don't want to come out of the bag. "Don't you realize this is the Hapsburg Palace?" I thought it was a hotel. "Vell, it is now a hotel." They had great chocolate cake in that Viennese hotel, I remember that. Anyway, who wants to be locked in a bag? You have to break out of your bag to keep alive.

[The studio engineers are now playing a tape of Yoko's new song, "Walking on Thin Ice."]

Listen to this, Jonathan. We were thinking that this song is so damn good that she should put her own single out, independently with me on the B side. I'd love to be on the B side of a hit record after all these years. Me just being the guitarist—I'm playing backwards guitar on this song. I'd settle for it any day. Yoko deserves it, it's been a long haul. I wouldn't fight about it at all.

And speaking of fighting—and this will make you laugh—Andy Warhol once wanted Yoko and me to wrestle at Madison Square Garden, and he'd film it!

You must be kidding. He wanted you two to wrestle? Maybe a sumo contest!

Anything. Just to show the great "peace and love" people having a good fight onstage—it might have been great!

Do you and Yoko have any plans now, not to fight in public, but maybe to tour together?

I don't know, maybe we will. It could be fun. Can you imagine the two of us now with these new songs . . . and if we did some of Yoko's early stuff, like "Don't Worry, Kyoko" or "Open Your Box" or "Why" from the Plastic Ono album—it's just her voice and my guitar and one bass and drums, and I hear all those licks coming out now from some of today's groups. So we just might do it. But there will be no smoke bombs, no lipstick, no flashing lights. It has to be just comfy. But we could have a laugh. We're born-again rockers, and we're starting over.

And you could also have your own late-night TV show . . . like The Captain and Tennille Show. *[Pop music artists "Captain" Daryl Dragon and Toni Tennille ("Love Will Keep Us Together," "Do That to Me One More Time") had an ABC TV variety series in the late seventies.]*

Yeh, of course we could. John and Yoko might do it one day. We often talk about that. It might be fun. But there's time, right? Plenty of time. Right now here we are in the Record Plant, talking to Jonathan Cott again for *Rolling Stone* . . . and it will be fun to be on the cover of *Rolling Stone*. It will be fun, won't it, to start 1981 like 1968?

"Look out kid / You're doin' it again."

Right. And who's going to be the first to go—Lennon or *Rolling Stone*? Who do you think's going to be around the longest? *Life, Time, Newsweek, Playboy, Look, Rolling Stone*? Let's face it, magazines come and go, record executives come and go, record companies come and go, film producers come and go. Artists come and go, too. What a life!

You know, the last album I did before *Double Fantasy* was *Rock 'n' Roll*, with the cover picture of me in Hamburg in a leather jacket. At the end of making that record, I was finishing up a track that Phil Spector had made me sing called "Just Because," which I really didn't know—all the rest of the songs I'd done as a teenager, so I knew them backwards—and I couldn't get the hang of it. At the end of that record—I was mixing it just next door to this very studio—I started spieling and saying, "And so we say farewell from the Record Plant," and a little thing in the back of my mind said, "Are you *really* saying farewell forever?" I hadn't thought of it then. I was still separated from Yoko and still hadn't had the baby, but somewhere in the back was a voice that was saying, "Are you saying farewell to the whole game?"

It just flashed by like that—like a premonition. I didn't think of it until a few years later, when I realized that I had actually stopped recording. I came across the cover photo—the original picture of me in my leather jacket, leaning against the wall in Hamburg in 1961—and I thought, "Is this it? Do I start where I came in, with 'Be-Bop-A-Lula'?" The day I first met Paul I was singing that song for the first time onstage. There's a photo in all the Beatles books—a picture of me with a checked shirt on, holding a little acoustic guitar—and I'm singing "Be-Bop-A-Lula," just as I did on that album.

It was like this little thing, and there was no consciousness in it. It was only much later, when I started thinking about it . . . you know, like sometimes you dream—it's like a premonition, but this was an awake premonition. I had no plans, no intention, but I thought, "What is this, this cover photo from Hamburg, this 'Be-Bop-A-Lula,' this saying goodbye from the Record Plant?" And I was actually *really* saying goodbye since it was the last track of the *Rock 'n' Roll* album—and I was so glad to get it over with—and it was also the end of the album.

It's like when a guy in England, an astrologer, once told me that I was going to *not* live in England. And I didn't remember that until I was in the middle of my immigration fight to stay in this country and when I thought, "What the hell am I doing here? Why the hell am I going through this?" I didn't plan to live here, it just happened. There was no packing the bags—we left everything at our house in England, we were just coming for a short visit . . . but we never went back.

I was in court, and people were saying I wasn't good enough to be here or that I was a communist or whatever the hell it was. So I thought, "What am I doing this for?" And then I remembered that astrologer in

London telling me, "One day you'll live abroad." Not because of taxes. The story was that I left for tax reasons, but I didn't, I got no benefit, nothing, I screwed up completely, I lost money when I left. So I had no reason to leave England. I'm not a person who looks for the sun like a lot of the English who like to get away to the South of France, or go to Malta or Spain or Portugal. George was always talking about, "Let's all go and live in the sun."

"Here Comes the Sun."

Right, he's always looking for the sun because he's still living in England. . . . And then it clicked on me, "Jesus, that guy *predicted* I was going to leave England!" Though at the time he said that to me, I was thinking, "Are you kidding?"

Sometimes you wonder, I mean really wonder. I know we make our own reality and we always have a choice, but how much is preordained? Is there always a fork in the road and are there two preordained paths that are equally preordained? There could be hundreds of paths where one could go this way or that way—there's a choice, and it's very strange sometimes.

And that's a good ending for our interview.

It was now four o'clock in the morning. The album's co-producer, Jack Douglas, was still sitting in front of the control board and remixing a couple of Yoko's songs; Yoko was napping on a studio couch; and John was talking to me about how happy he felt being able to live in New York City, where, unlike in England or Japan, he could raise his son without racial prejudice; of his memory of the first rock 'n' roll song he ever wrote, a takeoff on the Del-Vikings' "Come Go with Me," in which he changed the lines to "Come come come come / Come and go with me / to the peni-peni-tentiary"; and of some of the things he had learned on his many trips around the world during the past five years. As he walked me to the elevator, I mentioned to him how exhilarating it was to see Yoko and him looking and sounding so well. "I love her, and we're together," he said. "Goodbye, till next time."

JOHN LENNON

OCTOBER 9, 1940 – DECEMBER 8, 1980

ASTRID LINDGREN
The Happy Childhood of Pippi Longstocking

Stockholm, 1981

In *The Children of Noisy Village,* Astrid Lindgren narrates the adventures of six nine-to-eleven-year-olds (three boys, three girls) living in the Swedish farming area of Småland, where the author herself grew up. The children play in the linden tree's branches that connect two of three neighboring farms, celebrate holidays, visit grandparents, make huts by the lake, mingle with the animals (horses, cows, pigs, sheep, chickens, rabbits), and meet up with villagers like the shoemaker Mr. Kind, who thinks that "youngsters are a wild lot who should get spanked every day." It is a book that recalls and celebrates a kind of childhood that has become increasingly rare today. "Does Noisy Village really exist?" a young reader once wrote Astrid Lindgren. "For if it does," she added, "I don't want to live in Vienna anymore."

In *The Children of Noisy Village,* Lisa—the girl through whose eyes we see this childhood world—informs us:

> Britta and Anna gave me a storybook, and Olaf gave me a chocolate bar. He sat down next to me, and my brothers started teasing us.
>
> "Boyfriend and girlfriend, boyfriend and girlfriend!"
>
> They say that just because Olaf is not one of those silly boys who won't play with girls. He doesn't care if Karl and Bill do tease him; he plays with both boys and girls anyway. Karl and Bill want to play with girls, too, although they pretend they don't.

This episode suggests one of the unfortunate facts about the way one reads children's literature as a child: girls will read "boys'" books, but boys will refuse to read about girls. It is this immemorially ingrained categorization and seg-regation of children's books by sex that made me, when I was young, forgo the experience of reading classics like *Little Women, What Katy Did, Rebecca of Sunnybrook Farm, Anne of Green Gables, Caddie Woodlawn,* and *Strawberry Girl.* And it is only as an adult that I chanced to discover the *Pippi Longstocking* books by Astrid Lindgren.

I became curious about them after four of my closest women friends told me of the strong impression the character of Pippi Longstocking had made on them when they were young. Since the child is mother of the woman, I decided to find out about Pippi (and therefore about my friends) by reading the books, and thereby came upon one of the greatest characters in children's literature.

Like the name of Peter Rabbit, Pippi Longstocking's name is legion—e.g., Pippi Långstrump (Swedish), Pipi Ğūrāb-baland (Persian), Peppi Dlinnyjčulok (Russian), Ochame-na Pippi (Japanese)—and Astrid Lindgren's books about her have been translated into more than forty languages. She is certainly one of the most curious (and subversive) immortals of world literature. A freckled nine-year-old with carrot-colored hair worn in two tight braids, Pippi gets her name from the way she wears one black and one brown stocking with black shoes that are twice as long as her feet. When we meet her, she is living alone: her mother died when Pippi was very young and is now "an angel . . . up in heaven," and her father, a sea captain, has been blown overboard in a storm; but Pippi is sure he floated to shore on an island and is now king of the cannibals. Her little home, a ramshackle house called Villa Villekulla, is surrounded by "an overgrown garden with old trees covered with moss, and unmowed lawns, and lots of flowers which were allowed to grow exactly as they pleased." And this is the way Pippi lives her life—exactly as she pleases. She provides for herself with a suitcase filled with gold pieces and a chest of drawers that contains an illimitable supply of gifts. She tells herself when to go to bed, sleeps with her feet on the pillow and her head way under the covers, and because she doesn't receive letters, writes them to herself. Her motto is "Don't you worry about me. I'll always come out on top."

Pippi's only companions are a horse, which lives on her porch, and a monkey named Mr. Nilsson. She also befriends her next-door neighbors' children, Tommy and Annika—"good, well brought up, and obedient." When they first see Pippi, she is walking backward because she doesn't want to turn around to get home. "Why did I walk backward?" asks Pippi. "Isn't this a free country? Can't a person walk any way she wants to?" And Tommy and Annika realize that "this was not going to be one of those dull days."

There isn't a dull day in any of the three *Pippi Longstocking* books (*Pippi*

Longstocking, Pippi Goes on Board, Pippi in the South Seas) as Pippi turns into a Thing-Finder ("When you're a Thing-Finder you don't have a minute to spare") who uncovers articles like a rusty tin can and an empty spool of thread ("The whole world is full of things, and someone has to look for them"). She and her new friends Tommy and Annika become inseparable as they hide in a hollow oak tree, where they mysteriously find soda pop to drink, and go on picnics. Pippi is always leading the way to new adventures, and she is the possessor of great physical strength—she calls herself "the strongest girl in the world"—lifting up her horse with her hands, overpowering two policemen who come to take her to a children's home, wrestling with and defeating the strongest man in the world at the circus, exhausting and warding off two burglars, and taming a tiger at a fair.

Pippi lives completely outside bourgeois conventions. The teacher at school asks her to leave the classroom and come back only when she learns to behave. At a coffee party given by Tommy and Annika's mother, she eats all the cakes and shocks the ladies present with dramatically acted-out stories of her grandmother's maid who never swept under the beds. She washes her hair in a pool and has thereby "saved a visit to the hairdresser." She steps into a gutter—"I love gutters," she says—and wonders what's wrong with being soaked. To a teacher who asks: "You want to be a really fine lady when you grow up, don't you?" Pippi answers: "You mean the kind with a veil on her nose and three double chins under it?" When a supercilious, rich old lady named Miss Rosenblom gives out gifts only to the good and hardworking schoolchildren, demeaning all the others, Pippi does her own corrective examining, judging, and awarding of gold pieces. She is, moreover, contemptuous of money. After winning a hundred dollars in a wrestling contest, she says, "What would I want with that old piece of paper. Take it and use it to fry herring on if you want to."

When her sea-captain father shows up unexpectedly, he and Pippi immediately arm-wrestle, then dance and wrestle some more. And after climbing a tree in order to save two children from a burning building, she climbs back up the tree, raising her arms to the night sky while a shower of sparks fall on her, and dances wildly while singing an ecstatic song:

> The fire is burning,
> It's burning so bright,
> The flames are leaping and prancing.
> It's burning for you,

It's burning for me,
It's burning for all who are dancing!

Pippi always uses her powers wisely. When she, Tommy, and Annika visit her father on a South Sea island (spending "wonderful days in a warm wonderful world full of sunshine with the blue sea glittering and fragrant flowers everywhere") she is chosen to be a princess by the natives, but renounces her position immediately, saying, "I'm through with this throne business." She consistently refuses to join the compromised adult world, commenting: "Grown-ups never have any fun. They only have a lot of boring work and wear silly-looking clothes and have corns and minicipal taxes."

At the conclusion of the third volume, Pippi gives Tommy and Annika some pills (they are actually ordinary peas), which, she tells them, when taken in the dark after repeating a rhyme ("Pretty little chililug, / I don't want to get bug"), will make it impossible for them to grow up. After this little ritual, Tommy and Annika return home, where they can see through the window of Pippi's kitchen. And there, in a beautiful farewell—similar to Mary Poppins's final ascent into the heavens—we find Pippi sitting at the table with her head leaning against her arms:

> She was staring at the little flickering flame of a candle that was standing in front of her. She seemed to be dreaming.
>
> "She—she looks so alone," said Annika, and her voice trembled a little. "Oh, Tommy, if it were only morning so that we could go to her right away!"
>
> They stood there in silence and looked out into the winter night. The stars were shining over Villa Villekulla's roof. Pippi was inside. She would always be there. That was a comforting thought. The years would go by, but Pippi and Tommy and Annika would not grow up. That is, of course, if the strength hadn't gone out of the chililug pills. There would be new springs and summers, new autumns and winters, but their games would go on. Tomorrow they would build a snow hut and make a ski slope from the roof of Villa Villekulla, and when spring came they would climb the hollow oak where soda pop spouted up. They would hunt for treasure and they would ride Pippi's horse. They would sit in the woodbin and tell stories. Perhaps they would also take a trip to Kurrekurredutt Island now and then, to see Momo and Moana and the others. But they would always come back to Villa Villekulla.
>
> And the most wonderful, comforting thought was that Pippi would always be in Villa Villekulla.

"If she would only look in this direction we could wave to her," said Tommy.

But Pippi continued to stare straight ahead with a dreamy look. Then she blew out the light.

As the philosopher Gaston Bachelard wrote in *The Poetics of Reverie* (as if to describe this scene): "There are moments in childhood when every child is the astonishing being, the being who realizes the *astonishment of being*. We thus discover within ourselves an *immobile childhood, a childhood without becoming,* liberated from the gear-wheels of the calendar." And Bachelard continues: "In every dreamer there lives a child, a child whom reverie magnifies and stabilizes. Reverie tears it away from history, sets it outside time, makes it foreign to time. One more reverie and this permanent, magnified child is a god."

Certainly, Pippi Longstocking shares the physical strength of mythological and legendary child heroes like Hercules and Cúchulainn—the latter of whom contested with a hundred and fifty other youths and beat them all, calling himself "a boy with a difference!" And Pippi is indeed "a girl with a difference!" But, moreover, with her gold coins, her unending supply of presents from her chest of drawers, and her peas of immortality, she also resembles the Norse goddess of spring, the ever-young Iduna, a possessor of the golden apples of immortality, which she kept in a golden treasure chest that always remained full—apples that gave youth to the deities of Asgard.

On a less exalted but more important level, it is interesting to notice how the *Pippi Longstocking* books broke with the centuries-old tradition of depicting girls in children's literature. Generally speaking, girls in eighteenth- and nineteenth-century children's books were advised to be docile, submissive, self-sacrificing, pious, grateful, obedient, clean, virtuous, dutiful, modest, and retiring creatures. Rousseau set the familiar tone in *Emile* with his sententious comments concerning how Sophie should behave:

A man has no one but himself to consider, and so long as he does right he may defy public opinion; but when a woman does right her task is only half finished, and what people think of her matters as much as what she really is.

Women should be strong enough to do anything gracefully; men should be skillful enough to do anything easily.

Women should not be strong like men but *for* them, so that their sons may be strong.

A man seeks to serve, a woman seeks to please.

It is amusing to see her occasionally return to her old ways and indulge in childish mirth and then suddenly check herself, with silent lips, downcast eyes, and rosy blushes; neither child nor woman, she may well partake of both.

A virtuous woman is little lower than the angels.

Benighted as the author was with regard to Sophie's educational possibilities—he simply prescribed and subscribed to what in fact was the prevailing, obtuse point of view of his time—Rousseau was an inspired utopian prophet when he wrote of his educational ideas for Emile:

Teach him to live rather than to avoid death: life is not breath, but action, the use of our senses, our mind, our faculties, every part of ourselves which makes us conscious of our being. Life consists less in length of days than in the keen sense of living.

There is only one man who gets his own way—he who can get it single-handed; therefore freedom, not power, is the greatest good. That man is truly free who desires what he is able to perform and does what he desires. This is my fundamental maxim. Apply it to childhood, and all the rules of education spring from it.

The education of the earliest years should be merely negative. It consists, not in teaching virtue or truth, but in preserving the heart from vice and from the spirit of error.

You are afraid to see him spending his early years doing nothing? What, is it nothing to be happy, nothing to run and jump all day? He will never be so busy again all his life long.

He does not know the meaning of habit, routine, and custom; what he did yesterday has no control over what he is doing today; he follows no rule, submits to no authority, copies no pattern, and only acts or speaks as he pleases. So do not expect set speeches or studied manners from him, but just the faithful expression of his thoughts and the conduct that springs from his inclinations.

He has reached the perfection of childhood; he has lived the life of a child; his progress has not been bought at the price of happiness, he has gained both.

It is clear that Pippi Longstocking *is* Emile—the perfect fictional embodiment.

Needless to say, there were books earlier than *Pippi Longstocking* (first published in 1945) that presented fearless and free-thinking heroines: Susan Coolidge's Katy (who hated sewing and "didn't care a button about being called 'good'"), Louisa May Alcott's Jo (who had "blunt manners" and a "too independent spirit"), and Carol R. Brink's Caddie Woodlawn (who liked to run through the woods with her brothers). But each one of these girls ends up by having or deciding to renounce her tomboy ways. As Jo's father says on his return home: "I don't see the 'son Jo' whom I left a year ago . . . I see a young lady who pins her collar straight, laces her boots neatly, and neither whistles, talks slang, nor lies on the rug as she used to do. . . . I rather miss my wild girl; but if I get a strong, helpful, tender-hearted woman in her place, I shall feel quite satisfied."

Pippi Longstocking shares many of the qualities of the above characters; and, surprisingly, she also might be seen to derive certain of her characteristics and spirit from the nineteenth-century tradition of ministering evangelical child waifs who were written about in Religious Tract Society stories like *Little Meg's Children, Jessica's First Prayer,* and *Christie's Old Organ*— God-fearing, motherless orphans who were morally superior to the adults around them. (As Gillian Avery states in *Childhood's Pattern*: "Mothers have a constricting effect on the plot and on the children's activities; their love is so embarrassingly obvious that it can't be overlooked, it stands in the way of that independence that children like to imagine.")

But Pippi never compromises and always remains unreconstructedly herself, for she is free of what the anarchist educator Max Stirner called "wheels in the head"—the knowledge which used and owned the individual rather than that which was used *by* the individual. Pippi exemplifies what Stirner thought of as "self-ownership"—the state in which the person is free from those dogmas and moral imperatives that made him or her a "subservient and cringing" being—as well as what Wilhelm Reich called the "self-governing" character. Reich saw the patriarchal family structure as the ideological factory of the ruling order. (Think of Mr. Fairchild in Mrs. Sherwood's influential children's novel *The Fairchild Family,* published in 1818, who, after whipping his son, says: "I stand in place of God to you, whilst you are a child.") But among the Trobriand Islanders, Reich happily discovered a nonauthoritarian family structure that allowed young children either to remain with their parents during the day or to join with their friends in their own community—a miniature republic that functioned according to its own needs and desires. (Think of Pippi and Tommy and Annika on their various outings and voyage to the South Seas.) And like the dog-hero of William Steig's *Dominic*, Pippi Longstocking also partakes of what Reich saw as Jesus's true nature. As he wrote in *The Murder of Christ*: "Children who gleam with happiness are also born leaders of other children. The latter flock around them, love them, admire them, seek their praise and counsel. . . . Jesus knew that children have 'IT.' He loved children and he was childlike himself; knowing and yet naïve . . . streaming with love and kindness, and yet able to hit hard; gentle and yet strong, just as the child of the future is."

And this, too, is Pippi Longstocking.

* * *

I visited Astrid Lindgren in May 1981. She greeted me at the door of her Stockholm apartment wearing a blue pantsuit, a blue scarf, and a necklace of colored baubles. "They make me look like a Christmas tree, don't they?" she said, laughing, as she took me through the foyer into the living room, which was lined with books and which had naïve and landscape paintings by Swedish artists hanging on the wall. We sat down and chatted—she gave the immediate impression of a person who is open, energetic, unpretentious, and unafraid (as any author of *Pippi Longstocking* would have to be), and then I posed the predictable question: "How did Pippi come into the world?"

"I'm asked that all the time," she said, without impatience, in clear but hesitant English, "but I'll tell it to you as I've done before. In 1941 my then seven-year-old daughter Karin was sick in bed with pneumonia. Every evening when I sat by her bedside she would nag in that way children do: 'Tell me something!' And one evening, completely exhausted, I asked her: 'What should I tell?' And she answered, 'Tell me about Pippi Longstocking!' She had come up with the name right there on the spot. I didn't ask her who Pippi Longstocking was, I just began the story, and since it was a strange name, it turned out to be a strange girl as well. Karin, and later even her playmates, showed a strong love for Pippi from the very beginning, and I had to tell the story again and again. It went on like that for several years.

"Then one day in March 1944 it snowed in Stockholm, and in the evening as I was out for a walk, there was fresh snow covering a layer of ice. Well, I slipped and fell, spraining one of my ankles. I was forced to stay in bed for a time. To make time pass, I started to take down the Pippi stories in shorthand—since my office days I've been a capable stenographer, and I still write all my books first in shorthand.

"In May 1944 Karin was to celebrate her tenth birthday, and I decided I would write out the Pippi story and give her the manuscript for a birthday present. And then I decided to send a copy to a publisher. Not that I believed for one minute that they would publish it, but even so! The fact was, I was rather upset about Pippi myself, and I remember concluding my letter to the publisher with 'In the hope that you won't notify the Child Welfare Committee'—really because I had two children of my own, and what kind of a mother had they who wrote such books?

"Just as I had thought, I got the manuscript back, but while I was waiting for it, I wrote another book and sent it to the publishing house of Rabén & Sjögren, which in 1944 had announced a prize contest for girls' books. And it actually happened: I won second prize in the competition. I don't think I've ever been happier than on that autumn evening in 1944 when word came that I'd won. The next year, 1945, the same publishing house had a contest for children's books. I sent in the Pippi manuscript, and I received first prize.

"So maybe every children's book author should be sick in bed for a while. [Smiling] And when I write, I lie in bed, put the book down in shorthand, and I have the feeling that nothing outside exists, I'm just on my bed in my little room and I can go and meet the people I want to."

"Pippi Longstocking seems as if she's always been around," I said.

"Maybe she was just waiting for someone to pick her and to write about her," Astrid Lindgren replied with a smile.

I read her Reich's statement about the child of the future.

"That's Pippi!" she exclaimed. "Pippi says: I'm going to be happy and free and stronger than anybody. She has power, but she never misuses it. She's just kind. . . . But do you think that children of the future will be like that? I'd be very happy if I could believe that. I don't know what will happen to our world if there aren't any happy leaders being born."

"You've written many children's books," I continued. "And in many of them the idea of being happy as a child in summertime occurs over and over, and in a way, *Pippi in the South Seas* is really just a glorified summer outing. In your book *Bill Bergson Lives Dangerously*, for instance, you write: 'There were nooks and crannies to hide in, fences to climb over, winding small alleyways where you could shake off your pursuers; there were roofs to climb and woodsheds and outhouses in the back yard where you could barricade yourselves. As long as a town had all these advantages, it need not be beautiful. It was enough that the sun was shining, and that the cobblestones were feeling so warm and comfortable under your bare feet that you felt it was summer in all your body.'"

"I think you should feel everything in your whole body—whatever there is to feel," Astrid Lindgren responded. "In Sweden we especially need the summer. And when you look back at your childhood, you think it was always summer, in a way, because everything was at its best then. I want to feel summer in my whole body and in my heart."

"It's interesting," I added, "that in 1977 a controversial novel came out in Sweden by P. C. Jersild, called *Children's Island,* which tells of an eleven-year-old boy named Reine who refuses to go to municipal children's camp, and, since his mother has left for her own vacation, he returns to their empty apartment in the suburbs of Stockholm, where he hides out and spends his time reading *The Guinness Book of Records* and Donald Duck comics (apparently the favorite reading materials of Swedish schoolchildren at that time). On his first day alone he fakes a letter to his mother which goes: 'Hi Mom. It's great on Children's Island. We swim and play football. The food is yummy. This morning I got stung by a bee on my big toe (bravo, bravo!) but the nurse gave me some salve. Tonight we'll roast hot dogs outside.' And Jersild comments: 'That would have to be enough this time. [Reine] felt he'd finished with the whole summer in five lines.'

"Things have certainly changed since the days when you wrote *Pippi Longstocking* and the *Bill Bergson* series," I commented. "No matter how lonely some of your child characters might feel, they never seem to experience this suffocating sense of anomie and resignation and isolation."

"Things *have* changed," Astrid Lindgren replied. "I'm afraid that children don't play the way we did as children and as they do in my books. They participate in sports, but they don't *play.* Now they look at television. TV broadens the mind in one way but narrows it in another. It gives you more facts and words and information, but it limits your imagination. It's on a more superficial level than when a child reads a book, because he or she has to create his or her own pictures, which are more lovely and beautiful than you can ever see on TV. On the whole I think it's damaging if you can't control it. I met a mother in America who told me that her daughter had watched TV for eighteen hours one day! She must have been crazy at that point. And I'm sure that there are many homes in which parents don't speak to their children and children don't speak to their parents. I can't write for teenagers now, I don't know enough about them, they're completely unlike the Bergson children—there's no resemblance at all. When I was a child we didn't have cars, TV, radio, or even many films. So there was a lot of room for imagination!"

"You once said: 'That our Lord let children be children before they grew up was one of his better ideas.' And I wanted to know something about your own childhood, since you've also said that 'it is my childhood that I long to return to . . . and if I dare to be so bold as to speak of inspiration, I must say that it is there in my childhood home that I get many of the impulses that can later appear in a story.'"

"My father, Samuel August Ericsson," she explained, "was a peasant, a renter of a vicar's farm, and fell in love with my mother, Hannah from Hult, when he was thirteen and she was nine—and she remained his 'devotedly little beloved one' throughout their life together. She died eight years before him—we thought he'd die, too. But no, he said that some leave ahead, others leave later, there's nothing you can do. He enjoyed living, and he was sure that one day he'd meet her again, and he continued to love her and talk about her and to praise all her virtues. They were strong believers, which my brothers and sisters and I were not. In the Bible we read that there is no marriage in heaven, just angels. So I told my father about the 'little angel Hannah,' and he got quite angry at the thought that Hannah should be there as an angel and not belong to him!

"And I've written a memoir about my parents' love affair and about my childhood," Astrid Lindgren said as she got up to find a copy in one of the bookshelves [*Samuel August från Sevedstorp och Hanna i Hult*]. "It's never been translated into English, so perhaps you could find someone to do that, and then you can find out everything." (Thanks to Ann B. Weissmann, I did!)

Astrid Lindgren, the second of four children (three girls, one boy), was raised on a farm called Nås near the little town of Vimmerby in Småland. Her extraordinarily happy childhood was, as she tells us, filled with security and freedom: "security in having those two there, those who cared so much for each other and who were there all the time if we need them, but who—if we did not need them—left us free to roam around the fantastic childhood playground we had at Nås. Surely we were disciplined with order and the fear of God, as was the tradition of the time, but in our playful life we were wonderfully free and never controlled. And we played and played and played, and it is a wonder we didn't play ourselves to death. We were climbing like apes in trees and on roofs, we jumped from lumber piles and hay lofts so that our innards complained, we crawled through our dangerous subterranean tunnels in the sawdust heap, we were swimming in the river long before we knew how to swim, totally forgetting the imperative by our mother not to 'go further out than the navel.' But all four of us survived."

Free from nagging and free to play, the children, at age six, were still expected to learn how to thin fodder beets and cut nettles for the poultry. "Just go on, don't stop" was their mother's admonition when they started dreaming over the dish pail—a piece of advice Astrid Lindgren says she has taken to heart throughout her life. And the children, far from being sheltered from adult reality, learned about life from the servant girls and farmhands: "It was fun and it was instructive for a child to grow up as I did with people of varying habits and types and ages. Without them knowing it and without me knowing it myself, I learned something from them about the conditions of life and how problematic it can be to be a human being. I learned other things as well, for this was an outspoken sort of people who did not keep anything back just because children happened to be around. And we were there, my siblings and myself, for we had to bring them coffee while they were working the fields. That is what I remember best, the coffee breaks when all were gathered, sitting there at the edge of a ditch, drinking coffee and dunking their rye-bread sandwiches and exchanging thoughts about this and that."

Astrid and her siblings often used to run through a little stretch of forest and wind up visiting Stenbåcksroten, a group of small cottages where many outcasts of society lived—paupers, "coffee bitches" (women who were supposed to have gone mad from drinking too much coffee), and the village prostitute. There were vagabonds in their hayloft every night (probably the models for Paradise Oscar the tramp, who befriends the orphan boy Rasmus in the author's moving *Rasmus and the Vagabond*) who arrived in the twilight and bought some milk and bread for the night. And Astrid, always curious, often investigated local lore: "Our cow-tender told us that if we walked around the coffin house in the cemetery twelve times at twelve o'clock at night, the devil would appear in all his hideousness. 'And then it happens, then "Knös" comes to fetch one,' that was the saying. And of course we had to find out if that was really true, just as we had to find out about the coffee bitches and their wickedness toward children. I believe that we spent a great deal of our time exploring what was true and what was not true in this world."

Sundays were begrudgingly devoted to Sunday school and church, for which Astrid was forced to wear "freshly washed, coarse, black wool stockings" that she detested. (Perhaps the refusal of the five-year-old heroine of *Lotta on Troublemaker Street* to wear an itchy, striped sweater—Lotta cuts it to pieces with scissors and then runs away—is her author's fantasy revenge for having had to wear those hated stockings as a child!) But she looked forward to traveling to family parties at her grandmother's in a horse-driven *vurst*, the journey there smelling of "horses and sunbaked leather and the resin of the pine trees" . . . while the homebound journeys found her "half asleep watching the black forest under the light summer sky; and perhaps I remember even better going home from the Christmas parties, bedded down in the basketweave sleigh listening to the sleigh bells and looking up into the starry sky. . . . Yes, it was good to be a child in the age of horses." And then there were the fall and spring fairs in Vimmerby, when the streets were taken over by itinerant menageries and carnivals and were filled with candy-women, merchants, farmers, and horse dealers.

But even more than the people she grew up with, Astrid Lindgren most of all remembers nature: "The strawberry patches, the hepatica hills, the meadows with primulas, the blueberry lands, the woods where the linneas tinkled their pink bells in the moss, the pastures around Nås where we knew every path and every rock, the stream with the water lilies, the ditches, the creeks, and the trees—I remember those more than I remember the people. Rocks and trees were as close to us as living beings, and nature protected and nurtured our playing and our dreaming. Whatever our imagination could call forth was enacted in the land around us, all fairy tales, all adventures we invented or read about or heard about, all of it happened there, only there, even our songs and prayers had their places in surrounding nature."

But while she was "soaking up nature," Astrid was also introduced to "culture" when she was about five years old, by a little girl named Edith, the daughter of a cowhand and his wife, Kristin: "This girl Edith—blessed be she now and forever—read to me the fairy tale about the Giant Bam-Bam and the fairy Viribunda, and thus set my childish soul into a movement which has not yet completely ceased. The miracle occurred in the kitchen of a poor farmhand, and from that day on there is no other kitchen in the world."

Eventually, Astrid learned to read herself and ordered books for Christmas. Her first volume was *Snow White*, "with a chubby, black-tressed princess by Jenny Nyström on the cover; later, I bought *Among Leprechauns and Trolls* with the unforgettable illustrations by John Bauer. Imagine, to be the sole owner of a book—a wonder I didn't faint for pure happiness! I can still remember how these books smelled when they arrived, fresh from the printer; yes, I started by smelling them, and there was no lovelier scent in all the world. It was full of foretaste and anticipation."

At ten, Astrid went to a school that had a library, and began "devouring" everything: the *Iliad, Robinson Crusoe, Uncle Tom's Cabin, The Count of Monte Cristo, The Jungle Books, Huckleberry Finn*, among others. "And then all the wonderful books for girls. Imagine, there were so many girls in the world who were suddenly as close to oneself as ever any beings of flesh and blood! There was Hetty, the Irish whirlwind, and Polly, a jewel of a girl from New England, Pollyanna and Katy, not to mention Sara, the one with the diamond mines who became so wondrously poor and was freezing in her attic until Ram Dass came climbing across the roof with soup and warm blankets. And then of course Anne of Green Gables: oh, my unforgettable one, forever you will be riding the cart with Matthew Cuthbert beneath the flowering apple trees of Avonlea! How I lived with that girl! A whole summer my sisters and I played at Anne of Green Gables in the big sawdust heap at the sawmill; I was Diana Barry, and the pond at the manure heap was the Dark Reflecting Waves." She also confesses to having read mysteries, "tear-dripping" love stories, and religious books—"in my opinion, all of these books were good books, please notice that! But then, of course, I do not believe in the system of using children as literary critics."

She found it hard to find time to read as much as she wanted to, since "it was assumed that the children would help around the house. I was frequently put to rocking and singing to my youngest sister, who refused to go to sleep otherwise, and that was an ordeal if one had just come across a good book. But I managed. I sang from the book, page after page. It took more time than usual, of course, but I could do it. 'There is a woman alone in the woods and crying, tralalala'—my sisters still repeat that as an example of my exercises in singing and reading."

In school her classmates used to say, "You'll turn out to be an author when you grow up" or, more sarcastically, "You'll be the Selma Lagerlöf of Vimmerby." "That scared me so much," Astrid Lindgren recalls, "that I made a firm decision—never to write a book! It says already in Ecclesiastes that there is no end to the making of books, and I didn't feel that I would be the right person to increase the stacks of books further. I stuck to my decision until March 1944. But then that snow fell and made the streets slippery as soap. I fell, sprained my ankle, I had to stay in bed, and I had nothing to do. So what does one do? Maybe write a book? I wrote *Pippi Longstocking*. . . . That's why I write children's books. And it is all nothing but a continuation of what started in Kristin's kitchen that long ago."

Back in Astrid Lindgren's living room, I asked her about the old red farmhouse, surrounded by apple trees, where she was born and raised. "That house," I said, "must have been the archetype of all the houses that appear in your children's books: the little gray house by the lake in *Rasmus and the Vagabond*, the old white house with lilacs and cherry trees in *The Brothers Lionheart*, the white thatched cottage in the Garden of Roses in *Mio, My Son*, and of course, Villa Villekulla in *Pippi Longstocking*. As Bachelard writes in *The Poetics of Space*: 'There exists for each one of us . . . a house of dream-memory that is lost in the shadow of a beyond of the real past. . . . The places in which we have *experienced daydreaming* reconstitute themselves in a new daydream, and it is because our memories of former dwelling places are relived as daydreams that these dwelling places of the past remain in us for all time.'"

"That's wonderful!" Astrid Lindgren responded. "I love houses and I hate them when they go against what my dream house ought to be. I used to go to a place called Tällberg where there are wonderful old houses—peasant houses that seem as if they came up from the ground by themselves. And now there is one terrible, ugly house that destroys everything around it. Also, I bought the house where I was born, but now the town has spread into the wooded pastureland, and my old house is surrounded by things I don't like. But inside it's exactly as it was, since I've restored it—it's just as it was when I was a child."

"I've noticed that trees are also important in your books—the ones that connect the farmhouses in *The Children of Noisy Village*, the linden tree in which Rasmus perches in *Rasmus and the Vagabond,* and, of course, Pippi Longstocking's hollow oak."

"Trees mean a lot to me," Astrid Lindgren replied. "I once wrote an essay—it's in the book I just gave you—called 'Are There Different Trees?' A professor once asked that question—that's how close he was to nature! To me, there's nothing more personal or alive on earth than trees—with the exception of people and animals. And in my essay I quoted a number of verses by different poets about trees—we have trees in poems and songs and tales and myths.

"I also mentioned my favorite childhood trees: grandmother's white-heart cherry tree covered with big, yellowish-red berries, the equal of which might have grown in paradise but nowhere else. Then there was a particular apple tree outside our house, and we used to wake early and be the first outside to eat whatever apples had fallen down during the night. And then there was the 'owl tree,' for the owls had their nests there. But during the day it was our climbing tree. It was hollow, just like Pippi Longstocking's tree, but it was an elm, not an oak as in the *Pippi* books. And we loved it, even without the soda pop inside. My brother once put a hen's egg in the owl's nest, and the owl hatched a chicken for him. I even taught my little son when he was three years old to climb that tree; and he wanted to go up it every day, otherwise he'd cry in the evening. That tree is still there, though it's now aged and battered."

At the conclusion of her essay, she writes: "Even better, I know an ash tree that grew at the church of Vimmerby when this century was young. For under that tree they were sitting, my father and my mother, one April evening when snow was whirling around them, and my father asked my mother if she would share his life. Who knows what would have happened if that ash had not been standing there with a bench beneath it! Perhaps there would never have been a proposal, and that would have been sad for me." And then the author adds: "Far away in our unknown past we might have been creatures swinging from branch to branch, living in trees. Perhaps in the deepest depths of our wandering souls we long to return there, perhaps without knowing it we regret having ever left the crowns of the trees and stepping down onto earth. Who knows, perhaps it is pure homesickness that makes us write poems and songs of the trees and makes us dream of all the green forests of earth."

"I don't write books *for* children," Astrid Lindgren commented to me.

"I write books for the child I am myself. I write about things that are dear to me—trees and houses and nature—just to please myself."

"Listen to what Bachelard writes," I said. "'The water of the child, the child's fire, the child's trees, the child's springtime flowers . . . what a lot of true principles for an analysis of the world!'"

"How beautiful!" she exclaimed.

"And he also says: 'When the human world leaves him in peace, the child feels like the son of the cosmos.' And I've noticed that you've depicted many orphaned or foster children—Rasmus, Mio, Karlsson in *Karlsson-on-the-Roof*, and Pippi—all of them alone but in touch with what is real. I read somewhere that you once said: 'To be alone is best. There is no loneliness that frightens me. Deep down we all remain alone. Without loneliness and poetry I believe I could hardly survive.'"

"Did I say that?" Astrid Lindgren asked, laughing. "I don't remember, but it does sound like me. I think, however, that a great many children are lonely, even if they aren't orphans. It's a pity when the child has no adult—at least one—close to him or her in order to help the child to be happy and to develop."

"But all these children in your books do belong to someone," I commented. "Pippi has Tommy and Annika, Mio has the King in Farawayland, Karlsson has his friend Eric, Rasmus has Paradise Oscar the tramp, and Jonathan and Karl have each other in *The Brothers Lionheart*. I wanted to ask you about this last work because along with the *Pippi* books it's your most controversial, since it's about death—a subject children's literature, in this century at least, has tended to shy away from. Each of the brothers sacrifices himself for the other; and after their deaths, they find themselves together, first in the heavenly land of Nangiyala—where they have to battle evil forces that live outside their valley paradise. And when one of them has again to die, because he has been mortally wounded in battle, they both decide to die again in order that they can be together in another heavenly land where they will never be apart. . . . And I'm sure your father would have understood this book that reminds us that love is as strong as death," I added.

"Yes, the book came about in a very strange manner," she replied. "You know how you walk around with very diffuse thoughts, waiting for something to grow and be real? And I like to walk in cemeteries; it's very peaceful to go there and read the inscriptions. And one day I saw one that said:

Here lie two little brothers. And then I found other dead brothers lying together—never sisters—and that made me think of what happened to them, why they had to die so young. So I had this feeling and didn't know what to do about it. And then one early winter morning, on a train trip through Sweden, seeing a beautiful rose-colored sunrise over the snow, I suddenly knew what I wanted to write—more or less.

"I thought this book might be a comfort for children who were afraid of death, which many children are. When I was little and was told that after you die you go to heaven, I didn't find that very amusing, but thought it better than lying down in the earth and just being dead! But my grand-children have no such belief. I felt that one of them was afraid of death, and when I showed him the manuscript he smiled and said, 'Well, we don't know how it is, it could just as well be like that.'

"And I get lots of letters about *The Brothers Lionheart*—many from adults, too. One from a German woman doctor who had lost her nine-year-old daughter to leukemia. And this little girl had lived with the book the last years of her life, and it was her only comfort. When her two little rabbits died, the girl said, 'Oh, they're in Nangiyala now.' Many children have written to me saying, 'Now I'm not afraid of death anymore.' Even if it's just a tale, why shouldn't they have some comfort?

"Incidentally, I just got a letter yesterday from a Korean soldier who studied Swedish at the university there and who plans to translate *The Brothers Lionheart* into Korean. He writes: 'Spring rain falls outside the window and spring flowers growing outside the gray walls whisper to me in my ear: Throw away your green uniform, let us go out. But I can't, be-cause I'm a twenty-five-year-old Korean soldier.' It's wonderful to get a letter that begins that way. And I think that all soldiers should throw away their uniforms.

"I know, too, that people have told me that the *Pippi* books have changed their lives. But the best compliment came in a message on a scrap of paper that was given to me once by an unknown woman. All it said was, 'Thanks for brightening up a gloomy childhood.' And that satisfied me.

"Memory," concludes Astrid Lindgren in her essay on her childhood, "holds unknown sleeping treasures of fragrances and flavors and sights and sounds of childhood past! . . . I can still see and smell and remember the bliss of that rose bush in the pasture, the one that showed me for the first time what beauty means, I can still hear the chirping of the landrail in the rye fields on a summer evening and the hooting of the owls in the owl tree in the nights of spring, I still know exactly how it feels to enter a warm cow barn from biting cold and snow, I know how the tongue of a calf feels against a hand and how rabbits smell, and the smell in a carriage shed, and how milk sounds when it strikes the bottom of a bucket, and the feel of small chicken feet when one holds a newly hatched chicken. These may not be extraordinary things to remember. The extraordinary thing about it is the intensity of these experiences when we were new here on earth.

"How long ago that must be! Otherwise, how can the world have changed so much? Could it all really become so different in just one short little half-century? My childhood was spent in a land that no longer exists—but where did it all go?"

("But Pippi continued to stare straight ahead with a dreamy look. Then she blew out the light.")

ASTRID LINDGREN

NOVEMBER 14, 1907 – JANUARY 28, 2002

HENRY MILLER
Reflections of a Cosmic Tourist

Pacific Palisades, 1973

Henry Miller—"confused, negligent, reckless, lusty, obscene, boisterous, thoughtful, scrupulous, lying, diabolically truthful man that I am"; author of many famous and infamous books "filled with wisdom and nonsense, truth and falsehood, toenails, hair, teeth, blood, and ovaries" (his words)—has been called everything from "a counterrevolutionary sexual politician" (Kate Millett) to "a true sexual revolutionary" (Norman Mailer); an author who neglects "form and *mesure*" (Frank Kermode) to "the only imaginative prose writer of the slightest value who has appeared among the English-speaking races for some years past" (George Orwell).

Now eighty-two [1973], and in spite of recent illnesses still painting and writing, Miller is still accepting what he once called our Air-Conditioned Nightmare with joyful incredulity, still continuing to find out and tell us who he is. This past year marks the fortieth anniversary of the publication of the first Paris edition of *Tropic of Cancer* (Miller's first published book), and it is now indisputably clear that Miller's more than forty subsequent volumes must be read simply as one enormous evolving work—a perpetual bildungsroman—manifesting the always changing, yet ever the same, awareness and celebration of the recovery of the divinity of man, as well as of the way of truth which, Miller says, leads not to salvation but to enlightenment. "There is no salvation, really, only infinite realms of experience providing more and more tests, demanding more and more faith. . . . When each thing is lived through to the end, there is no death and no regrets, neither is there a false springtime; each moment lived pushes open a greater, wider horizon from which there is no escape save living."

229

Gentile Dybbuck (as he once called himself), patriot of the Fourteenth Ward (Brooklyn), American anarchist, Parisian *voyou*, cosmic
tourist in Greece, sage of Big Sur, Henry Miller is today an inhabitant of
an improbable-looking Georgian colonial house in Pacific Palisades, Los
Angeles—a house teeming with posters, paintings, sketches, and photographs, all tokens and traces of Miller's ebullient, peripatetic life.

There are a number of his radiant "instinctive" watercolors hanging in
the living room. ("If it doesn't look like a horse when I'm through, I can
always turn it into a hammock," he once said of his "method" of painting
in "The Angel Is My Watermark.") On one wall is a hand-inscribed poster
listing the names of scores of places Miller has visited around the world—
with marginal comments:

> Bruges—the Dead City (for poets)
> Imperial City, California (loss of identity)
> Pisa (talking to tower all hours)
> Cafe Boudou, Paris: Rue Fontaine (Algerian whore)
> Grand Canyon (still the best)
> Corfu—Violating Temple (English girl)
> Biarritz (rain, rain, rain)

In the kitchen, posted on a cabinet, is his Consubstantial Health Menu,
which announces favorite dishes: e.g., Bata Yaku! Sauerfleisch mit
Kartoffel-klösze, Leeks, Zucchini ad perpetuum, Calves' Liver (yum
yum) . . . and a strong warning: Please! No Health Food.

Across one end of his study is a floor-to-ceiling bookshelf containing
hundreds of his own works translated into scores of languages, while two
other walls are completely decorated with graffiti and drawings, all contributed by visitors, friends, and Henry himself: "Kill the Buddha!" "Let's
Case the Joint!" "Love, Delight, and Organ Are Feminine in the Plural!"
"The Last Sleeper of the Middle Ages!" "Don't Look for Miracles. You
Are the Miracle!"

Most fascinating of all is the author's famous bathroom—a veritable
museum that presents the iconography of the World of Henry Miller:
photos of actresses on the set of the filmed version of *Tropic of Cancer*,
Buddhas from four countries, a portrait of Hermann Hesse ("Most writers don't look so hot," Miller says. "They're thin blooded, alone with their
thoughts."), a Jungian mandala, Taoist emblems, a Bosch reproduction,
the castle of Ludwig of Bavaria, Miller's fifth wife, Hoki (from whom he's

now separated and about whom he wrote: "First it was a broken toe, then it was a broken brow and finally a broken heart"), the head of Gurdjieff ("of all masters the most interesting"), and, hidden away in the corner, a couple of hard-core photos "for people who expect something like that in here." (Tom Schiller's delightful film *Henry Miller Asleep and Awake* was shot in this bathroom and presents the docent author taking the viewer around on a guided tour.)

"I really hate greeting you like this, in pajamas and in bed," Miller says as I enter his bedroom. Smiling and talking with a never discarded bristly, crepitated Brooklyn accent and a tone of voice blending honey and *rezina*, he continues: "I just got out of the hospital again, you see. They had to replace an artificial artery running from my neck down to the leg. It didn't work, it developed an abscess, and so they had to take out both the artery and the abscess. I'm really in bad shape, no?" Miller says, laughing. "And this is all attributable to those damned cigarettes. I was an athlete when I was young—don't you know? I was good at track and a bicycle rider. I didn't smoke until I was twenty-five, and then it was incessant. And all my wives smoked, too. If I start again it means death. My circulation will stop, and they'll have to cut off my legs."

Again a smile and a gentle laugh. "Always Merry and Bright!"— Henry's lifelong motto.

"You'll have to speak to my left ear—the other one doesn't work. And I've lost vision in my left eye."

"Can you see me?" I ask.

"I certainly imagined you differently," Miller responds. "When I heard that someone named Jonathan was coming, I thought you'd be some tall, uptight Englishman with blond hair. But I'm glad I was wrong."

Henry, unlike his fellow expatriate novelist and namesake Henry (James)—it is impossible to think of two more wildly opposite types—is well known for his caustic Anglophobic attitudes. (Miller in a letter to Lawrence Durrell: "The most terrible, damning line in the whole of *The Black Book* is that remark of Chamberlain's: 'Look, do you think it would damage our relationship if I sucked you off?' That almost tells the whole story of England.") But strangely, it is the English Lawrence Durrell who, as a twenty-three-year-old writer and diplomat living in Corfu, wrote the then forty-three-year-old Miller an ecstatic fan letter after reading *Tropic of Cancer*, calling it "the only really man-sized piece of work this century can boast of." They have been close friends and correspondents for almost forty years, and in fact Durrell and his wife are expected this evening for dinner. (Durrell taught this past year at Caltech, one of the main reasons being to keep in close contact with his friend.)

Hanging on the wall alongside Henry's bed is a dramatic photo of a saintly looking Chinese man, whose face bears an uncanny resemblance to Miller's own.

"That's a photo of a Chinese sage I found in a magazine thirty years ago," Henry says, noticing my interest. "I framed it and kept it ever since. I regard him as an enlightened man. Even though he wasn't known."

"You yourself once characterized the French writer Blaise Cendrars as 'the Chinese rock-bottom man of my imagination,'" I mention, pulling out my little black notebook to check the quote.

"I'm sure Durrell christened me that," Henry says. "Are you sure I said that about Cendrars?"

"Absolutely, it's in my book here."

Henry looks at me bemusedly. "That's really something," he exclaims. "I should have realized this before. But with that book you really look just like that guy Columbo on television. Peter Falk plays him, and he seems a little half-witted, you know, a little stupid . . . not conniving but cunning. Yes, I'd like to be like that. That's my idea of a man! . . . Go right ahead with . . . what is it you want to ask me? . . . Amazing, just like that guy Columbo."

"This isn't really a question," I say, rummaging through the book, "but speaking of the Chinese, I'd like to read you a little story by Chuang-Tze, the disciple of Lao-Tze. I wrote it down to read to you because to me it suggests something very deep and basic about all of your work."

"Just read it loudly and slowly, please," Henry says.

Chuang-Tze writes: "The sovereign of the Southern Sea is called Dissatisfaction (with things as they are); the sovereign of the Northern Sea, Revolution; the sovereign of the Center of the World, Chaos. Dissatisfaction and Revolution from time to time met together in the territory of Chaos, and Chaos treated them very hospitably. The two sovereigns planned how to repay Chaos's kindness. They said, 'Men all have seven holes to their bodies for seeing, hearing, eating, and breathing. Our friend has none of these. Let us try to bore some holes in him.' Each day they bored one hole. On the seventh day Chaos died."

"That's a fantastic story," Henry says. "And it's interesting that you see that in my work."

"I was thinking of your idea of chaos as the fluid which enveloped you, which you breathed in through the gills. And of the fertile void, the chaos which you've called the 'seat of creation itself,' whose order is beyond human comprehension. And of the 'humanizing' and destruction of the natural order. And I was thinking, too, of your statement in *Black Spring*: 'My faltering and groping, my search for any and every means of expression, is a sort of divine stuttering. I am dazzled by the glorious collapse of the world!'"

"Yes, that's wonderful," Henry says. "I don't even remember some of these things you say I've written. Read some more from your notebook."

"I've been thinking about your obsession in your books with the idea of China, and that photo on the wall made me realize how much you look Chinese. 'I want to become nothing more than the China I already am,' you once wrote. 'I am nothing if not Chinese,' and you've identified *Chinese* with that 'supernormal life such that one is unnaturally gay, unnaturally healthy, unnaturally indifferent. . . . The artist scorns the ordinary alphabet and adopts the symbol, the ideograph. *He writes* Chinese.' And in many of your works you point over and over again to the fact that our verb 'to be,' intransitive in English, is transitive in Chinese."

"Yes, yes, that's become my credo. To be gay is the sign of health and intelligence. First of all humor: that's what the Chinese philosophers had, and what the Germans never had. Nietzsche had some, but it was morbid and bitter. But Kant, Schopenhauer . . . you can look in vain. Chuang-Tze is a genius, his marvelous humor comes out of all his pores. And without that you can't have humor. My favorite American writer, for instance, is the Jewish immigrant I. B. Singer. He makes me laugh and weep, he tears me apart, don't you know? Most American writers hardly touch me, they're always on the surface. He's a big man in my estimation.

"But speaking of the Chinese, I have intuitive flashes that I have Mongol and Jewish blood in me—two strange mixtures, no? As far as I know, I'm German all the way through, but I disown it. I believe that blood counts very strongly—what's in your veins. I've had that feeling. Because I'm a real German, and I don't like that. Not just because of the war . . . long before that: I was raised among them in a German-American neighborhood, and they're worse than the Germans in Germany. . . . Of course, there's Goethe, Schiller, Heine, Hölderlin, the composers. . . . Naturally they're wonderful.

"You know something? I was recently reading Hermann Hesse's last book, *My Belief.* And the very end of this book has to do with Oriental writers. He mentions how his perspective on life changed when he became acquainted with Lao-Tze, Chuang-Tze, and the I Ching, of course. And I discovered these writers when I was about eighteen. I was crazy about the Chinese. I have trouble, however, with the novels like *All Men Are Brothers*—too many characters and there's no psychology—everything is on the surface."

"One of my favorite books of yours, Henry, is *Big Sur and the Oranges of Hieronymus Bosch.* Your meditations on and descriptions of your friends and life in Big Sur are so serene and lambent, like some of the great Chinese poems. I wish it had gone on and on."

"The poets who retired in old age to the country," Henry reflects. "Yes, that's right. I've tried to model myself on the Chinese sages. And they were happy, gay men. I've heard that the old men in China before the Revolution used to sit out on river boats and converse, drink tea, smoke, and just enjoy talking about philosophy or literature. They always invited girls to come and drink with them. And then they'd go and fly a kite afterwards, a real kite. I think that's admirable. . . . We flew kites in Big Sur, but there we had big winds in canyons with birds being lifted by the updrafts. The kites got torn and smashed."

"I especially remember," I mention, "that passage in *Big Sur* where you describe the morning sun rising behind you and throwing an enlarged shadow of yourself into the iridescent fog below. You wrote about it this way: 'I lift my arms as in prayer, achieving a wingspan no god ever possessed, and there in the drifting fog a nimbus floats about my head, a radiant nimbus such as the Buddha himself might proudly wear. In the Himalayas, where the same phenomenon occurs, it is said that a devout follower of the Buddha will throw himself from a peak—*into the arms of Buddha.*'"

"Yes, I remember that," Henry says. "Your shadow is in the light and fog, overaggrandized; you're in monstrous size and you're tempted to throw yourself over."

"That reminds me of Anaïs Nin's comment," I mention, "that the figures in your books are always 'outsized . . . whether tyrant or victims, man or woman.'"

"That's true," Henry responds. "That's because I'm enthusiastic and I exaggerate, I adore and worship. I don't just *like*. I love. I go overboard. And if I hate, it's in the same way. I don't know any neutral, in-between ground."

Henry Miller's enthusiasms and exaggerations have led many persons to hold on to a distorted picture of the author as a writer only of six supposedly epigamic "sex" books (the *Tropics, Quiet Days in Clichy,* and *Sexus, Plexus,* and *Nexus*) for a reading constituency consisting primarily of GIs in Place Pigalle, existentialist wastrels, or academic "freaks" like Karl Shapiro (who called Miller the "greatest living author").

Of the above-mentioned works, *Tropic of Capricorn* is certainly one of the most original works of twentieth-century literature. And the fact that Henry Miller has been stereotyped so disparagingly is a peculiarity of American literary history, since his work is one that consistently evolves, perfectly exemplifying the ideas of rapturous change, metamorphosis, surrender, and growth.

"The angels praising the Lord are never the same," the great Hasidic Rabbi Nachman once said. "The Lord changes them every day." One of Henry Miller's favorite statements is that of the philosopher Eric Gutkind: "To overcome the world is to make it transparent." And it is as if with the transparency of angels that Miller reveals an unparalleled literary ability to disappear into the objects and persons of his attention and thereby to allow them to appear in an unmediated radiance. Miller's heightened identification with everything he notices is made even more powerful by means of an astonishing descriptive presentational immediacy and an attendant sense of magnanimity.

Consider his meditation in "The Cosmological Eye" on his friend Hans Reichel's painting, *The Stillborn Twins*:

> It is an ensemble of miniature panels in which there is not only
> the embryonic flavor but the hieroglyphic as well. If he likes you,
> Reichel will show you in one of the panels the little shirt which
> the mother of the stillborn twins was probably thinking of in her
> agony. He says it so simply and honestly that you feel like weeping. The little shirt embedded in a cold prenatal green is indeed
> the sort of shirt which only a woman in travail could summon
> up. You feel that with the freezing torture of birth, at the moment when the mind seems ready to snap, the mother's eye
> inwardly turning gropes frantically towards some tender, known
> object which will attach her, if only for a moment, to the world
> of human entities. In this quick, agonized clutch the mother
> sinks back, through worlds unknown to man, to planets long
> since disappeared, where perhaps there were no babies' shirts but

where there was the warmth, the tenderness, the mossy envelope of a love beyond love, of a love for the disparate elements which metamorphose through the mother, through her pain, through her death, so that life may go on. Each panel, if you read it with the cosmological eye, is a throwback to an undecipherable script of life. The whole cosmos is moving back and forth through the sluice of time and the stillborn twins are embedded there in the cold prenatal green with the shirt that was never worn.

Or read Miller's descriptions of the Paris photographs of the French photographer Brassai in "The Eye of Paris":

What strange cities—and situations stranger still! The mendicant sitting on the public bench thirsting for a glimmer of sun, the butcher standing in a pool of blood with knife upraised, the scows and barges dreaming in the shadows of the bridges, the pimp standing against a wall with cigarette in hand, the street cleaner with her broom of reddish twigs, her thick, gnarled fingers, her high stomach draped in black, a shroud over her womb, rinsing away the vomit of the night before so that when I pass over the cobblestones my feet will gleam with the light of morning stars. I see the old hats, the sombreros and fedoras, the velours and Panamas that I painted with a clutching fury; I see the corners of walls eroded by time and weather which I passed in the night and in passing felt the erosion going on in myself, corners of my own walls crumbling away, blown down, dispersed, reintegrated elsewhere in mysterious shape and essence. I see the old tin urinals where, standing in the dead silence of the night, I dreamed so violently that the past sprang up like a white horse and carried me out of the body.

Most persons seem to have forgotten (or have never known) not only passages like these but also the great reveries on Brooklyn, the pissoirs in Paris, and the madness of Tante Melia (all in *Black Spring*); the hymn to Saturnian effluvia and the talking-blues Dipsy Doodle passacaglia which tells the story of Louis the Armstrong and Epaminondas *(The Colossus of Maroussi)*; his dreamlike discovery of the secret street in "Reunion in Brooklyn"; the letters to Alfred Perlès and Lawrence Durrell; the prose poems describing Miller's obsession with painting *(To Paint Is to Love Again, The Waters Reglitterized)*; the *Hamlet* correspondence with Michel

Fraenkel (long out of print); and the essays on Balzac, D. H. Lawrence, Cendrars, and H. Rider Haggard. All of these have been overlooked in the still raging debate concerning Miller's problematic attitude toward women.

The recent Mailer/Miller/Millett literary fracas presented Kate Millett, in her book *Sexual Politics,* accusing Miller of depersonalizing women with his virulent and fear-ridden sexual attitudes, while Norman Mailer in *The Prisoner of Sex* defended him as a "sexual pioneer." According to Mailer, Millett distorts Miller's escapades and determinedly overlooks the author's omnifarious, picaresque humor. But in terms of getting to the roots of Miller's sexual attitudes, neither Millett nor Mailer comes close to the perspicacious criticism of Miller's friend of more than forty years, Anaïs Nin, or to Miller's own comments on these matters in his correspondence with various friends.

In her diaries Anaïs Nin often mentions the paradox between what she sees as her friend's gentle and violent writing, his veering from sentimentality to callousness, tenderness to ridicule, gentleness to anger. And she suggests that because of what she saw as Miller's "utter subjection" to his wife June (Mona, Mara, Alraune in his novels), Miller used his books to take revenge upon her.

Miller himself has written: "Perhaps one reason why I have stressed so much the immoral, the wicked, the ugly, the cruel in my work is because I wanted others to know how valuable these are, how equally if not more important than the good things. . . . I was getting the poison out of my system. Curiously enough, this poison had a tonic effect for others. It was as if I had given them some kind of immunity."

Sometimes, in his letters, we find Miller protecting himself, describing himself as "a little boy going down into the street to play, having no fixed purpose, no particular direction, no especial friend to seek out, but just divinely content to be going down into the street to see whatever might come. As if I did not love them! Only I also loved others, too . . . not in the way they meant, but in a natural, wholesome, easy way. Like one loves garlic, honey, wild strawberries."

But he is unsparing of himself as well: "The coward in me always concealed himself in that thick armor of dull passivity. I only grew truly sensitive again when I had attained a certain measure of liberation. . . . To live out one's desires and, in so doing, subtly alter their nature is the aim of every individual who aspires to evolve."

The idea of self-liberation—what psychologists like to call "self-actualization" or "individuation" or "creative being"—has always been Miller's great concern in all of his books, which progress from the *via purgativa* to the *via unitiva*. And even as his novels work counterclockwise (*Tropic of Cancer* tells of Miller's life in thirties Paris, *Tropic of Capricorn* and *The Rosy Crucifixion* of his earlier life in New York City), Miller gives, as he tells us, in "each separate fragment, each work, the feeling of the whole as I go on, because I am digging deeper and deeper into life, digging deeper and deeper into past and future. . . . The writer lives between the upper and lower worlds: he takes the path in order eventually to become that path himself."

This path is often filled with the "strong odor of sex," which, to Miller, is "really the aroma of birth; it is disagreeable only to those who fail to recognize its significance." And it is a path which leads to his rebirth at the tomb of Agamemnon—described in *The Colossus of Maroussi* as "the great peace which comes of surrender"—and to his rebirth at the conclusion of *Tropic of Capricorn*: "I take you as a star and a trap, as a stone to tip the scales, as a judge that is blindfolded, as a hole to fall into, as a path to walk, as a cross and an arrow. Up to the present I traveled the opposite way of the sun; henceforth I travel two ways, as sun and as moon. Henceforth I take on two sexes, two hemispheres, two skies, two sets of everything. Henceforth I shall be double-jointed and double sexed. Everything that happens will happen twice. I shall be as a visitor to this earth, partaking of its blessings and carrying off its gifts. I shall neither serve nor be served. I shall seek the end in myself."

And this amazing passage suggests, if not that Henry is a prototype of Norman O. Brown, at least something quite different from what Millett and Mailer are arguing about.

Henry Miller is hardly an enthusiastic supporter of psychological criticism. "This seeking for meaning in everything!" he once exclaimed. "So Germanic! This urge to make everything profound. What nonsense! If only they could also make everything unimportant at the same time." But I decided to ask him about the woman question anyway.

"Henry," I say, "Anaïs Nin wrote in her diaries that in *Tropic of Cancer* you created a book in which you have a sex and a stomach. In *Tropic of Capricorn* and *Black Spring*, she says, you have eyes, ears, and a mouth. And eventually, Anaïs Nin suggests, you will finally create a full man, at which point you'll be able to write about a woman for real."

"I don't remember her writing that," Henry responds. "That should have stuck in my head. That's quite wonderful. But it's interesting, isn't it? It's like that Chuang-Tze story you read me, about the drilling of the holes into Chaos, don't you know?" Henry smiles. "But if you saw Anaïs today I think she'd give you the feeling that I *am* a whole man today.

"Tom Schiller told me that there was a bomb scare in Copenhagen when they were going to show his film about me *(Henry Miller Asleep and Awake)*. A woman's lib group called up the theater to stop the film from being shown—they showed it anyway—but I want so badly to write a letter to the women who are against me. The woman I could write it to would be Germaine Greer. I adore her—the others I don't know—and I'd like to say: 'My dear Germaine Greer, isn't it obvious from my work that I love women? Is the fact that I also fuck them without asking their names the great sin? I never took them as sex objects. . . . Well, maybe I did at times, but it wasn't done with evil thought or with the intention of putting the woman down. It just so happened that there were chance encounters—you meet and pass, and that's how it sometimes occurred. There never was any woman problem in my mind.'"

"You've been criticized, perhaps validly," I say, "for portraying women either as phantasmagoric angels disappearing into the clouds or as down-to-earth whores. Or do you think I'm distorting the picture?"

"I don't think that's true. I really don't," he replies. "To talk jokingly about it: They're all layable, even the angels. And the whores can be worshipped, too. Naturally. That's what Jesus did. The famous religious leaders always spoke well of whores."

"Again, Henry," I say, "Anaïs Nin has said that in *Tropic of Cancer* you seemed to be fighting off the idea of Woman because there was a woman inside of you whom you couldn't accept."

"It was my mother," Henry replies without hesitation, "whom I couldn't accept. I was always the enemy of my mother and she of me. We never got along—never. Not till her dying day. And even then we were still enemies. Even then she was berating me and treating me like a child. And I couldn't stand it. And I grabbed her and pushed her back on the pillow. And then I realized the brutality of it—I didn't hurt her—but the very thought of doing this to such a woman! And then I went out to the hall and sobbed and wept."

"I saw a photo of your mother recently," I mention, "and she looked like a strong, handsome woman."

"You really think so? Is that so?" Henry says with interest. "I always think of her as a cold woman. . . . But sometimes I think Anaïs analyzes everything too much. She believes so much that she's had such great help from psychoanalysts, and I'm always saying: Fuck the analyst, that's the last man to see, he's a faker. Now he isn't a faker, he's honest, and there are wonderful men. I read Jung and I know that Hermann Hesse said he was indebted to Jung and Freud. I can't read Freud today, but when I was nineteen or twenty I fought a battle for him. Today I don't think it was worth wasting time on, but that's a prejudice again, and I don't deny that. I don't see why we haven't got a right to be prejudiced."

"But psychologically there are so many interesting things in your books, Henry," I say. "The conclusion to *Tropic of Capricorn*, for example, where you say that from then on you'd be both male and female—everything that happened would occur twice. Or the earlier, even more amazing 'Land of Fuck' interlude, which is a reverie about the purity and infancy of sexual desire, in which you seem to become the sexual process itself in an out-of-body journey."

"Yes," Henry agrees, "you're lifted out of the body of the narrative, you're floating somewhere and sex is something like x, y, z—you can't name it. You see, that was a windfall. Every so often you get a gift from above, it comes to you, you have nothing to do with it, you're being dictated to. I don't take credit for that interlude. . . . And the last part of *Capricorn* . . . yes, that was a wonderful passage. Sometimes I don't know what these things mean. They come out of the unconscious. It's interesting, these questions. No one picks these things out."

In order to lighten things up, I innocuously ask Henry about rock 'n' roll—something I assume he likes.

"I detest rock 'n' roll," he retorts passionately. "To me it's noise, I miss the beautiful melodies. But I suppose it's an omission. What rock 'n' roll musicians do you like?"

"I like Bob Dylan for one," I say, "and I was thinking that some of your work must have influenced someone like Dylan. Like that passage in 'Into the Night Life' from *Black Spring*."

"Do you have it there in your book?" Henry asks. "How does it go?" I read:

The melting snow melts deeper, the iron rusts, the leaves flower.
On the corner, under the elevated, stands a man with a plug hat,
in blue serge and linen spats, his white mustache chopped fine.
The switch opens and out rolls all the tobacco juice, the golden

lemons, the elephant tusks, the candelabras. Moishe Pippik, the lemon dealer, fowled with pigeons, breeding purple eggs in his vest pocket and purple ties and watermelons and spinach with short stems, stringy, marred with tar. The whistle of the acorns loudly stirring, flurry of floozies bandaged in Lysol, ammonia and camphor patches, little mica huts, peanut shells triangled and corrugated, all marching triumphantly with the morning breeze. The morning light comes in creases, the window panes are streaked, the covers are torn, the oilcloth is faded. Walks a man with hair on end, not running, not breathing, a man with a weathervane that turns the corners sharply and then bolts. A man who thinks not how or why but just to walk in lusterless night with all stars to port and loaded whiskers trimmed. Gowselling in the grummels he wakes the plaintiff night with pitfalls turning left to right, high noon on the wintry ocean, high noon all sides aboard and aloft to starboard. The weathervane again with deep oars coming through the portholes and all sounds muffled. Noiseless the night on all fours, like the hurricane. Noiseless with loaded caramels and nickel dice. Sister Monica playing the guitar with shirt open and laces down, broad flanges in either ear. Sister Monica streaked with lime, gum wash, her eyes mildewed, craped, crapped, crenelated.

"What a passage!" I exclaim. "That's certainly rock 'n' roll to me."

"I'm glad you liked that," Henry says, "but I have no way of knowing whether Bob Dylan was influenced by me. You know, Bob Dylan came to my house ten years ago. Joan Baez and her sister brought him and some friends to see me. But Dylan was snooty and arrogant. He was a kid then, of course. And he didn't like me. He thought I was talking down to him, which I wasn't. I was trying to be sociable. But we just couldn't get together. But I know that he is a character, probably a genius, and I really should listen to his work. I'm full of prejudices like everybody else. My kids love him and the Beatles and all the rest."

At this point, Robert Snyder walks into the room. Snyder is the di rector of an excellent two-hour film titled *The Henry Miller Odyssey*—a film in which Miller is shown in his swimming pool reminiscing about his childhood, playing Ping-Pong, bicycling around Pacific Palisades, revisiting old friends in Paris, and conversing with Durrell, Anaïs Nin, and other friends.

Henry has been a film buff ever since his days in Paris, and his essays on *Ecstasy,* Buñuel's *L'Age d'Or,* and the French actor Raimu are marvelous pieces of film criticism.

"Do you still see a lot of movies?" I ask.

"Well, as you can guess, I'm a little behind. Bob brought over a film to show here recently—a film that made me sob and weep: Fellini's *Nights of Cabiria.* I could see it again and cry again. And I just saw the original *Frankenstein* again. And of course, the original story ends at the North Pole where everything is ice, and that's the only proper ending for that monstrous story. It's really a work of art."

"There are films that you detest, Henry, aren't there?" Snyder asks.

"*Bonnie and Clyde!*" Henry exclaims. "Did I hate that! I was clapping to myself when they machine-gunned them to death at the end. Dynamite them! Blow them to smithereens! It was so vulgar, that film. I love obscenity but I hate vulgarity. I can't see how people can enjoy killing for fun. Also, there was a perverse streak there. There was a suggestion that the hero was impotent. I don't like that, I like healthy sex. I don't like impotence and perversion."

"What's perversion?" I ask.

"Well . . . what is it?" Henry laughs, confused. "You got me stumped for a moment. Perversion. Now you've got me stumped. Now I'm moralizing. Well, to get out of it nicely, I'd say it's what isn't healthy. I think you know what I mean, don't you?"

"Not exactly."

"Have you become so broad-minded—I'm not being sarcastic—that to you there's no such thing as perversion?"

"I have my preferences, but I wouldn't make a definite judgment."

"I once asked someone what he'd rather be: ignorant or stupid," Henry explains. "I'd rather be ignorant, but I've done stupid things every day of my life. I think we all do, don't you? Every day we're wrong about something. But I have no remorse, no regrets. That's what I call being healthy."

"Just to take you back for a minute, Henry," I say, "someone told me that you knew Gurdjieff when you were living in Paris. Is that true?"

"I wish I *had* met him," Henry replies, "because I think he's one of the greatest figures in modern times, and a very mysterious one, too. I don't think that anyone has ever come to grips with him yet. I was going to make a tour of France with one of my wives, and she didn't know how to ride a bike. So we went out to the park in Fontainebleau—and we drove around Gurdjieff's place, never knowing he was there. What a misfortune!"

"You often write about how it's possible to become aware and awake in the flash of a moment. This concern with being 'awake' was also important to Gurdjieff."

"I think there are two valid attitudes to this," Henry comments. "Because even in the Zen movement in Japan there are those who think you have to work at it, meditate, study hard, be ascetic. And then there's another group, whose attitude is exemplified by the story of the Master of Fuck. It was written by a famous American living in Japan, and it's about a young man whose parents sent him to become a Zen monk. He's a good student, disciplined, but after ten years he's not getting anywhere—he's not enlightened. After fifteen years he feels he'll never make it and so he decides to live the worldly life, leaves the monastery, and runs into a prostitute who looks wonderful. And in the middle of the fuck he attains satori. . . . I never thought of such a thing and naturally he didn't either, and that's why it happened. Do you know the quote from the Buddha: 'I never gained the least thing from unexcelled complete awakening, and for that very reason it is called that.'"

"Once you're awake, how do you keep awake?"

"I can't answer that question really. But: Do you believe in conversion and that it's sincere? Well, I do, I've seen it in people, and they don't have to struggle every day to hold on to it. It remains with you. I don't know if it ever really happened to me. But I think perhaps it did in Paris in 1934, when I moved into the Villa Seurat and was reading the books of Mme Blavatsky. And one day after I had looked at a photograph of her face— she had the face of a pig, almost, but fascinating—I was hypnotized by her eyes and I had a complete vision of her as if she were in the room.

"Now I don't know if that had anything to do with what happened next, but I had a flash, I came to the realization that I was responsible for my whole life, whatever had happened. I used to blame my family, society, my wife . . . and that day I saw so clearly that I had nobody to blame but myself. I put everything on my own shoulders and I felt so relieved: Now I'm free, no one else is responsible. And that was a kind of awakening, in a way. I remember the story of how one day the Buddha was walking along and a man came up to him and said: 'Who are you, what are you?' and the Buddha promptly answered: 'I am a man who is awake.' We're asleep, don't you know, we're sleepwalkers."

Henry is showing Robert Snyder some photographs. "Some fan of mine wanted to cheer me up," Henry says, "and so he sent me these post-card photos showing the house in Brooklyn where I lived from the age of one to nine. I spent the happiest times at that age, but these photos are horrible, they're like insanity. The whole street I grew up on has become like a jaw with the teeth falling out. Houses uprooted . . . it looks so horrible."

"What was your first memory of Brooklyn?" I ask.

"A dead cat frozen in the gutter. That was when I was four. I remember birds singing in the cage and I was in the high chair and I recited poems in German—I knew German before I knew English. I had three great periods in my life. Age one to nine was Paradise. Then 1930–1940 in Paris and Greece. And then my years at Big Sur."

"Why are you living here, Henry?"

"L.A. is a shithole. Someone selected the house for me and told me to move in. But it doesn't bother me because I have nothing to do with it. I'm in this house, this is my kingdom, my realm. It's a nice house, I have a Ping-Pong table, and when my leg was okay I used to play every day."

"Tell Jonathan about the new book you're working on," Bob Snyder interjects.

"It's called *The Book of Friends* and it's an homage I'm paying to close, intimate old friends. It begins when I was five years old—what happened seventy-five years ago is so fresh and vivid to me!—and it starts off with childhood friends. I always made friends easily—all my life, even now. And in this book I'm repeating myself often, overlapping, covering ground I've already written about, but from a different angle. It goes up to Joe Gray—an ex-pugilist, a stuntman, and stand-in for Dean Martin. An uncultured guy but a great reader. After reading my books, he started to read everything else. He died two years ago, and he was a great friend. With each friend, you know, I was different."

"The last thing I wanted to ask you about, Henry," I say, leafing through my little book, "was the initiation ordeal imposed by the Brotherhood of Fools and Simpletons—an ordeal you've humorously written about in *Big Sur*."

"The Brotherhood of Fools and Simpletons?" Henry wonders. "I've completely forgotten what that was all about."

"Well, the Brotherhood asks three questions of the initiates. The first is: 'How would you order the world if you were given the powers of the creator?' The second: 'What is it you desire that you do not already possess?' And the third: 'Say something which will truly astonish us!' How would you answer these questions?"

"Ah ha!" Henry exclaims. "That third question I borrowed from Cocteau and Diaghilev. They met in the dead of night and Diaghilev went up to Cocteau and said: '*Étonne-moi! Astonish me!*' The second question was a rhetorical question because there isn't any such thing. And the first question about ordering the world: I would be paralyzed. I wouldn't know how to lift a finger to change the world or make it over. I wouldn't know what to do."

Lawrence Durrell and his wife have arrived for dinner and are now chatting in the living room with Henry's daughter Val and his son Tony and Tony's wife. Henry appears in his bathrobe and speaks to Durrell with the generosity and gentleness that one might imagine a younger son would feel toward an adored older brother. And I am reminded of that beautiful letter Henry wrote to his younger friend in 1959, from *A Private Correspondence: Lawrence Durrell and Henry Miller*:

> Ah, Larry, it isn't that life is so short, it's that it's everlasting. Often, talking with you under the tent—especially over a vieux marc—I wanted to say, "Stop talking . . . let's talk!" For 20 years I waited to see you again. For 20 years your voice rang in my ears. And your laughter. And there, at the Mazet, time running out (never the vieux marc), I had an almost frantic desire to pin you down, to have it out, to get to the bottom. (What is the stars? Remember?) And there we were on the poop deck, so to speak, the stars drenching us with light, and what are we saying? Truth is, you said so many marvelous things I never did know what we were talking about. I listened to the Master's Voice, just like that puppy on the old Victor gramophone. Whether you were expounding, describing, depicting, deflowering or delineating, it was all one to me. I heard you writing aloud. I said to myself—"He's arrived. He made it. He knows how to say it. Say it! Continue!" *Oui, c'est toi, le cher maître.* You have the vocabulary, the armature, the Vulcanic fire in your bowels. You've even found "the place and the formula." Give us a new world! Give us grace and fortitude!

As they sit down at the table, Henry says to Durrell: "This guy here mentioned three terrific questions asked by my Brotherhood of Fools and Simpletons. I'd really forgotten them."

"What were they, Henry?"

"What were they, Jonathan?"

I repeat them.

"I bet I know how you'd answer the first," Durrell says, "about how you'd order the world."

"What would you think?"

"Like a Gnostic," Durrell says, "you'd wipe it out."

"I said that I wouldn't know what I'd do, I'd be paralyzed," Henry replies. "But sometimes I do think the world is a cosmic error of a false god. I don't really believe things like that but I like the idea. Life is great and beautiful—there's nothing *but* life—but we have made of the world a horrible place. Man has never handled the gift of life properly. And it is a crazy world, everything about it is absurd and wrong, and it deserves to be wiped out. I don't think it's going to last forever. I think there is such a thing as the end of the world or the end of this species of man. It could very well be that another type of man will come into being.

"You know," Henry turns to me, "Larry recently gave me a book to read called *The Gnostics*. It's written by a young Jesuit, of all people. And you know something . . . you were asking me before about rock 'n' roll and the happenings with young people in the sixties. Well, when all that was happening, I wasn't aware that it was a revolution. Now they look back and they call it that. But the hippies are like toilet paper compared with the Gnostics. They *really* turned the world upside down. They did fantastic things. They were deliberately amoral, unmoral, immoral, contra the government and establishment. They did everything possible to increase the insanity."

A toast is proposed to insanity.

Even in his early days in Brooklyn, Henry Miller saw through the Social Lie as easily as through Saran Wrap, embodying the alienating Lie as the Cosmodemonic Telegraph Company in *Tropic of Capricorn*. While gainsaying Ezra Pound's dimwitted social-credit economics in a famous essay filled with sublime truisms ("Money and How It Gets That Way"), Miller rejected any and all "political" paths (for which he has been often criticized), preferring instead to lambaste every irruption of corporate mentality in any number of pasquinades—one of his most delightful being his attack on American bread, from *Remember to Remember*:

Accept any loaf that is offered you without question even if it is not wrapped in cellophane, even if it contains no kelp. Throw it in the back of the car with the oil can and the grease rags; if possible, bury it under a sack of coal, bituminous coal. As you climb up the road to your home, drop it in the mud a few times and dig your heels into it. When you get to the house, and after you have prepared the other dishes, take a huge carving knife and rip the loaf from stem to stern. Then take one whole onion, peeled or unpeeled, one carrot, one stalk of celery, one huge piece of garlic, one sliced apple, a herring, a handful of anchovies, a sprig of parsley and an old toothbrush, and shove them in the disemboweled guts of the bread. Over these pour a thimbleful of kerosene, a dash of Lavoris, and just a wee bit of Clorox. . . .

And in *The Colossus of Maroussi,* he writes: "At Eleusis one realizes, if never before, that there is no salvation in becoming adapted to a world which is crazy. At Eleusis one becomes adapted to the cosmos. Outwardly Eleusis may seem broken, disintegrated with the crumbled past; actually Eleusis is still intact and it is we who are broken, dispersed, crumbling to dust. Eleusis lives, lives eternally in the midst of a dying world."

Miller has always chosen reality over realism, action over activity, intuition over instinct, mystery over the mysterious, being over healing, surrender over attachment, conversion over wishing, lighthouses over lifeboats, enlightenment over salvation, and the world-as-womb over the world-as-tomb. Strangely, cosmologists have recently given credibility to the intuition that we probably all exist within a universe composed of space and time created by the original, erupting, fecundating "big bang"— all of us and all of our worlds trapped inside the gravitational radius of a universe from which no light can escape.

In the forties, George Orwell criticized Miller's idea of passive acceptance as it was revealed in the image of the man in the belly of the whale (the world-as-womb)—an image which Miller first presented in his impassioned introduction to and defense of Anaïs Nin's then unpublished diaries. In "Un Être Etoilique," Miller wrote:

We who imagined that we were sitting in the belly of the whale and doomed to nothingness suddenly discover that the whale was a projection of our own insufficiency. The whale remains, but the whale becomes the whole wide world, with stars and seasons,

with banquets and festivals, with everything that is wonderful to see and touch, and being that it is no longer a whale but
something nameless because something that is inside as well as
outside us. We may, if we like, devour the whale too—piecemeal,
throughout eternity. No matter how much is ingested there will
always remain more whale than man; because what man ap-
propriates of the whale returns to the whale again in one form
or another. The whale is constantly being transformed as man
himself becomes transformed. . . . One lives within the spirit of
transformation and not in the act. The legend of the whale thus
becomes the celebrated book of transformations destined to cure
the ills of the world.

"The stars gather direction in the same way that the foetus moves toward birth," Miller has said. And his own books of transformations are remarkably in tune with the new cosmological perspectives of the universe.
Rather than regressing to agoraphobic passivity, his books continually
open themselves up to include and become a perpetually metamorphos-
ing personality, which itself becomes a "creation." "You have expanded the
womb feeling until it includes the whole universe," Miller wrote Durrell
after reading *The Black Book* for the first time, generously praising a fellow
author yet also accurately describing the direction of his own work.

Henry Miller has continued to foster his "cosmic accent" and his
mantic gift, but, like the Greek poet Seferiades, whom he praises in *The
Colossus of Maroussi*, his "native flexibility" has equally responded to "the
cosmic laws of curvature and finitude. He had ceased going out in all
directions: His lines were making the encircling movement of embrace."

As the world falls rapidly on its measured ellipse, Henry Miller is
writing, painting, and dreaming his life away in Pacific Palisades: "Some
will say they do not wish to *dream* their lives away," he writes in *Big Sur*.
"As if life itself were not a dream, a very real dream from which there is no
awakening! We pass from one state of dream to another: from the dream
of sleep to the dream of waking, from the dream of life to the dream of
death. Whoever has enjoyed a good dream never complains of having
wasted his time. On the contrary, he is delighted to have partaken of a
reality which serves to heighten and enhance the reality of everyday."

HENRY MILLER

DECEMBER 26, 1891 – JUNE 7, 1980

LOU REED
A New York State of Mind

New York City, 1989

Lou Reed, who died on October 27, 2013, in Amagansett, New York, at the age of seventy-one, was one of the most original and influential poetic and musical innovators in the history of rock 'n' roll. He was the lead singer and songwriter of the legendary rock band the Velvet Underground, for which he wrote such classic songs as "Sweet Jane," "Sister Ray," "Heroin," "I'm Waiting for the Man," and "Pale Blue Eyes"; and in his post-Velvet life he went on to record twenty-two remarkable and radically inventive solo albums.

From the beginning of his career, Reed entered into, explored, chron-icled, dramatized, commented on, criticized, and celebrated the seductive shadow side of the New York City psyche—particularly the demimonde of street hustlers, teenage runaways, transvestites, drug dealers, princesses and queens for a day, and other Bohemian, hipster, and punk denizens of the wild side of New York. A true *poète maudit*, Reed embraced Arthur Rimbaud's notion that "a poet makes himself a *seer* by a long, prodigious, and rational derangement of all the senses," and in so doing, Reed found a vital language for the poisons and ecstasies of urban life, communicating his vision of the body and city politic in tight, intense rock 'n' roll music and a poetry of fierce originality.

Released in 1989 and simply titled *New York*, Lou Reed's fifteenth solo album unflinchingly depicted with savage indignation and the fervency of a biblical prophet an AIDS-stricken city in which friends were continually "disappearing"—a desolation row of pestilential welfare hotels; of battered wives, crack dealers, TV bigots, racist preachers, and venal politicians; of kids selling plastic roses for a buck by the Lincoln Tunnel; of a Hudson River del-uged with garbage; and of bloody vials washing up on city beaches. In Lou

Reed's eyes, these were not the days of miracle and wonder, and in *New York's* "There Is No Time" he declared: "This is no time for Celebration / This is no time for Shaking Hands / This is no time for Backslapping / This is no time for Marching Bands."

"First we take Manhattan, then we take Berlin" Leonard Cohen had announced in his album *I'm Your Man*. For his part, however, Lou Reed scuttled and reversed that battle plan. In his 1973 album *Berlin* he first composed a song cycle that described and explored not a place but rather a state of mind—an inner world of private desperation as reflected in the self-destructive lives of a couple named Caroline and Jim. Sixteen years later in his album *New York* he then took on Manhattan—and New York City's other boroughs as well—in another song cycle that shifted its perspective in order to now describe and explore an outer world of public squalor and social despair.

The poet Kenneth Rexroth once wrote, "Against the ruin of the world, there is only one defense—the creative act." And the miracle and wonder of *New York* is that rather than conveying the sense of emotional numbness and dysphoria that characterized the world of *Berlin*, it instead, from its very first jolting chord, instantly communicated a mood of unexpected musical euphoria. With Mike Rathke and Reed himself on Pensa-Suhr custom guitars, Rob Wasserman on a Clevenger electric upright six-string bass, and co-producer Fred Maher on drums, and with Velvet Underground's Maureen Tucker playing percussion on two tracks (and Dion DiMucci adding a vocal flourish on the song "Dirty Boulevard"), *New York* provided a stunning example of unmediated, stripped-down, and elemental rock 'n' roll. "You can't beat guitars, bass, and drums," Lou Reed remarked in his album notes, and with this tightly meshed band he gave birth to an album that was both a shattering cri de coeur and an act of creative joy.

I interviewed Lou Reed in New York's Warner Bros. offices in early 1989. He was wearing jeans, boots, a black T-shirt, a casual gray Italian leather jacket, and a Rolex watch. "It's one of life's little pleasures," he told me with a laugh, adding, "it'll last forever." As will his words and music.

* * *

Your new album New York *depicts a city that seems to be profoundly and hopelessly sick.*

In my song "Endless Cycle" I say: "The bias of the father runs on through the son / and leaves him bothered and bewildered. . . . / The sickness of the mother runs on through the girl / leaving her small and helpless." There are such terrible images running through the album, like in "Xmas in February," the song about the abandoned, unemployed Vietnam vet, "the guy on the street with the sign that reads / 'Please help send this vet home' / But he is home." *But he is home!* I listen to that and think, Oh my God, what have I done? The images just come at you, and some of them were very hard for *me* to deal with.

You know, a hundred years ago another New York poet, Walt Whitman, had something quite different to say about the city. He wrote: "Mannahatta! How fit a name for America's great democratic island city! The word itself, how beautiful! how aboriginal! how it seems to rise with tall spires, glistening in sunshine, with such New World atmosphere, vista, and action! . . . A million people—manners free and superb—open voices—hospitality."

He should really see it now! Every day when I go outside I see the result of the emptying of the mental hospitals, of not having enough halfway houses, of having all kinds of services cut, of backing off on funding for schools and for food for kids, of holding out on just about anything . . . and here we are. You read me Walt Whitman, so let me read you a few lines from my song "Romeo Had Juliette": "I'll take Manhattan in a garbage bag / with Latin written on it that says / 'It's hard to give a shit these days' / Manhattan's sinking like a rock, into the filthy Hudson what a shock / they wrote a book about it, they said it was like ancient Rome." And I'm trying to make you feel the situation we're in—feel what it's like—and I don't think I'm the only one who feels this way. But what did Alfred Hitchcock say? "It's only a movie."

The tone of your song is sure different from the old Rodgers and Hart song "Manhattan" with its lines like "The great big city's a wondrous toy / Just made for a girl and boy. / We'll turn Manhattan into an isle of joy."

[Laughing] Yeah, that kind of tacky lyric is so hilarious that it was fun to try to reinvent it. But on the other hand I also have to say that on my last album [Mistrial] I had a song that I thought was really beautiful called "Tell It to Your Heart," and I thought it was a really nice paean to Manhattan ["Tell it to your heart, please don't be afraid / New York City lovers, tell it to your heart"]. There's a lovely image of my looking out across the river and seeing the neon Coca-Cola sign.

In 1929 the great Spanish poet Federico García Lorca spent a year in New York City, and in his book Poet in New York *described how he would walk around the city and see "crowds stagger sleeplessly through the boroughs as if they had just escaped a shipwreck of blood." And like you he also tried to make people become aware of and feel the social despair and awfulness of the life he saw around him, denouncing those who unconscionably ignored "the unredeemable half," and who raised their "mountains of cement" over the beating hearts of abandoned animals; a city of rust and ferment and a Hudson River "drunk on oil"; and Lorca declaims: "I spit in all your faces." This really sounds a lot like some of your songs on* New York.

That's great! That's wonderful! You're going to quote Lorca to me, well, I love it. Can I read back to you for a minute? In my song "Dirty Boulevard," it says: "Give me your tired, your poor, I'll piss on 'em / That's what the Statue of Bigotry says / Your poor huddled masses, let's club 'em to death / and get it over with and just dump 'em on the boulevard." Lorca, of course, was writing during the first year of the Depression, and I think that today we're heading toward another one. I also feel that the people who run things have knowledgeably and intentionally fucked the people who can't possibly defend themselves—the aged, the poor, the young, the old, women. Lorca was livid about the situation, and so am I.

What about the artists?

The artists can fend for themselves. I'm talking about a six-year-old kid who can't defend himself. And let's see: Let's take abortion back to the Supreme Court and take that away so that women can go play with coat hangers and get really fucked up. And of course what happens here will spread. How many people have to drop dead from AIDS? Why do they think that's not going to spread? Do they have to wait until AIDS works its way to the suburbs before the great middle class rises up and says Ohhh! Well, everybody should be saying Ohhh! right now. These are very scary and treacherous times even though people seem to think that everything's okay. But we're right in the middle of it. Why do you think people are taking crack? And where do you think the crime comes from? It's a hopeless, dead-end situation, and you've got to give to people, you can't just sit there saying things are good for *us*. That's an extraordinarily easy thing to say. That's no big thing, anybody can go outside and say that.

As Lorca wrote: "The other half hears me, devouring, pissing, flying in their purity."

Yeah, there's this vicious noncaring or, in some cases, a cavalier noncaring under the guise of something else. It's a complete disregard for the other guy or woman or child, and a complete rejection of any kind of humanity and an unrelieved viciousness for laughs. As Mike [Rathke] said when we were listening to the record one day, "That's what eight years of rape does to you."

Eight years of Ronald Reagan.

It really *is* the eight years of Reagan. And as I said, I'm trying to make you feel the situation we're in. And that's what this album is all about.

In your song "Spit It Out," which was on your 1986 album Mistrial, *you say that if there's a rage inside you or if you get so angry that you can't think or speak, you should "spit it out / and tell them where they can put it." And on your new song "There Is No Time" you say that this is no time to swallow anger and ignore hate.*

Yeah, I'm furious.

But it's been said that you can't really eliminate pain through anger because it's like trying to eat yourself from the inside out, and that when you've eaten yourself, the eater remains and he must be eaten as well. So you always remain unsatisfied.

Look, I'm not unaware of other points of view. It's very depressing in some ways because I'm one of those people who are *doomed* to continuously see the other person's point of view. I can see why he or she is right, I can see why I could be seen as being wrong. And then there's even a third, a fourth, a fifth point of view, and on and on. And you can just end up davening. But there are some points of view I really have, and I think that *New York* is a legitimate channel for them.

With regard to different points of view, I hope that you won't mind my saying that I did take issue with one of your songs, "Good Evening Mr. Waldheim," in which I thought that you were criticizing Jesse Jackson a bit unfairly.

Well, isn't it nice in a rock 'n' roll song to be able to give my position on something? I'm not trying to just get a rise out of somebody, but that's how I feel and I'm not kidding around, and you can feel the other way, that's your business, but we could spend the rest of our interview just debating this.

Maybe we should wait to do that till the next time around.

And of course we're allowed to disagree.

How long did it take you to write the songs on New York?

When I sat down to write the album, I didn't know that this was what it was going to be about. I started writing, and I'm watching what's happening, and I would write more, and I said to myself, "I think I can detect a trend, is this what I really want to write about because it seems to be." So that's where it wanted to go, and I only followed.

I spent almost three months writing those words. I put my whole weight on it, and I tried to find a way to surround the words properly, to surround them with the perfect setting for the jewels, so to speak, and to get the rhythm of the words working in the right way against the beat, and then get the nuances in the vocal so that listeners could hear the words—that was the raison d'être for this album. The lyrics should sound really simple and with a really easy flow to them, but it took a lot of re-writes to get it to that point.

How much rewriting did you do?

A lot. Rewriting really makes you focus. Haggling for weeks over a word. Just focusing. I tried all the vocals out before I ever went in the studio, and I've gotten pretty good at this, so that if I hear it in my head I ought to be able to sing it. But when we tried it out in the studio, sometimes I couldn't quite get it right because, as I said, there's so much rhythm going on in the words that is supposed to be working against the beat, and I could hear it clear as a bell in my mind but I couldn't always execute it. But whenever I found that I couldn't do it I didn't start tearing my lyric apart because I knew it was okay, I just knew that it was *me* who couldn't get into it, so we would keep at it until I did it right. It took hours sometimes, and it was maddening because I got so caught up trying to do it right that I'd lose the feel and the meaning of the words.

In the 1950s, some poets were reciting poetry to jazz, but for the most part I don't think it worked very well because it often sounded self-conscious and arty.

That's funny, you're the second person to make that comparison to what I was trying to do with my album. And I think it does try to do something like that but I hope it does a lot more because it should be rock 'n' roll, and *New York* is definitely a "quote" rock 'n' roll record, but it's my vision of what a rock 'n' roll record can be. It doesn't have to be a twenty-four-hours-below-the-belt type of experience all the time, though you should certainly be able to tap your foot to it and still follow it.

If the almost hilarious ferocity of the lyrics doesn't stop you dead in your tracks, I think that you could probably dance to your song "Hold On," with its Bo Diddley beat and your ecstatic guitar riff.

Yeah, that's one where the initial part of the song wasn't outstanding, but through the wonders of playing together, we stumbled on this very nice lick, and the really heavy-duty overdrive—the overloading of the amp—really takes your head off.

What kind of rock 'n' roll have you been listening to recently?

I don't find that much to listen to that works for me at the moment, but every once in a while I hear a song that just lays me out. On Bob Dylan's recent album *[Down in the Groove]* he sings a song that really killed me. It's called "Ninety Miles an Hour (Down a Dead End Street)," and in just that small amount of words the image is so devastating. I love stuff like that, and I try to fill my lyrics with things that are that immediate. It comes from being a fan of Raymond Chandler, like his line "That blonde was as attractive as a split lip." It's the visualization and the simplicity of the words. You say, Oh my God, how do you do that?

You have a lot of devastating images and words in New York. *How do you think people will respond to them?*

I just can't get involved with people telling me, Well, if you use this language you won't get on the radio and you won't get it on the Bible Belt, blah, blah, blah. You know, what's interesting about my situation is that unlike musicians like Clapton, Winwood, and so on, I've never gotten popular. I'm what they call a cult figure, and that's about where it is.

Except for "Walk on the Wild Side," which was a fluke. I don't have any overwhelming popularity, and I'm certainly not what you'd call a household word. I don't sell that many records, so there can't be so many people out there with an image of me. And I've been around so long that in any case an image must be kind of boring by now.

To your audience or to you?

To anyone. I mean, at this point what possible use could it be? I remember a reporter who once called me up and asked me all about my supposed "shocking" image. And I said to him, "Oh, come on, please, you're so parochial! Give us all a break." I mean, there's nothing shocking about "Wild Side" or any of my other songs. If you compare them with the writings of Hubert Selby Jr., William Burroughs, or Allen Ginsberg, none of my songs would be considered shocking. But it's just that this material is in rock 'n' roll—so it's that rock journalist's problem, not mine. And you know, I never thought that songs like "Heroin" or "Street Hassle" were pro-drug songs.

Some people think that in a way this tradition all began with Arthur Rimbaud's notion of the "rational derangement of all the senses."

Look, I'm forty-six years old now and I can't be bothered with that kind of stuff. And if I'm less concerned right now with derangement of all the senses, as you were calling it, let's just say that *I* might call it *just growing up.*

It sounds pretentious to say this, but I'm writing for an educated or self-educated person who has reached a certain level. I'm not aiming *New York* for fourteen-year-olds. See, I don't sell many records, so I know that the people who do buy them really want to hear them. And in my liner notes I say: there are fourteen songs and the album is fifty-eight minutes, so try to listen to it the first time from the beginning to the end because it was written, God forbid, around a theme, and the theme is running through it in a very specific order and is very tightly focused track-by-track, and the effect builds. So if you take one song out of context and put it on one of my other albums, you would get "x" effect, but when you listen to it here, where you have one song right after another coming at you, then you don't lose the effect of the song that came before, it's amplified, so that about three-quarters of the way through the album you go, Whoa!

How did you go about recording New York*?*

Almost all of the songs were done live, and we recorded them at Media Sound in New York in a tiny little room with an old Neve board. In the past, I've often had problems coming to grips with the technology in the studio, and it's taken years for me to learn how to use it as a tool and to get what I want out of it. Like sometimes I've wanted "x" out of it and at other times I've wanted "y" and often the two conflicted. Especially the conflict between the sound and the voice. Sometimes when I had multitudinous guitar parts I found out in retrospect that instead of expanding the thoughts they canceled each other out.

I mean, when we were recording *New York* there were instances in the studio when I'd come with yet the fiftieth guitar part and we'd then have to spend time taking things out. I would put down this guitar lick and go "Ah *hah,* listen to the tone of this, how do you like that part?" And Fred [Maher] or Mike [Rathke] would say to me, "It's a great part but unfortunately it just knocked the bass out and it's stepping all over the other guitar part and you can't hear either one now." "But don't you *love* it?" I'd say *[laughing],* and they'd say, "We love it but . . ." So the nice thing about our going minimal was that you could then hear the guitars *and* all the parts *and* the words *and* the full breath of the voice. But the dangerous thing about going minimal is that you'd better be good because your voice isn't going to be layered under tons of things.

You've always had a totally identifiable "Lou Reed voice."

Some people may not like my voice, though I think it has character. But it took me a while to get to the point where I could become a fan of my voice so that I was comfortable with it and could understand how it worked and what it was about and how to hear it, though sometimes I realized that I could hear something in it that the other guy couldn't. But I didn't want my records to sound as if the voice was over here while the music seemed to be in the next room over there. And on the other hand, I didn't want the voice to be buried so that God knows how anyone could figure out the words. I wanted you to be able to hear the words, and it's taken a long time and a lot of experience in the studio to get it so that it sounds like me. Because I always wanted it to sound like me, and that's not so easy. Not so easy.

The playwright and actor Sam Shepard recently remarked that "the trouble with modern rock 'n' roll is that it's lost its sense of humor. It's become so morbidly stylistic and sour—there's no joy in it. And I think it's disastrous that a genuine sense of humor has been smothered." And he added: "Take all those imitators of Lou Reed, for example: if they went back and listened to his early stuff, they'd see he had a whole different feel . . . plus he was a helluva writer. He could really write a lyric. He's been ripped off left, right, and center."

Why the word "was"? *[Laughing]* But that's nice of Sam.

Do you think you've been ripped off?

No, not for a second. I mean, everybody's heard everybody else, so many people are playing on the same sources. But it is sometimes kind of weird: I'll hear a group, and they'll be good, and I'm listening to them and realize that they sound like me. But in some ways it's like a "me" from a certain time, and it's weird because I'm over here now and I can't do that particular thing anymore, although I still enjoy it. But why wouldn't they want to do that, there's a lot to be said for that approach to things. I just wish that they would imitate it more and really get into the words, but you've got to know how to use them to do it.

Someone once said that a masterpiece's function is to create the energy for other people to create other masterpieces.

I'll settle for that. It's good to have examples and standards to either try to live up to or surpass. And in my life there have been some really important things that once someone bothered to tell or show me or give me an example of made things very clear and simple. At any point in my life if I heard someone else's song, it might have seemed so simple, but it really wasn't until I really knew it. Or to take another example: If you want to drink a bottle of club soda out of a cup, pick up the bottle and don't lift it over here and pour it over there but rather pour it over the cup. And something simple like that can be applicable to, say, an aesthetic or a life. You say: Oh . . . Right! And then you do it that way from that point on.

I remember a friend once offered me some very simple but wonderful advice, namely, that you should never smoke while you urinate and that you should come when you're called.

[Laughing] Well, this plumber out where I live said to me, "Don't believe anything you hear and half of what you see." He was serious—you know, small-town wisdom. And of course then there are other pieces of advice like "Don't shit where you sleep."

Or don't spit in the wind. In your song "Strawman" you say, "Spitting in the wind comes back at you twice as hard."

I went a long time trying to figure out whether it should be piss or spit and decided that spit was better. That's one of life's little things that you learn—you don't spit in the wind. You also don't get a mace gun and use it in the wind. So you can take this on all the different levels.

In your beautiful song "Coney Island Baby" you say that although the city is something like a circus or a sewer, one can still look up to see the "princess on the hill" and that the "glory of love just might come through." But on New York *one doesn't sense the possibility of salvation, and some people might take it to be extremely nihilistic.*

But it would be a shame if that's all they got out of the album. I think that people should be getting together and do something about the situation I'm describing. That's the salvation of it. Look at what's going on and then do something about it. Besides, don't people realize that the album's also funny, "leavened with humor"? *[Laughing]*

I really had to laugh at some of the lines in "Last Great American Whale" such as, "Some say they saw him at the Great Lakes / Some say they saw him off the coast of Florida / My mother said she saw him in Chinatown / but you can't always trust your mother." You know, Oedipus might have felt exactly the same way about his mother!

[Laughing] That's hilarious! And I think that some of the worst comments in the songs on *New York* are also hilariously funny at the same time. Some of the lines in "Hold On," for example, are straight out of the news, like "They shot that old lady / 'cause they thought she was a witness / to a crime she didn't even see" or "A cop was shot in the head by a ten-year-old kid named Buddha in / Central Park last week." I mean, what? And things like that are kind of funny in a very depressing way. We're so dulled to this. Take for instance the building that collapsed the other day in Manhattan.

The builders who were there, unlicensed with no permit, noticed a crack in the foundation as they were digging. So what do these large minds do? They dig a trench and then they put cinder blocks there, and the building collapses and I think it kills the owner of the building and a poor girl is caught under it. And they only have three inspectors to check on this shit! Isn't this hilarious at the same time that it's the worst thing you've ever heard?

You don't have to make anything up. In "Sick of You" I say: "I was up in the morning with the TV blarin' / brush my teeth sittin' watchin' the news / All the beaches were closed the ocean was a Red Sea / but there was no one there to part it in two / There was no fresh salad because / there's hypos in the cabbage / Staten Island disappeared at noon / And they say the midwest is in great distress / and NASA blew up the moon / The ozone layer has no ozone anymore / and you're gonna leave me for the guy next door."

That last line, which you sing with a little question mark on the word "door," really made me laugh, but there are a lot of your songs that make me laugh. One of my favorites is "High in the City" from your underappreciated 1984 album New Sensations, *in which you describe a couple—one of whom is carrying some mace, the other a knife—"hitting the streets" one night but avoiding walking down Sutton Place because "everybody there got an Akita"; and one of them advises the other to "watch out for that guy on your right / Seen him on the news last Saturday night / He was high in the city."*

Ah, you know that song, I'm so happy to hear that. I also thought it was so funny, but no one's ever mentioned to me that *they* thought it was funny. People don't seem to get it.

On that album you also have another wonderful song called "My Friend George" in which you sing about a childhood friend who likes music but who also likes to fight, and he tells you to avenge yourself for humanity and for the weak and the poor, and then says, "Well, the fight is my music . . . Can't you hear the music playing, the anthem, it's my call."

That's my favorite song on that album. I remember that when we were recording it, the engineer turned to me and said, "Do you have a friend named George?" And I said, "Of course not." One of the nice things about being a writer is that you can have a friend named George.

But do you think, like George, that the fight is your music and the anthem is your call?

I'd have to think about that for a while. Well, in fact I *have* been thinking about whether that is my call, and if it is I should be doing more than what I'm doing, like one record every two or three years is really not a lot.

But your album New York *is your fifteenth solo album. That's a career!*

But that's nothing because the songs and the writing and the stuff in my head don't stop just because I've done an album. I love playing around with words so much and putting them to music, and I do get such a great kick out of the guitar, but I really should move into poetry or short stories. Someone will say I should do a book, and I get close to it and then I back away from it. But it's not for lack of time, and it's not for not having it in my head, because it sometimes goes on all day, it just doesn't stop. Like I could go right back in the studio and do another album, and it's kind of a shame that you can't do that. But generally speaking I have to say that with most of my albums I've felt that I was behind myself, that the albums didn't represent where I really was when they came out. But on *New York* I'm not behind myself—that's where I am, that's what I'm capable of doing. On this album it wasn't a question of if I had more time or if I had more money I would redo this or that. We had all the time we needed to record it, and when the sessions ended, we all knew it was over. I gave it my best shot.

I personally think that the most astonishing song on New Sensations—*and it must be one of the most haunting ones you've ever written—is "Fly into the Sun," in which you express an apocalyptic longing for self-dissolution, declaring that "I'd welcome the chance to meet my maker / And fly into the sun. / I'd break up into a million pieces / And fly into the sun."*

Ah, well, yeah, it is apocalyptic. I work so hard on the words so that they'll come out a certain way. I mean, it's just the pleasure and the flow of them, and then you get into the thought. And it's so odd to me that people don't seem to get it, they don't understand it. You know, I do the records for myself but it's so nice to find out that sometimes there are people who get something from them.

In that song you also declare: "I would not run from the blazing light / I would not run from its rain" and that you'd see it as an end to misery and to worldly pain. There's a lot of humor in your songs, and occasionally some perfect days, but there's also a lot of "rage, pain, anger, hurt," as you say in your new song "Beginning of a Great Adventure."

Well, those are the emotions I was most familiar with.

Those are also the emotions that most infants and young children experience.

Except that they get pleasure too.

But you're saying that you don't?

I'm just saying that I didn't.

At the risk of being too personal, do you remember much about your earliest years?

No, but I'm glad.

But you do contact and touch on childhood feelings in some of your songs.

Well, I think that the artist reapproaches and goes back to all these things, asking questions like, What happened? What went on? Why am I this way? And what can I get from this? How can I use it for something? Can I get energy from it? How can I do something with it that isn't self-destructive? How can I speak of it maybe to other people who also feel that way? But I've found out about myself, and I'm not just one thing, I'm a whole slew of things. And when you write, you can leap into one particular pocket, as though that's you, but of course it isn't, even though for a song it may be.

My song "Legendary Hearts," for example, is one of my saddest. It's about not being able to live up to being an image of a Romeo with a Juliet. The girl in the song says, "Romeo, oh, Romeo, wherefore art thou Romeo," but "he's in a car or at a bar / or churning his blood with an impure drug / He's in the past and seemingly lost forever." And a lot of people are like that.

I'm reminded of the lines in your new song "Romeo Had Juliette": "The perfume burned his eyes, holding tightly to her thighs / and something flickered for a minute and then it vanished and was gone."

Isn't that sad? Every time people say to me "Romeo *and* Juliet," I say, No, it's "Romeo *had* Juliet" because I meant in the sexual way—it flickered for a minute and was gone. But of course that flicker is better than nothing.

Someone once remarked that a poem is either a kiss or a punch in the nose. There are a lot of punches on this album, but there doesn't seem to be a love song on it.

But there certainly is! If you look at the last song, "Dime Store Mystery," which is dedicated to Andy Warhol, whom I really miss and was privileged to have known, you'll find the line "I wish I hadn't thrown away my time on so much Human and so much less Divine." I think that that's one of the most stunning lines that I've ever written in my life, and I'm enormously proud of it. So when you say that there's no love song on the album . . . well, it's very true that there's no moon and spoon, but though it might sound tacky to put it like this I think that "Dime Store Mystery" is a supreme love song, and I'm talking about a love song to a vision of spirituality.

I gather that "Dime Story Mystery" was influenced by your having seen the film The Last Temptation of Christ, *which was Martin Scorsese's adaptation of Nikos Kazantzakis's controversial novel of the same name.*

What happened was that for years I had the title "Dime Store Mystery," along with a few lines, but I was never able to complete the song. And one night I happened to watch a television interview with Marty in which he was talking about his film, which I hadn't yet seen. The film was already being boycotted and censored and banned here and abroad, and Marty was defending his point of view in the most gracious and articulate manner that one could possibly imagine. And I was so struck by some of the things he was saying about the duality of Godly nature and human nature that I started writing them down, and I said to myself, That's what this song should be about. And I made the title "Dime Story Mystery, The Last Temptation."

So I wrote down a version of the song, and then I finally saw the film when Marty invited me to a private screening so that his friends didn't have to get killed by pickets *[laughing]*, and I sent the lyrics to him and told him that the film had really inspired me and that was how I came to write the song. And I thought that the song was done, but then I woke up one morning at six o'clock and my mind was saying, "That's not you at all, it's not right." So I sat up and started talking to myself and said, "Well what *is* it? Tell me what I should do." And then I rewrote the song again and yet again until I possessed it and felt that it was more mine and wasn't completely about the film.

The song talks about the physical against the spiritual, and about Vishnu and Buddha, and then all of a sudden it goes Whomp! and there's a big switch and you're in the present and you're talking about being in St. Patrick's Cathedral . . . and okay, what are you doing in St. Patrick's? Well, somebody must have died and there's going to be a funeral there the next day and "the bells will ring for you" [Andy Warhol's funeral took place at St. Patrick's on April 1, 1987], and this is told with the greatest amount of love.

In the title song of New Sensations, *you say: "I want the principles of a timeless muse / I want to eradicate my negative views / And get rid of those people who are always on a down."*

Ah! You probably want to know if those lines trumpet a new, mellow Lou?

Actually, I was going to ask you about the "timeless muse." Who or what is that muse?

Ah!

Is it the "princess on the hill" whom you mention in "Coney Island Baby"?

The timeless muse for me is . . . well, let me get into a personal thing for a minute. There was a time in my life when the ability to write wouldn't be there anymore, and I'd be panicked, thinking: It's gone, it's gone forever, it'll never be back. I was confused about where the talent came from, how it functioned, what it could do, what it didn't want to do, and where it was, and how it worked. And I thought of my friend, the poet Delmore Schwartz—God bless his soul—who wrote a wonderful essay on *Hamlet.* Some of his essays are kind of dismissed as lesser Delmore, but I think of them as higher Delmore, and moreover he said, "Even paranoids have enemies" and a lot of other worthy things. *[Laughing]* But in his *Hamlet* essay he points out that Hamlet came from an old upper-class family and began saying very disturbing things to his friend Horatio, such as, A woman is like a cantaloupe, open it and it starts to rot. And in this particular essay Delmore said that the real secret about Hamlet is that he was a manic-depressive, and a manic-depressive just *is*—like being right-handed or having brown hair. And that was the essence of Hamlet. It's either that or you view the play as though everybody is drunk from beginning to end.

So in my particular case, I finally realized that my talent just *is*— I didn't have to worry about it going away, I didn't have to do anything to try to amplify it or make things happen. All I had to do was just sit there and go about my business, and that I could do it like hanging upside down in a gym in gravity boots, and it would always be there for me. And then some days it isn't, but that doesn't mean it won't be there in an hour. The day I understood that I went through major changes, but it took a very long time for me to do so. In my album *New Sensations* I said that I wanted it to be there—I wasn't in touch with it at that point. But since then I *am*, which is just a blessing, because I had a little dream and I got it.

So who or what, ultimately, is the timeless muse?

The timeless muse for me is to be able to *tune in* or to have that thing just show up for me, and I am so, so lucky because I enjoy doing this kind of stuff so much. I want to be in touch with the timeless muse and I have to follow it because I get enormous satisfaction out of it. I did Honda and American Express commercials just so I can continue to make albums like *New York* and take the time off to write the way I really want to. But I don't have to be a big shot or rich. All I want to do is *more*. And I've got a motorcycle, see, and I can take off into the hills with it, and I really like that a *lot*.

In *New York* the Lou Reed image doesn't exist, as far as I'm concerned. This is me speaking as directly as I possibly can to whoever hopefully wants to listen to it. If someone accuses me of attacking my former image and says, "Oh, but you *once* said . . . ," then all I can now say is, "And what did *you* once say? And what did we all once say? And what might I say tomorrow?"

LOU REED

MARCH 2, 1942 – OCTOBER 27, 2013

OLIVER SACKS
The Neurology of the Soul

New York City, 1985

In 1926 an outgoing, carefree, and high-spirited twenty-one-year-old young woman, whom the British neurologist Dr. Oliver Sacks calls Rose R., began to have a recurring dream. And in this dream, in the words of Dr. Sacks, "she was imprisoned in an inaccessible castle, but the castle had the form and shape of herself; she dreamed of enchantments, bewitchments, entrancements; she dreamed that she had become a living sentient statue of stone; she dreamed that the world had come to a stop; she dreamed that she had fallen into a sleep so deep that nothing could wake her; she dreamed of a death which was different from death." Then one morning, after a night of dreaming this dream, Rose R. had difficulty waking up. Her parents, who had come to her bedside, found their daughter lying in bed, unable to speak, her eyes turned to the wardrobe mirror. "And there," as Dr. Sacks tells us, "she saw that her dreams had come true."

Forty years later, in 1966, the neurologist discovered her, along with a group of other mostly stuporous and transfixed patients ("human statues, as motionless as stones") in a ward of a New York hospital where he had begun to work—the forgotten survivors of a rare sleeping sickness called *encephalitis lethargica* that had broken out during World War I in all parts of the world and that, having affected some five million people within twelve years, vanished as mysteriously as it had arrived.

In 1969 Dr. Sacks, after much deliberation, decided to administer to these patients a drug—used to treat Parkinsonism—called L-dopa. And suddenly, as if in a "miracle" story or fairy tale when the spell or enchantment has been broken, "there burst forth the wonder, the laughter, the resurrection of Awakenings. Patients motionless and frozen, in some cases for almost five decades, were suddenly able, once again, to walk and talk, to feel and think, with perfect freedom. . . . One could not witness such 'awakenings' without feeling their legendary and fantastic quality, without thinking of the Sleeping Beauty, Rip Van Winkle, and other fictional and mythological parallels. The first awakenings nearly always gave intense and unmixed joy to the patients." (Oliver Sacks's accounts of these "rebirths" make up his book *Awakenings*—first published in 1973 and revised, expanded, and republished in 1983—one of the most profound, unsettling, compassionate, and beautifully written works of our time.)

But it soon became clear to Dr. Sacks that the side effects of L-dopa were bizarre and unpredictable, with each patient reacting to the drug in distinct and unique ways. Rose R., for example, now sixty-four years old and unable to comprehend and accept the loss of forty-three years, "reblocked" herself and fell, so to speak, back into her sleep and trance.

Another patient, whom Oliver Sacks calls Margaret A. (she was born in 1908 and had suffered from the sleeping sickness since her early twenties), found herself, under the influence of L-dopa, propelled from one extreme behavioral state to another (depression–mania, coma–frenzy). As Dr. Sacks reported her plight at that time: "*Both* poles, indeed, may simultaneously occur, and Miss A. will declare—within two or three minutes—that she feels wonderful, terrible, can see perfectly, is blind, cannot move, cannot stop moving, etc. Her will is continually vacillating or paralyzed; she wants what she fears, and fears what she wants; she loves what she hates, and hates what she loves. . . . In the presence of excitement and perpetual contradiction, Miss A. has split into a dozen Miss. A.s—the drinker, the ticcer, the stamper, the yeller, the swinger, the gazer, the sleeper, the wisher, the fearer, the lover, the hater, etc.—all struggling with each other to 'possess' her behavior. . . . The *original* Miss A.—so engaging and bright—has been *dispossessed* by a host of crude, degenerate subselves—a schizophreniform fission of her once-unified self."

A professor of clinical neurology at the Albert Einstein College of Medicine in New York and a consultant neurologist to a number of small New York hospitals, Dr. Oliver Sacks was born in London in 1933 into a medical family. (His mother was a surgeon and professor of anatomy, and his father, now ninety-one [1985], still sees patients as a general practitioner.) A bearded, bespectacled, almost rabbinical-looking man, Dr. Sacks speaks with a gentle stammer and a veritable twinkle in his eye. ("When I ask some of my patients, 'How old are you?'—he comments with a smile—"they'll reply, 'You tell *me!*'")

Unpretentious, courteous, jolly, and humane, he is a doctor who embodies and combines the "old-fashioned" qualities of wisdom teacher, healer, and artist; who speaks openly and unembarrassedly about a "neurology of the soul"; and whose prose style displays a remarkable sense of grace, strength, exactitude, and passion.

Drawing on a deeply felt knowledge of neurology, physics, cosmology, philosophy, Jewish mysticism, literature, and music (his two favorite bedside books are the dictionary and the Bible, and he is fond of quoting the German poet Novalis's dictum: "Every disease is a musical problem, every cure a musical solution"), Oliver Sacks has published three books during the past several years: *Migraine*—an expanded and updated version of his pioneering 1970 study (and one that led Israel Rosenfield to call Sacks "one of the greatest clinical writers of the twentieth century"); *A Leg to Stand On*—an account of how, having torn the quadriceps tendon of his thigh, he embarked on a pilgrimage through the "broken mosaic world" of the *patient,* with all its ontological terrors and convalescent grace ("To become a true doctor," he quotes the French philosopher Montaigne, "the candidate must have passed through all the illnesses that he wants to cure and all the accidents and circumstances that he is to diagnose. Truly I should trust such a man"); and, most recently, *The Man Who Mistook His Wife for a Hat and Other Clinical Tales*— a best-selling collection of twenty-four almost Gogolian- and Borgesian-like case studies about seemingly "untreatable" brain-damaged persons, such as a man who finds freedom from his uncontrollable tics, jerks, and grimaces only when he plays the drums or Ping-Pong ("Witty Ticcy Ray"); a woman who, though possessing the sensory faculties of her hands, can neither recognize nor identify any object she touches ("Hands"); a man who, although able to see colors, shapes, and shades of brightness, has lost all conception of imagery or faces ("The Man Who Mistook His Wife for a Hat"); and an ex-sailor who, thirty years after being discharged from the navy, finds it impossible to fathom the reality of persons or events appearing and occurring after 1945, and who is, for example, even unable to recognize Dr. Sacks from one moment's meeting to the next ("The Lost Mariner").

The philosopher and political scientist Hannah Arendt once wrote: "In acting and speaking, men show who they are, reveal actively their unique personal identities, and thus make their appearance in the human world." Yet in all these action-impaired patients, Oliver Sacks—through sympathy, dedication, patience, understanding, intuition, and faith—reveals how he has been able to discover and evoke "a living personal center, an 'I,' amid the debris of neurological devastation." And he has done so in a series of haunting tales that mix narration and meditation—as if to confirm Isak Dinesen's notion that "all sorrows can be borne if you put them into a story."

* * *

We sometimes read about certain patients who get so identified with their illnesses that they seem to be nothing but functions of them—like the Tourette's syndrome patient you refer to as "Witty Ticcy Ray," who says, "I consist of tics—there is nothing else."

Yes, that particular man suffered from all kinds of tics and grunts and involuntary cursing and shouting and stamping—it would attract outraged attention in the streets. And he came to me looking for a quick chemical answer, which I gave him: a drug called haloperidol (it's like L-dopa in reverse). Now, he was obviously sensitive to the drug, but he had bad effects from it as well. And he came back to see me, very upset by the whole business, because the magic hadn't worked; indeed the drug misfired, and many of his symptoms were worse. He then told me that he wasn't sure he *wanted* to be treated, saying, "I've had Tourette's since I was three. I consist of tics, and if you take them away I feel I won't be there." And it was at this point that he started referring to himself in the third person—not as "I" but as "Witty Ticcy Ray" or as the "Ticcer of Presidential Thruway." It was necessary for him to believe that there might exist a "nonticcy" identity. So a sort of imaginative and "existential" exercise was needed for some months until he felt he could face, enjoy, and even celebrate a life without tics. At that point we tried the same drug again, and it worked superbly. . . . It's worked superbly ever since.

It is in this sense of treatment that one wonders why you didn't originally want to become a psychiatrist instead of a neurologist.

Of course I'm interested in the psyche and in being. But, finally, I'm much too interested in the organic—in the relation between body and mind, between organs and being. It is insufficient to consider disease in purely mechanical or chemical terms; it must be considered equally in biological or metaphysical terms. In my first book, *Migraine,* I suggested the necessity of such a double approach, and I continue to develop this theme in my present work. Such a notion is far from new—it was understood very clearly in classical medicine. In present-day medicine, by contrast, there is an almost exclusively technical or mechanical emphasis, which has led to immense advances, but also to intellectual regression and a lack of proper attention to the full needs and feelings of patients. I hope that I may go a bit further than my colleagues in trying to look at the relationship of the disorder to the individual, at the struggle to endure and to maintain identity. The construct is finally dramatic and existential—the individual struggles to carry on in the face of a changing physiology.

I'm fond of browsing in the etymological dictionaries, and it pleases me that "will" and "well" are a sort of etymological double. And I think that *being* well—and certainly *getting* well—may require a will. In the case of Witty Ticcy Ray, at first he didn't *will* wellness . . . maybe he willed illness, and the *will* had to change before the drug could work. I think that the will to live or not live—sometimes thought of as something metaphysical—is terribly real, and I see it all the time.

In certain sixteenth- and seventeenth-century English poems, there was a tradition of organizing verses of three stanzas in such a way that the first dealt with memory, the second with understanding, and the third with will. But if memory goes—as it does in many of your patients—what happens to understanding and will?

It seems to me that will is the deepest thing in our being. And even in profound dementias, when the slate seems to have been wiped clean, there's this urge—something I practically equate with life itself—that is suggested in the last words of Samuel Beckett's novel *The Unnamable*: ". . . you must go on, I can't go on, I'll go on."

But will also depends on identity and memory, and if these are undermined by disease, one may see a strange sort of will-lessness or indifference. . . . Some of this is touched on in "The Lost Mariner"—a story of a man with profound amnesia due to Korsakoff's syndrome. This man, who seemed to have lost his past and his future and all sense of personal continuity, also seemed to have lost his will as well. . . . And I also tell of a man ("A Man of Identity") who had so lost his memory that he misidentified me as twenty different persons in the span of five minutes! And he would continually confabulate, invent stories—because, in some sense, he had lost his *own* story. One *must* have a story, one *must* have a narrative of one's life . . . otherwise one isn't alive.

I recently read a beautiful late essay by Freud called "Constructions in Analysis." And to Freud, a construction is not simply an interpretation, but rather a reconstruction of an early or repressed part of an infantile story—of how something was or might have been.

I think that medicine can't do without stories. This was the view of Hippocrates (who was supposedly the teacher of Thucydides); he said, in effect, that medicine couldn't be just science, it had to be history as well. And it's this insertion of history into science—this *conjunction* of personal narrative with physiology—that seems to me so essential in clinical medicine and clinical tales. The great Russian neuropsychologist A. R. Luria was a master in combining storytelling with science, and used to speak of "romantic science" in this connection.

There's a title of a play by Samuel Beckett—it's called *Not I*—that has always haunted me. And I'm especially interested in neurologic and organic problems that seem to destabilize the sense of "I" in some sort of way. In the case of the man I mentioned before who misidentified me as at least twenty different people, he was forced to invent scenes. Now, he was a part of every scene—one might say the one *stable* part of every scene. He began by seeing me as a customer. (In real life, he had worked in a delicatessen.) But then that broke down . . . it became clear that I wasn't a customer . . . and then he had to see me as someone else. But all of this kept breaking down. So, in *this* case, the attempted cure—the attempt to stabilize him—had in fact destabilized him, because all his stories were fictions. He needed his "true" story—but this he had lost. Whereas what Witty Ticcy Ray and I did together was to imagine and construct a possible life story—one not dominated by tics. And to that end, I acted as a kind of mirror that revealed his possibilities.

So your patients play an active part in their own treatment.

Yes, indeed. Some years ago I worked with a patient whose physical sense of balance had been so disturbed by Parkinson's disease that he walked with a precarious tilt to one side like a human Leaning Tower of Pisa. The man had been a carpenter, and when I showed him a videotape of his tilting walk, he was reminded of the spirit levels he had used in his work to tell whether a surface was straight. "Is there some sort of spirit level in the brain?" he conjectured. Parts of the inner ear are indeed like levels, and the man's homely analogy prompted a solution. We devised a pair of eyeglasses equipped with miniature horizontal levels extending forward from the bridge over the nose, and after some experimentation the man was able to use these spectacles to right his stance.

As a physician, how do you define your role in the patient's narrative?

Most of my patients are in homes for the aged and the chronically ill and suffer from the most severe forms of neurological damage. My work, my life, is all with the sick—but the sick and their sicknesses drive me to thoughts that, perhaps, I might not otherwise have. As Nietzsche said, "As for sickness, are we not almost tempted to ask whether we could get along without it?"

There's a part of me that almost *has* to organize clinical perception into a narrative, as well as theoretically. I tend to see most of my patients in the morning. Then, typically, I go for a walk in the New York Botanical Gardens. And while I'm there, I'm not consciously thinking about the patients I've just seen; but by the time I've returned to my office, the mass of things that have been told to me have taken the form of a story—a story that is the presentation of a problem, that investigates that problem, and that embeds all of my thoughts about it. Subsequently, I think, the patient comes to share the story, and the story gets modified. This comes back to what I was saying before about the need for a narrative. I think this need is absolutely primal. Children understand stories long before they understand trigonometry. And, for me, there is equally the need to tell a story and the need not to distort.

A friend of mine, who is a professor of pediatrics, says that, in her opinion, patients don't lie. And if they do, the lying is superficial and the truth is there on a deeper level. I do regard myself somewhat, sometimes, as a voice for the voiceless. And I feel that if my patients could speak, their individual stories would be what they would tell. Some of my students, incidentally, used to get a bit confused and would say to me, "Dr. Sacks, you talk like the patients and the patients talk like *you.*" *[Laughing]* Now, it's true that I don't talk entirely like a neurologist and that I do talk partly like a storyteller. But, on the other hand, I don't think that that makes me less of a neurologist.

Hippocrates was called the father of medicine, but he was also the father of medical *stories*, the father of case history. He gave us words like "prognosis" and "prodrome"—words that indicate that illness *has* a story and a narrative. And I think that, as at old-fashioned medical schools, you should be able to open any patient's chart and find his or her story. Of course, there's always a complex mixture between the patient's story and the doctor's rendering of the story. And the more that one can put the patient's own words in quotes, the better. But then it all has to be deepened and suffused with—though, one hopes, not distorted or reduced by—a physician's interpretation. But this kind of storytelling has rather disappeared in the past forty years. What we now get are a series of anonymous cases, presented in terms of percentages and so on (which, of course, are important), but the *individual* doesn't come through.

The limits of set, mechanical testing were strikingly brought out with some patients I once worked with—identical twins of subnormal intelligence, but with extraordinary powers of calculating or "seeing" numbers, instantly able to state dates or days of the week anytime in the last or next forty thousand years ("The Twins"). These rather mechanical feats—which are startling, but not of *really* deep interest—had been well documented in articles and even exhibited on television. But there was something else far more mysterious, which I came across only by accident, by being with them, knowing them, quietly, for a long time. I was working then on a ward where they were confined. One day I came across them talking to each other, with strange secret smiles on their faces—and their conversation consisted of swapping and savoring six-figure prime numbers. When I realized this, I was able to join in—with the help of a book of prime numbers—and then they went up bit by bit to swapping twenty-figure primes. This was amazing, quite beyond my understanding, indeed inexplicable by any account of mind—and it was something I was, so to speak, *allowed* to see or allowed the twins to reveal by abdicating a purely mechanical or professional role and permitting them to feel at ease, spontaneous, and intimate, in a very personal communion and contemplation. I always try to see my patients as *individuals,* which is not always practiced in a strictly medical or psychological setting.

William Osler, who was a very great physician, once said that "to talk of diseases is a sort of *Arabian Nights* entertainment." And this might sound either frivolous or monstrous if one didn't know that it came from Osler. And one might wonder in what sense it is true and what Osler meant by this. In my understanding, I think that it has to do with the fact that not only has every person with an illness or injury a story, and that not only are these stories interesting and varied, but that they also often have a quality of myth, of fairy tale, of dream. What interests me is the intersection between fact and fable. And in what appear to be the bleak rooms of clinics and chronic hospitals, I hear sagas, I see victims, I observe heroes, I witness great strivings of the human spirit.

How did you happen to get so interested in the idea of story and narrative?

I don't exactly know, but I think it can in part be attributed to my mother. She was trained in neurology and anatomy; and later, she became a professor of anatomy and surgery—she was, incidentally, the first Jewish woman to become a Fellow at the Royal College of Surgeons. Now, on the one hand, she loved anatomy, she loved minute detail . . . she had a tremendous feeling for this. I remember once saying that I had difficulty remembering the bones of the foot, and she said, "It's not a question of remembering but of understanding." And she drew me a foot—she drew me a whole *lot* of feet—and said, "Don't you see how the stresses must go and how it's like a bridge?" She immediately looked at it as an architect or like an engineer. But I couldn't see it; I didn't have that power.

So, she was my first tutor in anatomy, but she herself also loved to tell stories—rather disquieting ones, in fact, like D. H. Lawrence's "The Man Who Loved Islands" and Conrad Aiken's "Silent Snow, Secret Snow."

I've always associated your work with this latter story—about the little boy who, in the process of becoming autistic, sees and feels snow falling all around him when in fact it's sunny and springtime outside.

It's an extraordinary story, and what's so powerful about it, I suppose, is that on the one hand something terrible is happening to the boy, but it presents itself to him as a sort of sweetness.

I've been working mostly with older patients, yet, strangely, I just recently wrote up a story about a young man in his twenties ("The Autist Artist"). He had been variously described as idiotic and autistic, he had very severe epilepsy and temporal lobe seizures and brain damage, and there didn't seem to be any interaction with anything, until I took a copy of the magazine *Arizona Highways*, which I subscribe to because I love the desert. And, putting a pen in his hands, I opened up the magazine, showed him a photograph, and said, "Draw that!" And he immediately became sort of intense and quiet—the attendants had told me he wouldn't understand—and that was the beginning. His drawing revealed an extraordinary mixture of detail and comic exaggeration. In fact, in all of my work with autistic patients, the meeting point has never been in words, it's always been in play of one sort or another: one "meeting" was at the piano, another at a pool table. For I think that in the mode of play, one is no longer a composite of "drives," one is no longer driven at all.

I think the health resides in play or action; and whatever the problem, I try to bring out something central, something active, in all my patients. My story "Hands" is about this and nothing else—how, through being active, using them, a patient discovers she *has* hands.

This woman, who had long regarded her hands as useless lumps of putty, reached out one morning for a bagel. Impatient, hungry, instead of waiting passively and patiently, she acted—her first manual act in sixty years. After this act, progress was extremely rapid. She continued reaching out to explore the world. She asked for clay and started to make models; and eventually her attention, her appreciation, moved from objects to people.

I think of diseases as "Humean" and health as "Kantian." The philosopher David Hume affirmed that we are "nothing but a bundle or collection of different perceptions, succeeding one another with inconceivable rapidity, and in a perpetual flux and movement." And in this way, Hume is driven to consider man as passive and a spectator and not as an experiencer or active agent. The notion of action is so ostentatiously and absurdly absent that it was necessary for someone like Kant to make the idea of action central.

Writing about the Japanese puppet play known as Bunraku, Susan Sontag once commented that this kind of play shows us that "to act is to be moved." And I was thinking of Ida T. in Awakenings, *who, after taking L-dopa, says, "Wonderful, wonderful. I'm moving inside!"*

Even walking—something that would appear to be so mechanical, automatic, inexpressive, impersonal—is a movement of the soul. What is very characteristic of Parkinsonism, for example, is that the music of a style of walking goes away, and peculiar, robotic, puppetlike quality takes over such that a person actually feels that he or she is "walked"—the person isn't the "walker."

I took Susan Sontag's remark to include the idea of being "moved emotionally."

Absolutely. I'm reminded of one of my patients who would be "moved"—literally—by music that touched some emotional spring. The emotional spring is also a motor spring.

When I was first studying biology at Oxford, I was interested in animal movement, and particularly in the ways in which the characters of the animals seemed to enter their gestures—I was fascinated by the mechanics and the expressive quality of movement. When Clerk Maxwell was young, he would always ask about the "go" of things. And I've always been interested in the "go" of animals and peoples. Parkinsonism, for example, allows one to study "go," but as a pathological "go"—a "go" that is either haltered or driven.

And I've always had a passionate interest in the mechanisms of things: What makes a clock go? What makes the solar system go? But I've always also wondered what the inside of life is like, what it is to be a creature, to be a person. And I think that being a neurologist can bring these two interests together. Something has happened to someone's nervous system, and because of this, something has happened to someone's being.

So when something goes "wrong," so to speak, one can then examine what this reveals about the nature of being itself?

I suppose that diseases and disorders *do* provide a kind of vivisection . . . though that sounds like an awful word to use. But these are vivisections of *being,* hardly to be achieved in any other way—vivisections produced by nature in which our patients become our teachers. I think that medicine and philosophy are naturally close together, and that doctors must think philosophically and philosophers come to clinics! I regard my own work as a kind of clinical ontology.

OLIVER SACKS

JULY 9, 1933 – AUGUST 30, 2015

CARL SAGAN
Taking On the Cosmos

Los Angeles, 1980

"We are a way for the cosmos to know itself," Carl Sagan stated on *Cosmos: A Personal Voyage,* his recently broadcast thirteen-part series on public television. As he re-created journeys back in time and through the universe, speculating on its future and ours, Sagan continually reminded us that fresh knowledge of reality, even that which signals change, is inspirational, not dangerous.

In his essay "In Praise of Science and Technology," Sagan writes: "The most effective agents to communicate science to the public are television, motion pictures, and newspapers—where the science offerings are often dreary, inaccurate, ponderous, grossly caricatured or (as with much Saturday-morning commercial television programming for children) hostile to science." Sagan has attempted to correct this balance in his best-selling books and frequent appearances on television talk shows, but *Cosmos* has been his most ambitious and sustained undertaking to date. In the series, he used extraordinary special effects and a remarkably uncondescending, popular approach to present scientific information, displaying what one poet defines as the Homeric style: "eminently rapid, plain, direct in thought, expression, syntax, words, matter, ideas, and eminently noble." This proved to be an eminently suitable style with which to communicate deep and fundamental ideas about the universe to the close to 150 million people around the world who viewed the series.

In addition to his television work, Sagan is director of the Laboratory for Planetary Studies and is the David Duncan Professor of Astronomy and Space Sciences at Cornell University, where he also serves as associate director of the Center for Radiophysics and Space Research. He played a leading role in the *Mariner, Viking,* and *Voyager* expeditions, and he is the author of books such as *The Cosmic Connection; The Dragons of Eden,* for which he won a Pulitzer Prize; *Broca's Brain;* and *Cosmos,* which is based on the series.

Joining in the following interview is Ann Druyan, who, along with Steven Soter, contributed to the *Cosmos* scripts. The conversation took place at Sagan's Los Angeles home in August 1980 while he put the final touches on *Cosmos.*

* * *

In your book The Cosmic Connection, *you quote T. S. Eliot: "We shall not cease from exploration / And the end of all our exploring / Will be to arrive where we started / And know the place for the first time." I want to focus on the word "know" and ask you about knowing things for the first time, since this seems to be a seminal notion in your work.*

We start out a million years ago in a small community on some grassy plain. We hunt animals, have children, and develop a rich social, sexual, and intellectual life, but we know almost nothing about our surroundings. Yet we hunger to understand, so we invent myths about how we imagine the world is constructed—and they're, of course, based upon what we know, which is ourselves and other animals. So we make up stories about how the world was hatched from a cosmic egg, or created after the mating of cosmic deities or by some fiat of a powerful being. But we're not fully satisfied with those stories, so we keep broadening the horizon of our myths, and then we discover that there's a totally different way in which the world is constructed and things originate.

Today, we're still loaded down, and to some extent embarrassed, by ancient myths, but we respect them as part of the same impulse that has led to the modern, scientific kind of myth. But we now have the opportunity to discover, for the first time, the way the universe is in *fact* constructed, as opposed to how we would wish it to be constructed. It's a critical moment in the history of the world.

The Eliot quote also seems to suggest that, as explorers, human beings may exist to explain the universe to itself.

Absolutely. We are the representatives of the cosmos: we are an example of what hydrogen atoms can do, given fifteen billion years of cosmic evolution. And we resonate to these questions. We start with the origin of every human being, and then the origin of our community, our nation, the human species, who our ancestors were, and then the riddle of the origin of life. And the questions: Where did the earth and solar system come from? Where did the galaxies come from? Every one of those questions is deep and significant. They are the subject of folklore, myth, superstition, and religion in every human culture. But for the first time we are on the verge of answering many of them. I don't mean to suggest that we have the final answers—we are bathing in mystery and confusion on many subjects, and I think that will always be our destiny. The universe will always be much richer than our ability to understand.

For example, Io, one of Jupiter's big moons, was undiscovered until the seventeenth century. Until 1979, it was a point of light in the view of all but the few astronomers who had access to very large telescopes and could see the faintest mottling on the surface. Now we have thousands of detailed photographs showing features a kilometer across. We have passed from ignorance to knowledge of a whole world. Well, that's just one world. There are twenty other planets and moons we have since photographed. Twenty new worlds.

Freud wrote about the moment when an infant sees himself in the mirror for the first time.

That's a very good metaphor: we've just invented the mirror, and we can see ourselves from afar.

In the Cosmos *series, you stated that the fact that the universe was knowable was attested to in the sixth century B.C. in Greece.*

Sixth-century Ionia was, to the best of my knowledge, the first time there was a generally accepted view that the universe was subject not to the whims and vagaries of the gods but to generally applicable laws of nature that human beings were able to understand.

It wasn't until the 1960s that the first photograph of the whole earth was taken, and you saw it for the first time as a tiny blue ball floating in space. You realized that there were other, similar worlds far away, of different size, different color and constitution. You got the idea that our planet was just one in a multitude. I think there are two apparently contradictory and still very powerful benefits of that cosmic perspective—the sense of our planet as one in a vast number and the sense of our planet as a place whose destiny depends on us.

You've often quoted the Russian scientist K. E. Tsiolkovsky's statement: "The earth is the cradle of mankind, but one cannot live in the cradle forever."

I strongly dislike the notion that if things get absolutely rotten here, we can run away to somewhere else. I think it's a silly idea on economic *and* on moral grounds. Nevertheless, it's true, in my opinion, that the maturity of the human species will be connected with our ability to leave the earth, our mother, and seek our fortune in the galaxy . . . but not to abandon the earth, by any means. If we don't put our house in order, we'll never be able to explore the cosmos.

Life has had four billion years to develop through tortuous trial and error. But unlike biological evolution, which is fundamentally a random process and extremely wasteful in terms of lots of organisms dying, we don't have that opportunity. If we destroy ourselves, it may be a minor tragedy for life on the planet, but it's certainly a major tragedy for us. So we have to foresee the mistakes and avoid them. We can't stumble and then say, "I guess next time stockpiling fifteen thousand targeted nuclear warheads is not a good thing. I've learned from my mistake." I think there's a serious danger of our civilization destroying itself, and at least a possibility of our species destroying itself. But the destruction of all life on earth is unlikely, and certainly we can't destroy the planet. There's a hierarchy of destructibility.

Today, we can possibly destroy not only ourselves but also, it seems, some of our most intelligent hypotheses. More and more people, for example, are agreeing with Luther Sunderland, the New York spokesman for the "creationists" [anti-evolutionists]. Sunderland says: "A wing is a wing, a feather is a feather, an eyeball is an eyeball, a horse is a horse, and a man is a man."

The theory of evolution is the best explanation by far of the beauty and diversity of the natural world, and it's hard to see how evolution by natural selection wouldn't work. I think a fundamental problem with people who have trouble with the idea of evolution is the time perspective. You stand around, you watch a tree, and it doesn't turn into anything else. You say, "This evolution stuff is nonsense." But wait 100 million years and you will see something quite different. That instinctive feeling—"If I haven't seen it, it doesn't exist"—is, I think, behind some of the doubts on evolution. But it's also behind some of the doubts people have about special relativity. Special relativity says that if you travel close to the speed of light, your watch slows down and you can travel into the far future. Or quantum mechanics says that, in the realm of the very small, you can have a dumbbell-shaped molecule in this position or that position but not in any intermediate position. "Well, ridiculous, I never saw any rule that prevents me from turning a thing to any intermediary position I want."

This is an example of the inapplicability of common sense. Common sense works fine for the universe we're used to, for time scales of decades, for a space between a tenth of a millimeter and a few thousand kilometers, and for speeds much less than the speed of light. Once we leave those domains of human experience, there's no reason to expect the laws of nature to continue to obey our expectations, since our expectations are dependent on a limited set of experiences. The matter we're made out of was cooked in the center of stars. That's part of the disquiet a few people feel about evolution. Also, some people are annoyed by the idea that we are not the apex of the universe.

They'd rather be the apex than the ape.

If I thought the supreme coordinator of the universe had a special interest in making me and my brothers and sisters, that would give me a special significance. It would make me feel good, and also make me think that maybe I didn't have to take care of myself; someone much more powerful would do so. It's a tempting idea, but we have to be very careful not to impose our hopes and desires on the cosmos, but instead, in the scientific tradition and with the most open mind possible, see what the cosmos is saying to us.

On the question of creationism, it is true that natural selection as the cause of evolution is a hypothesis. There are other possibilities. The creationists argue that they're interested in fairness: they don't want only one of several competing doctrines taught in the schools. I applaud their interest in fairness, but I think that the first test is their willingness to teach Darwinian evolution in the churches. If they're worried that there isn't fair exposure of both sides, then it's quite remarkable how only one side is taught in the churches, the synagogues, the mosques, and, I might add, during the enormous number of hours on television devoted to presenting idiosyncratic belief systems.

In your books and throughout the Cosmos *series, you seem to be deeply committed to the idea of the relatedness and connectedness of all universal material.*

It's a truth of enormous power. Talk about things that ought to be shouted from the pulpits—this is surely one. The matter we're made out of was cooked in the center of stars. We're made of star stuff—the calcium in our teeth, the carbon in our genes, the nitrogen in our hair, the silicon in our eyeglasses. Those atoms were all made from simpler atoms in stars hundreds of light-years away and billions of years ago.

It's an astonishing thing, we're so tied to the rest of the cosmos. Cosmic rays that are produced in the death throes of stars are partly responsible for the mutations that have led to us—the changes in the genetic material. The origin of life was spurred by ultraviolet light from the sun and lightning, which in turn is caused by the heating of the earth by the sun. The connections are intricate and powerful and lovely. For those people seeking a cosmic tie-in, one exists. It's not the one the astrologers pretend, but it's much more elegant, and it has the additional virtue of being true.

I know you're not an avid consulter of astrologers.

I'd be all for it if there were any evidence for it, but there isn't. It's like racism or sexism: you have twelve little pigeonholes, and as soon as you type someone as a member of that particular group, as long as someone is an Aquarius, Virgo, or Scorpio, you know his characteristics. It saves you the effort of getting to know him individually.

In his book The Natural History of the Mind, *Gordon Rattray Taylor distinguishes, as you do not, between the mind and the brain, and he gives as examples things that he thinks can't be adequately explained by studying only the brain, such as altered states of consciousness, amnesia, artistic inspiration, imagination, inhibitions, pain, placebo effect, sight, smell, telepathy, willpower, and love.*

Talk about imagination! What a lack of imagination in the contention that those things can't be . . .

[Ann Druyan] . . . based on material reality.

Right. I mean, for example, he mentions altered states of consciousness. Look how psychedelic drugs, like alcohol, regularly produce altered states of consciousness. It's a simple molecule: C_2H_5OH. Put that in your system and suddenly you're feeling very different. Well, is that mystical, or does that have something to do with chemistry?

You're talking about what this chemistry causes rather than about what you're experiencing in that state of consciousness.

[Druyan] But why separate the dancer from the dance? Why separate the experience from what causes the experience? It's not necessary. The whole idea of science is to trust in reality and to interrogate nature so you can get answers, can step right up to the mirror—reality itself—and not turn away from it.

In The Dragons of Eden, *you write that "it is because of this immense number of functionally different configurations of the human brain that no two humans, even identical twins raised together, can ever be really very much alike. . . . All possible brain states are by no means occupied; there must be an enormous number of mental configurations that have never been entered or even glimpsed by any human being in the history of mankind." What do you think will enable human beings to occupy these configurations?*

Well, I don't know. There are many that may not be entered by a single person within the next thousand years.

What can human beings do to try to enter into these areas?

One thing to do is to mistrust the conventional perceptions. If you're interested in a new perception, you have to view with some degree of objectivity still-unspoken truths.

So the scientists you talk about in Cosmos *are quite subversive?*

Yes. As Alfred North Whitehead said, "It is the business of the future to be dangerous." Any new idea that doesn't threaten something isn't worth its salt.

Do you think the future is going to be dangerous?

Absolutely. The present is quite dangerous also, though. Let me give you an example. I think it's clear that none of the forms of government that exist in any of the two hundred or so countries on the earth today are applicable to the middle of the next century. Not a one. We have to get from here to there somehow. How can you do that without disturbing the here? The world is changing at an incredibly rapid pace. Human survival depends on dealing with those changes, but governments generally are concerned with changing nothing.

I think that any nation with a serious concern about the future would be busy inventing experimental communities to try, on a practical basis, to find the society that is going to work in the middle of the twenty-first century. I think the alternative communities of the sixties were a premonition, a spontaneous recognition by a lot of people that society, by and large, wasn't working, and that they had to see what else they could do. The larger society was unhappy with the idea of alternatives. The possibility of a better world is a rebuke. It says, "Why haven't you worked to make that change?" Since very few of us manage to make any significant changes, we tend to resist that exhortation.

[Druyan] There is a resistance to change, but there is no refuge from change in the cosmos. So it's a very grave problem.

So you're trying to wake people up a bit.

Those are highly ethical motivations. But a lot of my motivation is that understanding science is fun. It's communicable fun.

You don't want to be portentous.

Science, as communicated in some places, sounds as if it were the last thing in the world that any reasonable person would want to know about. It's portrayed as impossibly difficult to get into and a thing that sort of rots your brain for any good social interaction.

On his album Slow Train Coming, *Bob Dylan refers to scientists in a very disparaging manner.*

[Druyan] I take this very deeply to heart. The thing that I always loved about Dylan was the courage of his metaphors and the way he could cut to the bone of some kind of naked feeling. It always seemed very gutsy. And now it seems that he's turned away, he's blinded by the light, and so he looks for some easy explanation.

In The Dragons of Eden, *you quote St. Augustine of Hippo, who said, "I no longer dream of the stars."*

Just compare that with another quote: "To dance beneath the diamond sky with one hand waving free." Compare that with Augustine and with Dylan's latest incarnation.

Concerning your notion of the enormous amount of mental configurations in our brains, you've written: "From this perspective, each human being is truly rare and different, and the sanctity of individual human lives is a plausible, ethical consequence." This connects with another of your remarks concerning "the profound respect for other human beings and organisms as coequal recipients of this precious patrimony of 4.5 billion years of evolution." Both communicate a very Buddhist sense of the importance of the love for all sentient beings and creatures.

Don't you think that's just a logical extension? People certainly love their families, then distant relations, then friends. Then they have some degree of affection for their community, their tribe. One principal level of human identification right now is with the nation-state. Now, the obvious next identification is with all the people on the planet. But why is that the end? I mean, especially if we understand our common heritage, our genetic relationship to animals and plants. Why not a set of absolutely continuous dissolves, one animal to another? Don't we have some degree of sympathy and respect for all the living things on the planet? They are our cousins. It's such an obvious idea.

Your perspective is ethically far wider than the one we generally see operating today.

It's the time perspective point again. Most of human history was spent in hunter–gatherer communities. And in these kinds of communities today—there aren't many of them—you find a degree of cooperativeness, an absence of alienation that is unheard of in modern society. To ignore our social heredity is a serious mistake. There is a human capacity for good-natured cooperation that is simply not encouraged in modern society. That must change.

In the scientific world there are such subjects as particle physics, astrophysics, biophysics, and geophysics—all these compartmentalized and specialized areas. People working in any one of these areas are often afraid to make general statements about matters outside their domain. Yet in Cosmos, *you take on the entire cosmos!*

It's fun to do. It's certainly where the excitement is—on the border of two fields that haven't made much contact yet. The boundaries are arbitrary. Those things that separate, say, astronomy from geology, or chemistry from biology, or even mathematics from physics, these are man-made, human-invented boundaries. In the real world, these subjects flow into each other.

Everything is related. Suppose there's a computer that goes through the names of everybody in the country and randomly picks out one person, and you have to get in touch with that person. You have to call someone, who in turn has to call someone else, and so on. What's the average number of calls you'd have to make to get that targeted person? I mean, how many people could you call who would recognize you, even vaguely, so that you could say, "Hello, Charlie, sorry to bother you. I know you live in Omaha, but there's a guy in Fargo, North Dakota, I'm trying to get in touch with. Would you mind making one call for me?" How many people do you know who would make a phone call for you to someone he knows whom he could ask the same question? How many, just roughly? There are all sorts of mind-boggling things we can't even glimpse.

Maybe seventy or eighty.

Let's round it off to 100. Let's suppose that's true of everybody. So you know 100 people, and suppose each of them knows 100 people—only a few of whom are already on your list. So to get to 10,000 people, that's just two calls—100 times 100. To get to a million is three, to get to 100 million is four, and there are only 200 million people in the country.

So what is the moral of this example?

That it's not just some peculiar idea of the Buddhists. It's the truth: everything is connected.

The New York Times *reported not long ago that one bewildering outcome of quantum theory has led some scientists to speculate that the entire universe, "including the time in which it exists, may have been created by a spontaneous quantum fluctuation—a 'twitch' in the nothingness that preceded it." That sounds a lot like Buddhism, doesn't it?*

I agree. That does sound like an Eastern religion. And it may be based on a perfectly respectable scientific paper.

This kind of speculation leads to religious and philosophical questions, doesn't it?

All of science does. I think that's why we *have* religious questions: because we are naturally scientists. It's the only thing we do substantially better than other creatures. Even much of our music is an expression of feelings that we share with other animals but actualize because we're good at science and technology and they're not. And science and technology—surely no other animal on the planet has it, aside from termite nests and so on; that's a distinctively human ability. Feelings are not characteristically human—very likely animals have lots of deep feelings. It's thinking that's characteristically human. So I don't think you should be surprised that a religious idea turns out to have some scientific support.

But you've mentioned that science is still a myth.

Well, a myth is an attempt to pull together the best information that's available to explain the origin of something.

So there may possibly be a better myth than science in the future?

It's guaranteed. How likely is it that we live in the very year that the absolute truth is first found out about the cosmos? It would be a remarkable coincidence, considering how many years there are. It's much more likely that human knowledge is a set of successive approximations and that there are all sorts of things that we've gotten wrong, and all sorts of mind-boggling things that we can't even glimpse that will be the established fact in a century or two.

You're saying that there are ways of thinking that we know nothing about.

Must be. On many different levels the answer to that must be yes. T. S. Eliot talks about knowing a place for the first time. But there's a second and a third time. I think there's a continuum of fractional times. You always know the earth to some degree, you always know home to some degree, but you can always make significant increments in your knowledge of them.

So there's never a certitude?

There are two extremes to worry about. One is the extreme in which everything is known and there's nothing left to do. The other is where everything is so complicated you can never begin to do anything. We are lucky to live in a universe where there are laws of nature and things to discover, but they're not impossibly difficult, so we can understand them to some extent. But they're also difficult enough so that we're nowhere near understanding them all. There are exhilarating discoveries yet to be made. It's the best possible world.

[Druyan] The best possible cosmos!

CARL SAGAN
NOVEMBER 9, 1934 – DECEMBER 20, 1996

SAM SHEPARD
Lies of the Mind

Los Angeles, 1986

The theater critic Michael Feingold once remarked that the paradox of Sam Shepard consisted in his having "the mind of a Kafka trapped in the body of a Jimmy Stewart." It was Franz Kafka who wrote that "a book must be the ax for the frozen sea in us," and in the more than forty plays that Sam Shepard has written since 1964, this American playwright has been breaking open that frozen sea with an originality of vision, a jolting intermingling of humor and grief, a profound examination of the hopes and failures of the American family, and an astonishing ear for the cadences of the American idiom. With plays like *The Unseen Hand, Curse of the Starving Class, Buried Child* (for which he won the 1979 Pulitzer Prize), *True West, Fool for Love,* and the recent *A Lie of the Mind,* Shepard has cloaked himself in the mantle once worn by Eugene O'Neill and Tennessee Williams. He has also been a striking presence in films such as *Days of Heaven, Resurrection, Frances,* and *The Right Stuff.* In the words of *The Right Stuff*'s director, Phil Kaufman, "[Shepard] has a quality that is so rare now . . . a kind of bygone quality of the forties, when guys could wear leather jackets and be laconic and still say a lot without verbally saying anything."

Born Samuel Shepard Rogers III on November 5, 1943, in Fort Sheridan, Illinois, Shepard was an army brat whose family was stationed for various periods in South Dakota, Utah, Florida, and Guam and finally settled down on an avocado ranch in Duarte, California—an end-of-the-road valley town east of Los Angeles. At nineteen, he left his family and went to New York City as an aspiring actor and musician, started writing his superenergized, music-driven early plays, eventually moved to London, and now [1986] lives on a farm in Virginia. He is an intensely private person who shies away from journalists, preferring to allow transformed glimpses of himself to appear in his plays and in books like *Hawk Moon* and *Motel Chronicles*—collections of poems–meditations–dreams–journals.

In conversation, Sam Shepard is happy to speak directly about things that concern him and indirectly about issues of superficial or only "personal" importance. With an undeniably engaging blue-eyed squint and a kind of western-swing twang to his voice, he continually displays an unnerving, surprising, and charmingly boyish sense of humor. But most disarming of all is the way he unhesitatingly confronts, explores, and clarifies the most painful and sorrowful of matters—loss, separation, disillusionment, powerlessness, weakness, fear, lies.

In his most recent play, *A Lie of the Mind,* Shepard has made his most fearless, controlled, and deepest penetration into the realm of the American psyche. For in this story of two American families—with its revelations and reconciliations of the relationships between and among a violent son, his battered wife, and his angelic brother—the playwright shows how personal and social dreams and lies are one and the same, creating, as he once said Bob Dylan created, "a mythic atmosphere out of the land around us. The land we walk on every day and never see until someone shows it to us."

It was in an old-fashioned, unassuming drugstore on Canon Drive in Beverly Hills, California (one of Shepard's favorite "reading" haunts), and in the tearoom of the Chateau Marmont Hotel, in Hollywood, that the following interview took place in April 1986.

* * *

In many of your plays, your characters often perform music onstage, and the feel of your plays is often that of a jazz improvisation or of extended country, blues, or rock 'n' roll songs. When did your preoccupation with music begin?

My dad was a kind of semiprofessional Dixieland-type drummer, and I learned the drums from him. When I was about twelve, we bought our first Ludwig drum set from a pawnshop—a marching-band bass drum, great big tom-toms and big, deep snare drums. We stripped the paint off of them, varnished them, and then set them out in the orchard to dry.

I was in high school then in Duarte and started playing in a band called Nat's Cats. We performed old swing music, kind of Dixieland stuff, and gradually moved into rock 'n' roll. Trumpet, clarinet, drums—that was the trio. In this same high school that I went to, there was a student named

Mike Romero, who also played the drums. So this competition started—a kind of drum wars!—and I once went over to his place and stayed up all night and listened to jazz records for the first time. Then we played for hours, and I discovered what the left hand could do—letting the drum hand ride—because a rock 'n' roll drummer would turn the hand over and smash the snare drum, while the jazz drummer would hold the stick in his open palm so that he could get this snap out of it. Mike Romero was the guy who turned me on to that, and all of a sudden the drums opened up for me. And when I moved to New York City in 1963, I started playing drums for the Holy Modal Rounders.

I've always felt a great affinity with music. I've felt myself to be more of a musician than anything else, though I'm not proficient in any one instrument. But I think I have a musical sense of things . . . and writing seems to me to be a musical experience—rhythmically and in many other ways. But I don't think that that's so unusual. Most of the old guys had the same sense—Christopher Marlowe thought of himself as a musician. Just another musician killed at a bar [laughing] . . . and there's that theory that he was Shakespeare. . . . But I'm not sure that Shakespeare even existed. I think there was a whole cover-up for him.

You do?

Yeah. I think there's a big mystery about Shakespeare, but it's too late to confirm it. [Laughing] I mean, look at the plays, the way they suddenly shift gears—from the earlier period to those later tragedies. Something happened that nobody knows about. I think he was involved in something deeply mysterious and esoteric, and at the time they had to keep it under wraps. There's an awful lot of amazing insight in his plays that doesn't come from an ordinary mind. And there was a tremendous monastic movement at that time. Who knows what he was into?

Shakespeare didn't mince words either. "To be, or not to be" is right to the point. [Laughing] You can't get much more to the point than that. That is the question. Are you going to be here or not? What's the deal? Are you going to be or not be?

When did you make that decision?

Well, you decide that every day.

Do you sometimes wake up and wonder about it?

For me, it's been a process of overcoming a tremendous morning despair. It's been diminishing over the years. But I still feel this trace of this thing that I can't really track down.

Some people are just "up and at 'em!"

I've tried desperately to be like that—6:00 a.m. and bang! Feed the horses and milk the goats. I used to work a lot on ranches where I grew up, and I had to rise at 5:30 in the morning. In fact, there's something healthy about going against the grain of the laziness of the body.

In a prose poem you once wrote called "Rhythm," you make it sound as if everything is rhythm: "Oilcan rhythms, ratchet wrench rhythms. Playing cards in bicycle spokes. . . . Water slapping rocks. Flesh slapping flesh. Boxing rhythms. Racing rhythms. Rushing brooks . . ."

Well, it is, pretty much. But there's that distinction between tempo and rhythm, where tempo is a man-made invention. . . . In San Francisco, I once studied with an African drummer named Kwaku Dadey, who had been playing since he was seven years old in Ghana. I'd always thought that polyrhythm was an invention of contemporary jazz, but it turns out that it's an ancient African concept. And I remember that one day about eight of us got together to play congas: we played in rhythms of 5s and 6s and in 6/8, 3/4, and 4/4 time simultaneously. Everything stacked and piled up, and you had to carry some of the lines three or four measures to catch up, but eventually it all worked out. It was hard to believe!

There was no connecting principle?

Of course there was. Like the ocean. If you're playing an individual part and I'm playing an individual part and we can't figure out how these two are going to merge—assuming you're sticking to your part and I to mine—they just eventually merge. I don't know how. But the rhythmic structures underneath each one of these parts all somehow map out. And what's the principle of that? It's way beyond music. . . . That man was an amazing teacher, with an understanding of the crossroads and of how everything fits together. I learned a lot from him.

When I see your plays, I'm sometimes reminded of songs written by the Band.

I love Levon Helm—he's one of my favorite guys. You know, Levon once shot himself in the leg while practicing his quick draw! *[Laughing]* And there's another guy Levon once told me about who shot his nuts off—another drummer, by the way—and Levon said that he's never played the same since. *[Laughing]* Oh, boy! Carrying a .45 in your crotch when you're playing the drums is really asking for trouble!

Do you remember the Band's song called "Daniel and the Sacred Harp"? It tells the story of a guy who buys a magical instrument that he has no rights to, and while he's playing his heart out on it in a meadow, he notices that he's lost his shadow, perhaps his soul.

A bad sign. You know *Dr. Faustus*, by Christopher Marlowe? I'd love to make a film of that sometime. I even prefer it to Goethe's version because of Marlowe's incredible language.

You seem to like Marlowe a lot. When did you first read him?

I'll tell you—aside from assigned reading in high school, I didn't read any plays except for a couple of Brecht things when I was living in New York City. I avoided reading out of arrogance, really. But when I went to England in the early seventies, I suddenly found myself having a kind of dry spell. It was difficult for me to write, so I started to read. And I read most of the Greek guys—Aeschylus, Sophocles. I studied up on those guys, and I'm glad I did. I was just amazed by the simplicity of the ancient Greek plays, for instance—they were dead simple. Nothing complex or tricky, which surprised the hell out of me, because I'd assumed they were beyond me. But now I began to comprehend what they were talking about, and they turned out to be accessible.

They're a lot about the family romance, aren't they?

They're all about destiny! That's the most powerful thing. Everything is foreseen, and we just play it out.

You don't think a person can shape his own destiny?

Oh, maybe. But first you have to know what your destiny is.

When did you think you knew your own?

I'm not so sure I do. I'm not saying I know my destiny; I'm saying that it exists. It exists, and it can become a duty to discover it. Or it can be shirked. But if you take it on as your duty, then it becomes a different thing from dismissing it altogether and just imagining that it'll work itself out anyway. I mean, it will. But it's more interesting to try to find it and know it.

What was the first thing you ever wrote?

I remember that when I was a kid, I wrote a story about a Coke bottle. You know that in the old days Coke bottles had the name of the city where they were manufactured inscribed on the bottom—St. Paul, Dubuque, wherever. So I wrote this story about this bottle and its travels. It would get filled up in one town, someone would drink it and throw it out the window, and then it would get on a truck and go somewhere else.

You seem to have found your own voice, on the outskirts of Duarte, all on your own.

You know, Duarte was a weird accumulation of things, a strange kind of melting pot—Spanish, Okie, black, midwestern elements all jumbled together. People on the move who couldn't move anymore, who wound up in trailer camps. And my grandmother, my father's mother, was part something . . . maybe American Indian, I'm not sure what. She was real dark, with black eyes, and I don't know what that was all about—there was a cover-up somewhere back there.

But as far as my "voice" goes, I'm not so sure it's "mine." I had a sense that a voice existed that needed expression, that there was a voice that wasn't being voiced, if you want to put it like that. But is it "mine"?

Your most recent play, A Lie of the Mind, *seems like a real bringing together and transformation of many of your oldest and deepest "voices."*

That's twenty-one years of work there. It was a tough play to write, because I had the first act very clearly in mind, then went off on a tangent and had to throw away two acts and start again. And then it began to tell itself. Like a story you've heard a long time ago that's now come back.

A writer once stated, "Insight only occurs as a lightning-bolt. The text is the thunder-peal rolling long behind."

Did I write that? *[Laughing]*

No, the critic Walter Benjamin did. What was the lightning bolt for A Lie of the Mind?

The incredible schism between a man and a woman, in which something is broken in a way that almost kills the thing that was causing them to be together. The devastating break—that was the lightning bolt.

But isn't it this lightning bolt that woke them up? It seems as if Beth, the battered, brain-damaged wife, who appears to be crazy and living in a dream world, is in fact the clearest-seeing person in the play.

Yes, she's the most sensitive. I've had a couple of experiences of people very close to me who suffered brain damage and who underwent surgery. And the most startling thing in both of these cases was the sense of one's own helplessness in relation to what these two people were going through because of the innocence of their states. We use words all the time—we take them for granted—and suddenly you're faced with people who have no language. . . . It's gone. And you become aware that language is a learned function—it's an obvious fact—but at that moment you truly become aware of it, when you realize that it can be lost. Those people are on the open end of the stick. They're vulnerable and alive to the fact of language, while we're dead to it. We usually don't understand how it affects people and what kind of luxury it is to have language. So it shakes you up.

It's extraordinarily moving when Beth, pointing to her head, says, "This is me. This is me now. The way I am. Now. This. All. Different. I—I live inside this. Remember. Remembering."

It's interesting how you can be lost in an area like memory—memory is very easy to get lost in. Some things can't get lost, though, because they're based on emotional memory, which is a different thing from just trying to remember the name of a person or some fact. But to remember where you were touched has more of a reverberation. It remembers itself to you.

At the beginning of A Lie of the Mind, *Jake's talking to his brother, Frankie, on the phone, and the latter says, "Jake! Don't do that! You're gonna disconnect us again." And you notice how the word "disconnect" and later a word like "remember" almost act as ritualistic and key words in the play. Yet the words also pass by unnoticed because they're so well rooted in intense but simple colloquial speech.*

I think you have to start in that colloquial territory, and from there move on and arrive in poetic country . . . but not the other way around. I've noticed that even with the Greek guys, especially with Sophocles, there's a very simple, rawboned language. The choruses are poetic, but the speech of the characters themselves is terse, cut to the bone and pointed to the heart of the problem. It's like Merle Haggard tunes like "My Own Kind of Hat"—I do this, that, and some other thing, but I wear my own kind of hat. . . . Real simple.

A wisdom teacher once said that the most difficult barrier in one's life is the conquest of lying—lies of the mind.

But how do you come to see that? It's a hard pill to swallow that *everything* is a lie. Everything . . . even the truth! But if you even begin to approach that awareness, then something new takes place, because you start to see that there's another dimension of a relationship between yourself and the truth—the real truth as opposed to the real lies. Because everything, in a way, is suggestion: I suggest to myself that I'm brave, though it turns out that I'm a coward. But the suggestion is so powerful that I believe it, even in the face of my cowardice. The truth is that we can't face the truth, and it seems to me that the first step is to find out which is which. Because if you go off believing that one part is strong and it's actually weak, you're going to be in for a shock!

As when Jake beats his wife up?

The shock of that kind of violence *brings* something. I'm not in any way suggesting that violence is a way of catharsis—I don't believe that at all. Nor do I believe that acting out one's anger is necessarily going to clean you of it—if anything, it may just provoke more anger. But that kind of accidental confrontation, especially between men and women, can bring about—even if only temporarily—a kind of awakening. Because a man can believe himself to be in control of his emotions, yet in the flash of an eye he can lose it totally and be shocked into seeing what he's really made of. . . . But to get into that kind of thing with a woman is a cowardly act. And if he's a man at all and doesn't see that, there's no way he can be truthful with himself.

Doesn't Jake, by wounding Beth, make both him and her wake up?

But they wake up into a lostness. They're not found in that state—it's not like, "Oh, now I realize my situation and I know where to turn." It's a lostness. Lostness can be profoundly rejuvenating in a way—it's a desperate time and full of despair and all that—but being really lost can start something that's brand-new. Now, there are different kinds of lostness—you can be lost and not know what street you're on. You can be lost emotionally, you can be lost with other people, you can be lost in yourself. I think you continually turn around that circle—finding yourself lost and then getting relatively found.

To me, writing is a way of bringing things back together a little bit. If I can at least write something, I start to feel that I'm gathering out of that lostness something that has some kind of structure and form and something that, one hopes, can be translated to others. I don't know if you can ever get *totally* found—I've met people who are convinced that they know what direction they're going in, and they seem to be very together. But maybe they're believing in a lie. . . . A belief in a lie can be very powerful. And then again maybe some of it's true. . . . Who's to say?

Some of your characters do seem to have staked a legitimate claim in the realm of truth. Beth, for instance.

And they're the hardest ones to say anything about. It's much easier to define something that's bent and go with the way it's misshapen. But to define or give an impression of something or someone that's clean is very difficult.

You know, there's a great yearning to get back to that state, and there are all sorts of methods that have been developed for that purpose. I was just talking to an old friend of mine who's having a nervous breakdown—the last person in the world I ever thought would be in that state. And he told me that he was thinking of going on a vision quest. There's apparently a vision-quest cult based on the American Indian practice of going off for three days by yourself. And I said that that was great if it could serve the purpose of confronting the essentials. But I think it's incredibly difficult to do that today. If it happens accidentally, as it apparently did to Werner Erhard . . . well, then, he's a lucky man. But is that an excuse for starting an entire organization based on his personal breakthrough? I don't know. And I think that the question of death—of trying to take a truthful look at it—is missing in a lot of people's activities today. The health movement and jogging movement sometimes seem to me to reflect an incredible yearning to escape death—this fanatical thing of running to build up the body!

In his recent biography of you, the critic Don Shewey, who obviously greatly admires your work, makes several comments about your supposed macho image.

Just because machismo exists doesn't mean that it *shouldn't* exist. There's this attitude today that certain antagonistic forces have to be ignored or completely shut out rather than entered into in order to explore and get to the heart of them. All you have to do is enter one rodeo event to find out what that's all about . . . and you find out fast—in about eight seconds! So rather than avoid the issue, why not take a dive into it? I'm not saying whether it's good or bad—I think that the moralistic approach to these notions is stupid. It's not a moral issue, it's an issue of existence. Machismo may be an evil force . . . but what in fact is it?

I knew this guy down in the Yucatán who was so macho he decided to demonstrate to this princess he saw on the beach how *powerfully* he could swim. So he swam out into the ocean, got caught in the current and drowned himself. Now, *he* found out *fast*. What was that moment like when he suddenly realized that because of his vanity he was going to die? I know what this thing is about because I was a victim of it, it was part of my life, my old man tried to force on me a notion of what it was to be a "man." And it destroyed my dad. But you can't avoid facing it.

At the end of your play The Unseen Hand, *an old Wild West gunfighter, who's been brought back to life by Willie the Space Freak, reflects, "A man's gotta be still long enough to figure out his next move. . . . That's the great thing about this country, ya know. The fact that you can make yer own moves in yer own time without some guy behind the scenes pullin' the switches on ya." It's interesting that the American-pioneer myth and the spiritual mission and yearning you were talking about are often spoken of in exactly the same way. There seems to be a connection between these two things, such that true West equals true East.*

It's very strong, the connection between physical territory and inner territory. In America, we've run out of the former, and even though they talk about going to the moon and the planets as being an extension of that, it's going to wind up at the same borderline. Now, the spiritual notion talks about something that's more hopeful in a way, because the inner search doesn't come to some Pacific Ocean, where it just builds Los Angeles— it's a never-ending process. But it seems to me that there could be a real meeting between a true Western—meaning *Western Hemisphere*—spirit and the inner one, and it doesn't have to remain on the level of being courageous with the land anymore. The land's been discovered. There's a different kind of courage that's being called for now.

The poet William Carlos Williams once wrote, "The pure products of America / Go crazy." And some critics have seen your plays to be about these kinds of "real," indigenous, almost overly interbred Americans—now fragmented and deracinated.

I don't know. Insanity is something you're up against all the time. You always have to grapple with that. It's much easier to go crazy than to stay sane. Much easier. Insanity's the easy way out.

In your early writings, one finds a lot of harrowing depictions of demonic states and possession trances.

In those days, I had a lot of emotional earthquakes that I didn't understand because I was in the grips of them. I didn't realize even *that* much, I was just running wild with them and didn't know where they were taking me.

In your recent work—Fool for Love, A Lie of the Mind—*however, you've been clearly and consciously entering right into the earthquake zone.*

I had no choice. At a certain point, you've got to do that, otherwise you end up writing diddley-bop plays. Now, the ear of the typical psychological play doesn't have any reverberation anymore. Plays have to go beyond just "working out problems"—that's not the thing I'm talking about. What makes O' Neill's *Long Day's Journey into Night* such a great work, for instance, is that O' Neill moves past his own personal family situation into a much wider dimension. I read that play in high school, and I've always thought that that was truly the great American play. It's so overwhelmingly honest—O' Neill just doesn't pull any punches. You can't confront that play without being moved.

It's been said, in regard to that work, that children often live out the unconscious and fantasy lives of their parents.

Yes, but certain things that occur inside the family often leave marks on the emotional life that are far stronger than fantasy. What might be seen as the fantasy is, to me, just a kind of rumination on those deep marks, a manifestation of the emotional and psychological elements. Sometimes in someone's gesture you can notice how a parent is somehow inhabiting that person without there being any awareness of that. How often are you aware that a gesture is coming from your old man? Sometimes you can look at your hand and see your father. But it's a complex scheme—it's not that easy to pinpoint. Again, the thing is not to avoid the issue but to see that it exists.

Thinking of your brain-damaged character, Beth, in A Lie of the Mind *and of the deeply musical way she has of expressing herself, I recall a statement by the German poet Novalis that goes, "Every disease is a musical problem, every cure a musical solution."*

To me, music *and* humor are both very healing. . . . That's the trouble with modern rock 'n' roll, by the way: it's lost its sense of humor. It's become so morbidly stylistic and sour—there's no joy in it. And I think it's disastrous that a genuine sense of humor has been smothered.

When do you think the smothering began?

It began with the Doors! *[Laughing]* The Doors had *no* sense of humor—they were grim. Now, I knew Jim Morrison for a little while, and in fact he *did* have a sense of humor—a bizarre one—but he never really exhibited it onstage.

So what musicians do you like to listen to right now?

Billy Joe Royal, Ricky Skaggs, Stevie Ray Vaughan, Lou Ann Barton, the Blasters. I guess what I like is mostly country and western or else stuff that has a real blues feel to it. As far as straight-up-and-down rock 'n' roll goes, I don't think there's hardly anybody worth shaking a stick at anymore.

Guys like Clyde McPhatter used to sing their tail ends off! Today I only have a little hope for Texas bands. *[Laughing]* . . . Delbert McClinton's still doing some stuff . . . but melodically and rhythmically, it's not what it was. Take all those imitators of Lou Reed, for example: if they went back and listened to his early stuff, they'd see that he had a whole different feel . . . plus he was a helluva writer. He could really write a lyric. He's been ripped off left, right, and center.

Coming back to Jim Morrison—you know, he felt he had a curse on his head. Because when he was a kid, he was driving with his family outside Albuquerque. And there was an Indian on the side of the road. His family stopped, and Morrison went over to the Indian, and this guy—Morrison thought he was some kind of shaman—threw a whammy on him. That's probably when Jim Morrison lost his sense of humor. *[Laughing]*

Spells can be effective.

Their power lies in your believing them.

So how do you avoid the so-called powers of relentless and overintrusive fans?

Carry a gun! *[Laughing]*

Just don't carry it in your pocket! I can hear people saying, "His plays haven't been the same since."

Thanks for the warning. *[Laughing]*

I've noticed that the funniest moments in your plays are often intermixed with a sense of weirdness and sadness.

It's a double-edged thing. If you look at Buster Keaton and Harry Langdon and Stan Laurel, there's something tragic about them. The humor lies in their incredible innocence in the face of life, which doesn't make sense.

Someone once commented that life is tragic to those who feel and comic to those who think.

I think that to a certain extent that's true. One of the things I look for in actors is a genuine sense of humor. And if they have that, I immediately know that there's a kind of intelligence working there that you won't find in an actor who takes himself so seriously and who's so wrapped up in the Method that he can't see how ridiculous it is.

One of the characters in your play Curse of the Starving Class *says something like, "What's there to envy but an outlook?" One might envy your outlook.*

Well, I've seen people with better ones *[laughing]*, you know, people who never find fault with anybody, for whom everything's great, people who are positive all the time.

Not everyone, I gather, was totally positive about your first playwriting efforts in New York City.

Actually, there was only one guy who liked me *[laughing]*—Michael Smith of the *Village Voice*. Those first reviews were devastating. In fact, I was vulnerable then and was ready to pack it in and come back to California and get work as a hand on a ranch. But writing has been such a salvation for me for so long that it would be impossible for me to give it up now.

Too late to stop now.

Yeah, it's too late to stop now . . . Otis Redding. *There* was a great singer!

Has acting also been a salvation?

No, not at all. I don't have the same connection to it. With acting, I feel that I'm just struggling to get by. An actor is right on the edge, because all he has is the body. . . . Actually, I should say that acting and writing *are* related. I just don't feel the same sense of urgency about acting as I do about writing. I've never been able to write a play while I've been acting in a film. It's difficult to split your participation. You have to be very focused and fully occupied to write.

And then, of course, you've been directing your recent plays, too. Theoretically, you could actually be someone who directs himself acting in a play that you yourself have written.

Right. And I'm in the process of finishing a screenplay that I'm going to direct, but I'm not going to act in it.

Someone like Woody Allen does it all the time.

He can do it because in his roles he stands outside the character—he comments on the character rather than plays it . . . except in *Broadway Danny Rose*, where he does play a real character. And he's probably the best one around who can write, direct, and act. But I don't think I could direct myself acting, because, for me, the two things are diametrically opposed. I don't see how you can be inside and outside at the same time. Acting involves such a deep kind of penetration in, and directing demands an observation from the outside.

In Rolling Thunder Logbook, *you describe your first meeting with Dylan, commenting that the first thing he said to you was, "We don't have to make any connections," and you didn't know whether he was talking about you and him personally or about the movie you were supposed to be working on with him.*

Bob gets off the hook a lot with that approach. *[Laughing]* He's great, and I love working with him, but he would rather not commit than commit. *[Laughing]* I wish you could hear the tune he and I wrote together in the spring of 1985 ["Brownsville Girl"]. It's at least twenty minutes long—it's like a saga!—and it has to do with a guy standing on line and waiting to see an old Gregory Peck movie that he can't quite remember, only pieces of it, and then this whole memory thing happens, unfolding before his very eyes. He starts speaking internally to a woman he'd been hanging out with, recalling their meetings and reliving the whole journey they'd gone on—and then it returns to the guy, who's still standing on line in the rain. The film the song was about was a Gregory Peck western that Bob had once seen, but he couldn't remember the title. We decided that the title didn't matter, and we spent two days writing the lyrics—Bob had previously composed the melody line, which was already down on tape. He's already gone through different phases with the song. At one point, he talked about making a video out of it.

I told him that it should be an opera, that we should extend it—make it an hour and a half or so—and perform it like an opera. He's a lot of fun to work with, because he's so off the wall sometimes. We'd come up with a line, and I'd think that we were heading down one trail over here, and then suddenly he'd just throw in this other line, and we'd wind up following it off in some different direction. Sometimes it's frustrating to do that when you're trying to make a wholeness out of something, but it turned out okay.

You've actually done exactly that in many of your plays.

Yeah, but I'm trying to do it less than I used to. *[Laughing]*

Writing plays, playing music, acting, directing . . .

It's just been one step at a time. I don't deny that I've had some good luck. My dad had a lot of bad luck. I've had good luck. Luck is a part of it. But I don't know exactly how that works.

When critics say, "Well, Sam Shepard has now said everything he has to say in A Lie of the Mind—*where can he possibly go from here?" that is, in a way, sort of casting a little doubt spell, isn't it?*

Yeah, it's trying to do something to you, but you can't pay any attention to that, because you've got other things to do. Being surrounded by parasitic people who feed off of your work—well, I guess you've just got to accept it. And I suppose some parasites are okay, because they take things off of you. Once, in New Mexico, I observed these incredibly beautiful red-tailed hawks—with a wingspan of five feet—which start out gliding in these arroyos way down low. And these crows come and bother them—they're after fleas and peck at the hawks and drive them nuts, because they're looking for something else. And I watched a crow diving at and bothering this one hawk, which just flew higher and higher until it was so far up that the crow couldn't follow it anymore and had to come back down.

So the answer is to outfly them.

Yeah, outfly them. Avoid situations that are going to take pieces of you. And hide out.

SAM SHEPARD

NOVEMBER 5, 1943 – JULY 27, 2017

ELIZABETH TAYLOR
Passion

New York City, 1987

She has been called "the most beautiful woman in the world" and "the quint-essential movie star." Michael Jackson is supposed to possess a full-size mannequin of her in his home, which he dresses every day. But violet-eyed icon and legend that she has become, one often forgets that Elizabeth Taylor has appeared in almost sixty feature and television films since 1942, when, as a nine-year-old, she made her screen debut in *There's One Born Every Minute* and thereafter giving remarkable performances in movies such as *Giant, A Place in the Sun, Butterfield 8, Cat on a Hot Tin Roof, Reflections in a Golden Eye,* and *Who's Afraid of Virginia Woolf?* In the words of director Richard Brooks, with whom she worked on two films: "As an actress, she has a breadth and scope beyond what she has ever been credited with. Despite everything that's happened in her life, she has always survived. Time after time, they declared her buried in Hollywood, but she's always come back."

Born in London in 1932 to American parents, she moved with them to Los Angeles at the outset of World War II. Signing with MGM in 1943, this child beauty became a star at the age of twelve in *National Velvet* (1944) and has remained so to this day, through dramatic offscreen marriages, divorces, illnesses, and malicious gossip. Having recently lost forty-five pounds ("I'd avoided looking in the mirror for so long that I'd allowed myself to become really obese—and I didn't see it"), and having withdrawn from her addiction to Jack Daniels, Percodan, and Demerol at the Betty Ford Center in Rancho Mirage, Elizabeth Taylor was recently made a Knight of the French Legion of Honour and is, at fifty-five [1987], a beautiful and vital woman. She has been one of the first Hollywood stars to participate in HIV/AIDS activism, and in 1985 she cofounded the National AIDS Research Foundation, helping to raise more than $270 million for the cause. And she is one of the first celebrities to create her own collection of fragrances; when I met her in 1987 she was just beginning to launch what would become her best-selling perfume Passion.

The following conversation with Elizabeth Taylor took place in August 1987 at her suite in New York City's Hotel Plaza Athénée.

* * *

You were making films in Hollywood during the 1940s and 1950s. How has the movie business changed since then?

Well, there's no such thing as Hollywood, per se, it started breaking up when motion picture stars started constructing their own individual companies and working abroad. Hollywood was both an *idea* and the name for a creative idea. And it became very "in"—during the sixties and the seventies—to appreciate it artistically. But for a long time it was almost an *insult* to be considered a "Hollywood" actor. Even worse to be a *star*—God forbid, a *super*star. Stage actors would accuse people of selling out when they'd go to Hollywood.

Actually, I think the whole thing is a bunch of bullshit, and I always have. An actor is an actor whether it's in Hollywood, whether it's in Africa, whether it's on stage, television, or in film. Acting has to be generated from within—somewhere along the line it has to somehow end up being your creation, if you put anything of yourself into it. It has to go through a form of translation. And you take guidance and direction from the best people you are working with.

How does that happen for you?

I've never had an acting lesson in my life. But I've learned, I hope, from watching people like Spencer Tracy, Marlon Brando, Montgomery Clift, Jimmy Dean—all people who were finely tuned and educated in the art of acting. *They* were my education, and *directors* were my education. I found quite early on that I couldn't act as a puppet—there would be something pulling my strings too hard—and that I did my best work by being *guided*, not by being forced. And I suppose that really is just the *child* in me, wanting to be allowed to grow and develop at my instinctual sort of pace. But if you describe me as an actress, you'd have to say that I wasn't a distinctive actress as actresses go, because I'm certainly not a polished technician.

Many of your fans would disagree. But just as "Hollywood" was once used as a dismissive epithet, so today some "stage-actor" types often demean "television stars." I gather you wouldn't agree with that.

I've seen some splendid work on television. And I think it was your *"definitive"* stage actor, Larry Olivier, who said that he thought that one of the finest ways a person could learn was through the medium of television—especially the soaps, where the actors have to be so creative day in and day out. I mean, they can be handed twenty, thirty, forty pages every morning, and if someone's going through a season where he or she's the star, the actor doesn't get a letup, he has to keep churning it out and tapping his resources, exercising his memory. My son is currently doing a play and a soap at the same time, and it's like patting your head and rubbing your stomach at the same time. Now, when I first watched soaps, it was always a real giggle for me, and then I became enthralled. I thought this is *my* show—*General Hospital*, I mean, this is *karma*, this has *got* to be my first soap. *[Laughing]* So I watched *General Hospital* and really liked it so much and had such a fun time watching it that I one day was a surprise visitor on the show. And my God, I have such admiration for *that* form of art in *acting*. It's bloody hard work.

The actor Van Johnson once said that the old Hollywood studio was a kind of extended family.

It was like a big extended *factory*, I'm sorry to say. But if you like being smothered I guess it was a very productive family. I was nine when I made my first film in Hollywood, and I've always been very much my own person. I had my own mother and father when I was little. *They* were my family, not the bloody studio.

Was there a particular incident that stands out?

When I was fifteen and Louis B. Mayer started screaming at my mother and using swear words that I'd never heard before ("I took you and your fucking daughter out of the gutter"), I uttered *my* first swear word and told him that he didn't *dare* speak to my mother that way, and he and the studio could both go to hell, and that I was never going to go back to his office. And I left my mother there with her eyes shut, and I think she was sort of *praying*.

What happened after that?

I walked out of there in such a fury and in tears, and went to see my old friend and vice president Benny Thau, and he said, "You have to go back." And another vice president came and found me. Now *those* guys were my buddies, and they said, "Sweetheart, you have got to go back and apologize." And I said, "What for? *He* should apologize to my mother, I'm not going back in his office. I mean what I said and I don't care if you fire me now. It will mean that this is not my life. There's a lot out there for me that I'm interested in." I don't know where I found the independence. I totally winged it on my own and just took my career, with total knowledge and decision, and threw it out the window.

Louis B. Mayer was the deity of the studio and was one of the great icons of Hollywood history, and slightly mad, and he was frothing at the mouth in a temper, and I had no idea how he would take this from a pipsqueak. But I didn't care. I knew that he had done something very wrong. As it turns out they must have wanted or needed me. Otherwise they wouldn't have kept me. But that has occurred to me in hindsight. I was *used* from the day I was a child, and *utilized* by that studio. I was promoted for their pockets. I never felt that they were a haven, I always felt that they were a factory.

Did the studio try to change you in other ways?

My God, I had black hair—it was photographed blue-black it was so dark—and thick bushy eyebrows, and my mother and father had to stop them from dying my hair and plucking out my eyebrows. The studio even wanted to change my name to Virginia. They tried to get me to create a Joan Crawford mouth when I first began using lipstick at fifteen. They wanted, you know, Joan Crawford, the forties and everything. Every movie star, Lana Turner, all of them, painted over their lips, and I'm sure that some of them had perfectly fine, full lips—and thin eyebrows were the fad—and God forbid you do anything individual or go against the fad. But I did. I figured this looks absurd. And I agreed with my dad: God must have had some reason for giving me bushy eyebrows and black hair. I guess I must have been pretty sure of my sense of identity. It was *me*. I accepted it all my life and I can't explain it. Because I've always been very aware of the inner me that has nothing to do with the physical me.

But there is a connection between the two.

Eventually the inner you shapes the outer you, especially when you reach a certain age, and you have been given the same features as everybody else, God has arranged them in a certain way. But around forty the inner you actually chisels your features. You know how some people have a kind of downward pull, and some people have sort of an upward pull, and look stress free, while the others look as if they're just trying to carry the world on their shoulders. And you just want to say: shake your head, shake your body like a dog, and just get *rid* of all that. It doesn't need to bow you down. Life is to be embraced and enveloped. Surgeons and knives have nothing to do with it. It has to do with a connection with nature, God, your inner being—whatever you want to call it—it's being in contact with yourself and allowing yourself, allowing God, to mold you.

Were you always as free-spirited when you were a kid?

When I was a child in England they always used to say to my mother—and it used to bother me—that I was an "old soul." I had no idea what that meant, but apparently I used to frighten grown-ups, because I was totally direct. It was like my daughter as a baby, before she was a year old, would look at people, steadily, with those eyes of hers, and see people start to fidget, and drop things out of their pockets, and finally, unable to stand the heat, get out of the room. She was totally tapping into something that she was seeing that they didn't want touched.

It sounds almost feral.

As they say, "Don't look into a lion's eyes." I had that happen once when I was in a jeep in the bush of Africa, in Chobe—this was during my second marriage to Richard Burton. It was on an earth path at six in the morning. And I came upon this black-maned lion just in the middle of the forest, at this footpath crossroads. We were in this totally open jeep that belonged to the white hunter guard named Brian and myself. It was just him and me, no tour guide. No protection of any sort. And I said, "Go very slowly, just make as little sound as you can." And we got a little bit closer—so close, in fact, that I could see the hairs on this animal's body.

Now, I'm fascinated by cats. I used to have an Abyssinian cat—if you are a cat lover you'll know exactly what I mean. The tips have a little dark marking on them, and it gets lighter and lighter the closer it gets to the pelt. But the mane itself, around that lion's face—those huge amber eyes—was black. I'd never seen a painting or anything resembling this lion. I wanted to get really close. And the animal by this time was looking at me, and Brian, who would not look at him, said, "Elizabeth, stop staring into the cat's eyes." And I said, "Why?" and he said that that was the one thing that will make them pounce, it makes them very nervous. And I said, "I'm sorry, Brian, but I can't take my eyes away from this." And this cat and I are staring into each other's eyes. And there was no power in this world that could make me take my eyes *out* of that cat's eyes. I was *into* them. And I was *locked* into that cat. Finally the cat stood up—my eyes and his eyes still locked—and he kind of stretched. Brian's hands were starting to shake on the wheel. And the lion opened his mouth, and I saw these teeth, I could see like strings of saliva attaching the teeth as he yawned, and he let out a roar that didn't make me jump—because it's as if I knew what he was going to do—and I still kept staring at him and he sort of moved his eyes away from me, started very gently padding away from me, turned and looked at me again over his shoulder, and then just went into a very relaxed trot and disappeared into the bushes. . . . I can't tell you what a *trip* that was.

Do you have a special affection for animals?

I've always preferred animals to little girls or boys. I had my first horse— actually it was a Newfoundland pony—when I was three, and I loved riding, without anyone shackling me—riding bareback as fast as I could.

In Africa, I also had a troop of green monkeys in my living room. Every morning and every evening, for a period of two months, I would go to the lip of the forest, which was right near Richard's and my bungalow, and it was where the monkeys would go down and drink at the river. Now, I'm not foolhardy, and I don't even think that encounter with the lion was foolhardy, because I knew nothing was going to happen. I was very respectful of the monkeys. It took me about two or three weeks, but I would start making them unafraid of me with food. And I got them so they'd go up this two-story wall, and around the swimming pool, and into my living room, and just have them accept my presence and realize that I wasn't threatening. They were just gorgeous little, innocent creatures whom I sat and chatted with. There were about twenty of them in my small living room, with Richard in the bedroom—just the monkeys, who would reach out and touch my knee. So it wasn't just the MGM lion! And I became known amongst the local tribes as this strange Caucasian lady who spoke to animals. And so can my daughter, by the way. . . . But, of course, *you're* an animal and we're communicating. *[Laughing]*

You've obviously never liked to conform or be shackled.

As a child, I would go to concerts and listen to symphonies instead of the sort of "hot" music of the moment. I'd only seen one film before I was *in* one, and it was *Snow White and the Seven Dwarfs,* which I loved, and in fact I preferred to go to the ballet. And I hated school, so I was kind of an oddball. And as far back as my consciousness can remember—and unfortunately it's associated with pain but also with curiosity—I loved the color of electric heat and the heaters that were in the corridors and the kitchen—that sort of iridescent pink coral. And I was still a toddler, but I remember the fascination with that color and sticking my finger in it. I remember that *vividly.*

Didn't you get burned?

Of *course* I got burned. *[Laughing]*

When you made your first film you were ten years old . . .

Nine! Will you *stop* making me older than I'm supposed to be! *[Laughing]* Actually, when I was *just* nine, I was in a film before that that I've never even seen *[There's One Born Every Minute].* And that was with—oh, God, Hugh Herbert, Peggy Moran, and Carl "Alfalfa" Switzer, who was the little boy with the freckles who used to be in *Our Gang,* and they wanted me to play an American brat. But at that time I had a very English accent, and I remember putting on the accent they wanted because I guess I was good at accents even then. But the film was something I hated, and I told my parents I hated it. So they got me out of it. There was sort of a mutual agreement that if the producers didn't like me, and the family didn't like them, we could break it off. . . . Oh, God, that just reminded me! The casting director had said, "You've got to get rid of that child, because there's something about her that's sort of frightening. She's just too old. She's like an old soul. She's depressing." And I hear he got fired after *National Velvet.* But of course he had been totally right about that earlier film. Because I had been totally miscast, and that was not my future.

An unauthorized biography of you [Elizabeth Taylor: The Last Star] *by Kitty Kelley was published six years ago, and its thesis is, so to speak, that you were nurtured by the studio, that you didn't have a life of your own aside from it, and that you lived the parts that you played and played the parts that you lived.*

That's absolute bullshit! I had my own world, my parents were sensitive enough to me, and I had something going for myself that I was tapping into quite naturally and quite instinctively. And they *encouraged* my relationship with animals. In England, where I lived until I was eight years old—you'd have a certain formal time for mommy and daddy: but otherwise the nannies would structure your life. I didn't dig that kind of existence at all. My family, being American in this sort of formal society, were much more liberal with their time than most English parents. But as far as nannies were concerned, I did live the so-called upper-middle-class childhood. I rebelled against it, and found nature was the one place where I could do my own thing and where I could trip out, literally, as a kid.

You weren't lonely?

There were all these fantastic natural highs. Why would I be lonely?

You seem to rebel against any kind of authority figures—Louis. B. Mayer, your nanny . . .

That type, yeah. My nanny, for instance, was horrible! Her name was Frieda Edith Gill—it's so onomatopoeic: *Fr*ieda *E*dith Gill. I think she was probably very sweet, and I was rude in my rebellion. But I had my own identity and I probably was the biggest manipulator of all time. I got my own way so cunningly, because I can see that in my daughter, I can see it in myself. Yeah, I was probably the biggest manipulator ever born! I hadn't thought about this for ages, but I can see that little girl getting onto that horse, and going on that trip that she wanted to go on, and accomplishing it, though sometimes it would take hours to start the trip. My pony would run away and I'd have to wait for her to come back, or track her down. And sometimes I would be gone all day long. I knew that if it were into the evening I'd be up shit's creek without a paddle, so I'd, you know, get myself back one way or another. But it's strange, this is really turning into an interview about animals! *[Laughing]*

You're currently putting together a self-help book based on the tough times you went through. What was that period like for you?

Everything is just totally out of whack. It's just more than fatness and obesity, it's more than just not caring how I looked. It's in every line of my face. It's even in the texture of my hair. The main reason I was doing this book was that I hoped that I could reach somebody out there, even if it was just one human being. Weight loss, weight gain all have something to do with your*self.* It's deep loneliness, depression, lack of self-esteem that is the cause for overeating, drinking, taking pills, whatever—the necessary crutch. One makes up excuses. I used to think that drinking would help my shyness, but all it did was exaggerate all the negative qualities. The drinking and the pills just sort of dulled my natural enthusiasm. All you have to do is look at a picture of me from that time to know. Unfortunately, I don't have a good photographic record of myself from that period. I don't have anybody around me with cameras, because to me it's like war.

I imagine the paparazzi all around the world could put together a few volumes on you.

They're not photographers! They're not people! *[Laughing]*

What species are they?

These are cockroaches. . . . But actually they do take some very revealing photographs.

I gather you don't feel the same way about supposedly "revealing" unauthorized biographies of you—in particular, Kitty Kelley's book.

I don't read them, and I've never read Kitty Kelley's because I know there is nothing I can do about it. Why aggravate myself? I've been told that it's full of a bunch of lies. Fabrications. And real dirty, malicious stuff. But why go through the irritation when I know that legally in the sweet buggerall there is nothing I can do about it?

I saw her plugging her Frank Sinatra book on *The Phil Donahue Show.* And here I was, innocently watching television—I think I had a bad back or something, it was in the afternoon—and I heard her say something like, "Well, Elizabeth Taylor hasn't sued me so you know I was telling the truth." Well, back and all, whatever it was, I went through the ceiling of my house, I touched the roof of the sky. I called my lawyer. And he told me I had to read the book and sue her for every single untruth. That would mean not only spending money that I think is a waste of time, but it would mean bringing everything up, and it would mean the aggravation of reading it, knowing I can't do anything. So my hands are tied.

The press creates an idea, a star. You're theirs. They have created this monster. So what do you do? It becomes boring unless you tear it down. I've been on that yo-yo trip all my life. I've been rejected more times than you can imagine. But I've always been myself . . . except for the times when I almost lost myself.

What do you think allowed you to pull yourself away from the brink?

Something always made me save myself. Either the Betty Ford Center or going onstage to perform in the theater when many people didn't think I could do it. Or doing this, doing that, whatever. I mean I was pronounced dead, for God's sake, about twenty years ago. I was in the hospital on a respirator, and they were pulling this sort of rubbery, bloody substance out of my lungs, but the grunge created itself faster than the machine could work and pull this stuff out of my collapsed lungs. And I stopped breathing for five minutes. And I had a kind of near-death experience that you didn't talk about then because people would have thought you were crazy. It's amazing that I didn't have any permanent brain damage. (Don't you *dare* make any cracks!) I even had a chance to read my obits, and they were the best reviews I ever had. *[Laughing]* But unless you desire to live, you can be hit by that train. You can *induce* that train. I caught myself in that frame of mind, and because I love life, I caught myself doing that in time. And I jumped clear. Even when I was chemically *dead.* After five minutes I was able to jump clear.

Why couldn't Marilyn Monroe save herself?

I don't think Marilyn committed suicide. I don't think Marilyn was murdered. I think it was an accident. But she was playing with fire. I don't think she was as acutely aware of it as some of my other self-destructive friends.

I was thinking about some of the leading men you've played opposite in your films, such as James Dean, Montgomery Clift, Marlon Brando, Rock Hudson,

Richard Burton, Orson Welles, Henry Fonda, and Paul Newman. That's quite a group.

They don't make leading men like that anymore. And, you see, they were my teachers. Then, add the women in there and the directors and the cameramen and you have some hell of a school. Thank God, I hope I picked up something!

The movie Giant, *made in 1956, continually shows on television and finds a new and appreciative audience year after year. And in that film your two leading men are James Dean and Rock Hudson—the first representing the wild, outlaw type; the latter, the patriarchal, conformist type. And your character hovers and mediates between them. What were those two actors like to work with on that film?*

It's funny: I was very connected to both Rock and Jimmy, but they had no personal connection at all. I was very connected to them—but it was like on the left side and the right side. One on each side, I was in the middle, and it just would be like a matter of shifting my weight. I'd bounce from one to the other with total ease. And I'm glad it shows in the film, I hadn't even thought of it that way. It's been a long time since I've seen *Giant*. I don't look at old movies of myself. I don't even look at new ones of myself. But I loved Jimmy and I loved Rock. And I was the last person Jimmy was with before he drove to his death. . . . But that was a private, personal moment.

*In Paris not long ago, I happened to see two of your best films—*Reflections in a Golden Eye *and* A Place in the Sun—*the first of which also starred Marlon Brando, the second Montgomery Clift.*

For some reason the French think I'm a good actress, and I think that's really nice.

I've come across some excellent reviews of your work recently in this country as well.

Oh, that's bullshit! That's probably in due deference to my age or something like that. Come on! I don't keep clippings of any kind, but if I had them I would show you some reviews that I consider to be bitchy for the sake of being bitchy.

Well, I wanted to know what you thought of the notion, once expressed by a European director, that Marlon Brando and Montgomery Clift are the two antithetical sides of great American acting.

To me, they tap and come from the same source of energy. (Oh God. Marlon will kill me!) I think that they both have this acute animal sensitivity and they both have the vulnerability. God, you don't even have to *think* about it—you can *feel* it, especially when you're working with them. I always felt it in their work.

I think Monty was at a more refined state early on. But Marlon developed it, and wasn't as self-destructive. Marlon is still around, Marlon is still a great actor. You know, we can't speculate what would have happened to Monty's career. He's safe now. But then he wasn't safe. He was one of the best actors that the acting world has ever known. And his timing— I think he would be recognized more for that. His death came at an untimely, unheroic, unpoetic moment in his life. So instead of being revered as one of the most innovative actors the acting world has ever known, he's kind of shuffled aside. But, good God, all you have to do is look at some of his old films. Just look at him. Open a little door of your consciousness and you can be on his wavelength so easily. He just takes you along. That's a great art. And so simple. Actually the Big Daddy of them all, for me, was Spencer Tracy, with his simplicity and honesty and directness. Monty and Marlon took it from the Method—both of them were Method actors, as was James Dean—which was like a kind of religion with them, although I don't understand it because I've never had an acting lesson. But I think they were all spawned by Spence, who did it instinctively and naturally. He was a highly polished actor, and he had that kind of quietness that is part of the acting of a Method actor. They call it being introspective, although I call it a kind of quietness.

But today a "name" no longer carries a film. People used to go to the cinema to see a "John Wayne film." And you don't have that thing happening now except in the rock world, which has taken the event out of movies. The "event" is where the "star" is, and that's in concerts. I think that this has to do with the pace of things and with "pushing buttons" instead of getting dressed, getting behind the wheel, and making an event of going to the cinema—which is what Mike Todd did thirty years ago with *Around the World in 80 Days*. So again, the superstars are in concerts. And I think that's why very few of them have made successful transformation to film. I happen to love David Bowie and think he's a brilliant actor, onstage, and I love his movies. But I don't think he has been given artistic control in his films. But I think he's got great, good taste. . . . I love going to rock concerts, by the way, I love to lose myself in that vast wave of rhythm and body heat and get on the same vibe. And kids will say, "Hi, Liz." And I'll say hi, back. I get an outrageous kick out of the concerts.

You're not thinking of forming a band, are you?

Don't worry, I promise. I tried it, and I've listened to my singing voice, and I've promised myself that I'm really too generous a human being to do that to the populace! *[Laughing]* Nobody can make it sound like me, believe me.

You're not singing but you've just brought out a new perfume and eau de toilette under the name of Elizabeth Taylor's Passion.

And I know exactly why it's called Passion if you want to know, since they were pushing other names. I remember rambling on in some interview—don't ask me what about—and the interviewer had asked me what quality it was in me that made me the survivor that I was. And I had to think about it, since I'd never thought about it before. It's just always been there and I've taken it for granted, I guess. But I think it's my passion. My passion for life, for people, for caring . . . my passion for everything, which makes me sound a bit scatty at times because I get so easily diverted by my own thoughts. Life is just such an adventure to me that I'll allow myself to be taken along with passion by it all. It started when I was born, and I still have that childlike ability to allow myself to go off on these mental adventures, because I'm not afraid—as with the stories of the animals I told you about before. And that's why I fought for the name Passion. I couldn't allow them to call it Divine Extravagance, and I couldn't allow it to be called Fascination, which is a lovely name—to me it brings to mind a gorgeous Audrey Hepburn and violin music. It's a beautiful name, but it's not me. I'm not *fascinated* by things, I *dive* into them. One by fire. Like what I told you about when I was a toddler and crawling, I was so fascinated by the fire that I reached out and touched it. That's the difference between fascination and passion to me.

The word "compassion" means "with passion," though some people think the two words suggest opposite thoughts and feelings.

It's integral to the sense of passion, though I hadn't thought about it. You can't have passion of any kind unless you have compassion. That's one of the reasons why I get so furious about AIDS. How dare people consider themselves fully rounded human beings without compassion? And if they don't have passion, it means they are incapable of love. And if you look at the root of all the trouble and the legal bullshit that is going on, you can observe that the *lawmakers* are incapable of love. Of any kind. Or compassion of any kind. . . . But don't get me going on that—your tape recorder will start smoking!

ELIZABETH TAYLOR

FEBRUARY 27, 1932 – MARCH 23, 2011

STUDS TERKEL
Nothing but Listen

Although this conversation took place in 2001, a few years later than the other interviews here, I wanted to include it in this collection because it features one of the great listeners of our time.

New York City, 2001

"Now I will do nothing but listen," wrote Walt Whitman in "Song of Myself": "I hear the sound I love, the sound of the human voice." Today, no one has listened and captured this voice better than Studs Terkel, the greatest oral historian of modern times. In his twelve books of oral histories—including *Division Street: America, "The Good War," Race,* and, particularly, *Working*—Terkel reveals the inner and outer lives, attitudes, feelings, hopes, and regrets of stockbrokers, process clerks, piano tuners, waitresses, gas-meter readers, bar pianists, actors, prostitutes, and hundreds of other "ordinary" people (as he puts it) to create what have been called "documentary masterpieces." John Kenneth Galbraith has hailed him "a national treasure."

Now eighty-nine [2001], this forever-youthful man was raised in Chicago ("It's my kind of town"), where his mother ("a tough little sparrow") ran the Wells Grand Hotel near Cook County Hospital. The Wells was frequented by nurses, interns, labor organizers, and company men, and Terkel had dreams of becoming a concierge. In his early twenties he completed three "bleak" years at the University of Chicago Law School ("I was dreaming of Clarence Darrow and woke up to find Julius Hoffman and Antonin Scalia") and, after graduating, changed course and began playing a gangster in the radio serials of the thirties ("I was always getting killed") and working as a sportswriter. Years later he would play one in John Sayles's Chicago Black Sox film *Eight Men Out*.

In the early 1950s, Terkel played himself in a mostly improvised live-television program on NBC called *Studs' Place*. It was the beginning of the Korean and Cold Wars and *Red Channels,* a publication that exposed show-business figures "suspected" of being Communists or fellow travelers. ("If you were listed in that," he says, "you'd be dead.") Somehow, Terkel never made it into those pages. "People I love were in it—Arthur Miller, Zero Mostel, Lillian Hellman—but where was *me*? I felt like the blue-haired dowager who didn't make the social register!"

Nevertheless, Terkel finally got his wish: because he had signed anti–Jim Crow and anti-poll-tax petitions and attended "subversive" meetings in the 1930s and 1940s, he was soon blacklisted. His sponsor fired him, NBC terminated *Studs' Place,* and Terkel was out of a job.

Today, in hindsight and in a bittersweet way, he credits his subsequent good fortune to having been canned by NBC. As he says, "History happened, banality happened, goofiness happened, happenstance happened, life happened." So Terkel found himself working as a disk jockey for forty-five years, five days a week, at Chicago's WFMT, hosting a program that featured short stories, radio documentaries, interviews, and a catholic range of music—Woody Guthrie, opera arias, the blues, jazz, and, especially, the gospel music of Mahalia Jackson.

"I often played her songs on my radio show," he says. "And I got to know her well. So when she got an offer from CBS to do a live-radio broadcast, she said she'd do it only if I were the host. The show was to be broadcast from the CBS theater in Chicago's Wrigley Building before a live audience of about four hundred people. And during a dress rehearsal, a guy from CBS in New York came up to me and said, 'Mr. Terkel, this is just pro forma for you to sign.' I looked it over, and it was a loyalty oath ('Are you now or have you ever been,' et cetera). And I said that I wouldn't sign it. He said, 'But you have to.'

"Mahalia happened to be passing by, and she knew about my background and had once said to me 'Studs, you and your big mouth, you should have been a preacher.' So she said, 'Is that what I think it is, baby?'—meaning, 'Are you in trouble again?' I said, 'Uh-huh.' She said, 'Are you going to sign it?' I said, 'No.' 'But you *have* to sign it,' the CBS guy said. And Mahalia told him, 'He doesn't have to do anything that he doesn't want to do. You tell Mr. Big back in New York that if they fire Studs Terkel they'll have to find another Mahalia Jackson.'

"And you know what happened? Nothing! The guy disappeared. And what's the moral of this? That in her little finger, she had more Americanism than all the networks and advertisers put together."

Terkel admits to being a bit of a Luddite. He doesn't drive a car, has, of course, no driver's license ("I do have a library card"), and, of all the modern conveniences, approves only of the refrigerator ("How else could you freeze your martini glass?") and the washing machine ("I hate to see a woman slapping clothes against a rock"). He has just learned how to use an electric typewriter.

Meeting Studs Terkel today—which I did recently over a three-day period in New York—one encounters an ebullient, open-hearted, white-haired man wearing his trademarks: red socks, red vest, red-checked shirt, red T-shirt. He follows a regimen of two cigars and two Bombay gin martinis a day ("not until five o'clock"). Some people have called him a "garrulous old gabber." In fact, he is a wonderfully engaging raconteur, master of the sermon and the sound bite, whose asides, descriptions, and judgments of people can be devastatingly funny. But, most of all, Terkel is a humane, courageous, compassionate man: "What gives me hope is the people I meet," he says. "The great thing is when somebody stops me on Michigan Avenue and says hello. I say, 'It's me, Studs'—they know me. And they say, 'Listen, I'm never again gonna talk to a waitress the way I did'; or, 'Now I know what the interstate truck driver's work is like.' Stuff like that I find terrific. That's big-time to me."

* * *

The Spanish poet Antonio Machado once wrote, "To have a dialogue / First: ask a question / Then: listen."

That's it. Interviewing people, you're listening. And what do I find out? I think of Big Bill Broonzy, who I knew well and who I consider to be one of the very great country-blues singers. He was a carpenter and a welder. One day he taught a young guy how to weld and then he was fired. And what did he do? He chuckled. Now why did he chuckle at that moment? It's because it's a safety valve. It's like a blues lyric—laugh just to keep from crying. Bill's laughter—that's the thing you listen to when you talk to people: how they react. Why does somebody pause a long time, and come back to it later? I listen.

What do I compare myself to? A gold prospector. I hear about a person and put in my stake. Digging and digging and digging. And we start the interview. Then I dig up all this ore—a ton of ore—until I've got these thirty pages, single-spaced.

Well, you can't use all that. Now you've got to do the sifting. I sift, I've got a handful of gold dust in my hands. And I edit at the key moment. Then I'm a brain surgeon. You've got to do it elegantly, so you save what is the truth. You highlight it like a play. The words are the words of a person, though you can alter their sequence. And now I've got my gold dust. And then you put the interviews together to make a book, and then comes the sad part—what you've cut out. And so now you become the director of a play. You're three things: gold prospector, brain surgeon, director of a play.

Woody Guthrie had a sign on his guitar that read, "This machine kills fascists." Don't you think that's a bit like you are with your tape recorder?

Guerrilla journalist is what I am. I know my terrain—the people I meet—and I work on hunches. Like the colonial guys against the British redcoats. Like the Vietnamese were against us—*we* were the redcoats over there. One other American who was enamored with the tape recorder was Richard Nixon. I call us neo-Cartesians—I tape, therefore I am.

Walt Whitman and many nineteenth-century utopians proposed the idea of a community of love. What happened?

Regarding community: I always love to quote Einstein, because no one dares to contradict me. Einstein said—and I'm paraphrasing him—that community is what it's all about. People say that you lose your individuality, but, on the contrary, it strengthens it. Because part of you goes elsewhere, you see. A union is about community. That's the key. So if you have free markets, where's the community? We have the commercials aimed at the ghetto kids. You go to school and you learn to compete. The word is *compete,* you see? Is that why you go to school? I thought you go to school to enrich yourself, thus you enrich the community.

Let me tell you a story: I can't drive, so I take a bus to work each day. And at the bus stop one morning there was this very handsome couple who ignored me, and my ego was hurt, of course. The guy was right out of *Gentleman's Quarterly*—he has on a three-piece Brooks Brothers suit, Gucci shoes, and the *Wall Street Journal* under his arm. And she's a stunner, right out of *Harper's Bazaar,* and she had a copy of *Vanity Fair* under her arm. So the bus is late in coming, and I wanted to make friends, so I said, "Labor Day is coming up." It was the wrong thing to say. He looked at me as Noel Coward would have. Now I'm really hurt, so I said, "On Labor Day we used to march down Michigan Avenue, banners flying—

UAW, CIO. We'd sing 'Which Side Are You On?' and 'We Shall Not Be Moved' . . ." and the man turns to me and in a voice of ice says, "We despise unions." So now I'm the Ancient Mariner and fix him with my glittering eye, and I say to him, "How many hours do you work?" He says, "Eight." I say, "How come you don't work eighteen or twenty hours a day?" I take a step toward him, see. "You know why? Because four men got hanged back in 1886 at Chicago's Haymarket Square fighting for the eight-hour day for *you*." She dropped her *Vanity Fair,* and, very courtly, I picked it up and gave it back to her. "And back in the thirties," I added, "men and women got their heads busted for you."

It was the New Deal and the alphabet agencies like the WPA [Work Projects Administration] that saved the asses of the daddies and grand-daddies of the very ones who most condemn big government today. Ronnie Reagan's father worked for the WPA in Dixon, Illinois. So we have a case here of what I call a national Alzheimer's disease. The kids are deprived of their own history. We use euphemisms—like "downsizing," which is mass firing. I pick up the business section, which is a great thing to read if you are a nut. They say things are getting better. Motorola is laying off ten thousand. IBM lays off twenty thousand.

I'm an emotional yo-yo. I wake up in the morning and think, "We're not going to make it." Then I come across the individuals in my books, capable of extraordinary things. So I'm both. Despair, hope; despair, hope. There are these kids who get together with those labor guys in Seattle. And now Seattle is known for more than just Starbucks.

Two thousand and one years ago, there was a demonstration at the foot of Calvary. During the time of the Roman Empire, the number-one superpower in the world, there was a subversive sect known as Christians—twelve "crazies" who never carried a gun in their lives and who had a credo, "Love thy neighbor," or, if they were Americans, "De-stabilize them." And the people were scared of them because they were condemned by the Un-Roman Activities Commission. And there was the judge washing his hands. And the wife of Pontius Pilate, a good person, asked, "Why are you persecuting this good man?" And he said, "Will you stop nagging me, for Christ's sake?"

So I end my sermon by saying that this has been going on, and it will continue to go on and on and on. Why? Because some of us are crazy enough to have a dream of a world in which it would be easier for people to behave decently. And that's what it's all about.

We all know that everything is homogeneous. Long ago, cities were known for landmarks. When you took a train you knew you were in Pittsburgh, Chicago, or Cleveland. Today, you get off the plane, what do you see? Holiday Inn. Red Lobster. Pizza Hut. McDonald's.

This is a true story: When you're on a book tour, you get a little hazy after a while. And so I'm at a motel somewhere and say to the operator, "Could you please wake me up at six o'clock because I've got to get the eight o'clock plane to Cleveland." A long pause: "Sir, you *are* in Cleveland." *[Laughing]*

The character of the Fool—the king's jester—is sometimes shown in tarot cards wearing a crown. Like a mirror, he reminds the king of his follies and helps guard him against the sin of pride.

I *love* the Fool! I play the Fool a lot. If I could be known as the Fool, I'd settle for that. The Fool who speaks truth to power is the only one who can.

The yippies played the role of Fools.

Of course. The oldest and the strongest of the group was Dave Dellinger, a conscientious objector during World War II. He was the group's Gibraltar. Politically, Tom Hayden was a pretty hip guy. But the real clown, the most outrageous and wittiest of all of them, was Abbie Hoffman. He knew exactly what buttons to push that would drive Richard the Lionhearted—Mayor Richard Daley the First—crazy. Rumors spread that they were going to add LSD into Lake Michigan and thus get the Chicagoans all high and happy *[laughing]*, and people believed that. So, naturally, I got a tremendous kick out of some of the things they did—like throwing dollar bills from the balcony of the New York Stock Exchange or nominating a pig for president during the 1968 Democratic Convention. They were really showing how goofy we really are, and the way they did it was by playing the Fool.

But the yippies haven't completely lost. They're alive in Seattle, in Quebec, and now, at Harvard, where students engaged in a three-week sit-in to force the university to raise the wages of the janitors and custodians. And in Europe this year, students in almost every country celebrated May Day, protesting one thing or another. So I'm a Pollyanna here, but I think there has always been a "prophetic minority." And so Abbie is still alive, if I can be romantic about it.

What about Hunter S. Thompson?

He's nutty as a fruitcake. But I love him. He had seen me once on TV and was shocked that I could get away with what I was saying. So I got a call from him at two in the morning. He'd had a few drinks of Wild Turkey, and he said, "Goddamn it, Studs. Now listen: You're too valuable. Do you have your doors barred? Have you got your windows closed? They're out to kill you!" Yes, he's the perfect Fool.

In all your years of interviewing, who impressed you the most?

That's a tough one; it's like deciding which of my children I prefer. I could name Bertrand Russell, whom I visited in his cottage in northern Wales during the Cuban missile crisis. But that wasn't it. There was Chief Albert Luthuli, who preceded Nelson Mandela in the African National Congress. And that was very exciting. But the most indelible one was C. P. Ellis, Exalted Cyclops of the Durham, North Carolina, branch of the Ku Klux Klan. I had read somewhere that he and an African American woman named Ann Atwater were on the road together advocating unions for janitors. So I said to myself, "I've got to see this guy." He was reluctant at first, but finally he agreed. And he started telling me his story—a story of a wretched, miserable life—a story about his father, who got plastered on weekends and was a Klan member. C. P. supported himself pumping gas and running a bread route, and raised four children, one blind and retarded. His father died at the age of forty-eight.

C. P. Ellis took his Klan vows—poor white trash in a white robe—and now felt that he was *somebody*, like Jesse Jackson with Operation PUSH, who'd tell his followers, "You *are* somebody!" But Jesse was doing it to raise self-esteem. C. P. Ellis was doing it at the expense of somebody else. "The natural person for me to hate," Ellis says, "was the black person." By then the civil rights movement was under way, and there was one woman in town he hated, and she hated him, and that was Ann Atwater, who was leading a boycott against a Durham department store. She was leading the picket line and he was breaking it up with some young thugs, and it was a bloody event.

So this was the situation: Jimmy Carter was the president, and two million or three million dollars were being sent to the segregated Durham public schools, but for some reason, the school committee was integrated. So a black member said, "Let's invite the parents of all the kids of all the public schools"—so they invited the Klan as well as the NAACP, a crazy idea! And Ellis said, "I'm going." One of his friends said, "You're sellin' out the white race. That woman Ann Atwater will be there." But Ellis said, "I don't want the kids to fight forever."

Anyway, at the school meeting, someone said that they should form a committee. And one person said, "I nominate Ann Atwater as chairman." And then a black guy said, "I nominate C. P. Ellis as co-chairman because I think he's an honest man." Ellis and Atwater hated each other, but she had a young daughter and he had a son, so they agreed to work together. Soon, he was calling her by her first name. And then one day Ann showed up crying. "What are you crying about?" Ellis asked her. "It's my little girl. The kids at her school said that they heard her mother was going around with Klansmen, and they mocked her and hit her and she was crying." "That also happened to my boy," Ellis said. "They said that his father was going out with a black agitator, and they hit him with sticks and stones." The next thing you know, they're in the same boat and they're clinging to one another.

At that time Ellis had a job as a janitor at Duke University. And he started organizing a union. And guess what? Ann found out that he could sign up more people than anybody. He was even voted the union leader by a vote of four to one. He'd had only a fifth-grade education, but he and his union outnegotiated the lawyers who had attended Harvard and Yale and who had been sent down to break the union. So Ellis had found his vocation, his calling—a union organizer. And, as he said, "Now, I am somebody."

So there's your story. I find it biblical in its power. It's about sin, revelation, redemption, transcendence.

Your new book Will the Circle Be Unbroken? *reveals people's attitudes about death. How did you choose this subject?*

It was because of a conversation I had with Gore Vidal, whom I had interviewed a few years ago. We were sitting at the Ambassador East Hotel's bar. And he said to me, "Have you thought of doing a book about death?" And I said, "I'm accustomed to writing about life's uncertainties." What's it like to have been involved in the "Good War"—a mother's boy in the landing craft about to land in Normandy? What is it like to be a schoolteacher or a housewife or a storekeeper or a prostitute? What is it like to be black? Or to grow old? The subject of death, which is about a certainty, what's *that* like? How the hell do you know what it's like? "It's too much for me," I thought. "This should be left for a metaphysician." So I abandoned that idea.

Years passed, and after all the books, I wondered, "What's the next subject?" And I thought of Vidal, and although I started the book before my wife died last year—I'm not going to deny that her death played a role in this book—it just fell into place organically.

My first book of the new millennium is about death. But it's also about life. We know that life is finite, therefore all the more precious, so we should talk about it when it's fresh and alive. My book is about living here now. Heaven is maybe up there, but it can be down here as well.

Do you consider yourself an atheist?

I think of myself as an agnostic, but an agnostic is really a cowardly atheist. At the same time I envy those who have faith. Well, I have a faith, but they have a religious faith. The recurring phrase used by people in my book is "I am not religious, I am spiritual." And they don't mean just Buddhism or pantheism, they mean: "I want to believe, but not in something connected to an institution"—Catholic, Protestant, Jewish, Muslim, whatever it might be.

Do you believe in rebirth?

That comes up a lot in my book. But in no way did I laugh or mock or challenge people's experiences. People talk about reincarnation: What's a caterpillar? What about a butterfly? The whole thing about the book is to leave it open and give these people dignity. One undertaker talked about burying a homeless man in a tuxedo, saying, "In my funeral home we all go out first-class." I like that. So what is reborn? Well, we know we become compost or whatever. I believe in cremation, and I want my ashes and my wife's ashes strewn about in Bughouse Square in Chicago. Bughouse Square is like Hyde Park in London or Union Square the way it was years ago in New York City. On summer nights when I was young, I used to go up there and hear guys on their soapboxes—one guy was a Communist, one was a sky pilot, one sold sex-hygiene books. It was known for the hecklers, of course. I remember someone pointing his bony finger and saying, "If brains were bedbug juice, you couldn't drown a nit."

The Roman philosopher Seneca wrote: "Rehearse death. To say this is to tell a person to rehearse his freedom. A person who has learned how to die has unlearned how to be a slave."

That's not bad. In fact, that's pretty good. Do I fear death? My wife of sixty years is gone, along with all of my old friends. I have young friends, and they're wonderful. They're great, but they don't know the old songs. Every day when I wake up, I open up the paper to read the obits. It's like the old doggerel that goes: "I wake up each morning and gather my wits. / I pick up the paper and read the obits. / If my name is not in it / I know I'm not dead. / So I eat a good breakfast and go back to bed."

Where are my friends? There are one or two around, but they're ailing. Where are the Chicago columnist Mike Royko, the novelist Nelson Algren, the speechwriter Lou Frank? They're all gone. But I wanted to hang around because, as my late friend Jimmy Cameron put it, "Hope subsides, but curiosity remains." That's what I'd like my epitaph to read: "Curiosity did not kill this cat."

STUDS TERKEL

MAY 16, 1912 – OCTOBER 31, 2008

MARIE-LOUISE VON FRANZ
Forever Jung

Küsnacht, Switzerland, 1984

For many years, the intellectual reputation and discoveries of the psychologist Carl G. Jung lay hidden in the shadow cast by his former colleague, collaborator, and coexplorer of the unconscious, Sigmund Freud. (One is easily reminded of James Joyce's punning line about being "yung and easily freudened.") Some people—many of whom had obviously read few of his close to fifty major works—imagined Jung to be some kind of dotty Swiss doctor who dabbled in and promulgated occult and mystical ideals and who spent his time absorbed in theorizing about ESP and flying saucers.

In fact, Jung was the first person to introduce and develop the concepts and notions of "individualization" (what psychologists after him were to call "self-realization" and "self-actualization"); the "complex" (an actively charged group of ideas or images); the "collective unconscious" (the myth-creating aspect of the mind); the "archetypes" (the collective universal images and motifs of myths and dreams); the "extrovert/introvert" and "anima/animus" (the latter referring to the unconscious female and male components of men's and women's personalities); the four psychological "types" (thinking, feeling, intuition, sensation); the "active imagination" (the writing or painting of one's unconscious fantasies and one's responses to them); "synchronicity" ("A connecting principle / Linked to the invisible / Almost imperceptible / Something inexpressible," to quote the lines of the Police's song "Synchronicity I"); and the "Self" (the archetypal, ideal center of one's being, about which Jung beautifully wrote: "Somewhere there was once a Flower, a Stone, a Crystal, a Queen, a King, a Palace, a Lover, and his Beloved, and this was long ago on an Island somewhere in the ocean five thousand years ago. . . . Such is Love, the Mystic Flower of the Soul. This is the Center, the Self").

With the proper understanding and help of these concepts, Jung believed one could set out upon an interior journey, returning and bringing back to the light of consciousness the projections and shadow components of one's unconscious life in order to create a harmony between one's inner and outer realities. Taking this journey, Jung thought, was not merely some indulgent holiday outing but a vital necessity, lest our unexamined, darker life energies lead us inescapably to a self-willed and self-destructive worldwide catastrophe. But Jung also saw that in the human psyche was a divine inner nucleus, the eternal essence of God, which could not die. And over the door of his home in Switzerland, he inscribed the ancient oracular saying VOCATUS ATQUE NON VOCATUS DEUS ADERIT (Called or not, the god will be there).

A recent and fascinating two-hour film titled *Matter of Heart* (made by Mark and Michael Whitney and George and Suzanne Wagner, 1983) presents interviews with twenty-one of Jung's former students, colleagues, patients, and friends—all of them in their seventies and eighties. And of these many extraordinary people, probably the most remarkable is the Swiss analyst, lecturer, and writer Marie-Louise von Franz, who was, at different periods, Jung's patient and close collaborator.

When an ancient Chinese Buddhist monk once asked his teacher whether there was any difference between the message of the Patriarchs and that of the Buddha, the teacher replied, "When you cup water in your hands, it reflects the moon; when you gather flowers, your robe absorbs the fragrance." And it is in this sense that one might well say that Marie-Louise von Franz is probably Carl Jung's most important living disciple, her work fully embodying the essence of his teachings.

But in her own right, she is an original, continually surprising, and provocative thinker, as manifested in her many astonishingly perceptive books about such subjects as fairy tales ("They are the wisdom of cosmic matter out of which we are made"); creation myths ("The story of the origin of the world and the origin of the awareness of the world are absolutely coinciding factors"); the *puer aeternus* (the "eternal child" archetype, as seen in her brilliant, pathbreaking analysis of Saint-Exupéry's classic story *The Little Prince*); alchemy (her major elaboration of Jung's notion of this subject as both a "chemical" and a "psychological" process); time (an investigation of the various and contradictory ways it has been conceived—as flux, as eternal return, and as a universal pattern of synchronous events); and projection ("If we could see through all our projections down to the last traces, our personality would be extended to cosmic dimensions").

Marie-Louise von Franz resides, practices, and writes in a book-filled house on a hilly street overlooking Lake Zurich in the town of Küsnacht, Switzerland, where Jung also lived. She is a soft-spoken and strong-minded person whose presence, like her work, is simultaneously challenging and healing.

The following conversation took place in the study of her home in early 1984.

* * *

You once mentioned that the first time you met Jung, he told you about one of his patients who felt that she had actually been on the moon.

I met Jung when I was eighteen, and at that time he told me about a vision that one of his patients had had of being on the moon, and then the man on the moon grabbed her with his black wings and didn't let her go. She was possessed by this thin black figure, you see. And Jung talked as if this weren't just a vision but actually as if she really *had* been on the moon. So, having a rational nature, I got irritated and said, "But she wasn't on the real moon. That was just a vision," and Jung looked at me seriously and replied, "She *was* on the moon." And I said, "Wait a minute. It can't be. She wasn't on that satellite of planet earth, she wasn't up there." I pointed to the sky and he just looked at me again, penetratingly, and repeated, "She was on the moon." Then I got angry and thought, "Either this man's crazy or I'm stupid." And then I slowly began to realize that Jung meant that what happens psychologically is the *real* reality—I started to comprehend his concept of the reality of the psyche. And that was a big revelation.

Does this have something to do with the comment you once made that "There are indications that physical energy and psychic energy may be but two aspects of one and the same underlying reality"?

Yes, and that's really an idea that Jung developed toward the end of his life, and one that I have only worked out a bit more. It's possible, for instance, that what the physicists call "energy" may in fact be the less intense frequencies of something that, in higher frequencies and at higher degrees of intensity, manifests itself as psyche. So that in the future, science may well begin to speak of only one energy that has different modes of manifestation. The brain probably transforms energies in such a way that we experience everything in a three-dimensional space. But we know from physics, too, that there are many more dimensions.

Not long ago, a medical doctor published a paper about a woman, a simple woman who woke up one morning in her hospital bed and told the nurse that she had had the following dream. She saw a candle on the windowsill that was burning down, and it began to flicker and she got terrible anxiety and felt the great darkness coming. Then there was a moment of blackout, and again she saw a light; this time, however, the candle was outside the window, the wick burning quietly. She didn't comment on it, but four hours later she died. . . . The reality, you see, was that the light went out, but in another medium, it burned on.

In one of the Gnostic Gospels, Jesus says: "If you bring forth what is within you, what you bring forth will save you. If you do not bring forth what is within you, what you do not bring forth will destroy you."

That's just it. Jung once said that you can cure a psychotic patient if you can make him creative. In other words, if what is destroying him from within can be brought forth in writing or painting or some other form, then he can be cured. What we try to do is to help people bring forth the Self. That means their true latent personality, or, in Gnostic terms, the God image in man. And if one creatively works that out by drawing on one's unconscious and following one's own path, then one is saved; and that very same thing undermines and destroys us if we don't do it. So that saying of Jesus is completely to the point.

I wanted to contrast this with a comment made by Janet Malcolm, who, writing about Freudian psychoanalysis, states: "The unexamined life may not be worth living, but the examined life is impossible to live for more than a few moments at a time. To fully accept the idea of unconscious motivation is to cease to be human. . . . To 'make the unconscious conscious' . . . is to pour water into a sieve. The moisture that remains on the surface of the mesh is the benefit of analysis."

That's because psychoanalytical theory is such a narrow sieve that it can't catch much of the unconscious. If you have preconceived ideas about childhood traumas and so on and don't allow for miracles, then you're going to bring up very little. Jung approached the unconscious much more openly, realizing that it's the unknown psyche, as big as the cosmos, and that we should really look at what's there. And at the end of his life he was still certain that there was more and more to discover.

In your own work, I've noticed that you tend to observe psychic events and phenomena with a very wide and open perspective. By that I mean that when you examine conflicts, you don't brush over or overlook one aspect in favor of another. In your book Puer Aeternus, *for instance, you suggest that the child archetype—the image of the eternal adolescent—represents charm, spontaneity, creativity, and risk-taking; but at the same time you remark that it can also reflect a destructive form of infantilism and one's entrapment in a negative mother complex. As you write: "In analysis, one tries to disentangle and definitely destroy what is really childish and [at the same time attempt to save] creativity and the future life. But practically, this is something which is immensely subtle and difficult to accomplish." How, in fact, do you go about this?*

It's very difficult to talk and make a theory about; you just have to work at it with your feeling function. Let's say, for instance, that a *puer* case comes into your office and tells you that he has a new obsession—windsurfing, say. At first you might think, "Oh Lord, another of those childish, risky sports where he'll break his neck!" But then from the tone in his voice you might suddenly have another feeling, which would tell you, "No, there's something to it. There's life and liveliness in it. It's meaningful to him." Then you get into the same conflict that he's in—now *you* are in a conflict. So you say nothing. You listen to the dreams, and then through dream interpretation—the decisive factor is the last sentence of the dream—you deduce whether it's rather more childish or rather more constructive, and then you go with that . . . all the while holding back your own feelings that are battling within you. And in that way you allow for many more unexpected things to happen. So the word "should" should be excluded from psychology. Jung said when you use the word "should" it means you're helpless.

You've said that when a person is in a painful, unresolvable situation, he or she will often have to remain in that situation without recourse to "shoulds" or escapes or false solutions.

Yes, in order to let things happen whereby the unconscious has a say. When you're in such a situation, that's the moment that your ego must abdicate and admit, "I don't know what to do." And the analyst must also be honest enough to say, "I don't know either. But now let's look at what the unconscious psyche suggests." And then you generally find that it teaches us unexpected ways of getting out of a conflict—not directly, but in a tortuous manner. The unconscious is like a snake. Somebody comes in and tells you about a terrible conflict. And then he or she dreams about something *completely* different, as if the conflict were completely unimportant. So I just go along with that and say, "Well, let's not discuss your problem. Let's discover what the unconscious proposes. It says that you should do more painting on a Saturday." "No, I have to decide whether to get a divorce or not," the patient will exclaim. And I'll say, "No, let's postpone that decision. The unconscious suggests you should do a painting." You see, it's a very good strategy, it wants you to loosen up the ego and get it to be more open, and then it will clarify the issue.

You once wrote about a patient who came to see you, suffering from sexual impotence, but you treated him by analyzing his creative block instead.

I used that case to illustrate what I mean by the tortuous ways of the unconscious. That patient came with his impotence and complained that he had already tried all sorts of more direct methods—hormone injections and whatnot—and that nothing had helped. And then I said, "Let's see what your dreams say," and his dreams only talked about how his paintings weren't right and about how he should paint differently. So he said, "I've come to you for my impotence, not for that. Don't interfere with my paintings!" And I replied, "Well I'm very sorry, but the snake makes a detour; your dreams point to something else." So I finally got him to paint differently, which released his whole emotional life; and with that, sex functioned again.

In a way, I'm reminded of that Eskimo dance drama in which one "good" and one "bad" shaman play out their magical arts against each other. First, one emerges the victor, then the other; and if one gets "killed," his adversary brings him back to life, while forgoing his own life for a moment so that both can be in balance.

Exactly. Life is a play of opposites, and thus there is never a one-sided victory. That kind of victory is a catastrophe, really, because then one of the opposites is wiped out; but it will certainly come back destructively if you don't evoke it once more. That's why Jung said you can never solve a conflict, you can only outgrow it. It brings you to the next level of growth, to a higher form of consciousness, and then suddenly you say, "Funny, now I have *another* conflict, that previous conflict doesn't bother me anymore."

Freud tended to see in neurosis the relics of one's unresolved past, whereas I gather that Jung thought that it contained possibilities of future growth.

Yes, Jung even spoke of the blessing of the neurosis. For him, it was a chance for growth and individual development. You see, there are two kinds of suffering. One belongs to life, which always contains a certain amount of suffering. But there's also a childish suffering that is unnecessary. If you have the wrong conscious attitude, the unconscious will work against you, and you become like the dog that tries to catch its tail and runs about in circles meaninglessly.

It sometimes seems as if an ever-increasing number of people are running around in these circles.

Yes. Everybody talks about nuclear war and pollution, but our real problem is overpopulation. That's really the villain, but human beings don't like to face that. The unconscious thinks of genocide because there are too many people in the world. Before his death, Jung often said that he saw great catastrophes ahead. He had very dark forebodings. Certainly the world's situation doesn't look good. But one must give nature credit because it might invent something new, you see. At the time when Christianity came about, for instance, a wise politician in Rome would probably have had a very gloomy view about everything, too. Nine out of ten persons were slaves. The culture was at point zero, the economy was in an awful crisis. But he would certainly not have imagined that in Palestine a man would turn up who would change things with a new message. So maybe something of the kind will happen again today, and perhaps the unconscious will produce some saving movement.

In 1910 Jung wrote a letter to Freud in which he stated: "Only the wise are ethical from sheer intellectual presumption, the rest of us need the eternal truth of myth. . . . Two thousand years of Christianity can only be replaced by something equivalent."

Yes, that's what I was driving at. Maybe a new myth will arise in the most unexpected corner of the world. Jung always thought, for instance, that a black man would be the next Savior. So in some corner of Africa, perhaps a man will stand up and proclaim the new myth.

You've pointed out that in fairy tales, before a hero or heroine is born, there's often a period of sterility and depression during which the queen cannot give birth. And you've talked about the idea of depression in the sense of the ego pressing down into the unconscious.

Depression can be a very salutary thing, if one knows how to handle it. I myself was terribly depressed when I first went into Jungian analysis. I complained about it, and Jung just smiled and said, "Well, 'depression' comes from the Latin word *deprimere,* so if you're sad, just sit down and go into your sadness until something comes up from it. If you're depressed, you're too high up in your mind." And sometimes I'd sit for a whole afternoon just staring ahead of me. And then suddenly I had fantasies. Jung encouraged me to write them down, and the creative flow began.

You've written a wonderful book about creation myths that is, in fact, about the creative process itself. And in that book you state that the many stories of the origins of the universe and the origins of your awareness of the universe are absolutely coinciding factors. That's a fascinating and certainly a true idea, since we don't really know what happened before the beginning of creation.

The only thing we can describe is when we woke up to our awareness of the universe. And that's the moment when it became real. There are thousands of creation myths, and they're all variations and different facets of this basic process.

You write about myths that conceive of a creation-from-above or a creation-from-below, which reminds me of the Greek philosopher Heraclitus's statement that "the way up and the way down are one and the same."

Absolutely. Only when it comes from the below you have the experience that a creative idea or painting or whatever you are doing comes out of your belly. And when it comes from above, it seems as if it drops from the sky into your head—it's inspired from above, so to speak. But these are only qualitatively different feelings, they're the same thing, really.

You've asserted that "where there is a creative constellation in the unconscious, that is, when the unconscious has conceived a child, if we do not put it out in the form of creative work, we get possessed by it instead."

People get absolutely intolerable when they have a creative idea in their womb and can't bring it out. They're neurotic, aggressive, irritable, and depressed. So then one has to help them bring the child out.

You've also said that "every step forward toward building up more consciousness destroys a previous living balance."

I had in mind the fact that medieval man, in spite of all the horrors of the times, was at home in an explained world. He was contained in the revealed truth of the Catholic Church; and even if he was against it, he still believed in it. The birth of science, however, made man a homeless wanderer. It was necessary, it was a kind of progress, but it destroyed something.

You once pointed out that among the Australian aborigines, when the rice crop shows signs of failure, the women go into the rice field, bend down, and tell the grains of rice the story of their origins.

We have to have a conception of where we come from and where we are going—a wider conception—and then we can be at home in the world. And that's why historical and mythological knowledge is so important. In the Book of Enoch we read how angels had intercourse with human women and created giants. The angels taught the giants about magic, natural sciences, and technology, and then they nearly destroyed the earth. For this was a too-rapid invasion of new creative contents into the conscious world, and people suffered from inflated notions and ideas. Just like today, I recently read, for example, that soon we'll be putting electrodes into the brains of children so that they can learn better in school. Imagine that inflated idea!

I don't know. If someone told me that with these electrodes implanted in me I'd be able to speak any language in the world, I might be tempted!

If that were possible. But there would undoubtedly be drawbacks. You might be able to speak, but your memory might not be able to store things. Or maybe, suddenly one day, you'd develop terrible headaches and all sorts of side effects. The medical world doesn't save more people nowadays than it did before.

You once wrote that when the ego identifies with the Self and begins to think, "I've got the message! I've got the true meaning!" one winds up with pathological demagogues and pseudo-prophets. You mention Hitler, Charles Manson, and others as examples, stating, "They have inflicted infinite damage on the world because they have transformed normal inner experiences of the unconscious into morbid poison through inflated identification with them."

I think it's indisputable that Hitler was destructive, and Charles Manson, too. One step further and you'd meet them in the lunatic asylums. In the asylums you have a lot of so-called gifted people who have invented the *perpetuum mobile* and answered the world riddles and so on. I sometimes get letters from inhabitants of such clinics. They always have *the* great idea, but when you look at it it's completely hazy, completely fuzzy. They haven't worked it out.

There are some young people who identify with the unconscious and fall into the world of dreams and neglect to build up their actual personal lives, while some others believe that with terrorism they can change the world. But you can never do that without the help of the unconscious. You have to keep your critical mind intact, you can't just be naïve with the unconscious. That's why, for instance, in shamanism the young apprentice always needs a teacher, because if he stepped into the ghost world alone, he would fall for all sorts of traps. The unconscious doesn't want to trap us, it's not wicked. But it *is* difficult to deal with, and it's sometimes very hard to find out what it really wants to say.

You've made a connection between the psychotherapist and the shaman, and have said that a shaman has to have been wounded in order for him to heal. Since you're a therapist, perhaps you were wounded, too.

In my childhood I hated my mother and didn't get on with her. Perhaps she wasn't as bad as I thought, but she was extremely different from me, a very powerful person who wanted to make me what she thought I should be. She was a smashing extrovert and I'm a deep introvert. So that was part of my problem when I met Jung. And if I hadn't had depressions and that difficulty with my mother, I probably wouldn't have gone into Jungian psychology and learned about the unconscious, which released my creativity and which enabled me to help other people. If it hadn't been for the trouble with my mother, I would probably just have done what she wanted me to do, which was marry a rich man and have children.

*You've said that "people who don't know much about Jungian psychology think
it is something esoteric and aristocratic. They don't realize that the process moves
in two directions: (a) becoming more individual and less identical with the
emotions, and moving upward to greater differentiation; but also (b) integrating the man in the street."*

Yes. And that's why Jung could talk to anybody, even to half-wits. They
adored him, and he gave them analytical hours. Once, for instance, a person sent him a farmer's girl from a mountain village. She couldn't sleep,
she hadn't slept for a whole year, and even pills hadn't helped. And when
she turned up in his office, Jung saw at once that she was a half-wit and
completely uneducated, and he couldn't do any therapy with her. So he
took her on his knees and rocked her and sang her lullabies. And from
then on, she slept. When the person wrote to Jung asking, "How did you
cure her?" Jung replied, "I couldn't talk to her, so I sang her some lullabies."
And the person was furious because he thought Jung was lying!

You see, we still have Stone Age people and we have medieval people,
and it's much better that they get cured in a style appropriate to them. I
once, for instance, sent a patient to an exorcist. And if someone goes to a
voodoo doctor in Haiti, it may very well help. Certain people are on that
level, and they need to cured on that level.

*Recently, both Jung and Freud have come under attack for their so-called sexual
adventures or misadventures—as if these somehow negated all their theories
and teachings.*

It's so naïve that I can only laugh at it. And since Freud taught that one
shouldn't repress sexuality, then he shouldn't have repressed his sexuality
either. And for some reason I always smile when Freudians attack Jung
over the Spielrein affair [Sabina Spielrein, one of Jung's first patients, was
cured by Jung and became his lover].

Jung and Freud had theoretical differences. Their disagreement wasn't
only a personal affair. Not at all. And now Jung is becoming more and
more known. I mean, the number of Jungian analysts increases every year,
the interest in Jung increases, the sales of his books increase—everything
increases—and so, naturally, the opposition increases too. For a while I
noticed the Freudians were no longer against Jung. They thought he was
passé, finished. So they weren't aggressive anymore about him. But now
that terrible snake is raising its head again, to speak their language, so one

has to stamp it out. But young people are discovering Jung all over the world. I get a lot of letters from sixteen- and seventeen-year-olds who have begun to read Jung or my work, and they want to know more about it.

Freud, you know, was terrified of the flood of occultism, his attitude being that one should not provoke it. And it is true that nowadays there is a certain turning toward the unconscious, with the misuse of drugs, that is thoroughly unhealthy. Many people also sit absolutely dazed in front of the TV for hours and hours—and that's a kind of falling into the unconscious. But we need the unconscious. It's only a question of dealing with it in a healthy manner, though there will always be a certain number of individuals who'll do it the wrong way.

You've said that the first dream that one recalls from one's childhood "often sets forth in symbolic form the essence of an entire life or of the first part of life. It reflects, so to speak, a piece of the 'inner fate' into which the individual was born." And when I've asked friends of mine to recount their first remembered dreams, they've always been extraordinary.

They *are* amazing. You should read the four volumes of seminars that Jung gave on such dreams that adults remember from their childhood, and also a few dreams that little children have told their parents. Jung interprets them. And they're fascinating.

I remember one dream he talks about in which a little girl saw herself lying in bed and Jack Frost came in and pinched her in the belly. And Jung interpreted that as being most dangerous because the girl had no reaction when the demon of cold and winter was pinching her in the seat of emotions, the fire center. And do you know what happened? She eventually became schizophrenic, took a pistol, and shot herself in the belly. That's how she died. She executed herself. The cold hand of death. So there was a bit of fate anticipated already in the childhood dream. A bad one in that case. . . . The first dreams—one should make many more studies about them.

What about the idea of synchronicity? The recent rock and roll album by the Police is deeply involved with that idea.

I think it's one of Jung's key concepts, and one that will have great importance in the future. As you know, synchronicity is the simple coincidence of two factors that are connected, not causally but rather through meaning. Have you heard about the Einstein–Podolsky–Rosen paradox in physics? To put it in simple words is very difficult, but let's say you have two particles that have once been connected but are then separated. And let's say one is in New York City and the other is in Tokyo. Now, at the moment you alter the spin of the one in New York, the spin of the other in Tokyo appears altered, too—so quickly that even a light signal couldn't have been exchanged. In other words, one particle knows what the other one, thousands of kilometers away, is doing. This reveals the so-called inseparability of the universe. The same is true in psychology.

The ancient Chinese said that a person sitting alone in his room thinking the right thoughts will be heard a thousand miles away.

Yes, Confucius said that, and that is synchronicity. Everything is contained in the oneness such that everything is connected with everything else in a meaningful way. And the physicists are actually getting at it now from their angle.

Jung and you often refer to the fourfold structure of the psyche, and to the fact that each person contains an anima and an animus.

Yes. There's the feminine nature in man and the masculine nature in woman, so there are four of us in this room right now. And that fourfold structure—you find it in basic physical theories, in myths, in fairy tales, and endlessly in dreams and in art. I mean, think of all those fourfold mandalas and pyramids.

Why four?

I think that's a just-so story that we can't explain. The meaning of *one* has to do with the spiritual oneness of everything. *Two* has to do with polarity—yin and yang. *Three* generally is concerned with dynamic movement and processes, such that in fairy tales you read about three giants or coming upon three rivers. And with *four,* you arrive at completion: one, two, three, *four.* And that gives the feeling of complete reality.

Jung's formulation of the four functional "types"—thinking, feeling, intuition, sensation—has been criticized as fairly naïve and reductive, but it seems to make sense to me as a way of seeing certain strengths and weaknesses in a person.

Practically, I use them all the time. For me they're the great peacemaking instrument, because you can settle hundreds of quarrels by telling someone: "Now look here, you're a sensation type and have no fantasy, while your friend's an intuitive type and has no sensation, and that's why you clashed." You can always make peace between people by revealing that to them. A lot of friction and marriage troubles and troubles in offices are in fact typological misunderstandings.

Jung also posited the notion of "active imagination." What is that?

You have it out with a fantasy. Let's say you do a painting of a black fox; then you hang it over your bed and you talk to it and say, "Black fox, why have you come to me? What's your message?" And then you listen to what it says. This is a two-way process, not only to let it out as fantasy but then to let it in again by integration.

What about the notion of the "complex"?

Jung discovered the "complex," by which he meant a cluster of emotionally tuned representations generally surrounding an archetypal kernel. Quite simply, if you have a money complex, then with anything that has to do with money, you get emotional—people begin to tremble when they have to take change out of their pockets, for example. Or there's the inferiority complex. That's another one. There are many complexes. What is interesting is that whenever something touches the complex, people get cold or sweaty hands, say. There's a psychic *and* physiological reaction to it. And if you want to find out what complexes a person has, all you have to do is just remain absolutely silent and let the other person talk and talk and talk and you'll always end up with the complex. If you make an empty space, the complex walks in.

You yourself have dealt with subjects as diverse as alchemy, fairy tales, time, and number. I assume your classical education made that possible.

When I was young, I didn't know what I should study. I hesitated between mathematics, medicine, and classical languages. And then one night I dreamt that I was sitting on the Acropolis as a wanderer, with no money and a knapsack between my knees. The sun was shining, and suddenly, from the right, all the Olympic gods entered in a big procession, and they begged—they stretched out their hands begging. I opened my sack and

344

wanted to give them something, but I had nothing except a loaf of bread. So I cut the loaf into bits, and I gave every god a piece, apologizing and saying, "I'm very sorry, but that's all I have." And after that, I decided to study classical languages, because the gods wanted something from me.

What gods appeared to you?

All of them—Zeus and Hera and Hermes and Aphrodite. The whole bunch.

Which one do you feel most connected to now?

I've changed. It used to be Hermes. Now I'm interested in Aphrodite.

A very jealous goddess!

Yes. That's one of her less good traits. But she also has sublime love and erotic love, she has a whole scale and range. For me, now, this goddess has become dominant. There are no "shoulds" about it. I just try to follow the stream of life, and where there's the most life and energy, that's where I try to be.

MARIE-LOUISE VON FRANZ

JANUARY 4, 1915 – FEBRUARY 17, 1998

Acknowledgments

I am inestimably grateful to my editor, Erik Anderson, for his unflagging encouragement and acute editorial guidance, and I am also indebted to everyone at the University of Minnesota Press who helped make this book possible, in particular Kristian Tvedten, Laura Westlund, Rachel Moeller, Emily Hamilton, and Heather Skinner. Thanks also to Michel Vrana, who designed the book cover, and to my outstanding copy editor, Judy Selhorst.

For their invaluable help I thank Scott Moyers, Jyotsna Hariharan, and Zenyse Miller.

For their abiding generosity and support I give heartfelt thanks to Ann Druyan, Elizabeth Garnsey, Richard Gere, Uma Thurman, and Jann Wenner.

I express my immeasurable gratitude to my literary agents at InkWell Management, Michael V. Carlisle and Michael Mungiello.

In my interview with Bob Dylan in 1977, he told me: "The highest purpose of art is to inspire. What else can you do? What else can you do for anyone but inspire them?" And for their unabating inspiration I am grateful to Nina Bengtsson, Lili Chopra, Michael J. Cindrich, Doris del Castillo, Yolaine Destremau, Calle Dieker, Ernie Eban, Dina El, Mark Epstein, Raymond Foye, Laura García Lorca, Philippe Goldin, Tara and Daniel Goleman, Dina Haidar, Joanne Howard, Lorraine d'Huart, Robert Hurwitz, Pico Iyer, Gita and Sonny Mehta, Alice Michel, Josephine Michel, James Moffatt, Sydney Picasso, Viveka Ramel, Sharon Salzberg, Paula von Seth, Charles Shere, Dan Solomon, Shirley Sun, Nadia Tazi, Robert Thurman, Anne Waldman, Jane Wenner, and Sue Wunderman.

Publication History

"Chinua Achebe: At the Crossroads" was originally published in an extended form in Jonathan Cott, *Pipers at the Gates of Dawn: The Wisdom of Children's Literature* (New York: Random House, 1981; reprint, Minneapolis: University of Minnesota Press, 2020); copyright 1981 by Jonathan Cott.

Part I of "George Balanchine: Dancing with Mr. B" was published in *Visions and Voices* (New York: Doubleday, 1987); copyright 1978 by Jonathan Cott. Part II was published in *Rolling Stone* magazine, May 12, 1983; copyright 1983 by *Rolling Stone* magazine. Reprinted with permission.

"J. G. Ballard: Halos of Light" was originally published as "The Strange Visions of J. G. Ballard" in *Rolling Stone* magazine, November 19, 1987; copyright 1987 by *Rolling Stone* magazine. Reprinted with permission.

"Ray Davies: Afternoon Tea on Hampstead Heath" was published as "Q&A: Afternoon Tea with Ray Davies" in *Rolling Stone* magazine, November 26, 1970; copyright 1970 by *Rolling Stone* magazine. Reprinted with permission.

"Bob Dylan: Behind the Mask" was first published in "The Rolling Stone Interview with Bob Dylan, Part 1" in *Rolling Stone* magazine, January 26, 1978; copyright 1978 by *Rolling Stone* magazine. Materials from *Tarantula* (Macmillan) copyright 1971 by Bob Dylan. Materials from *Writings and Drawings* (Knopf) copyright 1973 by Bob Dylan.

"Oriana Fallaci: The Art of Unclothing an Emperor" was originally published as "Oriana Fallaci: The Rolling Stone Interview" in *Rolling Stone* magazine, June 17, 1976; copyright 1976 by *Rolling Stone* magazine. Reprinted with permission.

"Federico Fellini: The Language of Dreams" was published in *Rolling Stone* magazine, May 10, 1984; copyright 1984 by *Rolling Stone* magazine. Reprinted with permission.

"Theodor Geisel: The Good Dr. Seuss" was first published in an extended form as "The Good Dr. Seuss" in Jonathan Cott, *Pipers at the Gates of Dawn: The Wisdom of Children's Literature* (New York: Random House, 1981; reprint, Minneapolis: University of Minnesota Press, 2020); copyright 1981 by Jonathan Cott.

"Richard Gere: Face-to-Face" was originally published as "A Conversation with Richard Gere" in *Rolling Stone* magazine, April 25, 1985; copyright 1985 by *Rolling Stone* magazine. Reprinted with permission.

"Stéphane Grappelli: The Prince of Violins" was originally published as "Improvising with Jazz Violinist Stéphane Grappelli" in *Rolling Stone* magazine, May 19, 1977; copyright 1977 by *Rolling Stone* magazine. Reprinted with permission.

"Werner Herzog: Signs of Life" was published in *Rolling Stone* magazine, November 18, 1976; copyright 1976 by *Rolling Stone* magazine. Reprinted with permission.

"Mick Jagger: Some Girls" was originally published as "Mick Jagger: Jumpin' Jack Flash at 34" in *Rolling Stone* magazine, June 29, 1978; copyright 1978 by *Rolling Stone* magazine. Reprinted with permission.

"John Lennon: December 5, 1980" was recorded in 1980 and was first published as "John Lennon: The Last Interview" in *Rolling Stone* magazine, December 23, 2010; copyright 2010 by *Rolling Stone* magazine. Reprinted with permission.

"Astrid Lindgren: The Happy Childhood of Pippi Longstocking" was first published as "The Happy Childhoods of Pippi Longstocking and Astrid Lindgren," in Jonathan Cott, *Pipers at the Gates of Dawn: The Wisdom of*

Jonathan Cott has been a contributing editor at *Rolling Stone* since its inception and has written for the *New Yorker*, the *New York Times*, and the *Washington Post*. He is the author of twenty books, which have been translated into seventeen languages, including *Dinner with Lenny: The Last Long Interview with Leonard Bernstein*, *Susan Sontag: The Complete Rolling Stone Interview*, *Days That I'll Remember: Spending Time with John Lennon and Yoko Ono*, *There's a Mystery There: The Primal Vision of Maurice Sendak*, and *Pipers at the Gates of Dawn: The Wisdom of Children's Literature* (recently republished by the University of Minnesota Press). He has received Fulbright and Guggenheim Fellowships and lives in New York City.